BLOOM'S PERIOD STUDIES

BLOOM'S PERIOD STUDIES

American Fiction Between the Wars

Edited and with an introduction by
Harold Bloom
Sterling Professor of the Humanities
Yale University

CHELSEA HOUSE
PUBLISHERS
A Haights Cross Communications Company ®

Philadelphia

©2005 by Chelsea House Publishers, a subsidiary of
Haights Cross Communications.

A Haights Cross Communications Company ®

www.chelseahouse.com

Introduction © 2005 by Harold Bloom.

Printed and bound in the United States of America.

10 9 8 7 6 5 4 3 2 1

Library of Congress Cataloging-in-Publication Data applied for.

American fiction between the wars / [compiled by] Harold Bloom.
    p. cm. — (Bloom's period studies)
  Includes bibliographical references and index.
  ISBN 0-7910-8236-9 (alk. paper)
 1. American fiction—20th century—History and criticism. 2. World War, 2914-
1918—United States—Literature and the war. I. Bloom, Harold. II. Series.
 PS374.W65A84 2004
 813'.5209—dc22
                            2004027465

Contributing editor: Janyce Marson

Cover design by Keith Trego

Layout by EJB Publishing Services

All links and web addresses were checked and verified to be correct at the time of
publication. Because of the dynamic nature of the web, some addresses and links may
have changed since publication and may no longer be valid.

Every effort has been made to trace the owners of copyrighted material and secure
copyright permission. Articles appearing in this volume generally appear much as they
did in their original publication with little to no editorial changes. Those interested in
locating the original source will find bibliographic information on the first page of each
article as well as in the bibliography and acknowledgments sections of this volume.

Contents

Editor's Note

My Introduction discusses a sequence of Willa Cather, F. Scott Fitzgerald, William Faulkner, Ernest Hemingway, and Nathanael West, who in my judgment were the five greatest masters of American prose fiction in the years 1919–1941, when their country was not at war.

Sergio Perosa finds the mode of "tragic pastoral" in *The Great Gatsby*, while Sherwood Anderson is valued as an authentic American mythmaker by Benjamin Spencer.

Sinclair Lewis, superbly disillusioned by the myth of America, is surveyed by James Lea, after which Howard Levant praises John Steinbeck's *The Grapes of Wrath* as a fully matured work of art.

U.S.A., the massive trilogy of John Dos Passos, is judged as a cunning act of resistance to society and history by Charles Marz, while Phyllis Rose persuasively argues for the aesthetic eminence of Willa Cather.

Barbara Johnson's brilliant essay on Zora Neale Hurston's *Their Eyes Were Watching God* has rightly become the classic discussion of that work.

Faulkner's *The Sound and the Fury* is read as a study in damnation by Max Putzel, after which Tom Quirk demonstrates Cather's influence upon *The Great Gatsby*.

Randa Dubnick relates the rhetoric of Gertrude Stein to the visual structures of Cubism, while Robert A. Martin ponders the expatriate ambiguities of Hemingway's *The Sun Also Rises*.

The Great Gatsby is juxtaposed with Thomas Wolfe's *Look Homeward, Angel* by D.G. Kehl, after which Ronald Berman reflects that *A Farewell to Arms* is also a post-war novel.

Thomas Wolfe returns in Lisa Kerr's discussion of John Milton's influence upon *O Lost*, while Scott Fitzgerald's early novels are read thematically by Kirk Curnutt as the waste of youth.

In this volume's final essay, Ryuichi Yamaguchi gives a strong analysis of Faulkner's magnificent *Light in August*.

HAROLD BLOOM

Introduction

I

Willa Cather, though now somewhat neglected, has few rivals among the American novelists of this century. Critics and readers frequently regard her as belonging to an earlier time, though she died in 1947. Her best novels were published in the years 1918–31, so that truly she was a novelist of the 1920s, an older contemporary and peer of Hemingway and of Scott Fitzgerald. Unlike them, she did not excel at the short story, though there are some memorable exceptions scattered through her four volumes of tales. Her strength is her novels and particularly, in my judgment, *My Ántonia* (1918), *A Lost Lady* (1923), and *The Professor's House* (1925); fictions worthy of a disciple of Flaubert and Henry James. Equally beautiful and achieved, but rather less central, are the subsequent historical novels, the very popular *Death Comes for the Archbishop* (1927) and *Shadows on the Rock* (1931). Her second novel, *O Pioneers!* (1913), is only just short of the eminence of this grand sequence. Six permanent novels is a remarkable number for a modern American writer; I can think only of Faulkner as Cather's match in this respect, since he wrote six truly enduring novels, all published during his great decade, 1929–39.

Cather's remoteness from the fictive universe of Fitzgerald, Hemingway, and Faulkner is palpable, though all of them shared her nostalgia for an older America. She appears, at first, to have no aesthetic affinities with her younger contemporaries. We associate her instead with Sarah Orne Jewett, about whom she wrote a loving essay, or even with Edith Wharton, whom she scarcely resembles. Cather's mode of engaging with the

psychic realities of post–World War I America is more oblique than
Fitzgerald's or Hemingway's, but it is just as apposite a representation of the
era's malaise. The short novel, *A Lost Lady* (1923), is not out of its aesthetic
context when we read it in the company of *The Waste Land*, *The Comedian as
the Letter C*, *The Sun Also Rises*, *The Great Gatsby*, and *An American Tragedy*.
Subtler and gentler than any of these, *A Lost Lady* elegizes just as profoundly
a lost radiance or harmony, a defeat of a peculiarly American dream of
innocence, grace, hope.

Henry James, Cather's guide both as critic and novelist, died in
England early in 1916. The year before, replying to H.G. Wells, after being
satirized by him, James wrote a famous credo: "Art *makes* life, makes interest,
makes importance." This is Cather's faith also. One hears the voice of James
when, in her essay "On the Art of Fiction," she writes: "Any first-rate novel
or story must have in it the strength of a dozen fairly good stories that have
been sacrificed to it." Those sacrifices of possibility upon the altar of form
were the ritual acts of Cather's quite Paterian religion of art, too easily
misread as a growing religiosity by many critics commenting upon *Death
Comes for the Archbishop*. Herself a belated Aesthete, Cather emulated a
familiar pattern of being attracted by the aura and not the substance of
Roman Catholicism. New Mexico, and not Rome, is her place of the spirit,
a spirit of the archaic and not of the supernatural.

Cather's social attitudes were altogether archaic. She shared a kind of
Populist anti-Semitism with many American writers of her own generation
and the next: Sherwood Anderson, Theodore Dreiser, Ezra Pound, Thomas
Wolfe, even Hemingway and Fitzgerald. Her own version of anti-Semitism is
curiously marked by her related aversion to heterosexuality. She had lost her
first companion, Isabelle McClung, to a Jewish violinist, Jan Hambourg, and
the Jewish figures in her fiction clearly represent the aggressivity of male
sexuality. *The Professor's House* is marred by the gratuitous identification of the
commercial exploitation of Cather's beloved West with Marcellus, the
Professor's Jewish son-in-law. Doubtless, Cather's most unfortunate piece of
writing was her notorious essay in 1914, "Potash and Perlmutter," in which
she lamented, mock-heroically, that New York City was becoming too Jewish.
Perhaps she was learning the lesson of the master again, since she is repeating,
in a lighter tone, the complaint of Henry James in *The American Scene* (1907).
She repeated her own distaste for "Jewish critics," tainted as they were by
Freud, in the essay on Sarah Orne Jewett written quite late in her career,
provoking Lionel Trilling to the just accusation that she had become a mere
defender of gentility, mystically concerned with pots and pans.

This dark side of Cather, though hardly a value in itself, would not much matter except that it seeped into her fiction as a systemic resentment of her own era. Nietzsche, analyzing resentment, might be writing of Cather. Freud, analyzing the relation between paranoia and homosexuality, might be writing of her also. I am wary of being reductive in such observations, and someone perpetually mugged by Feminist critics as "the Patriarchal critic" is too battered to desire any further polemic. Cather, in my judgment, is aesthetically strongest and most persuasive in her loving depiction of her heroines and of Ántonia and the lost lady, Mrs. Forrester, in particular. She resembles Thomas Hardy in absolutely nothing, except in the remarkable ability to seduce the reader into joining the novelist at falling in love with the heroine. I am haunted by memories of having fallen in love with Marty South in *The Woodlanders*, and with Ántonia and Mrs. Forrester when I was a boy of fifteen. Rereading *My Ántonia* and *A Lost Lady*, now at fifty-four, I find that the love renews itself. I doubt that I am falling again into what my late and honored teacher, William K. Wimsatt, named as the Affective Fallacy, since love for a woman made up out of words is necessarily a cognitive affair.

Cather's strength at representation gives us Jim Burden and Niel Herbert as her clear surrogates, unrealized perhaps as figures of sexual life, but forcefully conveyed as figures of capable imagination, capable above all of apprehending and transmitting the extraordinary actuality and visionary intensity of Ántonia and Mrs. Forrester. Like her masters, James and Pater, Cather had made her supposed deficiency into her strength, fulfilling the overt program of Emersonian self-reliance. But nothing is got for nothing, Emerson also indicated, and Cather, again like James and Pater, suffered the reverse side of the law of Compensation. The flaws, aesthetic and human, are there, even in *My Ántonia*, *A Lost Lady*, and *The Professor's House*, but they scarcely diminish the beauty and dignity of three profound studies of American nostalgias.

Cather is hardly the only vital American novelist to have misread creatively the spirit of his or her own work. Her essential imaginative knowledge was of loss, which she interpreted temporally, though her loss was aboriginal, in, the Romantic mode of Wordsworth, Emerson and all their varied descendants. The glory that had passed away belonged not to the pioneers but to her own transparent eyeball, her own original relation to the universe. Rhetorically, she manifests this knowledge, which frequently is at odds with her overt thematicism. Here is Jim Burden's first shared moment with Ántonia, when they both were little children:

> We sat down and made a nest in the long red grass. Yulka curled
> up like a baby rabbit and played with a grasshopper. Ántonia

pointed up to the sky and questioned me with her glance. I gave
her the word, but she was not satisfied and pointed to my eyes. I
told her, and she repeated the word, making it sound like "ice."
She pointed up to the sky, then to my eyes, then back to the sky,
with movements so quick and impulsive that she distracted me,
and I had no idea what she wanted. She got up on her knees and
wrung her hands. She pointed to her own eyes and shook her
head, then to mine and to the sky, nodding violently.

"Oh," I exclaimed, "blue; blue sky."

She clapped her hands and murmured, "Blue sky, blue eyes,"
as if it amused her. While we snuggled down there out of the
wind, she learned a score of words. She was quick, and very eager.
We were so deep in the grass that we could see nothing but the
blue sky over us and the gold tree in front of us. It was
wonderfully pleasant. After Ántonia had said the new words over
and over, she wanted to give me a little chased silver ring she
wore on her middle finger. When she coaxed and insisted, I
repulsed her quite sternly. I didn't want her ring, and I felt there
was something reckless and extravagant about her wishing to give
it away to a boy she had never seen before. No wonder Krajiek
got the better of these people, if this was how they behaved.

One imagines that Turgenev would have admired this, and it would not
be out of place inserted in his *A Sportsman's Sketches*. Its naturalistic simplicity
is deceptive. Wallace Stevens, in a letter of 1940, observed of Cather: "you
may think she is more or less formless. Nevertheless, we have nothing better
than she is. She takes so much pains to conceal her sophistication that it is easy
to miss her quality." The quality here is partly manifested by an exuberance
of trope and a precision of diction, both in the service of a fresh American
myth of origin. Nesting and curling up in an embowered world of baby
rabbits and grasshoppers, the children are at home in a universe of "blue sky,
blue eyes." Heaven and earth come together, where vision confronts only the
gold of trees. Ántonia, offering the fullness of a symbolic union to him, is
rebuffed partly by the boy's shyness, and partly by Cather's own proleptic fear
that the reckless generosity of the pioneer is doomed to exploitation. Yet the
passage's deepest intimation is that Jim, though falling in love with Ántonia,
is constrained by an inner recalcitrance, which the reader is free to interpret
in several ways, none of which need exclude the others.

This is Cather in the springtide of her imagination. In her vision's early
fall, we find ourselves regarding her lost lady, Mrs. Forrester, and we are

comforted, as the boy Niel Herbert is, "in the quick recognition of her eyes, in the living quality of her voice itself." The book's splendor is that, like Mrs. Forrester's laughter, "it often told you a great deal that was both too direct and too elusive for words." As John Hollander shrewdly notes, Mrs. Forrester does not become a lost lady in any social or moral sense, but imaginatively she is transformed into Niel's "long-lost lady." Lost or refound, she is "his" always, even as Ántonia always remains Jim Burden's "my Ántonia." In her ability to suggest a love that is permanent, life-enhancing, and in no way possessive, Cather touches the farthest limit of her own strength as a novelist. If one could choose a single passage from all her work, it would be the Paterian epiphany or privileged moment in which Mrs. Forrester's image returned to Niel as "a bright, impersonal memory." Pater ought to have lived to have read this marvelous instance of the art he had celebrated and helped to stimulate in Cather:

> Her eyes, when they laughed for a moment into one's own, seemed to provide a wild delight that he had not found in life. "I know where it is," they seemed to say, "I could show you!" He would like to call up the shade of the young Mrs. Forrester, as the witch of Endor called up Samuel's, and challenge it, demand the secret of that ardour; ask her whether she had really found some ever-blooming, ever-burning, ever-piercing joy, or whether it was all fine play-acting. Probably she had found no more than another; but she had always the power of suggesting things much lovelier than herself, as the perfume of a single flower may call up the whole sweetness of spring.

It is the perfection of Cather's difficult art, when that art was most balanced and paced, and Mrs. Forrester here is the emblem of that perfection. Cather's fiction, at its frequent best, also suggests things much lovelier than itself. The reader, demanding the secret of Cather's ardour, learns not to challenge what may be remarkably fine play-acting, since Cather's feigning sometimes does persuade him that really she had found some perpetual joy.

II

It is difficult to imagine John Keats writing the fictions of Joseph Conrad, since there is nothing in common between the Great Odes and *The Secret Sharer* or *Heart of Darkness*. But such an imagining is not useless, since in some sense that was Scott Fitzgerald's accomplishment. *The Great Gatsby* does combine the lyrical sensibility of Keats and the fictive mode of Conrad, and makes of so odd a blending a uniquely American story, certainly a candidate for *the* American story of its time (1925). *Gatsby* has more in common with T.S. Eliot's "The Hollow Men," also published in 1925, than it does with such contemporary novels as the *Arrowsmith* of Sinclair Lewis or the *Manhattan Transfer* of John Dos Passos. Eliot's admiration for *The Great Gatsby* is understandable; the book, like the visionary lyric of Hart Crane, struggles against Eliot's conclusions while being compelled to appropriate Eliot's language and procedures. Fitzgerald, the American Keats, and Crane, even more the American Shelley, both sought to affirm a High Romanticism in the accents of a belated counter-tradition. The Keatsian belief in the holiness of the heart's affections is central to Fitzgerald, and *Tender Is the Night* owes more than its title to the naturalistic humanism of the Great Odes.

Fitzgerald's canonical status is founded more upon *Gatsby* and his best short stories, such as "Babylon Revisited," than it is upon the seriously flawed *Tender Is the Night*, let alone upon the unfinished *The Last Tycoon*. Oddly praised as "the best Hollywood novel" despite its manifest inferiority to Nathanael West's *The Day of the Locust*, *The Last Tycoon* is more an embryo than it is a torso. Edmund Wilson's affectionate overestimation of this fragment has been influential, but will fade away each time the book is actually read. *Tender Is the Night* demonstrates that Fitzgerald, unlike Conrad and Lawrence, cannot sustain too long a narrative. The book, though coming relatively late in his career, is Fitzgerald's *Endymion*, while *Gatsby* is, as it were, his *Fall of Hyperion*. Keats desired to write epic, but was more attuned to romance and to lyric. Fitzgerald desired to write novels on the scale of Thackeray and of Conrad, but his genius was more fitted to *Gatsby* as his mode of romance, and to "Babylon Revisited" as his version of the ode or of the reflective lyric.

The aesthetic of Scott Fitzgerald is quite specifically a personal revision of Keats's hope for Negative Capability, which Fitzgerald called "a romantic readiness" and attributed to his Gatsby. It is certainly part of the achievement of Fitzgerald's best novel that its hero possesses an authentic aesthetic dignity. By an effective troping of form, Fitzgerald made this a book in which nothing is aesthetically wasted, even as the narrative shows us everyone being humanly wasted. Edith Wharton rather nastily praised Fitzgerald for having created the "perfect Jew" in the gambler Meyer Wolfsheim. Had she peered closer, she might have seen the irony of her patrician prejudice reversed in the ancient Jewish wisdom that even Wolfsheim is made to express:

"Let us learn to show our friendship for a man when he is alive and not after he is dead," he suggested. "After that, my own rule is to let everything alone."

Whether Nick Carraway is capable of apprehending this as wisdom is disputable but Fitzgerald evidently could, since Wolfsheim is not wholly devoid of the dignity of grief. Lionel Trilling commended *The Great Gatsby* for retaining its freshness. After sixty years, it has more than retained its moral balance and affective rightness. Those qualities seem augmented through the perspective of lapsed time. What has been augmented also is the Eliotic phantasmagoria of the *Waste Land* imagery that is so effectively vivid throughout Fitzgerald's vision. Carraway begins by speaking of "what preyed on Gatsby, what foul dust floated in the wake of his dreams." These are also "the spasms of bleak dust," above which you perceive the blue and gigantic eyes of Doctor T.J. Eckleburg, which brood on over the dumping ground of the gray land. "My heart is a handful of dust," the monologist of Tennyson's *Maud* had proclaimed in a great phrase stolen by Eliot for his *Waste Land*. Fitzgerald's dust is closer to Tennyson's heart than to Eliot's fear:

> to where Myrtle Wilson, her life violently extinguished, knelt in the road and mingled her thick dark blood with the dust.
>   Michaelis and this man reached her first, but when they had torn open her shirtwaist, still damp with perspiration, they saw that her left breast was swinging loose like a flap, and there was no need to listen for the heart beneath.

Fitzgerald's violence has that curious suddenness we associate with the same narrative quality in E.M. Forster. Something repressed in the phantasmagoria of the ordinary returns, all too often, reminding us that Fitzgerald shares also in Conrad's sense of reality and its treacheries, particularly as developed in *Nostromo*, a novel that we know Fitzgerald rightly admired. *Heart of Darkness*, which Fitzgerald also admired, is linked to "The Hollow Men" by that poem's epigraph, and many critics have seen Carraway as Fitzgerald's version of Marlow, somewhat sentimentalized but still an authentic secret sharer in Gatsby's fate. Like the Eliot of "The Hollow Men," Fitzgerald found in Conrad a seer of the contemporary abyss of:

> Shape without form, shade without color,
> Paralysed force, gesture without motion;

or, in the language of *Heart of Darkness*: "A vision of grayness without form."

Writing to his daughter about the "Ode on a Grecian Urn," Fitzgerald extravagantly observed: "For awhile after you quit Keats all other poetry seems to be only whistling or humming." Fitzgerald's deepest affinity to Keats is in the basic stance of his work, at once rhetorical, psychological, and even cosmological. In both Keats and Fitzgerald, the perpetual encounter is between the mortal poet or man-of-imagination (Gatsby, Diver) and an immortal or perpetually youthful goddess-woman. Fitzgerald's women—Daisy, Nicole, Rosemary—are not so much American dreams as they are Keatsian Lamias or perpetually virgin moon-maidens. "Virginity renews itself like the moon" is a Keatsian apothegm of Yeats's and the quester in Fitzgerald would have concurred. The murdered Gatsby is truly Daisy's victim; rather more grimly, Diver is emptied out by his relationship with Nicole, and to some degree, by his repetition of that pattern with Rosemary.

This has been read as misogyny in Fitzgerald but, as in Keats, it tends largely to be the reverse. Confronting his immortal women, the Keatsian quester seeks what at last Keats himself obtains from the harshly reluctant Muse, Moneta, in *The Fall of Hyperion*: recognition that he is *the* poet in and for his own time. "I sure should see / Other men here; but I am here alone." Fitzgerald was greatly ambitious, but his audacity did not extend quite that far. Yet his surrogates—Gatsby and Diver—are no more deceived than Keats's poets are deceived. Daisy, Nicole, and Rosemary do not matter as personalities, not to us as readers and not much more to Gatsby or Diver. Gatsby, the more sublime quester, is allowed his famous touch of genius when he dismisses Daisy's love for her husband, the brutal Tom Buchanan: "In any case, it was just personal." Diver, less magnificently, also knows better, but is just as doom-eager as Gatsby. The inadequacies of the actual women do not matter, because the drive is not for satisfaction or for happiness. It is Freud's uncanny death-drive, which replaces the drive for self-preservation, and exists in a dialectical balance with the libido. Gatsby somehow chooses to die in his own fashion, while Diver chooses the death-in-life of erotic and professional defeat.

Tender Is the Night survives the weakness of its characterizations and the clumsiness of its narrative structure precisely because of Diver's own fated sense that there are no accidents. His character is his fate, and his relationship with Nicole is not so much a failed counter-transference as it is another pathetic version of the sublime Romantic vision of sexual entropy set forth overtly in Blake's "The Mental Traveller" and implicitly in James's *The Sacred Fount*: "And she grows young as he grows old." For the Blakean "young" we can substitute "whole," yet for the "old" we cannot quite substitute "weak" but something closer to Fitzgerald's "interior laughter," the quality in Diver that drives him down and out until he ends up practicing medicine in progressively smaller towns in the Finger Lakes Section of the Western Reserve of New York State. The pathos of that dying fall is anything but Keatsian, and may have been Fitzgerald's trope for his own self-destructiveness.

A curious self-appropriation, or perhaps indeliberate self-repetition, links the close of *Tender Is the Night* to the close of "Babylon Revisited," which seems to me Fitzgerald's most impressive single short story. On the day before he leaves the Riviera for America, after his rejection by Nicole, Diver spends all his time with his children: "He was not young any more with a lot of nice thoughts and dreams to have about himself, so he wanted to remember them well." The penultimate sentence of "Babylon Revisited" is "He wasn't young anymore, with a lot of nice thoughts and dreams to have about himself."

Whichever came first, the repetition is central to Fitzgerald. "Nice thoughts and dreams" are the essence, and Fitzgerald's regressive vision, like Gatsby's and Diver's and Charlie Wales's, is a Keatsian and Stevensian study of the nostalgias. Keats, staring at the face of the unveiled Moneta, prophesies the Stevens of *The Auroras of Autumn*, with his unabashed, Freudian celebration of the imago: "The mother's face, the purpose of the poem, fills the room." Charlie Wales, in "Babylon Revisited," longing for his daughter, remembers his dead wife as any man remembers his mother: "He was absolutely sure Helen wouldn't have wanted him to be so alone." As the last sentence of what may be Fitzgerald's most memorable story, it reverberates with a peculiar plangency in American Romantic tradition.

III

No critic need invent William Faulkner's obsessions with what Nietzsche might have called the genealogy of the imagination. Recent critics of Faulkner, including David Minter, John T. Irwin, David M. Wyatt, and Richard H. King, have emphasized the novelist's profound need to believe himself to have been his own father, in order to escape not only the Freudian family romance and literary anxieties of influence, but also the cultural dilemmas of what King terms "the Southern family romance." From *The Sound and the Fury* through the debacle of *A Fable*, Faulkner centers upon the sorrows of fathers and sons, to the disadvantage of mothers and daughters. No feminist critic ever will be happy with Faulkner. His brooding conviction that female sexuality is closely allied with death seems essential to all of his strongest fictions. It may even be that Faulkner's rhetorical economy, his wounded need to get his cosmos into a single sentence, is related to his fear that origin and end might prove to be one. Nietzsche prophetically had warned that origin and end were separate entities, and for the sake of life had to be kept apart, but Faulkner (strangely like Freud) seems to have known that the only Western trope participating neither in origin nor end is the image of the father.

By universal consent of critics and common readers, Faulkner now is recognized as the strongest American novelist of this century, clearly surpassing Hemingway and Fitzgerald, and standing as an equal in the sequence that includes Hawthorne, Melville, Mark Twain, and Henry James. Some critics might add Dreiser to this group; Faulkner himself curiously would have insisted upon Thomas Wolfe, a generous though dubious judgment. The American precursor for Faulkner was Sherwood Anderson, but perhaps only as an impetus; the true American forerunner is the poetry of T.S. Eliot, as Judith L. Sensibar demonstrates. But the truer precursor for Faulkner's fiction is Conrad, inescapable for the American novelists of Faulkner's generation, including Hemingway and Fitzgerald. Comparison to Conrad is dangerous for any novelist, and dearly Faulkner did not achieve a *Nostromo*. But his work of the decade 1929–39 does include four permanent books: *The Sound and the Fury*, *As I Lay Dying*, *Light in August* and *Absalom, Absalom!* If one adds *Sanctuary* and *The Wild Palms*, and *The Hamlet* and *Go Down, Moses* in the early forties, then the combined effect is extraordinary.

From Malcolm Cowley on, critics have explained this effect as the consequence of the force of mythmaking, at once personal and local. Cleanth Brooks, the rugged final champion of the New Criticism, essentially reads Faulkner as he does Eliot's *The Waste Land*, finding the hidden God of the normative Christian tradition to be the basis for Faulkner's attitude towards nature. Since Brooks calls Faulkner's stance Wordsworthian, and finds Wordsworthian nature a Christian vision also, the judgment involved necessarily has its problematical elements. Walter Pater, a critic in a very different tradition, portrayed a very different Wordsworth in terms that seem to me not inapplicable to Faulkner:

> Religious sentiment, consecrating the affections and natural regrets of the human heart, above all, that pitiful awe and care for the perishing human clay, of which relic-worship is but the corruption, has always had much to do with localities, with the thoughts which attach themselves to actual scenes and places.

Now what is true of it everywhere, is truest of it in those secluded valleys where one generation after another maintains the same abiding place; and it was on this side, that Wordsworth apprehended religion most strongly. Consisting, as it did so much, in the recognition of local sanctities, in the habit of connecting the stones and trees of a particular spot of earth with the great events of life, till the low walls, the green mounds, the half-obliterated epitaphs seemed full of voices, and a sort of natural oracles, the very religion of those people of the dales, appeared but as another link between them and the earth, and was literally a religion of nature.

A kind of stoic natural religion pervades this description, something close to the implicit faith of old Isaac McCaslin in *Go Down, Moses*. It seems unhelpful to speak of "residual Christianity" in Faulkner, as Cleanth Brooks does. Hemingway and Fitzgerald, in their nostalgias, perhaps were closer to a Christian ethos than Faulkner was in his great phase. Against current critical judgment, I prefer *As I Lay Dying* and *Light in August* to *The Sound and the Fury* and *Absalom, Absalom!*, partly because the first two are more primordial in their vision, closer to the stoic intensities of their author's kind of natural piety. There is an *otherness* in Lena Grove and the Bundrens that would have moved Wordsworth, that is, the Wordsworth of "The Tale of Margaret," "Michael," and "The Old Cumberland Beggar." A curious movement that is also a stasis becomes Faulkner's pervasive trope for Lena. Though he invokes the imagery of Keats's urn, Faulkner seems to have had the harvest-girl of Keats's "To Autumn" more in mind, or even the stately figures of the "Ode to Indolence." We remember Lena Grove as stately, calm, a person yet a process, a serene and patient consciousness, full of wonder, too much a unitary being to need even her author's variety of stoic courage.

The uncanniness of this representation is exceeded by the Bundrens, whose plangency testifies to Faulkner's finest rhetorical achievement. *As I Lay Dying* may be the most original novel ever written by an American. Obviously it is not free of the deepest influence Faulkner knew as a novelist. The language is never Conradian, and yet the sense of the reality principle is. But there is nothing in Conrad like Darl Bundren, not even in *The Secret Agent*. *As I Lay Dying* is Faulkner's strongest protest against the facticity of literary convention, against the force of the familial past, which tropes itself in fiction as the repetitive form of narrative imitating prior narrative. The book is a sustained nightmare insofar as it is Darl's book, which is to say, Faulkner's book, or the book of his daemon.

Canonization is a process of enshrining creative misinterpretations, and no one need lament this. Still, one element that ensues from this process all too frequently is the not very creative misinterpretation in which the idiosyncratic is distorted into the normative. Churchwardenly critics who assimilate the Faulkner of the Thirties to spiritual, social, and moral orthodoxy can and do assert Faulkner himself as their preceptor. But this is the Faulkner of the Fifties: Nobel laureate, State Department envoy, and author of *A Fable*, a book of a badness simply astonishing for Faulkner. The best of the normative critics, Cleanth Brooks, reads even *As I Lay Dying* as a quest for community, an exaltation of the family, an affirmation of Christian values. The Bundrens manifestly constitute one of the most terrifying visions of the family romance in the history of literature. But their extremism is not eccentric in the 1929–39 world of Faulkner's fiction. That world is founded upon a horror of families, a limbo of outcasts, an evasion of all values other than stoic endurance. It is a world in which what is silent in the other Bundrens speaks in Darl, what is veiled in the Compsons is uncovered in Quentin. So tangled are these returns of the repressed with what continues to be estranged that phrases like "the violation of the natural" and "the denial of the human" become quite meaningless when applied to Faulkner's greater fictions. In that world, the natural is itself a violation and the human already a denial. Is the weird quest of the Bundrens a violation of the natural, or is it what Blake would have called a terrible triumph for the selfish virtues of the natural heart? Darl judges it to be the latter, but Darl luminously denies the sufficiency of the human, at the cost of what seems schizophrenia.

Marxist criticism of imaginative literature, if it had not regressed abominably in our country, so that now it is a travesty of the dialectical suppleness of Adorno and Benjamin, would find a proper subject in the difficult relationship between the 1929 business panic and *As I Lay Dying*. Perhaps the self-destruction of our delusive political economy helped free Faulkner from whatever inhibitions, communal and personal, had kept him earlier from a saga like that of the Bundrens. Only an authentic seer can give permanent form to a prophecy like *As I Lay Dying*, which puts severely into question every received notion we have of the natural and the human. Darl asserts he has no mother, while taunting his enemy brother, Jewel, with the insistence that Jewel's mother was a horse. Their little brother, Vardaman, says: "My mother is a fish." The mother, dead and undead, is uncannier even than these children, when she confesses the truth of her existence, her rejecting vision of her children:

I could just remember how my father used to say that the reason for living was to get ready to stay dead a long time. And when I would have to look at them day after day, each with his and her single and selfish thought, and blood strange to each other blood and strange to mine, and think that this seemed to be the only way I could get ready to stay dead, I would hate my father for having ever planted me. I would look forward to the times when they faulted, so I could whip them. When the switch fell I could feel it upon my flesh; when it welted and ridged it was my blood that ran, and I would think with each blow of the switch: Now you are aware of me! Now I am something in your secret and selfish life, who have marked your blood with my own for ever and ever.

This veritable apocalypse of any sense of otherness is no mere "denial of community." Nor are the Bundrens any "mimesis of essential nature." They are a super-mimesis, an over-representation mocking nature while shadowing it. What matters in major Faulkner is that the people have gone back, not to nature but to some abyss before the Creation-Fall. Eliot insisted that Joyce's imagination was eminently orthodox. This can be doubted, but in Faulkner's case there is little sense in baptizing his imagination. One sees why he preferred reading the Old Testament to the New, remarking that the former was stories and the latter, ideas. The remark is inadequate except insofar as it opposes Hebraic to Hellenistic representation of character. There is little that is Homeric about the Bundrens, or Sophoclean about the Compsons. Faulkner's irony is neither classical nor romantic, neither Greek nor German. It does not say one thing while meaning another, nor trade in contrasts between expectation and fulfillment. Instead, it juxtaposes incommensurable realities: of self and other, of parent and child, of past and future. When Gide maintained that Faulkner's people lacked souls, he simply failed to observe that Faulkner's ironies were Biblical. To which an amendment must be added. In Faulkner, only the ironies are Biblical. What Faulkner's people lack is the blessing; they cannot contend for a time without boundaries. Yahweh will make no covenant with them. Their agon therefore is neither the Greek one for the foremost place nor the Hebrew one for the blessing, which honors the father and the mother. Their agon is the hopeless one of waiting for their doom to lift.

Faulkner writes tragic farce rather than tragedy, more in the mode of Webster, Ford and Tourneur than that of Shakespeare. In time, his genius or daemon may seem essentially comic, despite his dark houses and death drives. His grand family is Dickens run mad rather than Conrad run wild: the hideous saga of the Snopes, from the excessively capable Flem Snopes to the admirably named Wallstreet Panic Snopes. Flem, as David Minter observes, is refreshingly free of all influence-anxieties. He belongs in Washington D.C., and by now has reached there, and helps to staff the White House. Alas, he by now helps to staff the universities also, and soon will staff the entire nation, as his spiritual children, the Yuppies, reach middle age. Ivy League Snopes, Reagan Revolution Snopes, Jack Kemp Snopes: the possibilities are limitless. His ruined families, burdened by tradition, are Faulkner's tribute to his region. His Snopes clan is his gift to his nation.

IV

Hemingway freely proclaimed his relationship to *Huckleberry Finn*, and there is some basis for the assertion, except that there is little in common between the rhetorical stances of Twain and of Hemingway. Kipling's *Kim*, in style and mode, is far closer to *Huckleberry Finn* than anything Hemingway wrote. The true accent of Hemingway's admirable style is to be found in an even greater and more surprising precursor:

> This grass is very dark to be from the white heads of old mothers,
> Darker than the colorless beards of old men,
> Dark to come from under the faint red roofs of mouths.

Or again:

> I clutch the rails of the fence, my gore drips, thinn'd with
>   the ooze of my skin,
> I fall on the weeds and stones,
> The riders spur their unwilling horses, haul close,
> Taunt my dizzy ears and beat me violently over the head
>   with whip-stocks.
> Agonies are one of my changes of garments,
> I do not ask the wounded person how he feels, I myself
>   become the wounded person,
> My hurts turn livid upon me as I lean on a cane and observe.

Hemingway is scarcely unique in not acknowledging the paternity of Walt Whitman; T.S. Eliot and Wallace Stevens are far closer to Whitman than William Carlos Williams and Hart Crane were, but literary influence is a paradoxical and antithetical process, about which we continue to know all too little. The profound affinities between Hemingway, Eliot and Stevens are not accidental, but are family resemblances due to the repressed but crucial relation each had to Whitman's work. Hemingway characteristically boasted (in a letter to Sara Murphy, February 27, 1926) that he had knocked Stevens down quite handily: "... for statistics' sake Mr. Stevens is 6 feet 2 weighs 225 lbs. and that when he hits the ground it is highly spectaculous." Since this match between the two writers took place in Key West on February 19, 1926, I am moved, as a loyal Stevensian, for statistics' sake to point out that the victorious Hemingway was born in 1899, and the defeated Stevens in 1879, so that the novelist was then going on twenty-seven, and the poet verging on forty-seven. The two men doubtless despised one another, but in the letter celebrating his victory, Hemingway calls Stevens "a damned fine poet" and Stevens always affirmed that Hemingway was essentially a poet, a judgment concurred in by Robert Penn Warren when he wrote that Hemingway "is essentially a lyric rather than a dramatic writer." Warren compared Hemingway to Wordsworth, which is feasible, but the resemblance to Whitman is far closer. Wordsworth would not have written: "I am the man, I suffer'd, I was there," but Hemingway almost persuades us he would have achieved that line had not Whitman set it down first.

It is now more than twenty years since Hemingway's suicide, and some aspects of his permanent canonical status seem beyond doubt. Only a few modern American novels seem certain to endure: *The Sun Also Rises*, *The Great Gatsby*, *Miss Lonelyhearts*, *The Crying of Lot 49* and at least several by Faulkner, including *As I Lay Dying*, *Sanctuary*, *Light in August*, *The Sound and the Fury*, *Absalom, Absalom!* Two dozen stories by Hemingway could be added to the group, indeed perhaps all of *The First Forty-Nine Stories*. Faulkner is an eminence apart, but critics agree that Hemingway and Fitzgerald are his nearest rivals, largely on the strength of their shorter fiction. What seems unique is that Hemingway is the only American writer of prose fiction in this century who, as a stylist, rivals the principal poets: Stevens, Eliot, Frost, Hart Crane, aspects of Pound, W.C. Williams, Robert Penn Warren, and Elizabeth Bishop. This is hardly to say that Hemingway, at his best, fails at narrative or the representation of character. Rather, his peculiar excellence is closer to Whitman than to Twain, closer to Stevens than to Faulkner, and even closer to Eliot than to Fitzgerald, who was his friend and rival. He is an elegiac poet who mourns the self, who celebrates the self (rather less effectively), and who suffers divisions in the self. In the broadest tradition of American literature, he stems ultimately from the Emersonian reliance on the god within, which is the line of Whitman, Thoreau, and Dickinson. He arrives late and dark in this tradition, and is one of its negative theologians, as it were, but as in Stevens, the negations, the cancellings, are never final. Even the most ferocious of his stories, say, "God Rest You Merry Gentlemen" or "A Natural History of the Dead," can be said to celebrate what we might call the Real Absence. Doc Fischer, in "God Rest You Merry Gentlemen," is a precursor of Nathanael West's Shrike in *Miss Lonelyhearts*, and his savage, implicit religiosity prophesies not only Shrike's Satanic stance but the entire demonic world of Pynchon's explicitly paranoid or Luddite visions. Perhaps there was a nostalgia for a Catholic order always abiding in Hemingway's consciousness, but the cosmos of his fiction, early and late, is American Gnostic, as it was in Melville, who first developed so strongly the negative side of the Emersonian religion of self-reliance.

Hemingway notoriously and splendidly was given to overtly agonistic images whenever he described his relationship to canonical writers, including Melville, a habit of description in which he has been followed by his true ephebe, Norman Mailer. In a grand letter (September 6–7, 1949) to his publisher, Charles Scribner, he charmingly confessed: "Am a man without any ambition, except to be champion of the world, I wouldn't fight Dr. Tolstoi in a 20 round bout because I know he would knock my ears off." This modesty passed quickly, to be followed by: "If I can live to 60 I can beat him. (MAYBE)." Since the rest of the letter counts Turgenev, de Maupassant, Henry James, even Cervantes, as well as Melville and Dostoevsky, among the defeated, we can join Hemingway, himself, in admiring his extraordinary self-confidence. How justified was it, in terms of his ambitions?

It could be argued persuasively that Hemingway is the best short-story writer in the English Language, from Joyce's *Dubliners* until the present. The aesthetic dignity of the short story need not be questioned, and yet we seem to ask more of a canonical writer. Hemingway wrote *The Sun Also Rises* and not *Ulysses*, which is only to say that his true genius was for very short stories, and hardly at all for extended narrative. Had he been primarily a poet, his lyrical gifts would have sufficed: we do not hold it against Yeats that his poems, not his plays, are his principal glory. Alas, neither Turgenev nor Henry James, neither Melville nor Mark Twain provide true agonists for Hemingway. Instead, de Maupassant is the apter rival. Of Hemingway's intensity of style in the briefer compass there is no question, but even *The Sun Also Rises* reads now as a series of epiphanies, of brilliant and memorable vignettes.

Much that has been harshly criticized in Hemingway, particularly in *For Whom the Bell Tolls*, results from his difficulty in adjusting his gifts to the demands of the novel. Robert Penn Warren suggests that Hemingway is successful when his "system of ironies and understatements is coherent." When incoherent, then Hemingway's rhetoric fails as persuasion, which is to say, we read To *Have and Have Not* or *For Whom the Bell Tolls* and we are all too aware that the system of tropes is primarily what we are offered. Warren believes this not to be true of *A Farewell to Arms*, yet even the celebrated close of the novel seems now a worn understatement:

> But after I had got them out and shut the door and turned off the light it wasn't any good. It was like saying good-by to a statue. After a while I went out and left the hospital and walked back to the hotel in the rain.

Contrast this to the close of "Old Man at the Bridge," a story only two and a half pages long:

> There was nothing to do about him. It was Easter Sunday and the Fascists were advancing toward the Ebro. It was a gray overcast day with a low ceiling so their planes were not up. That and the fact that cats know how to look after themselves was all the good luck that old man would ever have.

The understatement continues to persuade here because the stoicism remains coherent, and is admirably fitted by the rhetoric. A very short story concludes itself by permanently troping the mood of a particular moment in history. Vignette is Hemingway's natural mode, or call it hard-edged vignette: a literary sketch that somehow seems to be the beginning or end of something longer, yet truly is complete in itself. Hemingway's style encloses what ought to be unenclosed, so that the genre remains subtle yet trades its charm for punch. But a novel of three hundred and forty pages (*A Farewell to Arms*) which I have just finished reading again (after twenty years away from it) cannot sustain itself upon the rhetoric of vignette. After many understatements, too many, the reader begins to believe that he is reading a Hemingway imitator, like the accomplished John O'Hara, rather than the master himself. Hemingway's notorious fault is the monotony of repetition, which becomes a dulling litany in a somewhat less accomplished imitator like Nelson Algren, and sometimes seems self-parody when we must confront it in Hemingway.

Nothing is got for nothing, and a great style generates defenses in us, particularly when it sets the style of an age, as the Byronic Hemingway did. As with Byron, the color and variety of the artist's life becomes something of a veil between the work and our aesthetic apprehension of it. Hemingway's career included four marriages (and three divorces); service as an ambulance driver for the Italians in World War I (with an honorable wound); activity as a war correspondent in the Greek-Turkish War (1922), the Spanish Civil War (1937–39), the Chinese-Japanese War (1941), and the War against Hitler in Europe (1942–45). Add big-game hunting and fishing, safaris, expatriation in France and Cuba, bullfighting, the Nobel prize, and ultimate suicide in Idaho, and you have an absurdly implausible life, apparently lived in imitation of Hemingway's own fiction. The final effect of the work and the life together is not less than mythological, as it was with Byron, and with Whitman, and with Oscar Wilde. Hemingway now is myth, and so is permanent as an image of American heroism, or perhaps more ruefully the American illusion of heroism. The best of Hemingway's work, the stories and *The Sun Also Rises*, are also a permanent part of the American mythology. Faulkner, Stevens, Frost, perhaps Eliot and Hart Crane were stronger writers than Hemingway, but he alone in this American century has achieved the enduring status of myth.

V

Nathanael West, who died in 1940 at the age of thirty-seven in an automobile accident, wrote one remorseless masterpiece, *Miss Lonelyhearts* (1933). Despite some astonishing sequences, *The Day of the Locust* (1939) is an overpraised work, a waste of West's genius. Of the two lesser fictions, *The Dream Life of Balso Snell* (1931) is squalid and dreadful, with occasional passages of a rancid power, while *A Cool Million* (1934), though an outrageous parody of American picaresque, is a permanent work of American satire, and seems to me underpraised. To call West uneven is therefore a litotes; he is a wild medley of magnificent writing and inadequate writing, except in *Miss Lonelyhearts*, which excels *The Sun Also Rises*, *The Great Gatsby*, and even *Sanctuary* as the perfected instance of a negative vision in modern American fiction. The greatest Faulkner, of *The Sound and the Fury*, *As I Lay Dying*, *Absalom, Absalom!*, and *Light in August*, is the only American writer of prose fiction in this century who can be said to have surpassed *Miss Lonelyhearts*. West's spirit lives again in *The Crying of Lot 49* and in some sequences in *Gravity's Rainbow*, but the negative sublimity of *Miss Lonelyhearts* proves to be beyond Pynchon's reach, or perhaps his ambition.

West, born Nathan Weinstein, is a significant episode in the long and tormented history of Jewish Gnosticism. The late Gershom Scholem's superb essay "Redemption through Sin," in his *The Messianic Idea in Judaism*, is the best commentary I know upon *Miss Lonelyhearts*. I once attempted to convey this to Scholem, who shrugged West off, quite properly from Scholem's viewpoint, when I remarked to him that West was manifestly a Jewish anti-Semite, and admitted that there were no allusions to Jewish esotericism or Kabbalah in his works. Nevertheless, for the stance of literary criticism, Jewish Gnosticism, as defined by Scholem, is the most illuminating context in which to study West's novels. It is a melancholy paradox that West, who did not wish to be Jewish in any way at all, remains the most indisputable Jewish writer yet to appear in America, a judgment at once aesthetic and moral. Nothing by Bellow, Malamud, Philip Roth, Mailer, Ozick can compare to *Miss Lonelyhearts* as an achievement. West's Jewish heir, if he has one, may be Harold Brodkey, whose recent *Women and Angels*, excerpted from his immense novel-in-progress, can be regarded as another powerful instance of Jewish Gnosis, free of West's hatred of his own Jewishness.

Stanley Edgar Hyman, in his pamphlet on West (1962), concluded that "His strength lay in his vulgarity and bad taste, his pessimism, his nastiness." Hyman remains West's most useful critic, but I would amend this by observing that these qualities in West's writing emanate from a negative theology, spiritually authentic, and given aesthetic dignity by the force of West's eloquent negations. West, like his grandest creation, Shrike, is a rhetorician of the abyss, in the tradition of Sabbatian nihilism that Scholem has expounded so masterfully. One thinks of ideas such as "the violation of the Torah has become its fulfillment, just as a grain of wheat must not in the earth" or Jacob Frank's "We are all now under the obligation to enter the abyss." The messianic intensity of the Sabbatians and Frankists results in a desperately hysterical and savage tonality which prophesies West's authentically religious book, *Miss Lonelyhearts*, a work profoundly Jewish but only in its negations, particularly the negation of the normative Judaic assumption of total sense in everything, life and text alike. *Miss Lonelyhearts* takes place in the world of Freud, where the fundamental assumption is that everything already has happened, and nothing can be made new, because total sense has been achieved.

Negatively Jewish, the book is also negatively American. Miss Lonelyhearts is a failed Walt Whitman (hence the naming of the cripple as Peter Doyle, Whitman's pathetic friend) and a fallen American Adam to Shrike's very American Satan. Despite the opinions of later critics, I continue to find Hyman's argument persuasive, and agree with him that the book's psychosexuality is marked by a repressed homosexual relation between Shrike and Miss Lonelyhearts. Hyman's Freudian observation that all the suffering in the book is essentially female seems valid, reminding us that Freud's "feminine masochism" is mostly encountered among men, according to Freud himself. Shrike, the butcherbird impaling his victim, Miss Lonelyhearts, upon the thorns of Christ, is himself as much an instance of "feminine masochism" as his victim. If Miss Lonelyhearts is close to pathological frenzy, Shrike is also consumed by religious hysteria, by a terrible nostalgia for God.

The book's bitter stylistic negation results in a spectacular verbal economy, in which literally every sentence is made to count, in more than one sense of "count." Freud's "negation" involves a cognitive return of the repressed, here through West's self-projection as Shrike, spit out but not disavowed. The same Freudian process depends upon an affective continuance of repression, here by West's self-introjection as Miss Lonelyhearts, at once West's inability to believe and his disavowed failure to love. Poor Miss Lonelyhearts, who receives no other name throughout the book, has been destroyed by Shrike's power of Satanic rhetoric before the book even opens. But then Shrike has destroyed himself first, for no one could withstand the sustained horror of Shrike's impaling rhetoric, which truly can be called West's horror:

> "I am a great saint," Shrike cried, "I can walk on my own water. Haven't you ever heard of Shrike's Passion in the Luncheonette, or the Agony in the Soda Fountain? Then I compared the wounds in Christ's body to the mouths of a miraculous purse in which we deposit the small change of our sins. It is indeed an excellent conceit. But now let us consider the holes in our own bodies and into what these congenital wounds open. Under the skin of man is a wondrous jungle where veins like lush tropical growths hang along over-ripe organs and weed-like entrails writhe in squirming tangles of red and yellow. In this jungle, flitting from rock-gray lungs to golden intestines, from liver to lights and back to liver again, lives a bird called the soul. The Catholic hunts this bird with bread and wine, the Hebrew with a golden ruler, the Protestant on leaden feet with leaden words, the Buddhist with gestures, the Negro with blood. I spit on them all. Phooh! And I call upon you to spit. Phooh! Do you stuff birds? No, my dears, taxidermy is not religion. No! A thousand times no. Better, I say unto you, better a live bird in the jungle of the body than two stuffed birds on the library table."

I have always associated this great passage with what is central to West: the messianic longing for redemption, through sin if necessary. West's humor is almost always apocalyptic, in a mode quite original with him, though so influential since his death that we have difficulty seeing how strong the originality was. Originality, even in comic writing, becomes a difficulty. How are we to read the most outrageous of the letters sent to Miss Lonelyhearts, the one written by the sixteen-year-old girl born without a nose?

> *I sit and look at myself all day and cry. I have a big hole in the middle of my face that scares people even myself so I cant blame the boys for not wanting to take me out. My mother loves me, but she crys terrible when she looks at me.*
>
> *What did I do to deserve such a terrible bad fate? Even if I did do some bad things I didnt do any before I was a year old and I was born this way. I asked Papa and he says he doesnt know, but that maybe I did something in the other world before I was born or that maybe I was being punished for his sins. I dont believe that because he is a very nice man. Ought I commit suicide?*
>
> *Sincerely yours,*
Desperate

Defensive laughter is a complex reaction to grotesque suffering. In his 1928 essay on "Humor," Freud concluded that the above-the-I, the superego, speaks kindly words of comfort to the intimidated ego, and this speaking is humor, which Freud calls "the triumph of narcissism, the ego's victorious assertion of its own invulnerability." Clearly, Freud's "humor" does not include the Westian mode. Reading Desperate's "What did I do to deserve such a terrible bad fate?" our ego knows that is it defeated all the time, or at least is vulnerable to undeserved horror. West's humor has *no* liberating element whatsoever, but is the humor of a vertigo ill-balanced on the edge of what ancient Gnosticism called the *kenoma*, the cosmological emptiness.

Shrike, West's superb Satanic tempter, achieves his apotheosis at the novel's midpoint, the eighth of its fifteen tableaux, accurately titled "Miss Lonelyhearts in the Dismal Swamp." As Miss Lonelyhearts, sick with despair, lies in bed, the drunken Shrike bursts in, shouting his greatest rhetorical setpiece, certainly the finest tirade in modern American fiction. Cataloging the methods that Miss Lonelyhearts might employ to escape out of the Dismal Swamp, Shrike begins with a grand parody of the later D.H. Lawrence, in which the vitalism of *The Plumed Serpent* and *The Man Who*

Died is carried into a gorgeous absurdity, a heavy sexuality that masks Shrike's Satanic fears of impotence:

> "You are fed up with the city and its teeming millions. The ways and means of men, as getting and lending and spending, you lay waste your inner world, are too much with you. The bus takes too long, while the subway is always crowded. So what do you do? So you buy a farm and walk behind your horse's moist behind, no collar or tie, plowing your broad swift acres. As you turn up the rich black soil, the wind carries the smell of pine and dung across the fields and the rhythm of an old, old work enters your soul. To this rhythm, you sow and weep and chivy your kine, not kin or kind, between the pregnant rows of corn and taters. Your step becomes the heavy sexual step of a dance-drunk Indian and you tread the seed down into the female earth. You plant, not dragons teeth, but beans and greens."

Confronting only silence, Shrike proceeds to parody Melville of *Typee* and *Omoo*, or Somerset Maugham's version of Gauguin in *The Moon and Sixpence*:

> "You live in a thatch but with the daughter of a king, a slim young maiden in whose eyes is an ancient wisdom. Her breasts are golden speckled pears, her belly a melon, and her odor is like nothing so much as a jungle fern. In the evening, on the blue lagoon, under the silvery moon, to your love you croon in the soft sylabelew and vocabelew of her langorour tongorour. Your body is golden brown like hers, and tourists have need of the indignant finger of the missionary to point you out. They envy you your breech clout and carefree laugh and little brown bride and fingers instead of forks. But you don't return their envy, and when a beautiful society girl comes to your but in the night, seeking to learn the secret of your happiness, you send her back to her yacht that hangs on the horizen like a nervous racehorse. And so you dream away the days, fishing, hunting, dancing, kissing, and picking flowers to twine in your hair."

As Shrike says, this is a played-out mode, but his savage gusto in rendering it betrays his hatred of the religion of art, of the vision that sought a salvation in imaginative literature. What Shrike goes on to chant is an even more effective parody of the literary stances West rejected. Though Shrike calls it "Hedonism," the curious amalgam here of Hemingway and Ronald Firbank, with touches of Fitzgerald and the earlier Aldous Huxley, might better be named as an aesthetic stoicism:

> "You dedicate your life to the pursuit of pleasure. No overindulgence, mind you, but knowing that your body is a pleasure machine, you treat it carefully in order to get the most out of it. Golf as well as booze, Philadelphia Jack O'Brien and his chest-weights was well as Spanish dancers. Nor do you neglect the pleasures of the mind. You fornicate under pictures by Matisse and Picasso, you drink from Renaissance glassware, and often you spend an evening beside the fireplace with Proust and an apple. Alas, after much good fun, the day comes when you realize that soon you must die. You keep a stiff upper lip and decide to give a last party. You invite all your old mistresses, trainers, artists and boon companions. The guests are dressed in black, the waiters are coons, the table is a coffin carved for you by Eric Gill. You serve caviar and blackberries and licorice candy and coffee without cream. After the dancing girls have finished, you get to your feet and call for silence in order to explain your philosophy of life. 'Life,' you say, 'is a club where they wont stand for squawks, where they deal you only one hand and you must sit in. So even if the cards are cold and marked by the hand of fate, play up, play up like a gentleman and a sport. Get tanked, grab what's on the buffet, use the girls upstairs, but remember, when you throw box cars, take the curtain like a dead game sport, don't squawk.'"

Even this is only preparatory to Shrike's bitterest phase in his tirade, an extraordinary send-up of High Aestheticism prayer, of Pater, George Moore, Wilde, and the earlier W.B. Yeats:

> "Art! Be an artist or a writer. When you are cold, warm yourself before the flaming tints of Titian, when you are hungry, nourish yourself with great spiritual foods by listening to the noble periods of Bach, the harmonies of Brahms and the thunder of Beethoven. Do you think there is anything in the fact that their names all begin with a B? But don't take a chance, smoke a 3 B pipe, and remember these immortal lines: *When to the suddenness*

of melody the echo parting falls the failing day. What a rhythm! Tell
them to keep their society whores and pressed duck with oranges.
For you *l'art vivant*, the living art, as you call it. Tell them that
you know that your shoes are broken and that there are pimples
on your face, yes, and that you have buck teeth and a club foot,
but that you don't care, for to-morrow they are playing
Beethoven's last quartets in Carnegie Hall and at home you have
Shakespeare's plays in one volume."

That last sentence, truly and deliciously Satanic, in one of West's
greatest triumphs, but he surpasses it in the ultimate Shrikean rhapsody, after
Shrike's candid avowal: "God alone is our escape." With marvelous
appropriateness, West makes this at once the ultimate Miss Lonelyhearts
letter, and also Shrike's most Satanic self-identification, in the form of a letter
to Christ dictated for Miss Lonelyhearts by Shrike, who speaks absolutely for
both of them:

> *Dear Miss Lonelyhearts of Miss Lonelyhearts—*
> *I am twenty-six years old and in the newspaper game. Life for me is*
> *a desert empty of comfort. I cannot find pleasure in food, drink, or*
> *women—nor do the arts give me joy any longer. The Leopard of*
> *Discontent walks the streets of my city; the Lion of Discouragement*
> *crouches outside the walls of my citadel. All is desolation and a vexation*
> *of spirit. I feel like hell. How can I believe, how can I have faith in this*
> *day and age? Is it true that the greatest scientists believe again in you?*
> *I read your column and like it very much. There you once wrote:*
> *'When the salt has lost its savour, who shall savour it again?' Is the*
> *answer: 'None but the Saviour?'*
> *Thanking you very much for a quick reply, I remain yours truly,*
> *A Regular Subscriber*

"I feel like hell," the Miltonic "Myself am Hell," is Shrike's credo, and
West's.
       What is the relation of Shrike to West's rejected Jewishness? The
question may seem illegitimate to many admirers of West, but acquires
considerable force in the context of the novel's sophisticated yet unhistorical
Gnosticism. The way of nihilism means, according to Scholem, "to free
oneself of all laws, conventions, and religions, to adopt every conceivable
attitude and to reject it, and to follow one's leader step for step into the
abyss." Scholem is paraphrasing the demonic Jacob Frank, an eighteenth-

century Jewish Shrike who brought the Sabbatian messianic movement to its final degradation. Frank would have recognized something of his own negations and nihilistic fervor in the closing passages that form a patter in West's four novels:

> His body screamed and shouted as it marched and uncoiled; then, with one heaving shout of triumph, it fell back quiet. The army that a moment before had been thundering in his body retreated slowly—victorious, relieved.
>
> (*The Dream Life of Balso Snell*)

> While they were struggling, Betty came in through the street door. She called to them to stop and started up the stairs. The cripple saw her cutting off his escape and tried to get rid of the package. He pulled his hand out. The gun inside the package exploded and Miss Lonelyhearts fell, dragging the cripple with him. They both rolled part of the way down the stairs.
>
> (*Miss Lonelyhearts*)

> "Alas, Lemuel Pitkin himself did not have this chance, but instead was dismantled by the enemy. His teeth were pulled out. His eye was gouged from his head. His thumb was removed. His scalp was torn away. His leg was cut off. And, finally, he was shot through the heart."
>
> "But he did not live or die in vain. Through his martyrdom the National Revolutionary Party triumphed, and by that triumph this country was delivered from sophistication, Marxism and International Capitalism. Through the National Revolution its people were purged of alien diseases and America became again American."
>
> "Hail the martyrdom in the Bijou Theater!" roar Shagpoke's youthful hearers when he is finished.
>
> "Hail, Lemuel Pitkin!"
>
> "All hail, the American Boy!"
>
> (*A Cool Million*)

He was carried through the exit to the back street and lifted into a police car. The siren began to scream and at first he thought he was making the noise himself. He felt his lips with his hands. They were clamped tight. He knew then it was the siren. For

some reason this made him laugh and he began to imitate the
siren as loud as he could.

(*The Day of the Locust*)

All four passages mutilate the human image, the image of God that
normative Jewish tradition associates with our origins. "Our forefathers were
always talking, only what good did it do them and what did they accomplish?
But we are under the burden of silence," Jacob Frank said. What Frank's and
West's forefathers always talked about was the ultimate forefather, Adam,
who would have enjoyed the era of the Messiah, had he not sinned. West
retains of tradition only the emptiness of the fallen image, the scattered spark
of creation. The screaming and falling body, torn apart and maddened into a
siren-like laughter, belongs at once to the American Surrealist poet, Balso
Snell; the American Horst Wessel, poor Lemuel Pitkin; to Miss
Lonelyhearts, the Whitmanian American Christ; and to Tod Hackett,
painter of the American apocalypse. All are nihilistic versions of the
mutilated image of God, or of what the Jewish Gnostic visionary, Nathan of
Gaza, called the "thought-less" or nihilizing light.

West was a prophet of American violence, which he saw as augmenting
progressively throughout our history. His satirical genius, for all its authentic
and desperate range, has been defeated by American reality. Shagpoke
Whipple, the Calvin Coolidge-like ex-President who becomes the American
Hitler in *A Cool Million*, talks in terms that West intended as extravagant, but
that now can be read, all but daily, in our newspapers. Here is Shagpoke at
his best, urging us to hear what the dead Lemuel Pitkin has to tell us:

> "Of what is it that he speaks? Of the right of every American boy
> to go into the world and there receive fair play and a chance to
> make his fortune by industry and probity without being laughed
> at or conspired against by sophisticated aliens."

I turn to today's *New York Times* (March 29, 1985) and find there the
text of a speech given by our President:

> But may I just pause here for a second and tell you about a couple
> of fellows who came to see me the other day, young men. In 1981,
> just four years ago, they started a business with only a thousand
> dollars between them and everyone told them they were crazy.
> Last year their business did a million and a half dollars and they
> expect to do two and a half million this year. And part of it was

because they had the wit to use their names productively. Their business is using their names, the Cain and Abell electric business.

Reality may have triumphed over poor West, but only because he, doubtless as a ghost, inspired or wrote these Presidential remarks. The *Times* reports, sounding as deadpan as Shrike, on the same page (B4), that the young entrepreneurs brought a present to Mr. Reagan. "'We gave him a company jacket with Cain and Abell, Inc. on it,' Mr. Cain said." Perhaps West's ghost now writes not only Shagpokian speeches, but the very text of reality in our America.

SERGIO PEROSA

The "Tragic Pastoral"

This isn't just an epigram—life is much more successfully looked at from a single window, after all.   —GG, p. 169.

1

There is a remarkable difference in quality between *The Beautiful and Damned* and *The Great Gatsby*. But the road from the ambitious early attempt to the later achievement is short, going by way of an unhappy experience in the theater and the writing of a comparatively limited number of stories.

The project for a real play, something quite different from the college musicals or the adolescent melodramas, engaged the writer for more than a year. The results, however, were unequal to the effort expended, and *The Vegetable, or from President to Postman* (published by Scribner's in 1923) was a complete failure.[1] Popular success escaped Fitzgerald in the theater, as it had escaped, in spite of his greater efforts, Henry James. But even in this unlucky attempt, a critic can detect at least one positive element of renewal, a stage of a process through which Fitzgerald moved to a maturer position as a writer.

The Vegetable is only a light comedy, pleasingly written with the vague intention of staging a political satire. Nevertheless, if we examine its motives more closely, we can see that the subject of the play is again an indictment of the fallacy of dreaming, a denunciation of our irrational illusions. The play

From *The Art of F. Scott Fitzgerald*, by Sergio Perosa, translated by Charles Matz and the author. © 1965 by the University of Michigan.

lacks a unified development and a truly dramatic pace. It often descends to pure farce; but its informing idea and its final "message" is a definitive affirmation of realism and inner sincerity such as cannot be encountered previously in Fitzgerald's works.

The single ambition of the protagonist, Jerry Frost, who works for a railroad company, is to become a postman. This ambition seems ridiculous to his wife, father, and sister-in-law, all of whom contribute to making his life miserable with their continual upbraiding. Harassed and distressed by their reproaches, he nevertheless remains faithful to his ambition. After being visited by a bootlegger he dreams of becoming President of the United States. Most likely, he has drunk too much; all of the second act of the play takes place presumably in his dream, as in Shaw's *Man and Superman*. To Jerry Frost this long dream sequence soon becomes a frightful nightmare. He has been pushed to make war by ambitious generals and has been barred from the treasury by his miserly father; he has given up the whole state of Idaho, which has risen in rebellion against him, in exchange for some unknown islands and can only laugh when a Supreme Court justice, followed by all the Senators, stands up at hearing a jazz song which he takes for the national anthem. He has made fun of the army, political oratory, the inner divisions of Europe, and the American federal system. But this is not the life that Jerry Frost had wanted; it is a life that has been imposed on him. Thus, when he is accused of high treason, his sudden awakening to everyday reality is a form of liberation to him. Having learnt his lesson, in the third act he flees from home and does not reappear until he has become what *he* had wanted to become—a happy, self-satisfied postman, who can assert his own independence and personality over his relatives. His wife has been taught a lesson, too, and she welcomes her husband home.

It is clear that the plot is forced and mechanical, and it is equally evident that the three acts do not add up to a structural unity. Neither the central situation nor the method of presentation is original. The satire is often crude and the frequent *boutades*, puns, or wisecracks are clearly derived from the more brilliant ones of Oscar Wilde and Shaw. The discredit into which the play has fallen is, therefore, understandable: but in our context, it is worthwhile emphasizing the real novelty of intent with which Jerry Frost is portrayed.

Jerry Frost is the down-to-earth man, having no excessive illusions or ambitions in life, who asserts himself through the "realistic" side of his nature. In his acceptance of his own limitations, he achieves happiness and self-respect, after both of them have been put in jeopardy by absurd dreams or impossible pretentions. On the title page of the published version of the play Fitzgerald had placed an epigraph taken from "a current magazine":

"Any man who doesn't want to get on in the world, to make a million dollars, and maybe even park his toothbrush in the White House, hasn't got as much to him as a good dog has—he's nothing more or less than a vegetable." Jerry Frost, then, remains a "vegetable," and Fitzgerald intended perhaps to made fun of him as well. But this "vegetable" shows us the absurdity of the American myth of success. Frost's self-realization is in his doing what his innermost spirit tells him he wants to do. He does not get very far toward the world, and he does not make a million dollars. But his character betrays a positive, realistic side—the side that was so lacking in Anthony and his predecessors.

The serious aspect of his character, set against the background of a flippant farce with satirical intents, is perhaps one of the reasons for the play's failure. The "moralistic" assumption—either latent or consciously present—is difficult to reconcile with all the superficial elements that were included in the play to suit the popular tastes or the requirements of Broadway. But even this ambiguity and uncertainty represented a step forward. Jerry Frost has the virtue of accepting reality as it comes and is content with what he can get, without indulging in impossible dreams, pointless struggles, or Pyrrhic victories. He lives in the realm of everyday life, not in the eternal "carnival by the sea." He pays the penalty for his weakness in the second act, but then his wisdom triumphs over the world's folly, and he can become what he wanted to be—a simple, happy, efficient postman. He has realized his fate by accepting the simple virtues of his nature, and this "realistic" solution seems quite new in Fitzgerald's works.

It was still a way of burning incense before Mencken's disdainful frown, and in fact, Fitzgerald joined Mencken again in the denunciation of the vulgarity and ridicule of the contemporary popular myths. He offered Mencken a tribute of great esteem, and possibly a personal form of alliance. This coincidence with Mencken's crusade, however, is a passing one, and fortunately too, because the young writer had to follow his own intimate creative development by beating new paths and different roads. Yet even this temporary coincidence was a further step toward maturity. Even in *The Vegetable*, perhaps, Fitzgerald was experimenting with a form of dramatic foreshortening, of quick and concise action, of immediacy of response, such as he was later to achieve in *The Great Gatsby*. In this rather marginal experiment, in the waste of energy itself, not everything was lost,—just as not everything was lost in the stories which were written during, or soon after, the composition of the play. In most of them Fitzgerald was dealing with themes and motives and availing himself of techniques that he had already thoroughly exploited in the previous works. But a slow development toward the new novel is at times discernible, and this makes the stories interesting and significant, even when their purely aesthetic value seems rather poor.[2]

For the most part they are commercial stories, written for money, "fantasies" thrown together in a few hours, dealing with situations and characters which are wearily brilliant, repetitious, or pointless. It is clear that the writer had neither the time nor the willingness to try new things. Like a trump card, he held the novel up his sleeve, while satisfying for a while the public taste. And if the public had a taste for frivolity, Fitzgerald knew that he had better condescend to frivolity and repetition.

"The Popular Girl,"[3] for instance, deals again with the theme of the flapper, while "Rags Martin Jones and the Pr-nce of W-les"[4] reworks the formula of the rich boy who has to stage an elaborate fantasy to win the love of his flapper—as was the case in "The Offshore Pirate." "Gretchen's Forty Winks"[5] avails itself of autobiographical elements, while "Not in the Guide Book"[6] is a kind of advertising copy. "Dice, Brass Knuckles and Guitar"[7] is nothing more than a series of vapid humorous notes, and "Our Own Movie Queen,"[8] suggested and at least partly written by his wife Zelda, is nothing more than social chatter.

They are *divertissements* which are not even amusing, and they often melt into "fantasies," if we want to adopt Fitzgerald's definition for many of them. In "John Jackson's Arcady"[9] we are confronted with the theme of the prodigal son, whose homecoming brings peace and new faith to the long suffering father, who had been on the verge of despair. "The Curious Case of Benjamin Button" is merely an exercise in ingenuity. The germ for this story (which Fitzgerald found in a remark of Mark Twain and then in a note of Samuel Butler) is provided by the idea of a man born old, who grows younger as the time goes on, until he becomes a child. Once the situation is set in motion, each comic or farcical episode is possible and justifiable—if we accept the premises.[10]

Even a "fantasy," however, can serve a better purpose or can be put to a larger task, as is the case with the well-known story. "The Diamond as Big as the Ritz,"[11] where the theme of overpowering wealth is dealt with on the level of romantic fable. The story, foreshortened in eleven brief sections, follows the fantastic adventure of a boy who is a guest and at the same time a victim of an extremely wealthy family living in a secluded valley, and it is anything but negligible, either from the point of view its theme or of its artistic realization. It is in fact a variation on the motive of excessive wealth seen as the corrupting element which destroys both the dream of love and the need for purity. We are closer here to *The Great Gatsby* than to *The Beautiful and Damned*, because this same motive will be given fuller development in Fitzgerald's next novel. But hero the theme is unfolded and, as it were, analyzed in its bare form, in its essence, without the concurrence of other elements. The corrupting power of money is gradually revealed to the boy, but his discovery becomes the focal point of the tale, toward which every other interest is centered. As in the two novels the end of the fable is complete ruin, so great that it turns upside down the fabulous valley and destroys almost all its inhabitants. Only the boy, John, who remains uncorrupted despite his acceptance of the impossible dream of a boundless luxury, and his innocent girl-friend, purified by love, save themselves. The "moral," of course is that only purity of mind and sincerity of emotion resist the subtle corruption of money, and this is the lesson that Nick Carraway will learn, but with greater scepticism, in *The Great Gatsby*.

In bringing out the moral sense of such a parable, unfolded in its barest essence, there was the danger of making an abstract study of it, or of preaching a lay sermon about it. Fitzgerald avoided this danger, however, exactly because he gave the story the air of a fable or of a fantastic dream. Seen as such, the dream becomes credible because it is complete and isolated in its own frame, with no direct relationship with reality. The dreamy atmosphere sets off, as though in a show case, the events of the story, which acquire a kind of abstract and unreal distance. They are seen as detached from everyday life, perfectly consistent within their own frame of reference, and they are contemplated through the dazzled eyes of the boy. This focal length permits the action to unfold in obedience only to its own rationale, quite apart from any transposition on the level of actuality, which would have flawed the absolute purity of the fable:

Afterward John remembered that first night as a daze of many colors, of quick sensory impressions, of music soft as a voice in love, and of the beauty of things, lights and shadows, and motions and faces. There was a white-haired man who stood drinking a manyhued cordial from a crystal thimble set on a golden stem. There was a girl with a flowery face, dressed like Titania with braided sapphires in her hair. There was a room where the solid, soft gold of the walls yielded to the pressure of his hand, and a room that was like a platonic conception of the ultimate prison—ceiling, floor, and all, it was lined with an unbroken mass of diamonds, diamonds of every size and shape, until, lit with tall violet lamps in the corners, it dazzled the eyes with a whiteness that could be compared only with itself, beyond human wish or dream. (*Stories*, pp. 11–12.)

Such a perspective required from the author a certain capacity for objective detachment and an awareness of the possibilities provided by the use of symbolic devices. Fitzgerald proved equal to the occasion, so that the central idea of the story—the isolation and distortion of values which are typical of the very rich—is made evident by the symbol of the huge diamond and of the secluded valley, which is first the retreat and then the instrument of ruin for those who had found every reason and justification for living in it.[12] The symbolism, it should be noted, is still mechanical and rather simple here. And yet Fitzgerald's intuition—that the very rich are different and isolated from the rest of the human race and that they have to pay a penalty for it—is developed with rigorous consistency. For the first time, Fitzgerald was able to use a "controlling center" with thematic precision, by having the story recorded by the protagonist and filtered through his impressions. He set the center of interest in the sensitivity of the boy, and in this way he could confer a dreamy atmosphere on the story, and develop its theme as it gradually opened itself to John: If Fitzgerald, because of his total disinterest, could not tell the *how* and the *why* of so much wealth, he was able to make it visible and present through the dazzled and bewildered reactions of the boy; and this is quite sufficient for us to feel the inescapable burden under which the characters in "The Diamond as Big as the Ritz" must be buried.

The same theme, as we have hinted, was to reappear in *The Great Gatsby;* but it had to be dealt with, if not yet completely resolved, in realistic and not merely "fantastic" terms, before being ready for a maturer treatment. A breakaway from fable devices is already recognizable in "The Adjuster" and in "The Baby Party."[13] which takes up a theme of domestic comedy, developed along the slender thread of an argument between two old friends after a quarrel among their children. But it is also significantly present in three more stores—"Winter Dreams," "'The Sensible Thing,'" and "Absolution"—which bring us up to *Gatsby*.

The first two of these stories can be properly seen as attempts to come to terms with the new material that Fitzgerald was to utilize in the novel. They are, in a way, preliminary studies or tentative sketches, leading to a fuller awareness of the possibilities of a given subject matter. They might even serve by way of introduction to the novel, with all the merits and defects that introductions usually have. While clarifying many points that would reappear in *Gatsby*, they might predispose or condition our interpretation of the novel from an all-too-narrow point of view. In both of them we find the motive of a youthful dream of love which can be realized only when enough wealth has been somehow accumulated, and in both of them the financial success of the poor hero brings only the failure of the ideal of love. In

"Winter Dreams"[14] there is no doubt about the eventual failure. Young Dexter, although he has risen from caddy on the golf course to successful industrialist, is still unable to win the lasting love of irresponsible Judy, and his illusion of eternal beauty collapses when he discovers that the girl herself has lost all her charm. Money alone has not permitted him to fulfill his childhood dream. Like Anthony, he has tried to find an escape into the army, and like Anthony and Gatsby, he has failed to realize the "destructiveness of time." He has not been able to stop the fleeting moment of beauty and love, and nothing is left him but a deep regret for a youthful illusion which the present has shattered:

> "Long ago," he said, "long ago, there was something in me, but now that thing is gone. Now that thing is gone, that thing is gone. I cannot cry. I cannot care. That thing will come back no more." (*Stories*, p. 145.)

The ending of the story is more melancholy, perhaps, than hopelessly romantic, even if we are reminded of Poe at his least successful, and the style does not always reach the heights of the emotion that it would convey. In "'The Sensible Thing,'"[15] on the other hand, George O'Kelly, suddenly enriched, obtains an apparent victory in winning back the love of Jonquil, who had left him because he was poor. But even for him this apparent victory is but a sign of a subtler defeat, since it is won at the cost of an incurable loss: the loss of sentimental freshness and youthful emotion. For George O'Kelly as well, the passing of time had deprived his love of any charm and significance, and the longed-for wealth cannot bring back the lost moment:

> But for an instant as he kissed her he knew that though he search through eternity he could never recapture those lost April hours. He might press her close now till the muscles knotted on his arms—she was something desirable and rare that he had fought for and made his own—but never again an intangible whisper in the dusk, or on the breeze of night....
> Well, let it pass, he thought: April is over. April is over. There are all kinds of love in the world, but never the same love twice. (*Stories*, p. 158.)

In this second story, moreover, the theme is developed with greater skill and with a better awareness of its implications. In "Winter Dreams" the protest was hopelessly sentimental, and stylistically, it was resolved in awkward repetitions and digressions, with a deadly monotony of diction. "'The Sensible Thing,'" instead, seems to be more evenly balanced and better organized from a structural point of view. It portrays people that are at least more credible than those in the preceding story, George and Jonquil are more cautious and less given to talk than Dexter and Judy, and they are seen against a more realistic background. They refrain from the excited tone and the exasperated individualism of the earlier characters, and in the end they are willing to accept a form of compromise. Their refusal to make great scenes results in a melancholy humanity, such as we will meet again in the character of Gatsby. In the novel, however, the story developed from these slender suggestions into tragedy and even myth: here the writer was preparing and adjusting only the materials, the canvas, and the thread for the story that he was to weave. But we are slowly approaching that condition of happy perception that is responsible for the greatness of *Gatsby;* and with "Absolution," according to Fitzgerald's own admission, we have a discarded prologue of the novel itself.[16]

The interest of this story might be limited to its role as a possible explanation for the character of Gatsby; but one cannot neglect the fact that some technical devices of the novel are first encountered here. A young boy is driven by his father's harshness to tell two lies in confession, while the priest who hears them is involved in a deep moral and religious crisis. But what might interest us here is the fact that the story is practically represented by a long flashback sequence (the same technique used for relating Gatsby's and Daisy's past in the novel); the crisis of the priest, moreover, is not properly analyzed, but rather suggested by a careful correspondence of symbols (the Swedish girls, for instance, that appear at the beginning and at the end). Gatsby's "mystery" is not explained by this story, but here we can find all the promises for the technical and stylistic maturity of the novel, just as in the previous two stories we could easily recognize the first signs of its theme. But early thematic attempts and stylistic warnings cannot explain the balanced perfection of *The Great Gatsby*. We can only say that the ferment of ideas and the wealth of motives that can be found in these stories serve to set off in relief its unique quality.

2

In *The Great Gatsby* the motive of an impossible dream of love which riches cannot fulfill after the right moment has passed forever, finds its definitive consecration. Fitzgerald reveals the tragic implications of that dream by organizing the plot around an agonizing conflict of the moral and social order and by enlarging its meaning on the symbolic level of legend and myth. The story of Gatsby and Daisy, Nick and Jordan, Tom and Myrtle has a common origin with the similar adventures of so many of Fitzgerald's heroes and heroines. But it is no longer dependent on contingent reasons, nor is it the result of psychological distortions which are typical of individuals who turn their backs on reality. The story is rooted in an objective frame of references and thus acquires an individual, realistic meaning which is immediately apparent on the literal level. But it attains an even larger significance on the symbolic level by carrying to its tragic solution a conflict of characters which has a "universal" implication and a representative value. Hence its legendary and, at least partly, mythic quality, although we have always to remember that both legend and myth are resolved in, or spring from, the actual development of the story.

Only a careful examination of this structure—a thematic analysis, that is, developing step by step with an analysis of the manner of presentation— can render justice to the original and revolutionary quality of the novel. It is the method of presentation as well as its substance which is new, and this fact must be duly stressed; it is only in this way that T.S. Eliot's well-known statement about the novel—that *Gatsby* was "the first step that American fiction has taken since Henry James ... "[17]—can be meaningful.

At the time of composing his third novel, Fitzgerald felt that he had "grown at last." To both Edmund Wilson and John Peale Bishop he wrote of his new work with enthusiasm. He was convinced that he was writing something "wonderful," "something *new*—something extraordinary and beautiful and simple and intricately patterned."[18] His inspiration came so quickly as he worked that he finished the book in only ten months. In November 1924 the manuscript was already in the hands of the publisher, and yet he continued smoothing and polishing it so that in February of the following year he modified the structure of Chapters VI and VII by cutting and adding material and by rewriting an entire episode. It was only when the book was published on April 10, 1925, that Fitzgerald's labor to give it an organic form was completed.[19]

According to the outline that he had made,[20] Fitzgerald divided the material into nine brief chapters, in such a way that the climax comes in the fifth chapter (the "dead middle of book," as he called it). The first four chapters act as a slow introduction and preparation, while the last four mark the development of the story to its tragic conclusion at a quickened pace. In this brief span, by a masterful use of foreshortening, are encompassed the events of a single summer and the facts that precede them. These are evoked and reconstructed by the narrator, Nick Carraway, who learns about them and tells them in bits and pieces. Many flashbacks alternate in this way with the straight narration, and they give the motivations for the events represented, as well as provide a fuller basis for their understanding. From the dramatic immediacy of the present we are brought back to the past and referred to what might explain or motivate the action, reminded of its premises, recalled to its psychological reasons. In this superimposition and reciprocal influence of the two temporal levels, we are already confronted with an amplitude of perspective which makes the novel breathe.

In the first three chapters—to follow the action more closely in its development—the main characters are defined in their respective milieux and according to the moral or social positions that they represent. They are not described or "portrayed," however, as in the previous novels, but are represented in action and *through* their actions. Fitzgerald presents them at three different parties, given in different places at distinct times, in order to show immediately their various psychological natures, their diverse aspirations and ambitions, and the different social environments from which they spring and which they somehow embody. The method of presentation is, in other words, typically dramatic; the various characters are defined in action during three big scenes, as Nathaniel Hawthorne had done in *The Scarlet Letter*. Hawthorne's novel had been actually built on and around three "theatrical" scenes, which were staged on a "scaffold" (a kind of stage), and it could be easily staged in the theater. Melville had used the dramatic method of presentation in *Moby Dick*, and his novel has been often staged in the theater. The tendency to organize a novel in dramatic form, or to stress its dramatic possibilities with the use of theatrical devices, is actually present in most American fiction. It was to reappear in all its force in the last great novels of Henry James, who actually passed through a theatrical experience before writing them, and who built a theory of the "dramatic scene." This amounts to saying that at the very beginning of his new novel Fitzgerald had placed himself squarely within a fictional tradition, or at least trend, whose premises and assumptions were already firmly established.

Early in the novel Nick Carraway is defined as the *perfect* narrator. He has learned from his father to suspend judgment (which is an essential element for "objectivity"), he has been accustomed to listening to people who take him into their confidence, he maintains a "sense of the fundamental decencies," and possesses a good share of human sympathy and understanding. He can be "within and without, simultaneously enchanted and repelled by the inexhaustible variety of life." A son of the Middle West, he is now working in the East, having come back from the war disenchanted, but not feeling at ease in a surrounding which is foreign to him. Hence the precious detachment of his vision. But it is he who hints at Gatsby and suggests him, he who puts us in contact with Tom and Daisy Buchanan, who live on the other side (the fashionable side) of a bay on Long Island Sound. He thus becomes a participant in the story, a kind of fictional "go-between," who can be at the same time "within and without."

At the first party, Tom and Daisy betray to Nick their innermost natures. Strong and immeasurably rich, self-reliant, careless and ruthless, reactionary and arrogant, Tom has a "touch of paternal contempt in his voice." Daisy is also careless and self-reliant, but she is sophisticated and mildly genteel. She dawdles with Nick and her friend Jordan Baker, she teases Nick and is witty at times. And yet, under the cover of their genteel manners and the courtesy of their social talk, Nick, who feels himself "uncivilized" and would prefer "to talk about crops or something," does not fail to perceive a very different reality. Tom keeps a mistress, who telephones him at dinner, Jordan eavesdrops shamelessly, Daisy has sudden fits of impatience. Nick's first impulse is to "to telephone immediately for the police." His detachment from the Buchanans is not only social or geographic, it is moral. He draws back "confused and a little disgusted" before what seems to him "a rather distinguished secret society," and it is through his eyes that we have the first glimpse of Gatsby, alone and thoughtful in his garden, on the other side of the bay.

We have then, in the second chapter, a description of the "valley of ashes," halfway between the bay and New York. It is a desolate spot, a kind of waste land, overlooked by a gigantic pair of eyes on an advertising sign— a chance symbol,[21] but none the less effective, of the spiritual bareness and blindness of the world. This forms a prelude to the sordid atmosphere of moral disorder which broods over this chapter, and at the same time it offers a kind of thematic anticipation, for the final tragedy will take place in that valley, Myrtle, Tom's mistress, lives there, and he takes her to their apartment in New York, dragging Nick along. The second party, in New York, takes place, among vulgar and squalid people, in an atmosphere of moral disorder: Nick gets drunk, and in this way he records the events in a distracted and confused narration which reflects the intrinsic and moral disorder of the scene. This second party contrasts greatly with the "genteel" party in the first chapter and reveals the complete baseness of Tom, who, while amusing himself all the time with Myrtle, has no intention of divorcing Daisy. Like an autocratic and violent master, he wants to keep both women.

Gatsby now appears on the scene, after many hints and indirect suggestions. He is also shown (in Chapter III) against the background of a party on the grounds of his fantastic house ("a factual imitation of some

Hotel de Ville in Normandy"), to which a "menagerie" of people comes uninvited. There is an aspect of vulgarity in Gatsby's party, too, for his unknown guests behave "according to the rules of behavior associated with an amusement park." In the eyes of Nick, who has been regularly invited, the pretentious pomposity of this wealth is not lost. But Gatsby, far from participating in the drunken sprees of his guests and from identifying himself with the crowd of people, is melancholy and aloof. His isolation has something suspect and at the same time attractive about it. We sympathize with his evident timidity, his subdued tone. With the self-conscious courtesy with which he asks for an interview with Jordan Baker, who is present at the party. A comic automobile accident ends the elaborate "pageant" of his party, and this is a forewarning of the tragedy that will take place further along in the story.

Nick and Jordan wearily begin an affair and as "mediators" between the main characters, they make a meeting—or rather a collision—possible between East and West Egg, between Tom's and Daisy's "hard malice" and the dreamy vulnerability of Gatsby. In the fourth chapter, we have the preparations for the meeting. Gatsby reveals more and more of his contrasting aspects of modesty, ambiguous power, and questionable respectability, until Jordan discovers his secret—his lifelong love for Daisy. He has made his fortune for her, and for her he has bought his house in West Egg and given his parties (in the hope of meeting her by chance). This dubious gangster, who is supposed to be a murderer or a spy, reveals thus the dreamy aspect of his nature, his sentimental dedication, which in part redeem his coarse manners and his shady background, while Daisy's aloofness and carelessness are already marked by the fact that she has never yet appeared at one of his parties.

It is significant that their first meeting has to take place in the neutral ground of Nick's house (Chapter V); when the three of them move to Gatsby's enormous mansion, Gatsby after a passing moment of enthusiasm, of overwhelming self-satisfaction, begins to entertain a doubt "as to the quality of his present happiness." "Fulfillment destroys the dream—as Fitzgerald himself was to write. A long-cherished, sentimental illusion can be shattered by a mere brush with reality, or at least reduced to smaller dimensions." Gatsby's enormous dream is bound to suffer from any contact with reality.

This conflict between the expectations of Gatsby and the objective situation, however, is not simply an inner conflict. In the four chapters that follow it becomes also a conflict between external forces and social interests. Gatsby is ruined not only because of his inability to accept reality as equal to or sufficient for his dream; he is also defeated by Tom's "hard malice" and Daisy's irresolute carelessness.

The sixth chapter marks a pause in the narration. In the galley proofs, Fitzgerald described at some length the relation between Gatsby and Daisy, who told Nick of her willingness to "run off" with Gatsby. But in the final revision Fitzgerald chose to let the reader guess at the nature of the relationship, and to fill the void he skillfully added the "truthful," although incomplete, story of Gatsby's past.[22] We learn thus that Gatsby is a self-made man, an unscrupulous parvenu with no distinction or social background. He had met and lost Daisy in his youth, and his lifelong aim has been to recapture her, to become again acceptable to her. But he has no social or cultural tradition, and he remains a "newly rich" outsider. The point is important: it is from this angle that Tom chooses to attack Gatsby when he begins to suspect the truth.

At another party in Gatsby's mansion (Chapter VI), Tom, who has already snubbed him cruelly in the course of a casual encounter, manages to show him his utter hostility and contempt. This party should have marked Gatsby's triumph, but it proves a failure. Humiliated by Tom, Gatsby discovers with dismay that Daisy is unhappy and uncomfortable among his guests;[23] yet even in his disillusionment, he clings desperately to his impossible dream of "repeating" the past. The present does not come up to his expectation, and Gatsby abandons himself to an idyllic evocation of his first meeting with Daisy—his only way of actually "repeating" the past.

His faith, however, has been shaken, and he can no longer rely on his dream for support: he becomes an easy prey. He closes his house to please Daisy,[24] but he wants to come to a showdown with Tom—he wants Daisy herself to deny her past, to repudiate her love for Tom. On a sultry August afternoon, in the presence of Nick and Jordan, Gatsby confronts Tom in open battle (Chapter VII). But the struggle is not only for Daisy: each of the two wants to preserve and reaffirm his own attitude to life, the inner motivations of his own behavior, and Daisy's irresolution can only favor the man who is not utterly dependent on her. Enraged by the double prospect of losing wife and mistress at the same time (he has had a quarrel with Myrtle) of an athlete and hardened by his lifelong habit of command, Tom succeeds in striking Gatsby's weakest points until he makes him incapable of further resistance. In his purity Gatsby wants to be sincere and honest, and he reveals to everyone the secrets of his past, regardless of the consequences. He wins Nick's approval, but not Daisy's. Faced with those unpleasant revelations, and with Gatsby's avowal of a complete, unchanging love, she keeps her ground and does not move to meet him.

Abused by Tom and wounded by Daisy, Gatsby has already lost his battle. The automobile accident that happens under the spectral eyes of Dr. Eckleburg in the valley of ashes—on the ground that brings together both victors and vanquished—merely seals Gatsby's defeat. Daisy, who is at the wheel of Gatsby's car, runs over Myrtle who has rushed toward the car believing it to be Tom's, and Gatsby takes upon himself the whole responsibility for it. Shaken by these events Daisy hides behind the protection of her husband, without telling him the truth, and she remains with him, while Gatsby "is left standing there in the moonlight—watching over nothing":

Daisy and Tom were sitting opposite each other at the kitchen table, with a plate of cold fried chicken between them, and two bottles of ale. He was talking intently across the table at her, and in his earnestness his hand had fallen upon and covered her own. Once in a while she looked up at him and nodded in agreement.

They weren't happy, and neither of them had touched the chicken or the ale—and yet they weren't unhappy either. There was an unmistakable air of natural intimacy about the picture, and nobody would have said that they were conspiring together. (GG, pp. 274–75.)

Disturbed by this sight, Nick tells Gatsby of his admiration for him, but Tom puts Myrtle's husband on the track of Gatsby, who is murdered in the swimming pool (Chapter VIII). The murder might even seem superfluous, since Gatsby has already completed the cycle of his destiny. But fate is so bitterly cruel to him that it has in store the final humiliation—only Nick and a chance visitor attend his funeral (Chapter IX), and the latter recites a disconsolate epitaph on Gatsby: "The poor son of-a-bitch." Nick has broken his affair with Jordan, and in a final scene, a sort of elegiac fading-away, he is left to reconsider the story. He has learned a personal lesson, and he is now qualified to see the tragic and symbolic dimensions of the story, to bring forth its moral and universal significance as—a latter day Horatio over Hamlet's body.

Thus, the tragic dimension of the story becomes evident through a careful plot disposition, while Nick's reconsideration (or the author's reconsideration filtered through Nick) allows us to see its inherent richness of symbolic connotations. Superficially, the novel deals once more with the failure of a dream of love, which cannot be fulfilled or made to last by the acquisition of money. But Gatsby's failure has a deeper and more complex motivation in a subtle interplay of human and social conflicts, and his constitutional weakness finds a tragic counter part in them. Gatsby, too, is a hopeless dreamer, like Anthony before him and he clings stubbornly to his impossible illusion. But he has been strong enough to shape his own life and to acquire sufficient wealth and his struggle for success is a real one, ruthless and even dishonest. He *might*, after all win his battle, because he has prepared himself for it. But in his very strength, his sentimental purity is impaired. Gatsby builds his own fortune and puts himself, as it were in a bargaining position with Tom and Daisy, because he has somehow fulfilled her expectations of luxury and wealth. He is in any sense a self-made man, but he wants still to spring from "a Platonic conception of himself" and remain pure to his motives, at least.

His motives, however, may be pure, and yet he has to resort to dubious means to make his fortune; he is thus brought to foul the purity of his actions, and the "foul dust that floated in the wake of his dreams" envelops him in the end. If he is still a dreamer, in other words, he can accept the ethics of the "pioneers" and conform to it. If he is not linked with his parents, he is linked with Dan Cody ("the pioneer debauchee, who during one phase of American life brought back to the Eastern seaboard the savage violence of the frontier brothel and saloon"), and he shares the basic assumptions of Dan Cody's ethics. He can be faithful to his dream but to fulfill it he has to revert to questionable means, renounce his scruples, compromise with the world and its evil ways.

He is no longer a "youngster" or a "philosopher" and he cannot be a "young girl," as has recently been suggested by a modern critic.[25] He is definitely superior to Anthony, and he lives in a world of mature achievement, where one's wealth is no longer "easy money." On the practical side, he is a grown man who knows how to attain his practical aim. But for this very reason, the purity of his motivation is compromised by an acceptance of the ways of capitalist society. In this cleavage, therefore, between the innocence of his dream and the corruption of his practical ways, is to be found Gatsby's hamartia, his tragic flaw.

If this were all, however, Gatsby would be bound to become a pathetic failure, like Anthony. His failure is tragic, instead, because his attempt is thwarted by Tom's and Daisy's organized forces. His inner and psychological conflict coincides with an overt struggle where he is again bound to fail because his psychological and practical resistance has been weakened and because his dream interposes too much on his straightforward path. Daisy of course, is no longer a flapper—or she is a flapper still, but with a far greater power of offense than her predecessors. If, like Gloria she has made her choice, and has chosen security and wealth four years with Tom have hardened her character and made her careless and ruthless in her malice, Gatsby's dreamy attachment has no chance with her.

He asks too much of her, far more than she could actually give him, and this sentimental claim makes him partly responsible for her reaction. But she has taken on Tom's "hard malice" and his sense of spiteful superiority, and she comes to identify herself with him when he attacks Gatsby. In this sense Gatsby counts on her as an ally when he is actually confronted with another enemy. On the other hand, Tom is the dramatic antithesis of Gatsby. Born rich, he cares only for himself and his possessions (including Daisy, not so much as a wife but as someone or something that belongs to him), and he makes almost a natural right of his constitutional corruption. He has so successfully shaped Daisy's mind that she accepts his values and can even tolerate his frequent and open infidelities. At the crucial moment, only in Tom can she find a support for her weakness and her cowardice. Quite rightly, Nick puts them together in his moral judgment:

> They were careless people, Tom and Daisy—they smashed up things and creatures and then retreated back into their money or their vast carelessness, or whatever it was that kept them together, and let other people clean up the mess they had made.... (GG, p.300.)

After the car accident, as we have seen, they appear to Nick to be "conspiring together." And it has been a conspiracy, even if unconscious, in which Gatsby has been trapped. He has "paid a high price for living too long with a single dream," but he has also been defeated by the organized opposition of his antagonists. He has been brought against a wall of incomprehension, and he could not strike through their masks. He wanted to repeat the past, and the present itself fails him. He wanted to make up for his loss, and a greater loss awaits him. He wanted to be true to his own inner self, without realizing that the conflict was so much more of contrasting social and moral positions than of mere persons.

In Gatsby's moral ambiguity there is a also a touch of greatness. If this greatness lies in the unspoiled purity of his feeling, despite his soiled hands and his service of "a vast, vulgar and meretricious beauty," it is of no avail if confronted with the corruption of those traditionally "very rich," with the shamelessness of those who still know how to use force and exercise a *droit de seigneur.* "They are a rotten crowd—Nick shouts to Gatsby—. You're worth the whole damn bunch put together." He is confronted with a rotten crowd, and they are instrumental in bringing about his defeat: his failure is no longer the result of his own weakness alone. Nick makes this clear with his passionate outburst and with his moral opposition to Tom and Daisy. Gatsby is crushed in a moral conflict between two contrasting conceptions of the world, which is reflected in his geographical division from Tom and Daisy. Gatsby's mansion and Nick's cottage are on this side of the bay (both geographically and symbolically), while Tom and Daisy weave the threads of their net across the water, in East Egg or in New York.

This geographic opposition makes the moral division of the four characters symbolically concrete, but even their social contrasts are brought to bear in the development of the story. Gatsby, who is compared and equated with Trimalchio, remains a parvenu to the end. And this social detail speeds, if it does not actually determine, his ruin. Tom is opposed to Gatsby as a rich man by birth and tradition who hates and holds in contempt the lack of taste and manners of the newly rich. Tom himself is coarse and vulgar, of course, besides being corrupt (his relation with Myrtle admits of no doubt about it) but with Daisy he knows how to strike a detached attitude, how to impress her with his superior manners and superficial aloofness. He can be effectively ironical about Gatsby's display of wealth, his yellow car, the "menagerie" of people who frequent his house, the gaudiness of his dress, the vulgarity of his parties. Gatsby's elaborate formality of speech just missed being absurd," we are told and his pseudo-British expression "old sport" annoys Tom greatly. Daisy absorbs from her husband some of his annoyance and fastidiousness, and she feels uncomfortable at the party to which Gatsby invites her. She feels uneasy, too about his display of wealth, and it is significant that Gatsby's first move after they have met is to rid himself of the "menagerie"[26]

During that hot summer, we have to remember, Daisy lives in dark and cool rooms, "shadowed well with awnings." Gatsby does not feel at ease in her house (Chapter VII), and there is a social disparity between them that Daisy could overcome in her youth, but which she finds difficult to accept now. The social tone of Tom, Daisy, and Jordan is sophisticated and blasé, and they have no sympathy for Gatsby with his childish and impulsive sentimentality. Gatsby is outside their world from the very beginning, and his attempt to separate Daisy from her "aristocratic" background and surroundings is doomed to fail. The disparity of social levels from which they spring makes it impossible for him to satisfy her deeply rooted need for gentility and social distinction.

This social contrast between the opposing characters plays a remarkable part in *Gatsby*, and it is therefore clear why Gatsby's defeat, determined as it is by a complex interplay of inner and outer factors, becomes tragic and not merely pathetic. Too many forces, besides his sentimental weakness, are at work against him for him to escape his doom. He is doomed for having lived too long with a single impossible dream, defeated by social opposition, trampled down by a world of moral corruption and carelessness. But if he does not escape his fate a "possible" redemption is clearly indicated, and a gleam of hope is left at the end.

The many conflicts that cause the ruin of Gatsby leave Jordan as well as Tom and Daisy unchanged. But to Nick they open the way for a beneficial return home. Both Nick and Jordan (narrator and *ficelle* on the technical level) do not in fact remain on the edges of the plot, but participate in it, contributing to its clarification and at the same time involved in its development. Their own affair, wearily begun and dragged on, sets off in relief Gatsby's absorption in his love for Daisy; it is highly significant that Nick is moved to break off his affair with Jordan when Gatsby's love is painfully wrecked. Detaching himself from Jordan, who belongs completely to Tom's and Daisy's world and like them, is "careless" and "incurably dishonest," Nick perhaps avoids a similar destiny. At the same time, Gatsby's ruin, while saving Nick from a protracted compromise on the moral level, drives him home to the Middle West, where his innate "honesty," still uncorrupted, can find a better ground in which to flourish. Before it is too late, Nick leaves the East, which has the likeness of a nightmare for him now—and his choice is a moral one, a way to salvation. In the East, owing to his intermediate position between the various characters, he has been offered many allurements that might have meant ruin for him as well. Jordan was after all a trap, which might have brought him on Tom's and Daisy's side. Tom and Myrtle had tried to involve him in their corruption (Chapter II). Daisy had fascinated him, too, with her beauty and her verve. Gatsby, on the other side, had offered him a job ("a rather confidential sort of thing") that would have drawn him into his world of questionable business transactions. And yet Nick resists all the various suggestions and maintains his intermediate position without compromising his own integrity. His only concession to *their* code of behavior is his short-lived affair with Jordan. Thus, Nick is free to condemn the conduct of Tom and Daisy, even if at the end he can be persuaded to shake their hands. He feels strongly attracted by Gatsby and defends the purity of his hopeless attempt and his generous behavior, without sharing his assumptions. He is willing to let him meet Daisy in his own cottage, he is sensible of his "greatness," but he refuses his moral compromise between pure motives and shady means. He stays with him to the bitter end, but then goes home, and his return to the Middle West is a clear proof of his independence of judgment and moral integrity.

He saves himself through Gatsby's ruin; in his incorrupted honesty Nick is given the task of commenting on the story and of throwing into relief its legendary or mythical aspects. If he goes back to the Middle West, it is because it represents for him the positive side of a moral dilemma. In the geographic contrast between East and West, Nick perceives symbolically a wider significance: this contrast foreshadows a moral one between corruption and innocence, between economic power and homely virtues, urban sophistication and closeness to nature, "culture" and simplicity. As custodian of tradition and moral values, the West finds in its contact with the East the negation and perversion of these values. It is in this sense that Nick's choice becomes meaningful:

> After Gatsby's death the East was haunted for me.... distorted beyond my eyes' power of correction. So when the blue smoke of brittle leaves was in the air and the wind blew the wet laundry stiff on the line I decided to come back home. (GG, p. 298.)

If he returns home, it is because the story which he has witnessed implies a typical parable in which East and West are set up as two contrasting moral polarities:

> I see now [says Nick] that this has been a story of the West, after all—Tom and Gatsby, Daisy and Jordan and I, were all Westerners, and perhaps we possessed some deficiency in common which made us subtly unadaptable to Eastern life. (GG, p. 298.)

All excited by the East, but the East has "a quality of distortion." West Egg appears to Nick "as a night scene by El Greco," and so it must have appeared to Gatsby as well. Some of the characters have succumbed to the East, some have adapted themselves to it, some flee from it to save themselves and find shelter in the West. The West itself, of course, is tainted by the far-reaching tentacles of the East,[27] and Nick is right in observing that *his* Middle West was "not the wheat or the prairies or the lost Swede towns, but the thrilling returning trains of *his* youth." The returning trains come from the East with a burden of insinuating and subtle corruption—and it might be worth remembering that in college Nick belonged, after all, to the same society that Tom did; he might have been as predisposed to corruption as Tom was. But if Nick was not (at the very beginning, Gatsby represented for him "everything for which *he had* an unaffected scorn"), it is also because, in spite of his words, he was faithful to "the wheat" and "the prairies."

The point is that this complex adventure transcends, in its deeper nature, the literal limitations, the mere formulation of the facts as they are on the page. Going on with his disconsolate comment at the end, Nick realizes that Gatsby's illusion can be identified with the illusion or the dream of the early Dutch settlers, entranced by their vision of the New World:

> As the moon rose higher the inessential houses began to molt away until gradually I became aware of the old island here that flowered once for Dutch sailors' eyes—a fresh, green breast of the new world. Its vanished trees, the trees that had made way for Gatsby's house, had once pandered in whispers to the last and greatest of human dreams: for a transitory enchanted moment man must have held his breath in the presence of this continent....

And as I sat there brooding on the old, unknown world, I thought of Gatsby's wonder when he first picked out the green light at the end of Daisy's dock. He had come a long way to this blue lawn, and his dream must have seemed so close that he could hardly fail to grasp it. He did not know that it was already behind him, somewhere back in the vast obscurity beyond the city, where the dark fields of the republic rolled on under the night.

> Gatsby believed in the green light, the orgiastic future that year by year recedes before us.... (GG, p. 301.)

The houses, as we see, become "inessential", what matters is that Gatsby's story is identified with that of the pioneers. The trees have vanished, but his dream or his illusion repeats, in a modern context, their dream, which might have been after all an illusion, of building a new life for themselves, a new place in history where they could renew the past. The "green light" cherished by Gatsby is not only on Daisy's dock—it is also the green light of the "orgiastic future." And that future recedes before us year by year. If it is not already behind us, in the past, "in the vast obscurity beyond the city," in the dark fields.

In this way, Gatsby's adventure is based on a traditional motive of the American experience, divided between the yearning for innocence and the compromises of reality, between the idyllic vision of the West and the corruption of the urban civilization of the East. All experience in America—

whether historical, legendary, or literary—seems to be characterized by a pendular movement between these two poles: Fenimore Cooper and Thoreau, Mark Twain and Hemingway, Robert Frost and so many modern writers have all relied on that contrast for their works. *The Great Gatsby* clearly belongs to this tradition, both for its literal theme and for its larger symbolic significance. In his well-known preface to the novel.[28] Lionel Trilling speaks quite rightly of the legendary and mythical aspect of Gatsby's story. The legend is that of the "young man from the provinces," thwarted by his contact with the city (the East). They myth is, the typical American myth of the geographic and moral juxtaposition between the two poles of the nation to which a symbolic meaning is attached: the innocence of the flowering fields of wheat, the corruption and sterility of the city.

According to a well-known definition of Jacques Barzun,[29] all the characters, whether real or imaginary, who express and embody destinies, aspirations, or attitudes typical of man, or of a particular section of mankind, are to be considered "mythical." In this limited sense of the word. *The Great Gatsby*, both in its action and in its characters, can be said to be mythical. They do express and embody "attitudes, aspirations, and destinies" in many ways typical of the American experience, and thus they allow us to detect in the "literal" sense of the story a larger significance of symbolic connotations.

3

The Great Gatsby says or suggests all this. And it does it with a maturity and an economy of expressive means which must be duly emphasized, because they represent an important step forward and a real turning point in Fitzgerald's fiction.

The maturity lies in Fitzgerald's detachment of vision, in his objective rendering and in his skillful construction of the plot. The economy of means is achieved through a perfected use of foreshortening and of the "dramatic scene." The superior quality of the language gives the final touch to the book.

Gatsby vibrates with the intensely personal participation of the author, who infuses into his characters the warmth and depth of his own feeling. But this does not imply an immediate identification of the writer with his characters, as could be said of Amory or, to a lesser degree, of Anthony. Although making use of his own experiences, as every writer does, Fitzgerald *lent* them to his characters in *Gatsby* without linking himself to them. He projected them in imaginary figures who move by their own force and live their own "life" independently of him. Gatsby's dream might have been, partly, Fitzgerald's own dream, too. But it becomes step by step the dream of a whole nation, as we have seen, and it acquires a meaning which exceeds any autobiographical interpretation. Gatsby was originally drawn from a man Fitzgerald knew;[30] Daisy seems to have very little in common with Zelda, while Nick, Tom, Wilson, Myrtle, Wolfsheim, and the other characters are all objective creations. The fact that they are "filtered" through the eyes of a narrator undoubtedly added sharpness to Fitzgerald's objective rendering; and this is the first and all-important technical device which accounts for his detachment of vision.

The narrator gives a personal flavor to the story, and at the same time he allows the writer to attain a balance between the representation of character and incident. Henry James has already warned that in a successful work of art there is no possible distinction to be made between characters and incidents: "What is character but the determination of incident?—he had written—What is incident but the illustration of character?"[31] Too often, in the preceding novels, the fusion between these two elements had failed because the character was defined a priori by a "portrait," and the story unfolded according to the initial *donnée*. In *Gatsby* the two components are harmoniously developed in close relationship. The action is represented through "dramatic scenes" in which the characters are "illustrated" by their actions, and the incidents are in turn "determined" by their inner psychologies. Both incidents and characters are shown as they appear to Nick, and he can define them only by seeing them in a single moment of vision, where no distinction is possible between what the characters *do* and what they *are*. What they do tells us what they are; and what they are shows us what they can do. Nick is the only one to be defined at the beginning, on account of the obvious function that he has to perform: then the dramatic scene is responsible for the parallel development of the story and of the characters.

In this view, the supposed deficiencies of the book are easily accounted for. Edith Wharton, relying on her own method of composition, held that we should know more of Gatsby's past and his early career. And Fitzgerald himself agreed with John Peale Bishop that there was "a BIG FAULT" in the novel he had given "no account (and had no feeling about or knowledge of) the emotional relation between Gatsby and Daisy from the time of their reunion to the catastrophe." He felt that he had concealed the fault with "blankets of excellent prose."[32] But in the light of what has been said it is evident that the ambiguity of the relation between Gatsby and Daisy is revealed indirectly by the events that follow, when his dissatisfaction with the bourgeois, compromise of secret adultery is contrasted with her careless indecision. There is no account of their relation, but its deeper sense is dramatically made evident; and in the same way, Gatsby's clumsy attempts to regain and then defend the possession of Daisy are a clear indication of the instability and suffering of his youth. What is not "reported" is clearly suggested, and sometimes the suggestion carries more weight and significance—as in these cases—than would a diffuse treatment. As we know, moreover, these "omissions" were deliberate: Fitzgerald did not use "Absolution" as a prologue to the novel, and he cut out of the proofs his references to the relation between Gatsby and Daisy. In both cases, again, nothing was lost if we keep in mind the particular type of foreshortening that Fitzgerald used in the story.

The technical devices he used in *Gatsby*—foreshortening, the dramatic scene, the narrator, the mutual interdependence of character and incident—account for the formal perfection and the novelty of the book, and they must be properly understood if one wants to avoid the pitfalls of rash criticism. It is at this point that the influence of Henry James and Joseph Conrad becomes of paramount importance. If it was not a completely conscious influence, it was an indirect lesson that Fitzgerald drew from both writers, and in particular from Conrad, and neither of them can be ignored if we want to see the reasons that account for the success of *Gatsby* and for its novelty in the corpus of Fitzgerald's works.

His infatuation with Wells and Mackenzie had lessened, his interest in Dreiser had dwindled away, and he had discovered the ethical purpose of Mencken's "literary revolution."[33] In the short period between *The Beautiful and Damned* and *Gatsby* Fitzgerald had become interested in other writers—in Anatole France, Stephen Crane, Willa Cather, Edith Wharton, and, above all, Joseph Conrad.[34] They were all writers who were particularly interested in, and even obsessed by the problems of literary form, who strongly believed in the craft of fiction and in the art of the novel. Writing about *The Beautiful and Damned*, Edmund Wilson had maintained that Fitzgerald "had been given imagination without intellectual control of it" and that he had labored under "a desire for beauty without an aesthetic ideal." Responding to the advice of his "intellectual conscience," in his third novel Fitzgerald had set himself the task of "an attempt at form," refraining carefully "from trying to 'hit anything off.'"[35] He had developed a form of intellectual control over his material and proposed to himself an aesthetic ideal which can be traced back to the informing principles not only of Conrad or Edith Wharton but of their "master," Henry James.

Henry James had strongly advocated, both in theory and in practice, the principle of the "*craft* of fiction" and of the "*art* of the novel" by stressing the need for a formal awareness on the part of the writer. He had emphasized in his essays on the novel and in his prefaces the necessity of an indirect approach through the use of a narrator involved in the story, or of a disinterested observer, who would filter the story itself through his impressions and feelings. He had then inferred from it the principle of the "dramatic scene," with the corollary of foreshortening and of the limited point of view. Eliminating the principle of an omniscient author, and consequently his personal intrusions in the novel, he had reduced the value of the great fictional "frescoes" in favor of a dramatic type of novel, in which a series of quick and meaningful scenes—"pageants" or *tableaux vivants*— would resolve and exhaust the complex shades of the action and define the psychologies of the characters. He detached himself in this way from a typically nineteenth-century tradition and opened the way to the modern novel. His ideal, as has been noted, was to endow the novel with dramatic immediacy, to represent the action in its unfolding, "here and now." The practical result was an awareness of the need for selection and the fictional importance of a dramatic structure. As Joseph Warren Beach has remarked:

> The dramatic method is the method of direct presentation, and aims to give the readers the sense of being present, here and now, in the scene of action.... Description is dispensed with by the physical stage setting. Exposition and characterization are both conveyed through the dialogue and action of the characters.
>
> .   .   .
>
> The restricted point of view is listed among the elements that make for the realization of the dramatic ideal.... The fundamental impulsion to dramatic concentration in general is the desire to secure in the novel something equivalent to the dramatic present in the play. The limitation of time tends to produce the effect of the dramatic Now, the limitation of place, the dramatic Here; the "center of interest" concentrates the attention, as in the drama, upon these particular people or this particular person now present here. And finally, the restriction of the point of view carries to its full logical outcome the esthetic idea of the limited center of interest.[36]

Willa Cather, Edith Wharton, and Joseph Conrad not only knew, but conformed to these principles in their works. Conrad himself had enlarged the task and the role of the narrator involved in the story, by bestowing on him the ability of "imagining" scenes at which he had not been present, and by admitting the principle of a concurrence of several narrators of the story;

furthermore, driven by a desire for verisimilitude, Conrad had advocated the principle of the "chronological muddlement," arranging his stories not as a chronological sequence of events, but as a series of gradual discoveries made by the narrator. Ford Madox Ford, who worked with Conrad and collaborated with him on some early novels, has left us an enlightening explanation of this theory:

> It became very early evident to us that what was the matter with the novel, and the British novel in particular, was that it went straight forward, whereas in your gradual making acquaintanceship with your fellows you never do go straight forward. You meet an English gentleman at your golf club. He is beefy, full of health, the moral of the boy from an English Public School of the finest type. You discover gradually that he is hopelessly neurasthenic, dishonest in matters of small change, but unexpectedly self-sacrificing, a dreadful liar.... To get such a man in fiction you could not begin at his beginning and work his life chronologically to the end. You must first get him in with a strong impression, and then work backwards and forwards over his past.... That theory at least we gradually evolved.[37]

There is no evidence that Fitzgerald had read much of James when he wrote *Gatsby*, although he knew *The Portrait of a Lady* and *What Maisie Knew* (and possibly James's own prefaces to them). But he had read *A Lost Lady* (1923) and *My Antonia* (1918) by Willa Cather—two novels in the Jamesian manner that have points in common with *Gatsby*—and had become an even greater admirer of Edith Wharton.[38] Moreover, we have every reason to believe that he was perfectly acquainted with Conrad's methods, and while writing *Gatsby* be had "just re-read," by his own admission,[39] Conrad's preface to *The Nigger of the 'Narcissus.'* In this well-known and important preface, Conrad had expounded his "impressionistic" principles ("Fiction ... appeals to temperament.... Such an appeal to be effective must be an impression conveyed through the senses.") and had maintained that the art of fiction "must strenuously aspire to the plasticity of sculpture, to the colour of painting, and to the magic suggestiveness of music." The task which the writer had to achieve was "by the power of the written word to make you hear, to make you feel— ... before all, to make you *see*." In a "single-minded attempt" of this kind the writer would "hold up unquestioningly, without choice and without fear, the rescued fragment before all eyes in the light of a sincere mood ... and disclose its inspiring secret: the stress and passion within the core of each convincing moment." All the truth of life was then to be found in "a moment of vision, a sigh, a smile."[40] Conrad's principles were clearly based on certain assumptions of James's theory of the novel, and through his words, therefore, Fitzgerald could have at least a glimpse of James's lesson.

In this way the process of evolution that brought the author to an awareness of the *craft* of fiction and of the novel as an art form becomes clear, and in the technical and formal excellence of *Gatsby* we are able to single out some precise derivations. For his narrator, Fitzgerald used the "modified point of view" developed and advocated by Conrad. Nick is not present in all the scenes, and he reconstructs what he has not witnessed through other sources: Jordan Baker, the *ficelle* (who tells him about Daisy before her marriage). Gatsby (who reveals to him some of his own past). Gatsby's father and servants, Michaelis (who reports to him Wilson's desperate behavior). In addition, Nick draws upon his imagination when he describes Gatsby's death and his youthful idyll with Daisy. From Conrad, again, Fitzgerald got the technique of the "chronological distortion" of the events, beginning with a "strong impression" of the protagonist and of the situation, and then moving "backwards and forwards" to unravel the past from the present, the truth from the appearance, the motivation from the act. The chronological order of *Gatsby* is not so complicated as that of *Lord Jim*, for example, but it does give the reader the sense of a "reconstruction," as close as possible to the truth, of the events.[41] Typical of Conrad, too, is the predilection for the indirect allusion, the ability to suggest character and situation by simple hints, the "magic suggestiveness" of the "written word" which allows Fitzgerald to hold up "unquestioningly" his rescued fragments and to disclose "the stress and passion" within the core of his convincing moments. However indirect unconscious, must be taken into consideration.[42]

The technical device of a *ficelle* (Jordan Baker), who somehow supports the narrator in his task, seems to be clearly derived from James, even if Fitzgerald gave Jordan not only a *technical* function in the novel, but a thematic significance as well, in contrast with the requirement of the "master" himself. And the use of foreshortening and compression, of the dramatic scene filtered through an observer, is perfectly in keeping with James's principles and with James's advice to suppress all the substance and all the surface in favor of an allusive treatment:

> To give the image and the sense of certain things while still keeping them subordinate to his plan, keeping them in relation to matters more immediate and apparent, to give all the sense, in a

word, without all the substance or all the surface, and so to summarise and foreshorten, so to make values both rich and sharp, that the mere procession of items and profiles is not only, for the occasion, superseded, but is, for essential quality, almost "compromised"—such a case of delicacy proposes itself at every turn to the painter of life who wishes both to treat his chosen subject and to confine his necessary picture.[43]

The Great Gatsby is governed by this principle and informed by this "delicacy." The picture is "confined" and the chosen subject is "treated" so that its art becomes "exquisite." "The mere procession of items and profiles" is almost compromised, but the values have been made both rich and sharp. The foreshortening is so conscious, and the compression so much sought after, that the effect comes close to James's aesthetic ideal—"to the only compactness that has a charm, to the only spareness that has a force, to the only simplicity that has a grace—those, in each other, that produce the *rich* effect."

In this complex interplay of literary influences or suggestions Fitzgerald was nonetheless able to speak with his own voice, and he explored the ways of the dramatic scene or of the "magic suggestiveness" with his own vehicle—a highly refined and mature prose, musically alive, sober and controlled in its diction but rich in effectiveness. In *This Side of Paradise* the stylistic pattern was given by the sentence. In *The Great Gatsby* it is represented by the period, almost a rhythmic clause rounded-off and self-contained, subtly scanned in the transitions from one sentence to another, opening at times in effective flow. Of the many possible illustrations (and quite a few are already there in the previous pages), two will suffice at this point. One is the central scene of the accident, when Myrtle Wilson is run over by Daisy at the wheel of Gatsby's car, a scene compressed and foreshortened, seen from a close angle of vision:

> The "death car" as the newspaper called it, didn't stop; it came out of the gathering darkness, wavered tragically for a moment, and then disappeared around the next bend. Mavromichaelis wasn't even sure of its color—he told the first policeman that it was light green. The other car, the one going toward New York, came to rest a hundred yards beyond, and its driver hurried back to where Myrtle Wilson, her life violently extinguished, knelt in the road and mingled her thick dark blood with the dust. (GG, pp. 268–69.)

The crucial incident of the novel is given in three quick sentences. It opens with the sight of the speeding car, which has already a connotation of death, and whose swerving is actually reproduced in the movement of the first sentence. The car disappears immediately, and in the second sentence we have a pause, marked by the appearance of that clumsy name—Mavromichaelis—which seems almost a personification of the absurdity of things. There is a vague hint at the color of the car, the sudden mention of the policeman and then "the other car" rushes on the scene in the third sentence—another image of speed which comes slowly to a standstill. Following the steps of its driver, we are brought to the cruel discovery of Myrtle's body, weirdly kneeling on the road, and the scene closes on that gruesome image of her *thick, dark blood* mingling with the *dust*. The three sentences seem to mark the three steps of a musical progression, scanned in the last line by the sharp beat of the monosyllables.

This passage might be linked with the scene when Gatsby's body is found in the swimming pool:

> There was a faint, barely perceptible movement of the water as the fresh flow from one end urged its way toward the drain at the other. With little ripples that were hardly the shadows of waves, the laden mattress moved irregularly down the pool. A small gust of wind that scarcely corrugated the surface was enough to disturb its accidental course with its accidental burden. The touch of a cluster of leaves revolved it slowly, tracing, like the leg of transit, a thin red circle in the water.
>
> It was after we started with Gatsby toward the house that the gardener saw Wilson's body a little way off in the grass, and the holocaust was complete. (GG, p. 287.)

In this case, we are given at first an almost elegiac image, modulated in four short sentences on the suggestion of a faint and peaceful movement ("faint barely perceptible movement of the water," "fresh flow," "little ripples," "hardly the shadows of waves," "a small gust of wind that scarcely corrugated the surface," "the touch of a cluster of leaves"). Then our attention is drawn on "a thin red circle in the water," and here the undulating and dancing movement is interrupted by the clean cruel break of a matter-of-fact enunciation: "It was after we started with Gatsby...."

With equal skill a single sentence is sufficient to suggest Wolfshelm's moral character, when he is made to say: "I understand you're looking for a business gonnection [*sic*]," "'Her voice is full of money,'" Gatsby says of

Daisy, and in that single phrase we perceive the depth of his love and his disconsolate disenchantment, his awareness of her basic weakness. Many other of these brilliant touches could be quoted to illustrate the concision and the "magic suggestiveness" of Fitzgerald's language in *The Great Gatsby*. After the effective and witty list of Gatsby's guests—a *tour de force* which tells us more about them and about Gatsby himself than an elaborate description—Fitzgerald can bring Nick back to his role of sober narrator with a sharp statement: "All these people came to Gatsby's house in the summer." In the summer: this single statement, far from being a casual remark, conveys all the melancholy sadness of Gatsby's "tragic pastoral"—of a memorable novel, to which Arthur Mizener's definition seems perfectly appropriate.

NOTES

1. The play was begun in the autumn of 1921 and completed the next spring. It was revised during the summer of 1922 (with the title of *Gabriel's Trombone*) and rewritten completely after some producers had refused it. In April 1923, however, Sam Harris decided to produce it, and it opened at the Apollo Theater of Atlantic City, N.J., in November. It was a complete failure and was dropped a week later. Its final title might have been suggested by a passage of Mencken in his essay. "On Being an American," cf. W. Goldhurst, *op. cit.*, p. 88, and Mencken's general influence is apparent in many passages. A reviewer felt justified in writing that "the spirit of the play is an obvious act of deference to Mencken's virulent contempt for the American people," cf. *FSP*, p. 156. In 1922, F. had staged a short play for the St. Paul Junior League, called *The Midnight Flapper*. Cf. *FSP*, pp. 146–48, and *AA*, pp. 93–94.

2. F. wrote few stories in 1922–23, and in 1924–25 he had to make up for it by composing, chiefly for financial reasons, a good number of them, which often do not come up to his standards. "I really worked hard as hell last winter"—he wrote to Wilson—"but it was all trash and it nearly broke my heart as well as my iron constitution" (*Letters*, p. 341). "I've done about 10 pieces of horrible junk in the last year ... that I can never republish or bear to look at—cheap and without the spontaneity of my first work," we read in a letter to J.P. Bishop, *ibid.*, p. 356.

3. *SEP*, February 11 and 18, 1922: uncollected.

4. *McCall's*, July 1924, then in *ASYM*.

5. *SEP*, March 15, 1924, then in *ASYM*.

6. *Woman's Home Companion*, November 1925, uncollected.

7. *Hearst's International*, May 1923, uncollected.

8. *The Chicago Sunday Tribune*, June 7, 1925, uncollected.

9. *SEP*, July 26, 1924; reprinted in pamphlet form, *John Jackson's Arcady*. A Contest Selection, arranged by Lilian Holmes Strack (Boston: W.H. Baker, 1928), 8 pp.

10. The story appeared in *Collier's*, May 27, 1922, and was included in *TJA*. "This story was inspired by a remark of Mark Twain's to the effect that it was a pity that the best part of life came at the beginning and the worst part at the end ..."—F. wrote, *ibid.*,

p. 192.—"Several weeks after completing it, I discovered an almost identical plot in Samuel Butler's Notebooks.'"

11. *SS*, June 1922, then in *TJA*. The background of this story was provided by F.'s visit to the ranch of his friend Sap Donahoe in Montana (cf. *FSP*, p. 52), but the idea of a secluded valley might have been derived from Samuel Johnson's well-known *Rasselas*.

12. On F.'s early use of symbolism, cf. J.E. Miller, Jr., *op. cit.*, pp. 49–51, and Marius Bewley, *The Eccentric Design* (London, 1959), p. 259.

13. *Hearst's International*, February 1925, then in *ASYM*. For a more serious treatment of a similar theme, see the story "The Adjuster" (1925), in which the protagonist, however, Luella Hemple, matures through suffering and saves her husband, and the general tone is tragic rather than comic. Cf. K. Eble, *op. cit.*, p. 105, and W. Goldhurst, *op. cit.*, pp. 197–99.

14. *The Metropolitan Magazine*, December 1922, then in *ASYM*. F. himself was to call it later "a sort of first draft of the Gatsby idea," cf. A. Turnbull, *op. cit.*, p. 133.

15. *Liberty*, July 5, 1924, then in *ASYM*.

16. *The American Mercury*, June 1924, then in *ASYM*. On April 15, 1934, F. was to write to John Jamieson: "It might interest you to know that a story of mine, called 'Absolution' ... was intended to be a picture of his [Gatsby's] early life." *Letters*, p. 509; cf. also *ibid.*, p. 164. Strangely enough, K. Eble (in *op. cit.*, p. 32) considers it "the most 'naturalistic' story F. ever wrote." For its Catholic element, cf. Henry Dan Piper, "The Religious Background of *GG*," in Frederick J. Hoffman (ed.), *GG: A Study* (New York, 1962), pp. 321–34.

17. *CU*, p. 310. Writing to Scribner's on October 31, 1933, T.S. Eliot somewhat modified his original statement; he wrote that *GG* had *interested* him more than any American novel he had read since Henry James.

18. *CU*, pp. 264 and 269; *FSP*, p. 170.

19. See F.'s own introduction of *GG* (New York: The Modern Library, 1933), p. ix, and *FSP*, p. 164. Originally, the title of the book was to be *Among Ash Heaps and Millionaires*, then *Trimalchio in West Egg* (with the two variants: *Trimalchio* and *On the Road to West Egg*). Two other possibilities were *Gold-hatted Gatsby* and *The High-bouncing Lover*, both suggested by the four lines attributed to Thomas Parke D'Invilliers, which figure in the title page. Cf. *Letters*, p. 169. In the galley proofs, the title was still *Trimalchio*, and Gatsby is identified with this character at the beginning of Chapter VII of the book. Their relationship is analyzed by P.L. Mackendrick in *The Classical Journal*, XLV (1950), pp. 307–14: Mackendrick sees in F. and Petronius two writers of protest and denunciation, and finds similarities of *method*, *aim*, and *experience* in them.

20. In a MS note the subject matter is clearly divided into nine chapters: "I. Four characters & Landscape. Gatsby suggested. / II. Two more characters. New York. / III. The Party. Gatsby. Summer passes. / IV. The Guests. Wolfshiem [*sic*]. The Past. / V. The Meeting. / VI. More of Gatsby's past. The second party. / VII. The Buchanans. The Playa. The Filling Station. / VIII. The Rest of the Past. Murder of Gatsby. / IX. Wolfshiem. The Funeral (for a total of 48,000 words)."

21. This symbolic image was suggested to the writer by a tentative jacket for the novel which had been sent to him, and which "he wrote into the book," cf. *Letters*, p. 166.

22. The information which is here given about Gatsby's past is actually learnt by Nick *after* Gatsby's tragedy (Chapter VIII): this is a clear indication that F. *wanted* as much as possible to avoid describing the actual nature of the relationship between Gatsby and Daisy. The same device had been used by Henry James in *The American*,

where Newman and Mme de Cintré are "ignored" by the writer soon after their engagement.

23. In the galley proofs the episode was slightly different. Tom and Daisy arrive at the party spontaneously, and while Daisy tries openly to "separate" Gatsby from his guests, Tom tries to identify him with them: "He's just like them," he tells Daisy. It is worth noting, also, that part of Gatsby's past was here related in the first person, and not reported by Nick.

24. In the galley proofs Daisy tells Nick that she wants to run off with Gatsby, and the same information is given by Gatsby, who refuses, however, to "run off" with her. It is not simply that Daisy must break her marriage; she must actually deny its existence. Refusing a bourgeois compromise, Gatsby remains "pure," but puts himself in an impossible situation. For F.'s revisions on the galley proofs, cf. also *Letters*, pp. 171–74.

25. Cf. Leslie A. Fiedler, "Some Notes on F.S.F.," in *An End to Innocence* (Boston, 1955), pp. 176–83, and in *Love and Death in the American Novel* (New York, 1960). Fiedler sees in *GG* "an eastern drama": F. himself, however, says that it is "a history of the West."

26. Gatsby's complete lack of taste shows in his way of dressing (he wears for instance "a white flannel suit, silver shirt, and gold-colored tie ..."), in his cars, in his house, in the display of impossible shirts to Daisy when she visits his house, and in his ill-timed offer of a profitable and "rather confidential" job to Nick, soon after Nick has been asked to bring him and Daisy together.

27. Cf. Malcolm Cowley, Introduction to *Three Novels by F.S.F.* (New York, 1953), p. xiv, and J. Aldridge, "The Life of Gatsby," in *Twelve Original Essays on Great American Novels*, ed. by Carl Shapiro (Detroit, 1958), pp. 230–31.

28. Lionel Trilling's preface was prepared for the New Directions edition of *GG* (1945), and then developed into an essay, now in *The Liberal Imagination* (New York, 1950), in A. Kazin (ed.), *op. cit.*, etc. Trilling's interpretation was immediately taken up and discussed by Malcolm Cowley in *The New Yorker* and popularized in many reviews of the book (*Kenyon Review*, *Sewanee Review*, etc.). The "mythic" character of Gatsby is also stressed by William Troy, *op. cit.*

29. Jacques Barzun's essay, "Myths for Materialists," where his theory was expounded, is discussed at length in Marius Bewley, *op. cit.*, p. 271. Cf. also Richard Chase, *The American Novel and Its Tradition* (New York, 1958); Chase sees in Gatsby the vehicle of a "pastoral" ideal, like Franklin, Natty Bumppo, and Huck Finn, and he stresses his "legendary" character. Forerunners of Gatsby's "divine madness," according to Chase, can be found in Julien Sorel, Don Quixote, and Hamlet (!). Chase seems far closer to the truth when he places *GG* halfway between the *novel* and the *romance*; to stress its "romantic" aspect it is quite unnecessary to go back to Hamlet. On the subject, cf. also Robert Orstein, "F.'s Fable of East and West," *College English*, XVIII (1956), pp. 139–43, and K. Eble, *op. cit.*, pp. 96–97.

30. *FSP*, p. 171 and *Letters*, p. 358: "I never at any one time saw him [Gatsby] clear myself"—F. had written to John Peale Bishop, August 9, 1925—"for he started as one man I knew and then changed into myself—the amalgam was never complete in my mind."

31. Cf. his essay "The Art of Fiction," now in *The Future of the Novel*, ed. by Leon Edel (New York, 1956), pp. 15–16.

32. *Letters*, pp. 341–42 and p. 358. Both Edith Wharton (*CU*, p. 309) and John Peale Bishop thought that Gatsby had been "blurred" by the mystery about his past; both E. Wharton and H.L. Mencken thought that the book was "no more than a glorified anecdote" (cf. *CU*, p. 309, and W. Goldhurst, *op. cit.*, p. 79).

33. Cf. *Letters*, pp. 356 and 374; see p. 305 for F.'s waning admiration for Wells and Mackenzie ("The war wrecked him [Mackenzie] as it did Wells and many of that generation," we read for instance in a letter to J.P. Bishop, April 1925), and cf. F.'s essay "How to Waste Material," in *AA*, pp. 117–22, for his waning admiration for Mencken ("His idea had always been ethical rather than aesthetic," p. 118).

34. He had praised Anatole France in two letters to J.B. Cabell (*Letters*, p. 466 and p. 468) and in a review of Grace Flandrau's *Being Respectable*, in *The Literary Digest*, March 1923, pp. 35–36 (cf. J.E. Miller, *op. cit.*, p. 69). To Galsworthy F. had said that he considered A. France and Conrad the two greatest living writers (cf. *FSP*, p. 132). Stephen Crane was praised at the end of a review of Thomas Boyd's *Through the Wheat*, in *The New York Evening Post*, May 26, 1923—the same review began with a quotation from Conrad's *Youth*. Willa Cather had been praised in an interview in 1924, now in Charles E. Baldwin, *The Men Who Make Our Novels* (New York, 1924), p. 167. For F.'s admiration for Edith Wharton, cf. *FSP*, p. 154, and K. Eble, *op. cit.*, p. 87.

35. Cf. Wilson's essay in *The Bookman*, March 1922, and Ch. E. Baldwin, *op. cit.*, p. 167. Cf. also *Letters*, p. 163 (where F. speaks of *GG* as "purely creative work" and as "a consciously artistic achievement"), p. 430 (for *GG* being "detached") and p. 480 (where *GG* is described as being written "in protest against my own formless two novels").

36. J.W. Beach, *The Twentieth Century Novel: Studies in Technique* (New York, 1932), pp. 181–82, and 193 and *passim*. For Henry James's theories, cf. his essay "The Art of Fiction," already quoted, and his Prefaces to the New York Edition of his works, now collected in *The Art of the Novel* (London, 1934), with an extremely useful introduction and index by R. P. Balckmur. On this and related questions, see also Wayne C. Booth's invaluable study *The Rhetoric of Fiction* (Chicago, 1961).

37. F.M. Ford, *Joseph Conrad: A Personal Remembrance* (Boston, 1924), pp. 136–37, as quoted in J. E. Miller, *op. cit.*, p. 95. Parts of this book are also reprinted in F.J. Hoffman (ed.), *GG: A Study*.

38. It is significant that *GG* was originally meant to have a Middle West and New York Locale, and to take place in the 1880's, as is the case with many works by E. Wharton (cf. F.J. Hoffman, *op. cit.*, p. 322). For similarities between *GG* and *A Lost Lady*, *see Letters*, p. 507, and Maxwell Geismar, *The Last of the Provincials* (Boston, 1947), p. 166. For a comparison between F. and E. Wharton, see F.J. Hoffman, in *English Institute Essays* (New York, 1950).

39. Cf. F.'s introduction to the Modern Library *GG*, p. x. It might be worth noting that Conrad had visited America in 1923 (see *FSP*, p. 158). References to Conrad are particularly frequent in F.'s letters: cf. *Letters*, p. 211 ("Conrad has been, after all, the healthy influence on the techniques of the novel"), p. 246 ("an author's main purpose is 'to make you see'"—as Conrad had written in the preface to *The Nigger of the 'Narcissus'*), p. 301 and p. 362 (a new reference to Conrad's preface, as in p. 309), p. 462 (for F.'s idea of Conrad's pessimism), and p. 482 (May or June 1925: "God! I've learned a lot from him"). Cf. also *CU*, pp. 262 and 288 (a reference to *Lord Jim*). As early as 1923 F. had "discovered" that Conrad was superior to Wells; in *CU*, p. 179, we find an entry which might be easily referred to *GG*:

"Conrad's secret theory examined: He knew that things do transpire about people. Therefore he wrote the truth and transposed it to parallel to give that quality, adding confusion however to his structure. Nevertheless, there is in his scheme a desire to imitate life which is in all the big shots. Have I such an idea in the composition of this book?"

40. Cf. Joseph Conrad, Preface to *The Nigger of the 'Narcissus'* (1897), reprinted in F.J. Hoffman (ed.), *GG: A Study*, pp. 59–64. In his essay "One Hundred False Starts" (1933), F. was to quote Conrad's second statement, *AA*, p. 136. On Conrad's impressionistic theory, see my essay "Stephen Crane fra naturalismo e impressionismo," in *Annali di Ca' Foscari*, III (Milan, 1964).

41. As J.W. Beach (*op. cit.*, p. 363) had done for *Lord Jim*, J. E. Miller (*op. cit.*, p. 97) has worked out a diagram of the sequence of events in *GG*, "allowing X to stand for the straight chronological account of the summer of 1922, and A, B, C, D, and E to represent the significant events of Gatsby's past," which runs as follows: X, X, X, XCX, X, XBXCX, X, XCXDX, XEXAX (each group of letters indicates a chapter).

42. F. disclaimed an influence of Henry James on *GG*, cf. *Letters*, p. 480: in the same passage, however, he makes it clear that he *had* read *The Portrait of a Lady*. He had also read Conrad's essay on James (see his letter to Maxwell Perkins, *circa* June 1, 1925, in *Letters*, p. 187), and already in 1922 he had read *What Maisie Knew*, *see ibid.*, p. 333.

43. Cf. Henry James, *The Art of the Novel*, p. 14. According to James, a *ficelle* represented "a relation that has nothing to do with the matter ... but everything to do with the manner" (cf. *ibid.*, p. 342).

BENJAMIN T. SPENCER

Sherwood Anderson:
American Mythopoeist

It is not surprising that during the past generation Sherwood Anderson's literary reputation should have suffered an eclipse, for the renascent American literature which he envisioned and in part exemplified half a century ago was rooted in the soil and in a sense of wonder and mystery alien both to the realism which preceded it and to the sophisticated naturalism that followed it. To be sure, his work has rarely evoked the degree of condescension found in the dictum of Miss Susan Sontag, who, somewhat ironically upbraiding Anderson for taking himself too seriously, recently dismissed *Winesburg, Ohio* as "bad to the point of being laughable." In view of her addiction to the New Wave of French fiction, with its commitment to sensory surfaces and psychic fragmentation as contrasted with Anderson's concern for inwardness and identity, her verdict is inevitable.

That such a reversal in his literary fortunes would occur Anderson himself surmised over forty years ago. Acknowledging himself to be not a great writer but rather a "crude woodsman" who had been "received into the affection of princes," he prophesied that "the intellectuals are in for their inning" and that he would be "pushed aside." And indeed, though more judiciously than Miss Sontag, estimable critics have concurred in assigning Anderson a lesser rank than did his early contemporaries. Soon after the author's death Lionel Trilling, while confessing a "residue of admiration" for his integrity and his authenticity as the voice of a groping generation,

From *American Fiction 1914 to 1945*, Harold Bloom, ed. Originally published in *American Literature* 41, no. 1 (March 1969). © 1969 by Duke University Press.

nevertheless adjudged him too innocent of both the European literary heritage and the role of ideas in psychic maturity. More recently Tony Tanner, in an analysis of the naïveté of American writers, found in Anderson a distressing example of such writers' penchant for "uncritical empathy" and for dealing in discrete moments of feeling without that "exegetical intelligence" which has shaped all durable literature.

Between these two extremes of detraction grounded on the one hand in an aversion to "meaning" and on the other in an intellectualization of art through formal control and complexity, Anderson has consistently had, as a recent volume assessing his achievement shows, his body of apologists. Faulkner, Van Wyck Brooks, Irving Howe, Malcolm Cowley have been among those who have found a distinctiveness and a distinction in the best of his work, especially when it is related to the literary atmosphere of the first quarter of the century. Indeed, Anderson himself throughout his career could never separate his writing from its national context, and this cisatlantic cultural context impelled him toward the mythic, toward the archetypal and the elemental, rather than toward the urban and sociological. Repeatedly he spoke of his love for America, sometimes as "this damn mixed-up country of ours," sometimes as a land "so violent and huge and gorgeous and rich and willing to be loved." Moreover, he thought of himself as representatively and comprehensively "the American Man," as he wrote Brooks, explaining that by virtue of his varied occupational background he could take into himself "salesmen, businessmen, foxy fellows, laborers, all among whom I have lived." But not only did he feel himself to be "a composite essence of it all"; he also could experience, he declared with Whitman-like assurance, an "actual physical feeling of being completely *en rapport* with every man, woman, and child along a street" and, in turn on some days "people by thousands drift[ed] in and out" of him. Like Whitman, too, he contained multitudes and contradictions; he was, as he said, a compound of the "cold, moral man of the North" and "the warm pagan blood of the South ... striving to become an artist" and "to put down roots into the American soil and not quite doing it."

In reiterating through the second and third decades of the century his view that the crucial deficiency among American writers was that "Our imaginations are not yet fired by love of our native soil," Anderson had in mind of course more than the affirmation of a simple American pastoralism. The "soil," indeed, included the darker lives of the people who lived on it or near it; or, as he wrote to Dreiser in the mid-1930s, the redemption of such lives must lie so far as the writer is concerned not in any philosophical or ideological projection from his pen but in telling "the simple story of lives" and by the telling, counteracting the loneliness and "terrible dullness" that afflicted the American people. He had in mind, no doubt, such a story as the first which he had drafted for *Winesburg*, as he later related its genesis in "A Part of Earth"—a story called "Hands," in which he conveys the pathetic misunderstanding of the character whom he described as the "town mystery" of Winesburg, Wing Biddlebaum, whose hands reached out to others like "the wings of an imprisoned bird." Later the same motif is repeated in the hero of *Poor White*, whose loneliness and vague ambition impel him to a restless wandering and finally to an awkward and alienated marriage, and in the heroine of *Kit Brandon*, whose intense loneliness Anderson asserts to be characteristic of American life. Indeed Anderson's return to his native "soil" led him to the discovery of what he called "the loneliest people on earth," and his sensitive treatment of these people has led the novelist Herbert Gold to call him one of the purest poets of isolation and loneliness. To Irving Howe he seemed to have expressed the "myth" of American loneliness. Even with this theme, therefore, the mythopoeic Anderson apparently had initially found his imaginative stance. He was not, of course, in the strict etymological sense of the word a "mythopoeist," a maker of myths; but his imagination achieved its finest expression in narratives such as "Death in the Woods" or in parts of *Dark Laughter* where the preternatural or archetypal not only gave it unity and direction but also evoked a connotative style approaching the idiom of poetry. The term is therefore broadly used here as the most adequately comprehensive one to indicate the orientation and mode of Anderson's fiction as contrasted with those of such contemporary naturalists or realists as Dreiser and Lewis.

II

This persistent concern with loneliness both in Anderson's own life and in that of his characters, Lionel Trilling has asserted, is in part traceable to his excessive reliance on intuition and observation and to his unfortunate assumption that his community lay in the "stable and the craftsman's shop" rather than in the "members of the European tradition of thought." That Anderson was only superficially and erratically involved with the literary and philosophical past of Europe is undoubtedly true. As late as 1939 he could declare that he did not know what a "usable past" is, and that his concern was rather to live intensely in the present. In effect Anderson was emphasizing the inductive and the autochthonous as primary in the literary imagination, as Emerson, Thoreau, and Whitman had done before him, or, in anticipation of William Carlos Williams, he was committing himself to the principle that only the local thing is universal. By concentrating on the elemental tensions of provincial life he was assuming, as Mark Twain had done with the Mississippi, that the archetypes of human character and situation would most surely emerge, and that by returning to "nature" or the "soil" American literature would find at once its uniqueness and its authenticity. Hence his dismissal also of recent European art as a model for American artists. How irrelevant is Whistler's pictorial mode, he wrote in the 1920s, to a valid expression of the "rolling sensuous hills ... voluptuously beautiful" in California; and how silly are those painters who follow Gauguin when the varied life and color of New Orleans is available to them. The "half-sick neurotics, calling themselves artists" as they stumbled about the California hills, apparently resembled the "terrible ... shuffling lot" of Americans he later observed in Paris. Yet from writers whom he venerated as the great fictional craftsmen of Europe—Turgenev, Balzac, Cervantes—he induced what seemed to him to be the fundamental principle for a durable American literature: indigenous integrity. These authors were "deeply buried ... in the soil out of which they had come," he asserted in *A Story Teller's Story*; they had known their own people intimately and had spoken "out of them" with "infinite delicacy and understanding." With this indigenous commitment, Anderson believed, he and other American writers could belong to "an America alive ... no longer a despised cultural foster child of Europe."

Though Anderson found only a limited relevance for the cisatlantic writer in the literary modes and cultural traditions of Europe, he was by no means indifferent to the American past. His involvement lay deeper than the love which he professed to Gertrude Stein for "this damn mixed-up country of ours"; it approached, indeed, a mythic assent to what he viewed as a liberating cultural destiny often reiterated from the early days of the Republic—a belief in what his younger contemporaries Pound and Fitzgerald praised as the old largeness and generosity which they felt had marked the antebellum national character. The substance and inclination of Anderson's nationality may be inferred from the names of the five Americans whom he concluded, in an evening's discussion with his wife, to be the greatest his country had produced: Jefferson, Lincoln, Emerson, Whitman, and Henry Adams. For Lincoln and Whitman, as well as for Twain and Dreiser, he confessed a special affinity because they, with origins like his own, had had to take time to put roots down in a thin cultural soil and, ingenuous and confused, to confront a "complex and intricate world." The somewhat unexpected inclusion of Henry Adams may be accounted for by the common anxiety that both authors felt not only about the shattering effects of the machine on the older American values but also about the redemptive agency of some new mythic force which would bring unity out of multiplicity in American life. A more sustained influence, however, Anderson felt in Whitman, whose attempt to supplant a narrow and repressive Puritanism with large democratic vistas of brotherhood and loving perceptions he believed had been betrayed by later generations of American authors. Like Whitman he tried to project the democratic beyond concept into myth— into man's link with primordial forces of earth and into an eventual return to what the older poet in "Passage to India" had called "reason's early paradise."

Though early in his literary career Anderson was puzzled that Twain had not generally been placed with Whitman "among the two or three really great American artists," he was especially drawn to the Missouri author as a salient example of the American writer's plight and failure. In Twain he perceived a literary pioneer whom the "cultural fellows," as he termed them, had tried in vain to get hold of. Yet ironically, despite Twain's brave achievement and his bold disregard of literary precedent, Anderson sadly observed, he had never been able to attain full literary stature because the America which nurtured him was a "land of children, broken off from the culture of the world." As a part of this, Twain seemed to Anderson to have been caught up in the country's dominant shrillness and cheapness, with his literary talent thereby perverted and dwarfed. But an additional factor in Twain's failure seemed to Anderson to be his voluntary removal during the latter half of his literary life to the East, where he became subservient to what the latter termed the "feminine force" of the "tired, thin New England atmosphere." It is not surprising, therefore, that in *Dark Laughter* Anderson, through his hero Bruce Dudley, should charge Twain with deserting the imaginatively rich Mississippi River milieu and reverting to childhood or trivial themes which could be summed up as "T'witchetty, T'weedlety, T'wadelty, T'wum!" By ignoring the "big continental poetry" of rivers before it was choked off by the invasions of commerce, Twain in Anderson's eyes was in part responsible for the fact that the great River had become a "lost river," now "lonely and empty," and perhaps symbolic of the "lost youth of Middle America." Indeed *Dark Laughter* may be viewed as Anderson's mythopoeic projection of the repressed Dionysiac forces which the early Twain at times adumbrated and then gradually abandoned for genteel values and concerns. At the heart of the book is Anderson's elegy for a literary ancestor who should have expressed the mythic force of the heartland but who lost his touch with elemental things.

For Anderson, therefore, America evoked both intense devotion and recurrent despair—perhaps an inevitable dualism in one whose deepest cultural convictions were grounded in an antebellum version of the

American dream as articulated by his five greatest Americans. Jeffersonian as
he essentially was, he inclined to trace the confusion and vulgarity of his age
to the displacement of the agrarian base of American society. This older
America he could envision in *Windy McPherson's Son* as a kind of pastoral
paradise, a land of milk and honey wherein the shocks of abundant corn were
"orderly armies" which the American pioneer had conscripted from the
barren frontier, as it were, "to defend his home against the grim attacking
armies of want." It was this agrarian faith, he wrote in *Mid-American Chants*,
that had lured the immigrant races westward and had developed a deep
affinity with the earth spirit, with the fields as "sacred places" in whose
fertility the impulses to human aggression had vanished. And as small
organic centers in this agrarian richness, he felt, there had developed the
Midwestern villages, which, in turn, had nurtured a vital individualism
whereby both men and women lived with courage and hope and with a pride
in craftsmanship and independence such as that joyously possessed by
Sponge Martin in *Dark Laughter*. Hence Anderson's characterization of
Bidwell, Ohio, the setting of much of *Poor White*: it was a pleasant and
prosperous town whose people were like a "great family," and, like those in
other Midwestern towns in the 1880s, were undergoing a "time of waiting"
as they tried to understand themselves and turned inward to ponder the
utopianism of Bellamy and the atheism of Ingersoll.

The snake which had crept into this agrarian Eden and its village
culture was, in Anderson's reiterated view, a new reliance on the external
benefits supposedly conferred by technological progress rather than on the
inner resources conferred by Nature and the Soul on the Emersonian and
Thoreauvian and Whitmanian self. On this contest of the humane self and
the nonhuman machine most of Anderson's major works revolve—especially
Windy McPherson's Son, *Winesburg*, *Poor White*, *Dark Laughter*, and *Beyond
Desire*. During his youth, Anderson told a college audience in 1939, the
increasing obsession with getting ahead had resulted in a pervasive confusion
through the identification of happiness with possessions. Inevitably the
towns had become tainted with a competitiveness and greed which left them,
as he phrased it in *Windy McPherson's Son*, "great, crawling slimy thing[s]
lying in wait amid the cornfields." Young Sam McPherson's success in
Chicago, like Anderson's, brought its disenchantment with such "blind
grappling for gain"; having "realised the American dream" in its perverted
form at the end of the century, Sam felt impelled toward the larger quest of
seeking truth—toward the risks of that "sweet Christian philosophy of failure
[which] has been unknown among us." Because of a ruthless greed whetted
by the new industrialism, Anderson suggests in the novel, "Deep in our

American souls the wolves still howl." The consequent dehumanization of
the old communities could be seen in both city and village. Reflecting on the
brutal crowds in New York, Sam is no doubt expressing Anderson's attitude
when he concludes that "American men and women have not learned to be
clean and noble and natural, like their forests and their wide, clean plains."
And in villages like Winesburg, as Anderson declared in his *Memoirs*, the
blind faith in machines had not brought beauty but had left a residue of
fragmented grotesques villagers who, as he explains in introducing the stories
of *Winesburg*, in the disintegration of the agrarian community had been
driven to seize upon some narrow or partial truth and, in a desperate attempt
to sustain their lives, to make it an obsessive and destructive absolute. In a
disconsolate mood of acceptance Anderson conceded in his *Memoirs* that "it
may just be that America had promised men too much, that it had always
promised men too much." In effect he was conceding the subversion of a
major myth—one fused by his own experience from the old dream of the
garden, Jeffersonian agrarianism, Transcendentalism, the repudiation of
Puritanism, and the pastoral abundance of the West. His vision of a land
where the earth and brotherhood would allow the satisfaction of the basic
human desires had yielded to the reality of masses of "perverse children," lost
and lonely.

III

Anderson's mythic focus, however, lay below the national or politico-
economic level. America and the West were at last but symbolic media or
indices for him, as they had been for the Transcendentalists—transient
entities to be valued only to the degree that they proved instrumental in
releasing the deific forces of primal satisfactions of man's being. This
assumption Anderson made clear in his early days as a writer by insisting in
the *Little Review* that the so-called "new note" in American literature was in
reality "as old as the world," involving as it did the "reinjection of truth and
honesty into the craft" of writing and also the "right to speak out of the
body and the soul of youth, rather than through the bodies and souls of
master craftsmen who are gone. [¶] In all the world there is no such thing
as an old sunrise, an old wind upon the cheeks...." Similarly, as he later
recalled in his *Memoirs*, he and other members of the Chicago group during
the First World War were, above all, trying "to free life ... from certain
bonds" and "to bring something back," including the "flesh" which the
genteel realism of the preceding generation had excluded. In short, they
wished to divert American literature from what they conceived to be its

secondary focus on the socio-political and redirect it to the primary and recurring experiences—to what Anderson in his later years was willing to call "the great tradition" which, he said, goes on and on and is kept straight only with difficulty. "All the morality of the artist," he concluded, "is involved in it."

Convinced as he was that the greatest obstacle to the return to the "oldness" and the "great tradition" lay in the fidelity to fact espoused by the realistic school, Anderson insisted that American writers look primarily within themselves, for "there is this common thing we all have ... so essentially alike, deep down the same dreams, aspirations, hungers." In effect Anderson was urging a mythopoetic approach to the same native scenes that Howells and Twain had often depicted. Like Conrad, he believed that "the artist descends within himself" and "appeals to that part of our being which is not dependent on wisdom" by speaking to "our capacity for delight and wonder, to the sense of mystery surrounding our lives; to our sense of pity, and beauty, and pain...." In the Midwestern lives about him Anderson found the "dreams, aspirations, hungers" which could evoke the "sense of mystery ... of pity, and beauty, and pain," and the transatlantic understanding and approval which his stories had elicited confirmed his belief that the American writer could best strike the universal note through such an emphasis. That the "subjective impulse" and the imagined world should take precedence for the author over fact he continued to affirm throughout his life, proclaiming consistently the satisfactions that he had found as a "slave to the people of ... [his] imaginary world."

As the clearest repository of archetypal emotions and situations Anderson, like Hawthorne and Twain before him, used the small town or village for his settings. In the commonplace Midwest world, he wrote in 1918 in "A New Testament," there is a "sense of infinite things." As an illustration of this "sense" he proffered his story "In a Strange Town," in which the persona observes an ordinary couple—a woman and a man accompanying her to place her husband's coffined body on the train. The people are of no importance, he explained in a comment on the story, but they are involved with Death, which is "important, majestic." The very strangeness of the town, he also explained, served to afford a kind of aesthetic distance in which the irrelevant and superficial disappeared and the elemental constants of mortality emerged. To be sure, Anderson at times and for the most part in nonfictional works, did view the town, both Midwestern and Southern, in a sociological perspective. But even here he frequently sounded mythic overtones, as he did in his perceptive remark in *Home Town* (1940) that the small community had always been the "backbone of the living thing we call America" because it lies halfway between the cities (which breed ideas) and the soil (which breeds strength).

On this soil as an autochthonous matrix Anderson consistently relied for the vital norms of his stories as well as of the villages themselves, enclosed as they generally were with their cornfields. It was the soil which in his belief gave the "power" to life and literature (to use Emerson's dual terminology from "Experience") as the towns and cities gave the "form." The towns and villages, therefore of *Winesburg* or *Dark Laughter* and *Poor White*, rich as they may be in human archetypes, are never autonomous, but always have their traffic with the surrounding fields and woods. Acknowledging the "bucolic" in his nature, Anderson spoke of himself as a "Western novelist" and of his region as the "corn-growing, industrial Middle West." It is "my land," he wrote in 1918 to Van Wyck Brooks. "Good or bad, it's all I'll ever have." But only incidentally was he concerned with its industrial aspects; for what he wished to do, he said, was to "write beautifully, create beautifully ... in this thing in which I am born"—indeed, to "pour a dream over it." His perspective was thus visionary; his imagination was committed to distant vistas, not merely democratic but essentially mythic. Stirred during the years of the Chicago renaissance by something new and fresh in the air, as he said in the *Little Review*, he was convinced that "the great basin of the Mississippi ... is one day to be the seat of the culture of the universe." The current industrialism of the region he interpreted in a quasi-mythic figure as a cold and damp winter beneath whose lifeless surface something was "trying to break through." Envisioning that vernal rebirth in the West when "newer, braver gods" would reign and a new and joyous race would develop, he composed his *Mid-American Chants*—essentially a volume of free-verse hymns extolling an American paradise where nature and man were one. In the very term "chants" Anderson suggested both the style and purpose of his poems. Eschewing both the elegiac disenchantment with the region to be found in Master's Spoon River Anthology and the virile bravado of Sandburg's contemporaneous *Cornhuskers*, these visionary poems in their diction and movement and tone are Anderson's most explicit venture into the mythopoeic strain.

In the *Chants* Anderson essentially invoked the earth spirit, as he wrote in "Mid-American Prayer," with its Indian memories and rites to supplant the Puritanism dominant in the region and to remind the Midwestern people of the "lurking sounds, sights, smells of old things." The theme of the repressive sterility of New England was, indeed, and oft-reiterated one in Anderson's most prolific years, for he had come to feel that the major mission of the Midwestern writer, as he explained in his *Memoirs*, was on behalf of a new race to put "the flesh back in our literature" and thereby to counteract the "feminine force" of the older section. The New England notion of

America was not blood deep, he asserted in a Lawrentian vein in *A Story Teller's Story*; and since blood will tell, the increasingly thinner blood of the Northeastern man must yield to that type more richly blended from the "dreaming nations" which had settled the Midwest. In place of an "old-maid civilization" derived from a cold, stony New England, Anderson saw emerging from the "rich warm land" and polyglot racial strains a kind of Dionysiac brotherhood in which the humane spirit of Lincoln would be the heroic and brooding presence. Thus, as he wrote in *Dark Laughter*, the "whole middle American empire" would be restored as a land of rivers and prairies and forests "to live in, make love in, dance in."

Despite Anderson's invocation of rivers and forests and the "old savages" therein "striving toward gods," the dominant symbol in *Mid-American Chants* was the pastoral cornfield—a symbol indigenous to the country as a whole, though especially so to the Upper Mississippi Valley. Confessing himself to be a "kind of cornfed mystic," Anderson was always moved by the sight of a cornfield, and later in his life at Marion, Virginia, he remarked that such fields were distinctively American. Not surprisingly, the cabin where he chose to do his first writing in Virginia was, as he wrote Stieglitz, a "deserted one in a big cornfield on top of a mountain. Cowbells in the distance, the soft whisper of the corn." Nearly a decade earlier, in *Windy McPherson's Son* he had protested the popular conception of corn as being merely the feed for horses and steers; instead the shocks of corn stood for him as majestic symbols of a land in which man had been freed from hunger. Yet two years later, in *Mid-American Chants* the cornfields moved from a mere symbol of well-being into the sacramental: they became a "sacred vessel" filled with a sweet oil which had reawakened man to a sense of the beautiful, old things. Moreover, the long aisles of corn in their orderly planting not only signified man's conquest of the forest; they seemed even to run to the throne of the gods. "Deep in the cornfields the gods come to life," he wrote in "War," / "Gods that have waited, gods that we knew not." In the cornfields, indeed, Anderson found a new impulse to prayer through what he felt to be their mythic reincarnation of the earth spirit; in them he found an elemental vitality to counteract the sterile religious tradition of New England. Back of the "grim city," Chicago, he saw "new beauties in the standing corn" and, in "Song to New Song," dreamt of "singers yet to come" when the city had fallen dead upon its coal heap. Or again, in "Song for Lonely Roads," he reasserted his faith that "The gods wait in the corn, / The soul of song is in the land." During these years, indeed, as he wrote in one of his letters, he felt that "a man cannot be a pessimist who lives near a brook or a cornfield"; and in another he confessed to the "notion" that none of his writing "should be published that could not be read aloud in the presence of a cornfield."

IV

By the 1930s, and especially with the stringencies of the economic depression, Anderson's corn gods had proved illusory. In his earlier romantic commitment to the divinely organic he had construed the machine as a seductive threat to a Mid-American reunion with the earth. In those days he could still believe in the triumph of the egg—to use the title of one of his volumes which contains the story "The Egg," a humorous treatment of the effort of the persona's father to subdue a simple egg by standing it on end or forcing it into a bottle. His humiliating defeat, one may suppose, may be taken to reflect Anderson's earlier view of the futility of human attempts to contain or subdue the primal, organic forces of nature. From a similarly organic perspective the inventor-hero of *Poor White* (1920), appearing at evening and pantomiming with his flailing arms and mechanical strides the motions of his cabbage-planting machine, becomes for the farmers a frightening specter whose grotesque movements are a graphic index to consequences which Anderson felt must follow the replacement of the organic by the mechanical. As imposed behavior and technological demands had succeeded freedom and personal pride in craftsmanship, he commented in *Poor White*, men and women had become like mice; and in *Dark Laughter* he spoke of the "tired and nervous" cities, with their "murmur of voices coming out of a pit." Over a decade later in his Southern novel *Kit Brandon* only a few of the mountain girls seemed to him to have retained a self-respect and proud individualism akin to that of "the day of America's greater richness." Of this older richness another symbol was the horse, which as a boy in the livery stable he had found to be the most beautiful thing about him and superior to many of the men with whom he had to deal. In the industrial era, he wrote in *A Story Teller's Story*, since machines had supplanted horses, his own nightmare as a writer was that of being caught as a prisoner under the "great iron bell"—that is, we may interpret, under the great humanly wrought inanimate doom. Perhaps his vivid story "The Man Who Became a Woman," in which a young boy whose devotion to the horse Pick-it-boy has cleansed his lustful thoughts and dreams and who, mistaken for a girl at night in the stable loft by the drunken horse-swipes, flees naked to the neighboring slaughterhouse yard and undergoes a kind of traumatic burial in the skeleton of a horse—perhaps this story reflects something of the psychic effect on Anderson of the destruction of his mythopoeic America. At any rate, even by the time of the publication of *Horses and Men* (1925), in which he celebrated both the vibrant fascination of the horse and the innocence of youth, he confessed to Stieglitz that he had learned at last that horses and men are different and that in the confrontation of human dilemmas the equine would no longer "suffice."

Though by the mid-1920s Anderson felt obliged to abandon many of the mythic assumptions of his Midwestern years, he could not renounce entirely the demands of his mythopoeic imagination. During the last fifteen years of his life, therefore, he sought new centers and media for a viable myth which would bring unity and beauty to his life. This he found in the mill towns of the new industrial South and in the girls who worked therein. Formerly the South had been for Anderson New Orleans and the southern Mississippi, where the dark, ironic laughter of the Negroes had seemed to express for him an elemental spontaneity and a vital sense of life—a "touch with things" such as stones, trees, houses, fields, and tools, as Bruce Dudley enviously concedes in *Dark Laughter*—which made the members of a subject race humanly superior to the sterile life about them. In the later Southern novels the Negroes have all but disappeared, and though the mill girls, who as a vital center supplant them, are too much at the mercy of their factory world to embody any mythic assurance, they do point to a redemptive feminine principle which Anderson, like Henry Adams, found in his later years the surest counteragent to the disintegrating power of the machine. It was the American woman, he concluded in the 1930s, who alone could reintroduce the "mystery" which a technological age had dispelled and without which "we are lost men." Since American women at their best had not yet been "enervated spiritually" by the machine or accepted from it a "vicarious feeling of power," perhaps women, he argued in his book entitled by that phrase, might rescue the American man "crushed and puzzled" as he was in a mechanical maze.

Yet, just as Anderson's phrase "perhaps women" suggests an acknowledged tentativeness in his later mythic formulations, so his treatment of the machine in his late works often discloses a new ambiguity. As his recourse to woman for salvation reflects Adams's adoration of the Virgin, so his discovery of the poetry as well as the power of the machine follows the example of another of his five "greatest Americans," Whitman, who abandoned the pastoral milieu of "the splendid silent sun" to discover the poetry of ferries and locomotives and crowded streets. Yet Anderson, with his earlier sustained distrust of the machine, could not free himself from an ambivalence in his later years; he felt both awe and impotence, he confessed, in the presence of the vast order and power and beauty of machinery, and his tribute to Lindbergh as an emergent culture hero, the new type of machine man, as well as his sympathetic portrayal of the speed-obsessed Kit Brandon, the heroine of a late novel, betrays an uneasiness not present, say, in his characterizations of Sponge Martin and the Negroes in *Dark Laughter*. Yet watching the superb technology of the whirling machines, his hero Red Oliver, in *Beyond Desire*, no doubt reflected much of Anderson's later attitude by confessing that he felt "exultant" and that here was "American genius" at work—America at "its finest." Two years earlier, in 1930, Anderson had declared that he would no longer be "one of the ... protestors against the machine age" but henceforth would "go to machinery" as if it were mountains or forest or rivers. Hence his poem to the beneficence of the automobile and his attempts to catch the excitement of the cotton mills in his "Machine Song" or "Loom Dance." Yet he also felt impelled to express the more sinister admixture of fear and awe experienced in the presence of the textile machines, whose hypnotic speed and incessant shuttle rhythms could induce in Molly Seabright, a mill girl in *Beyond Desire*, an indifference and confusion which led to a loss of identification with the human world about her. Modern American industry, he concluded ambivalently in *Perhaps Women* (1932), was indeed a "dance," a "flow of refined power," to which men lifted up their eyes in worshipful adoration. Surely in such statements the failure of Anderson to approach the machine as if it were mountains and rivers is manifest. The earlier mythopoeic imagination has become bifurcated into myth and poetry; the validity of the myth is not felt, and the poetry is an act of will rather than of imagination. In this bifurcation and desiccation one may no doubt find much of the explanation for Anderson's decline in his later years.

V

To his inclination and commitment to a mythopoeic approach to American experience both Anderson's literary achievements and his shortcomings may ultimately be traced. From the time of the First World War until his death at the beginning of the Second, he consistently aligned his writing with a focal purpose summarily stated in *A Story Teller's Story*: "It is my aim to be true to the essence of things." In probing for the "essence" he ran the romantic risk of neglecting the existential substance of American experience, and hence one may feel, as Lionel Trilling has asserted, a deficiency of the sensory and concrete in his work. If one adds to this mythic concern for patterns and forces behind the phenomenal world Anderson's addiction to the psychic and intuitive as the arbiters of reality, one approaches what to

Anderson seemed the "poetic" factor in the mythopoeic imagination. Hence neither the region nor the nation was a substantial entity for him; neither ideologies nor sociological formulas were significant norms for his fictional perspective. The "new note" in American literature, as he said, was really a return to the old sensations and desires; and hence his women have few social concerns or ambitions, nor are they regional types: Aline Grey and Clara Butterworth and Kit Brandon play their roles rather as versions of the White Goddess reasserting primal humanity, as did Adams's Virgin.

Anderson's style, like his larger fictional perspective, is an organic product of his mythopoeic approach. Rooted in the naive, in wonder, in the mystic and the intuitive, his expression shapes itself subjectively from emotions or associations, as Tanner has shown, at the expense of tight syntax, controlled structure, and purified or precise diction. And yet Anderson's vagaries are, for the most part, those which he inherited (and somewhat intensified) through a major native tradition initiated by the Transcendentalists and involving in its course Whitman, Twain, Stein, and Salinger. If from Anderson's pen this style becomes one in which each sentence affords only a fragmentary glimpse, as Tanner contends, perhaps the limitation is in part explained by Anderson's conclusion that in an immense land where all men are strangers to one another, the writer can "only snatch at fragments" and be true to his "own inner impulses." That a cisatlantic orientation may be necessary to the full comprehension of Anderson's style, with its indigenous tone and idiom, is suggested by Gertrude Stein's contention that "Anderson had a genius for using the sentence to convey a direct emotion, this was in the great american [*sic*] tradition, and that really except Sherwood there was no one in America who could write a clear and passionate sentence." Early in his career Anderson in "An Apology for Crudity" asserted that if American writing were to have force and authenticity, it would have to forgo objectivity for the "subjective impulse," and that an honest crudity would have to precede the "gift of beauty and subtlety in prose." However consciously stylized and contrived his own apparent artlessness may be, his "subjective impulse" extended outward like Whitman's in an effort to catch "the essence of things," and his reputation will be most secure among those who can accept the mythopoeic assumptions which nurtured and shaped his imagination.

JAMES LEA

Sinclair Lewis and the Implied America

That Sinclair Lewis recorded the social history of a major sector of the American population in the first third of the twentieth century is a generally accepted literary axiom. An ear for the rhythms of Midwestern speech and a descriptive power which E.M. Forster likened to that of photography combined with intelligent curiosity to produce in him one of the country's most astute social critics. Especially during the decade of the twenties, the mirror which his novels held up to the material crassness and spiritual befuddlement of middle-class Americans established Lewis as a forceful cultural commentator, a best-selling novelist and the darling even of those whom he damned.

But Sinclair Lewis wrote—or, we should say created—another sort of American history as well. In the work of most social satirists, criticism of the contemporary world derives in large part form the writer's assumption that there was, or is, or could be a better world. Lewis assumed that there *had* been a better world, or at least a better America, and that his twentieth century had betrayed the potential for freedom and productive happiness implicit in the people, life, and very land itself of eighteenth- and nineteenth-century America. Sheldon Grebstein has observed that "the theme of Lewis's serious books, beginning with *Main Street*, is disillusionment." But disillusionment is more than a theme; it is the tonal foundation of Lewis's major works. Lewis's picture of a banal present is underpinned by his concept

From *American Fiction 1914 to 1945*, Harold Bloom, ed. Originally published in *Clio* 3, no. 1 (October 1973). © 1973 by Robert H. Canary and Henry Kozicki.

of a more meaningful past, a concept which is manifested both in implication by contrast and in detailed representation throughout his principal novels. The center-stage actions of Lewis's novels—the struggling of Carol Kennicott, the blustering of George Babbitt, the soul-searching of Neil Kingsblood—are always played against a back-drop depicting the America that has been, and that by extension could be, but is being perverted.

To aid the process of delineating the character of the American past which is continuously implied by Lewis, I have chosen to examine seven novels which present an interesting historical chronology through the periods in which they are set. *The God-Seeker*, although not published until 1949, is Lewis's only work that follows Sir Walter Scott's classic definition of the historical novel. Its action is laid between 1830 and 1856. *Main Street* (1920) covers the years 1907 to 1920, *Babbitt* (1922) the years 1920 to 1922. *Arrowsmith* (1925) is set between 1897 and 1923, and *Elmer Gantry* (1927) between 1902 and 1926. *Dodsworth* (1929), called by some Lewis's last great novel, covers the years 1903 to 1928. *Kingsblood Royal* (1947), lying far beyond the limits of Lewis's "golden decade" with respect to quality as well as to publication date, treats the period 1944 to 1946. While Lewis calls upon his vision of the American past in other novels, these seven offer particularly illuminating examples of the methods by which he describes what may be called his Implied America.

When Sinclair Lewis was a boy, in the late years of the nineteenth century, Sauk Centre, Minnesota, was only two generations removed from the crude huts and the cavalry stockade of the early plains pioneers. It is quite probable that when he boarded the train for New Haven and the lifetime that lay beyond, he took with him at least a germinating sense of the land which earlier eyes had seen and earlier feet had walked. This imaginative perspective, reinforced by the sort of research which stood behind every Lewis novel, appears in the setting and characters of *The God-Seeker*. In this, the last Lewis novel published during the author's lifetime, Aaron Gadd traces in microcosm the trail of the Yankee missionaries and merchants who settled the northern plains in the mid-1800s. Physically, Aaron moves from his boyhood home in Clunford, Massachusetts (where his American lineage is firmly established in the person of his grandfather, a Revolutionary War veteran) to a missionary post among the Sioux and Chippewa, and from there to the growing frontier camp which becomes St. Paul, where he sets up shop as a housing contractor. In the course of his progress, Aaron is identified— either directly or by association—with most of the forces which shaped the character of the American frontier as Lewis sees it represented in pioneer Minnesota. Perhaps more idealistic than many of the early migrants, Aaron departs Massachusetts "to go west! To bring order and civilization to the aborigines!" Traveling by train, river boat, canoe, and horseback to his job at the Mission, he encounters the fur-traders, voyageurs, gamblers, soldiers, preachers and barons of commerce who are writing the history of the territory. His frontier mentors are Caesar Lanark, one of the traders who "pioneered the way for a lot of scoundrels who want to butcher the Indians at once, instead of gently pasturing them and milking them over the years." Squire Harge, the missionary whose mission is to impose his own Christianity upon a people with a centuries-old cultural identity of their own, and the St. Paul carpenter Seth Buckbee, whose social posture in the free, new land is supported by his belief that "the Irish and the Scandinavians were as shiftless as the Injuns." Among them and the proud but desperate Indians, and on the face of the Minnesota wilderness, Aaron finds his place alongside other frontiersmen, "men with stars in their heads and solid boots on their feet, men with a sense of elevated piety and of slick politics and land-options, in their violent and everwestering lives."

If Aaron Gadd's physical travels and his contact with the western up-and-comers seem to reflect the movements of the Yankee pioneers, his spiritual progress represents the development of Lewis's ideal of the nation-builder. Beginning in a youthful innocence shaped by his father's New England Puritanism, Aaron is seized by a religious conviction and a missionary fervor which are perhaps similar to the fever for free land and a free life which drove more than one mid-nineteenth-century easterner westward. His service at the Mission loosens his resolution and implants in his mind grave doubts about the superiority of his creed and his white race. His escape to St. Paul and his success as a carpenter in a town where building is as much a function of the heart as of the hands mark his initiation into that class of men who neither advertised nor traded but actually produced the flesh and bone of America. Aaron's representative spiritual completeness is not realized, however, until he takes the ultimate democratic step and helps his own employees organize a labor union. So Aaron Gadd—and, Lewis seems to say, all those who helped shape "a just, orderly and enduring commonwealth"—travels the circle from the innocence of externally ordered youth to the dawning human awareness of autonomous manhood.

The God-Seeker must be judged one of Lewis's weaker novels. But in the consideration of his formulation of an American past clearly in contrast with his American present it holds an important place. In this novel Lewis establishes his idea that the crassness and pettiness of the twentieth century are both a perversion of the ideals of a time when "men cast longer shadows" and at the same time directly traceable to it. For as Aaron Gadd ascends to success on the Minnesota frontier, Lewis continues to remind us that "the future history of Minnesota, like that of every other state in the Union, would be the inept struggle of mechanics and farmers and shopkeepers to get back a little of what they never intended to give away in the first place." *The God-Seeker* probably should not be read as Lewis's "final statement," but rather as an indication of his late recognition of the need for a preliminary statement. The total impact of the body of Lewis's major work resides not only in its social character, but in its historical character as well; it is in *The God-Seeker* that Lewis gives substance to that age of promise against which his age of disillusionment is measured.

From this level of historical perspective, we read more than irony in the frontispiece note to *Main Street*: "Main Street is the climax of civilization. That this Ford car might stand in front of the Bon Ton Store, Hannibal invaded Rome and Erasmus wrote in Oxford cloisters ... Our railway station is the final aspiration of architecture." For Lewis seems to consider it very important that we understand that the life and times of Gopher Prairie which he is about to present are of historical value in a double sense: they are a representation both of what we are and of what we have made out of what we could have been. Main Street does not exist as an independent construct, but as a point on the continuum of time, accountable to the past and to the future.

The Implied America makes briefer appearances in *Main Street* than in *The God-Seeker*, but it appears early. The novel opens with a description of Carol Milford (later to be Mrs. Will Kennicott) standing "on a hill by the Mississippi where Chippewas camped two generations ago." It is 1907, and the Chippewas Lewis refers to are the sons and grandsons of the Chippewas whose hunting grounds Aaron Gadd had walked. In those two generations, much has changed; the Indians and the frontiersmen are gone, although their presence remains woven into the fabric of the era: "She saw no Indians now ... Nor was she thinking of squaws and portages, and the Yankee fur-traders whose shadows were all about her."

Main Street, of course, marked Lewis's turn, as Robert J. Griffin phrases it, from "the celebration of national potentialities to the castigation of national failings." Lewis's five novels which preceded it were buoyant little books of apprenticeship, and, except for *The Job* (1917), they are rarely discussed today. In those early novels, Lewis treated the escape of the young innocent from the village into the outside world, a sort of idealized spiritual autobiography. By 1920, however, his vision seems to have panned down from the fresh leaves fluttering in the blue sky to the roots of life in America and the native soil in which they were sunk.

While Lewis's five apprenticeship novels dealt with the native Midwestern villager confronting the smug big city establishment, *Main Street* relates the confrontation between urban naïveté and small-town smugness. Carol Kennicott was brought up in "Mankato, which is not a prairie town, but in its garden-sheltered streets and aisles of elms is white and green New England reborn." Her childhood is delightfully secure, her education—both at home and at Blodgett College—is entertaining and shallow. She steps out on the trail to Gopher Prairie garbed in Aaron Gadd's Yankee innocence and idealism, a cultural pioneer armed with the Good Book-and-broadaxe of her own Romantic self-assurance.

Though she finds the plains no longer menaced by outraged Indians; though "the days of pioneering, of lassies in sunbonnets, and bears killed with axes in piney clearings, are deader now than Camelot"; still Carol encounters history in Gopher Prairie. There is the sense of the seemingly eternal land, into which she retreats in her most desperate moments. There are the Scandinavian farmers, belying the calendar by clawing the earth as their pioneer predecessors had done fifty years before: "a forest clearing pathetic new furrows straggling among stumps, a clumsy log cabin chinked with mud and roofed with hay."

There are the last frontiersmen, the Champ Perrys, whom Carol sees as merely another possible means to her end, but whom Lewis suggests are the remnants of an age degraded by "the era of aeroplanes and syndicalism." And there are the records of the Minnesota Territorial Pioneers. Carol muses for a moment over the years when Gopher Prairie consisted of four cabins and a stockade, when men and women lived with difficulty and vigor and a certain buoyancy, now lost. For Carol, stranded in an America which is "neither the heroic old nor the sophisticated new," the past is a panacea which she frivolously schemes to reclaim.

For Sinclair Lewis, the past is yesterday's reality. Miles Bjornstam is its only vitally extant embodiment in the novel. His socialism is the modern echo of the dead frontier equalitarianism. In a sense, he is a tragic anachronism, caught, as Mark Schorer would say, between "the individual impulse for freedom and the social impulse to restrict it." Bjornstam no sooner abandons his freedom of foot and spirit for an attempted accommodation with twentieth-century domesticity than he is crushed. When he leaves Gopher Prairie to find a new starting place, his directions are northward to Alberta and backward to the frontier past. Bjornstam's judgment upon the town, Lewis suggests, is the judgment of American history upon the Main Street of the American present.

For all its high towers of commerce and sprawling circumference of modern economic splendor, the city of Zenith, as Lewis depicts it in *Babbitt*, is built over a pit. Located in Lewis's mythical Midwestern state of Winnemac, Zenith was "an ancient settlement in 1897, one hundred and five years old, with two hundred thousand population." By 1920, it is a city on the make, rudely displacing its nineteenth-century buildings with "clean towers ... thrusting them from the business center," re-surfacing its land— formerly a "wilderness of rank second-growth elms and oaks and maples"— with the "bright roofs and immaculate turf and amazing comfort" of Floral Heights. If in 1856, Aaron Gadd's St. Paul was on its way to becoming "the most mammoth, gorgeous and powerful metropolis on this globe," Zenith is Lewis's unpleasant representation of what the realization of such a goal can produce.

Turning from his examination of the mid-American village to a study of the mid-American city, Lewis finds a social phenomenon inflated to the bursting point with the hot air of its own gusto. Zenith has long since lost touch with its agricultural beginnings; that aspect of its history is no longer even relevant. For generations its citizens have occupied themselves with the manufacturing of products, the buying and selling of property, the lending of money and other vocations which contribute to the collection of masses of people into easily manipulable units. In the process, they have all but eradicated the city's link with the land and their own link with their forebears. For their own purposes, they have no history: in Zenith in 1920, Lewis writes, "an old house is one which was built before 1880."

The result of Zenith's exorcism of its past to make room for a booming present and a "promising" future is reflected in the befuddlement which creeps into the soul of George Babbitt. Outwardly brash and blustering, Babbitt inwardly represents a population in limbo, at a point in history when, as Walter Lippman has written, "they have lost the civilized traditions their ancestors brought from Europe and are groping to find new ways of life." Cut off from a vital past, they have lost the vitality to pursue their personal dreams: Babbitt is a real estate salesman who has dreamed of being a lawyer; Paul Riesling is a roofing salesman who has dreamed of playing the violin; even Chum Frink, author of versified pap and "Ads That Add," has once dreamed of being a poet.

It seems that Zenith's pioneer past is all the more conspicuous because of its absence in the present. Modernity's hollowness and shallowness go unrelieved, except when Babbitt discovers the restorative effects of a vacation in the Maine woods with Paul Riesling. It is a return to the frontier for Babbitt, a chance to touch "something sort of eternal" that has eluded him in the city. The woods invite Babbitt's dreams of what is strangely like an idealized frontier life: "If he could but take up a backwoods claim with a man like Joe, work hard with his hands, be free and noisy in a flannel shirt, and never come back to this dull decency!" The plague of city life disappears as Babbitt imagines "Moccasins—six-gun—frontier town—gamblers—."

But in the end it is too late for Babbitt. The frontier is too far past. He can't draw from it sufficient courage to face down the forces of materialism that Zenith can marshall at the first sign of individual diversity. At the end of the novel, there is a quiet note of hope as Babbitt encourages his son to "Tell 'em to go to the devil!" But Babbitt disappears again into the crowd of faces—mindless behind their smiles—of Americans who have severed themselves from history.

In April, 1926, Sinclair Lewis was awarded the Pulitzer Prize for his ninth novel, *Arrowsmith*. With considerable malice aforethought, he rejected the award on the grounds that he would not be bought off by an agency of the tasteless American literary establishment. Given the probability that after the Pulitzer debacle of 1920 Lewis would have welcomed any opportunity to snub the Columbia University trustees, it is nonetheless interesting that *Arrowsmith* gave him that opportunity. For Martin Arrowsmith is also a man who will not be bought off by the establishment, and this is only one of the traits which mark him as Lewis's most nearly autobiographical character.

With this novel, Lewis undertook a series of studies of the professional person that developed from Arrowsmith the doctor through Gantry the preacher to Dodsworth the retired manufacturer and others. Each of these different characters moves in a milieu in which the historical past, Lewis' Implied America, plays a significant role. In Arrowsmith, the role is dual, incorporating history both as personal lineage and as a standard for the measurement of modern contrasts.

The story of Martin Arrowsmith opens sometime in the early nineteenth century, with a brief vignette in which a fourteen-year-old girl is driving a wagon westward. Despite the pleadings of her fevered father and her responsibility for a horde of younger brothers and sisters, she presses on: "There's a whole lot of new things I aim to be seeing!" The girl turns out to be Martin Arrowsmith's great-grandmother, and thus Lewis establishes an historical referent for Arrowsmith's character, linking him personally to the past.

Because he has a new story to tell, Lewis revolves his artistic gels a few turns and sheds a new light on Winnemac and Zenith. As he describes it, the character of Zenith's contemporary population has not changed noticeably since Babbitt, but Lewis works to re-establish the area's historical groundings. Prior to taking a satiric crack at the University of Winnemac,

Lewis explains that the state's tradition goes back to the Revolutionary War. Zenith, as we learned earlier, was founded in 1792—the year Kentucky joined the Union—but outlying counties were not settled until 1860. (Of Elk Mills, Martin's hometown, we learn nothing directly.) Then, having established that Winnemac is to a notable degree rooted in history and that Martin Arrowsmith is very much rooted in it, Lewis seems to drop the matter. His chief interest in this novel is the development of a contemporary pioneer stalking the frontier of science.

Hazard offers an interpretive construct of American history as representing three stages of pioneering: the regional stage, in which man attempts to control nature; the industrial stage, in which man attempts to control the labors of his fellow men; and the spiritual stage, in which man attempts to control himself. She suggests that Arrowsmith contains elements of all three stages, that Martin's ancestors were the regional pioneers, that his contemporaries are the industrial pioneers and that he becomes a spiritual pioneer in the manner of the Transcendentalists when, at the end of the novel, he resigns wealth and celebrity in New York and goes off to the Vermont woods to pursue pure science. Hazard's speculation should be extended somewhat, for from his first practice in the plains village of Wheatsylvania, Martin is seeking first of all to serve his fellow man. There is, therefore, a strain of the spiritual pioneer running in him throughout.

But Lewis is treating modern science in much the same way he treated the physical wilderness in *The God-Seeker* and the cultural wilderness in *Main Street*—that is, as an untracked space in which man could leave prints as deep and as permanent as he could make them. Martin Arrowsmith remains the regional pioneer in this open domain, much as Miles Bjornstam remains one in the broad lands beyond the short horizons of Gopher Prairie. Both of them occasionally pass through the clutches of their industrial contemporaries, sometimes with tragic consequences. But in the end each succeeds because each is free. For Martin this freedom is the fruit of the dogged determination inherited from his pioneer great-grandmother. Arrowsmith is characterized as Lewis may have characterized himself: a solitary and beleaguered spiritual survivor of the frontier past.

Although *Elmer Gantry* is set between the years 1902 and 1926, the voice of the narrator obviously speaks from the late years of that span. In the chapters dealing with Elmer's days as a student at Terwillinger College and as a rising young cleric, the voice is almost reflective in tone: "His Mother was able to give Elmer the three hundred dollars a year which, with his summer earnings in harvest field and lumber-yard, was enough to support him in Terwillinger, in 1902." Speaking not in the past tense but in a sort of past-imperfect, Lewis writes of Gritzmacher Springs, the home of Terwillinger College: "The springs have dried up and the Gritzmachers have gone to Los Angeles, to sell bungalows and delicatessen." On the day of Elmer's ordination ceremony, "It was 1905; there was as yet no Ford nearer than Fort Scott." The author's sense of historical distance becomes clearer when he writes: "In the virginal days of 1905 section gangs went out to work on the railway line not by gasoline power but on a handcar, a platform with two horizontal bars worked up and down like pump-handles." This impression of a distance in time and place between the narrative voice and the action of the novel is one which Lewis manages to achieve in several pieces of his fiction. One effect of this device is to raise the reader above the plane of the story, to give him a share in the author's omniscience, to allow him to view plot and characters in the temporal context in which the author has placed them. Rather than weaving historical dates and events into the narrative, Lewis alludes to their presence outside the narrative. By this means, the action of the novel is historically anchored, and, at the same time, the reader is aware that the action is distinct from, but contiguous to, other events of its time.

The clarification of this distinction is particularly important to the reading of *Elmer Gantry*, for in this novel Lewis has created his least sympathetic character. Elmer is a universal type, rather than a character representative of some national epidemic of the heart. He is the operator immemorial, egocentric and ruthless. He is Squire Harge with no core of sincere religious zeal; he is Juanita Haydock with no limit to his perfidy; he is Babbitt with no suspicion of his fallibility. Elmer Gantry's prototype is the ahistorical Ananias.

But Elmer does not move independently of history. There are around him the identifiable characters of the twenties: Billy Sunday, Amiee Semple McPherson, and others. And there is the suggestion that historical perspective itself can be manipulated, as when Katie Jonas, of Utica, New York, acquires enough money to be able to put on the aristocratic home, lineage, and name of Sister Sharon Falconer.

So while *Elmer Gantry* is set before Lewis's ubiquitous backdrop of history, the relationship between the present and the past is somewhat different in this novel from that in those novels we have previously examined. Lewis is describing here not so much a society brought to its present state by its betrayal of its own past, as a phenomenon—Elmer—emerging in a society that is as historically ready for him as its early-nineteenth-century counterpart was ready for the revivalists of that time.

Maxwell Geismar has offered the idea that the plots of Lewis's early

apprenticeship novels turn on the confrontation between the aristocratic
Easterner (or his tradition) and the Western democratic hero, and that the
novel's complications arise from this conflict of cultural values. By
comparison, *Dodsworth* turns largely upon the confrontation between a
johnny-come-lately American and an historically imposing Europe. By the
time *Dodsworth* was published in 1929, Sinclair Lewis's fame and increasing
fortune had allowed him to make several trips to Europe and to get glimpses
both of Europeans at home and of Americans away from home. The sense of
contrast which such glimpses aroused in him, and the notion that between
the American and his European heritage was a gulf even wider than the one
which separated the American from his own national past, were manifested
in Lewis's thirteenth novel.

Dodsworth is another admirable frontiersman who has outlived his
time. The Champ Perrys of *Main Street* were of this sort, lost in an age when
their courage and determination no longer had the focus provided by
torturing elements and belligerent Indians. In the industrial twentieth
century, Dodsworth has pioneered new designs and techniques in the
building of automobiles. He has outfought the industrial reactionaries and
the financial bamboozlers, and he has lasted long enough to see the
Revelation, the product of his own work and bearing the stamp of his own
imagination, become a world-famous motorcar. By 1925, he has become the
victim of advancing civilization; his outpost on the leading edge of the
industrial frontier has been overrun from behind by a more efficient—albeit
less refined—technology. Dodsworth at age fifty is an analogical national
soul who has experienced the rigors of regional and industrial pioneering and
now—like America in the 1920s—stands at the threshold of a new spiritual
frontier and a new self-perception.

Dodsworth's European experience is Lewis's idealization of a post-
pioneer America learning to live comfortably and unobtrusively with itself.
From a posture of boom-time smugness rooted in the mood of *Main Street*—
"Three guests had come in these new-fangled automobiles, for it was now
1903, the climax of civilization"—Sam evolves through self-doubt to an
ultimate new sense of his place in the commonality of human experience.
Europe is a testing ground on which his personal character—and, by
implication, America's national character—is tried. His first considered
reaction to Europe is historically framed. Though he is enchanted by the
atmosphere of England and disgusted by the superficiality of the Continental
salons, he—like Irving's Geoffrey Crayon a century earlier—is unequivocally
impressed by the air of solid permanence which he senses in old Europe. He
finds Paris "stately, aloof, gray with history, eternally quiet at heart for all its

superficial clamor." This captain of American industry responds to Europe with the shrinking awe of a small child: "Gee ... this town has been here a long time, I guess.... This town knows a lot.... I wish I did!" He reflects on the lost bliss of his egocentric American ignorance. "Life was a lot simpler then. We knew we were It. We knew that Europe was unbathed and broke, and that America was the world's only bulwark against Bolshevism and famine."

Dodsworth becomes first defensive, then contemplative in response to Europeanism's challenge to Americanism. In defense, he calls not upon America's "steel-and-glass skyscrapers and miraculous cement-and-glass factories and tiled kitchens and wireless antennae and popular magazines," but upon the tradition of his national past: "the tradition of pioneers pushing to the westward, across the Alleghenies, through the forests of Kentucky and Tennessee, on to the bleeding plains of Kansas, on to Oregon and California, a religious procession, sleeping always in danger, never resting, and opening a new home for a hundred million people."

After the disintegration of his marriage, and under the subtle tutelage of Edith Cortwright, Sam achieves a stability of perspective which suggests a new Lewis vision of the place of America in the history of the world. Sam is no longer unsure of himself as "the rich American ... uncouth and untraditional" in comparison to the European cultural heritage. Fully aware of his failings, he learns to revel in being "a most American American." After despair and self-denunciation, Sam can gloat "I am real!"

Dodsworth, in the chronology of Lewis's Implied America, marks a shift in setting and characterization from the Midwest of the Kennicotts and the Babbitts and an expansion in the scope of Lewis's historical perspective. No longer does a ponderous American history loom behind a frantic modern Zenith, reducing its loftiest self-serving ambitions to sheerest banality. In this novel, Lewis's vision of the entire American character, past and present, is re-adjusted through a thoughtful comparison with European civilization. Dodsworth himself is "not a Babbitt, not a Rotarian, not an Elk, not a deacon." He is as sound and sympathetic an American character as Lewis created before 1930. When, at the conclusion of the novel, Sam establishes something of a hold on happiness, he becomes complete as Lewis's post-pioneer American, still endowed with his natural awkwardness, perhaps, but possessed of a new historical and societal equilibrium. *Kingsblood Royal* was a highly topical novel when it was published in 1947, since it deals with racial tension in the small Midwestern city of Grand Republic. It also provides a chronologically and thematically satisfactory culmination to this study of Lewis's use of an implied American past. In the central plot device in the novel—Neil Kingsblood's discovery of his own past and that discovery's effect upon him and those around him—Lewis seems to have found a feasible working model of his own sense of history and the individual's relationship to it.

In 1944, Neil Kingsblood has "always wanted to be a frontiersman, an Astor Company trader of 1820 on the Minnesota border," but his life is a world and a couple of World Wars away from the frontier. It is his father's unlikely theory that the family line may carry the blood of Henry VIII which puts Neil on the trail of the genealogy of his mother's ancestors. He is excited enough to press his research when he learns that this great-great-great-grandfather was one Xavier Pic, "a voyageur for the Hudson's Bay Company," a man belonging "not to evening and mist and gossiping cowbells but to alert mornings on the glittering rapids of unknown rivers." Neil's investigation gives form to the desire of a more mature post-war America to ally itself with a national past which, two decades before, it had been happy to ignore.

The startling discovery that Xavier Pic was a full-blooded Negro—thereby making Neil a Negro by legal definition—opens the door to another exercise in spiritual pioneering, and also lays the foundation for Lewis's explication of his own hypothesis on the relationship of the past to the present. As Neil determines to testify to his racial status, regardless of the cost, the confluence of forces which time brings to bear upon the equilibrium of any given moment becomes apparent. The mixture of blood lines in Neil's ancestry is like the mixture of social, political and economic forces which, along with the whims of countless individuals, accounts for the character of an age. The inevitable conclusion to the story, with Neil waging a valiant but futile fight for his rights as a human being, rounds out not only Lewis's condemnation of racism in America, but also his implication that a nation must be willing to recognize and act upon the obligations imposed by its own past.

The chronological domain of these seven Sinclair Lewis novels spans more than a century of American history. During that century, America changed more radically in structure and character than any other nation had ever changed in an equal amount of time. The Upper Midwest passed from a state of wilderness to a state of prosperous modernity, and Lewis took it as one of his artistic tasks to chronicle that passage. As an observer of American life, he planted himself squarely in the twentieth century, but his vision ranged backward to the beginning and forward to the unknown but hopeful future. In *The God-Seeker*, he attempted to capture the flavor of optimism and expectancy and the nearly equal potentialities for glory and for ruin which pervaded the nineteenth-century frontier. He warned his readers to look carefully upon those pioneers, for what they did and saw and said would count for something in the development of the quality of the years which followed theirs. *Main Street*, *Babbitt*, *Arrowsmith*, *Elmer Gantry*, and *Dodsworth*, written amidst the fury of the decade in which they were set, described the harvest which the twentieth century was reaping from its own reckless tending of the national garden. *Kingsblood Royal* suggested the degree of courage which is necessary for a people to ride successfully the crest of their own history.

It would be presumptuous, even silly, to suggest that the body of Sinclair Lewis's novels constitutes a grand epic of the American Midwest. But the evidence of his attention not only to documentary accuracy but also to historical perspective in the recording of his era's manners and meanness clearly implies that Lewis was generally and artistically conscious of the prominent role which history plays in the affairs of his most memorable characters.

HOWARD LEVANT

The Fully Matured Art:
The Grapes of Wrath

The enormous contemporary social impact of *The Grapes of Wrath* can encourage the slippery reasoning that condemns a period novel to die with its period. But continuing sales and critical discussions suggest that *The Grapes of Wrath* has outlived its directly reportorial ties to the historical past; that it can be considered as an aesthetic object, a good or a bad novel per se. In that light, the important consideration is the relative harmony of its structure and materials.

The Grapes of Wrath is an attempted prose epic, a summation of national experience at a given time. Evaluation proceeds from that identification of genre. A negative critical trend asserts that *The Grapes of Wrath* is too flawed to command serious attention: the materials are local and temporary, not universal and permanent; the conception of life is overly simple; the characters are superficial types (except, perhaps, Ma Joad); the language is folksy or strained by turns; and, in particular, the incoherent structure is the weakest point-the story breaks in half, the nonorganic, editorializing interchapters force unearned general conclusions, and the ending is inconclusive as well as overwrought and sentimental. The positive trend asserts that *The Grapes of Wrath* is a great novel. Its materials are properly universalized in specific detail; the conception is philosophical, the characters are warmly felt and deeply created; the language is functional, varied, and superb on the whole; and the structure is an almost perfect

From *John Steinbeck*, Harold Bloom ed. Originally published in *The Novels of John Steinbeck: A Critical Study*. © 1974 by The Curators of the University of Missouri.

combination of the dramatic and the panoramic in sufficient harmony with the materials. This criticism admits that overwrought idealistic passages as well as propagandistic simplifications turn up on occasion, but these are minor flaws in an achievement on an extraordinary scale. Relatively detached studies of Steinbeck's ideas comprise a third trend. These studies are not directly useful in analytical criticism; they do establish that Steinbeck's social ideas are ordered and legitimate extensions of biological fact, hence scientific and true rather than mistaken or sentimental.

The two evaluative positions are remarkable in their opposition. They are perhaps overly simple in asserting that *The Grapes of Wrath* is either a classic of our literature or a formless pandering to sentimental popular taste. Certainly these extremes are mistaken in implying (when they do) that, somehow, *The Grapes of Wrath* is sui generis in relation to Steinbeck's work.

Trends so awkwardly triple need to be brought into a sharper focus. By way of a recapitulation in focus, consider a few words of outright praise:

> For all of its sprawling asides and extravagances, *The Grapes of Wrath* is a big book, a great book, and one of maybe two or three American novels in a class with *Huckleberry Finn*.

Freeman Champney's praise is conventional enough to pass unquestioned if one admires *The Grapes of Wrath*, or, if one does not, it can seem an invidious borrowing of prestige, shrilly emotive at that. Afterthought emphasizes the serious qualification of the very high praise. Just how much damage is wrought by those "sprawling asides and extravagances," and does *The Grapes of Wrath* survive its structural faults as *Huckleberry Finn* does, by virtue of its mythology, its characterization, its language? If the answers remain obscure, illumination may increase (permitting, as well, a clearer definition of the aesthetic efficacy of Steinbeck's ideas) when the context of critical discussion is the relationship of the novel's structure to materials.

Steinbeck's serious intentions and his artistic honesty are not in question. He had studied and experienced the materials intensely over a period of time. After a false start that he rejected (*L'Affaire Lettuceburg*), his conscious intention was to create an important literary work rather than a propagandistic shocker or a journalistic statement of the topical problem of how certain people faced one aspect of the Great Depression. Therefore, it is an insult to Steinbeck's aims to suggest that somehow *The Grapes of Wrath* is imperfect art but a "big" or "great" novel nevertheless. In all critical justice, *The Grapes of Wrath* must stand or fall as a serious and important work of art.

The consciously functional aspect of Steinbeck's intentions-his working of the materials-is clarified by a comparison of *The Grapes of Wrath* with *In Dubious Battle*. Both novels deal with labor problems peculiar to California, but that similarity cannot be pushed too far. The Joads are fruit pickers in California, but not of apples, the fruit mentioned in *In Dubious Battle*. The Joads pick cotton, and in the strike novel the people expect to move on to cotton. The Joads become involved in a strike but as strikebreakers rather than as strikers. Attitudes are less easy to camouflage. The strikers in *In Dubious Battle* and the Okies in *The Grapes of Wrath* are presented with sympathy whereas the owning class and much of the middle class have no saving virtue. The sharpest similarity is that both the strikers and the Okies derive a consciousness of the need for group action from their experiences; but even here there is a difference in emphasis. The conflict of interest is more pointed and the lessons of experience are less ambiguous in *The Grapes of Wrath* than in *In Dubious Battle*. The fact is that the two novels are not similar beyond a common basis in California labor problems, and Steinbeck differentiates that basis carefully in most specific details. The really significant factor is that different structures are appropriate to each novel. The restricted scope of *In Dubious Battle* demands a dramatic structure with some panoramic elements as they are needed. The broad scope of *The Grapes of Wrath* demands a panoramic structure; the dramatic elements appear as they are needed. Therefore, in each case, the primary critical concern must be the adequacy of the use of the materials, not the materials in themselves.

Steinbeck's profound respect for the materials of *The Grapes of Wrath* is recorded in a remarkable letter in which he explained to his literary agents and to his publisher the main reason for his withdrawing *L'Affaire Lettuceburg*, the hurried, propagandistic, thirty-thousand-word manuscript novel that preceded *The Grapes of Wrath*:

> I know I promised this book to you, and that I am breaking a promise in withholding it. But I had got smart and cagey you see. I had forgotten that I hadn't learned to write books, that I will never learn to write them. A book must be a life that lives all of itself and this one doesn't do that. You can't write a book. It isn't that simple. The process is more painful than that. And this book is fairly clever, has skillful passages, but tricks and jokes. Sometimes I, the writer, seem a hell of a smart guy-just twisting this people out of shape. But the hell with it. I beat poverty for a good many years and I'll be damned if I'll go down at the first little whiff of success. I hope you, Pat, don't think I've double-

crossed you. In the long run to let this book out would be to double-cross you. But to let the bars down is like a first theft. It's hard to do, but the second time it isn't so hard and pretty soon it is easy. If I should write three books like this and let them out, I would forget there were any other kinds.

This is Steinbeck's declaration of artistic purpose-and his effort to exorcise a dangerous (and permanent) aspect of his craft. Much of the motivation for Steinbeck's career is stated in this letter. After all, he did write *L'Affaire Lettuceburg*; and "tricks and jokes," detached episodes, and detached ironic hits, as well as a twisting of characters, are evident enough in much of Steinbeck's earlier work. But the depression materials were too serious to treat lightly or abstractly, or to subject to an imposed structure (mistaken idealism, nature worship, a metaphysical curse, a literary parallel). Such materials need to be in harmony with an appropriate structure.

From that intentional perspective, the central artistic problem is to present the universal and epical in terms of the individual and particular. Steinbeck chooses to deal with this by creating an individual, particular image of the epical experience of the dispossessed Okies by focusing a sustained attention on the experience of the Joads. The result is an organic combination of structures. Dramatic structure suits the family's particular history; panoramic structure proves out the representative nature of their history. To avoid a forced and artificial "typing," to assure that extensions of particular detail are genuinely organic, Steinbeck postulates a conceptual theme that orders structure and materials: the transformation of the Joad family from a self-contained, self-sustaining unit to a conscious part of a group, a whole larger than its parts. This thematic ordering is not merely implicit or ironic, as it is in *The Pastures of Heaven*, or withheld to create mystery as in *Cup of Gold* or *To a God Unknown*. Steinbeck chances the strength of the materials and the organic quality of their structure. And he defines differences: the group is not group-man. The earlier concept is a "beast," created by raw emotion ("blood"), short-lived, unwieldy, unpredictable, mindless; a monster that produces indiscriminate good or evil. The group is quite different-rational, stable, relatively calm-because it is an assemblage of like-minded people who retain their individual and traditional sense of right and wrong as a natural fact. Group-man lacks a moral dimension; the group is a morally pure instrument of power. The difference is acute at the level of leadership. The leaders have ambiguous aims in *In Dubious Battle*, but they are Christ-like (Jim Casy) or attain moral insight (Tom Joad) in *The Grapes of Wrath*.

The Grapes of Wrath is optimistic; *In Dubious Battle* is not. That the living part of the Joad family survives, though on the edge of survival, is less than glowingly optimistic, but that survival produces a mood that differs considerably from the unrelenting misery of *In Dubious Battle*. Optimism stems from the theme, most openly in the alternation of narrative chapter and editorial interchapter. While the Joads move slowly and painfully toward acceptance of the group, many of the interchapters define the broad necessity of that acceptance. Arbitrary plotting does not produce this change. Its development is localized in Ma Joad's intense focus on the family's desire to remain a unit; her recognition of the group is the dramatic resolution. ("Use' ta be the fambly was fust. It ain't so now. It's anybody. Worse off we get, the more we got to do.") Optimism is demonstrated also in experience that toughens, educates, and enlarges the stronger Joads in a natural process. On the simplest, crudest level, the family's journey and ordeal is a circumstantial narrative of an effort to reach for the good material life. Yet that is not the sole motive, and those members who have only that motive leave the family. On a deeper level, the family is attempting to rediscover the identity it lost when it was dispossessed; so the Joads travel from order (their old, traditional life) through disorder (the road, California) to some hope of a better, rediscovered order, which they reach in Ma's recognition and Tom's dedication. Their journey toward order is the ultimate optimistic, ennobling process, the earned, thematic resolution of the novel.

I do not intend to imply that Steinbeck pretties his materials. He does not stint the details of the family's various privations, its continual losses of dignity, and the death or disappearance of many of its members. On the larger scale, there is considerable objective documentation of the general economic causes of such misery-a circumstantial process that lifts *The Grapes of Wrath* out of the merely historic genre of the proletarian novel. Optimism survives as the ultimate value because of the will of the people to understand and to control the conditions of their lives despite constant discouragement.

This value is essentially abstract, political. Steinbeck deepens and universalizes it by developing the relationship between the family unit and "the people." The family is made up of unique individuals. "The people" embraces a timeless entity, a continuing past, present, and future of collective memory-but free of any social or political function. Time lag confounds the usefulness of "the people" as a guide for the present. The Joads and others like them know they may keep the land or get new land if they can kill or control "the Bank," as the old people killed Indians to take the land and controlled nature to keep it. But "the Bank" is more complicated an enemy than Indians or nature because it is an abstraction. (That buccaneering capitalism is an abstract or allegorical monster of evil is left to implication in *In Dubious Battle*. Steinbeck is far more directly allegorical in characterizing "the Bank" as an evil, nonhuman monster. Consequently there is, I think, a gain in horror but a relative loss of credibility.) So the Okies submit to dispossession in Oklahoma (forced by mechanized cheaper production of cotton) and to the huge migration into California (encouraged by landowners to get cheap field labor), motivated by the time lag that confuses them, for none of them comprehends the monstrous logic of modern economics. Despite their ignorance, in a process that is unifying in itself and is second only to survival, the families work at some way of preventing against "the Bank." The older, agrarian concept of "the people" is succeeded in time by the new concept of the group, an instrument of technology and political power-an analogue that works. Steinbeck makes this succession appear necessary and legitimate by a representation that excludes alternate solutions. The permitted solution seems a natural evolution, from people to group, because it is a tactic, not a fundamental change in folkways. Its process is long and painful because the emotive entity, "the people," needs to feel its way toward redefinition as the group-the abstract, political entity which emerges as an organic, particularized whole. This is brilliant literary strategy, in its grasp of operative metaphor and its avoidance of an overly obvious, loaded opposition. Steinbeck is scrupulously careful to keep to precise and exact circumstantial detail in this developed metaphor. Concretely, the panicky violence of "the Bank" is the reverse of the fact that (seemingly by habit) the Joads are kind to those who need their help and neighborly to people who are like them. The metaphor is persuasive.

Steinbeck is quite as scrupulous in the use of allegory as a way of universalizing an abstract particular. In his earlier work this method can produce a tangibly artificial, forced result, but allegory is a credible and functional device in *The Grapes of Wrath*. The turtle episode in chapter 3 is justly famous. Objectively, we have a fully realized description of a land turtle's patient, difficult journey over dust fields, across a road and walled embankment, and on through the dust. The facts are the starting point; nature is not distorted or manipulated to yield allegorical meaning. The turtle seems awkward but it is able to survive, like the Joads, and like them it is moving southwest, out of the dry area. It can protect itself against a natural danger like the red ant it kills, as the Joads protect themselves by their unity. The turtle's eyes are "fierce, humorous," suggesting force that takes itself easily; the stronger Joads are a fierce, humorous people. When mismanaged human power attacks, as when a truck swerves to hit the turtle, luck is on the animal's side-it survives by luck. The Joads survive the mismanagement that produced the Dust Bowl and the brutalizing man-made conditions in California as much by luck as by design. The relation to the Joads of the life-bearing function of the turtle is more obscure, or perhaps overly ambitious. The factual starting point is that, unknowingly, the turtle carries an oat seed in its shell and unknowingly drops and plants the seed in the dust, where it will rest until water returns. The most obvious link in the Joad family is the pregnant Rose of Sharon, but her baby is born dead. Perhaps compassion is "born," as in Uncle John's thoughts as he floats the dead baby down the flooding river in its apple box coffin: "Go down an' tell 'em. Go down in the street an' rot an' tell 'em that way. That's the way you can talk.... Maybe they'll know then." (The reversal of values is evident in the reversed symbolism; the river bears death-not life, the coffin-not water to seeds in the earth.) But this appeal is strained, too greatly distanced from the factual starting point. The link works in the restricted sense that Ruthie and Winfield are "planted," and will perhaps take root, in the new environment of California. At this point the careful allegory collapses under its own weight, yet care is taken to join the device to the central narrative. In chapter 4, Tom Joad picks up a turtle, and later Casy remarks on the tenacity of the breed:

> "Nobody can't keep a turtle though. They work at it and work at it, and at last one day they get out and away they go-off somewheres.

This recognition of the turtle's purposeful tenacity interprets and places the preceding interchapter in the central narrative. Tom calls the turtle "an old bulldozer," a figure that works in opposition to the threatening insect life the tractors suggest as self-defeating, destructive tools of "the Bank." Again, a purposeful turtle is opposed to homeless domestic animals, like the "thick-furred yellow shepherd dog" that passes Tom and Casy, to suggest precisely the ruined land and the destruction of the old ways of life on the most basic, animal level, where the wild (or free) animal survives best. These and other supporting details extend the exemplum into the narrative; they continue and deepen Steinbeck's foreshadowing, moralizing insight naturally, within the range of biological imagery. It is true, allowing for the one collapse of the allegory, that none of Steinbeck's earlier work exhibits as profound a comprehension of what can be done to "place" an allegorical narrative device.

The turtle interchapter is masterful enough. Steinbeck does even more with an extended instance of allegorizing-the introduction of the lapsed preacher, Jim Casy, into the Joad family. Casy has a role that is difficult to present within the limits of credibility. Casy may look too much like his function, the Christ-like force that impels the family toward its transformation into the group. If the novel is to have more significance than a reportorial narrative of travel and hardship, Casy's spiritual insights are a necessary means of stating a convincing philosophical optimism. The technical difficulty is that Casy does not have a forthright narrative function. He drops out of the narrative for almost one hundred and fifty pages, although his presence continues through the Joads' wondering at times what had happened to him. When he reenters the novel, he is killed off within fifteen pages-sacrificed for the group in accord with his Christ-like function, with a phrase that recalls Christ's last words. In spite of the obvious technical difficulty in handling such materials, Steinbeck realizes Casy as fully as any of the major Joads. Casy's struggle with himself to define "sin" to include the necessary facts of the natural world lends him a completely human aspect. He earns the right to make moral statements because he bases all judgments on his own experience. This earned right to "witness" serves to keep Casy human, yet it permits him to function as if he were an allegorical figure. This is a brilliant solution, and Casy is Steinbeck's most successful use of a functional allegorical figure in a major role. His narrative sharpness contrasts amazingly with the dim realization of Sir Henry Morgan or Joseph Wayne.

Even Casy's necessary distance is functional rather than arbitrary. He exists outside the narrative in the sense that he travels with the Joads but he is not a member of the family, and there is no danger of confusing his adventures with theirs. Further, by right of his nature and experience, he has the function of being the living moral conscience of "the people." He travels with the Joads to witness the ordeal of the Okies, to understand its causes, and to do what he can to help. Steinbeck's convincing final touch is that, at the end, Tom Joad aspires to Casy's role. In this shift, Steinbeck manipulates allegory, he does not submit to its rigid quality, for Tom is not like Casy. Tom is far more violent, more capable of anger; having been shown the way, however, he may be more successful as a practical missionary than Casy. One might say that if Casy is to be identified with Christ, the almost human god, Tom is to be identified with Saint Paul, the realistic, tough organizer. The allegorical link by which Tom is "converted" and assumes Casy's role is deeply realized and rich with significance, not simply because it is a technical necessity, but because it is a confirmation of Casy's reality as a man and a teacher. The parallels to Christ and Saint Paul would be only and technical facts if they were not realized so profoundly. The trivial fact that Casy has Christ's initials dims beside this more profound and sustained realization.

Function, not mere design, is as evident in the use of characterization to support and develop a conflict of opposed ideas-mainly a struggle between law and anarchy. The one idea postulates justice in a moral world of love and work, identified in the past with "the people" and in the present with the government camp and finally with the union movement, since these are the modern, institutional forms the group may take. The opposed idea postulates injustice in an immoral world of hatred and starvation. It is associated with buccaneering capitalism, which, in violent form, includes strikebreaking and related practices that cheapen human labor.

The Joads present special difficulties in characterization. They must be individualized to be credible and universalized to carry out their representative functions. Steinbeck meets these problems by making each of the Joads a specific individual and by specifying that what happens to the Joads is typical of the times. The means he uses to maintain these identities can be shown in some detail. The least important Joads are given highly specific tags-Grandma's religion, Grandpa's vigor, Uncle John's melancholy, and Al's love of cars and girls. The tags are involved in events; they are not inert labels. Grandma's burial violates her religion; Grandpa's vigor ends when he leaves the land; Uncle John's melancholy balances the family's experience; Al helps to drive the family to California and, by marrying, continues the family. Ma, Pa, Rose of Sharon, and Tom carry the narrative, so their individuality is defined by events rather than through events. Ma is the psychological and moral center of the family; Pa carries its burdens; Rose of Sharon means to ensure its physical continuity; and Tom becomes its moral conscience. On the larger scale, there is much evidence that what happens to the family is typical of the times. The interchapters pile up suggestions that "the whole country is moving" or about to move. The Joads meet many of their counterparts or outsiders who are in sympathy with their ordeal; these meetings reenforce the common bond of "the people." Both in the interchapters and the narrative, the universal, immediate issue is survival-a concrete universal.

On the other hand, the individualized credibility of the Joads is itself the source of two difficulties: the Joads are too different, as sharecroppers, to suggest a universal or even a national woe, and they speak an argot that might limit their universal quality. (It is a curious fact that Steinbeck attempts to create a so-called "universal language" in *Burning Bright*, a far more theory-ridden novel than *The Grapes of Wrath*. In any event, the attempt produces a fantastic, wholly incredible language.) Steinbeck handles these limitations with artistic license. The narrative background contains the Joads' past; their experience as a landless proletariat is highlighted in the narrative foreground.

The argot is made to seem a typical language within the novel in three ways: it is the major language; people who are not Okies speak variations of their argot; and that argot is not specialized in its relevance, but is used to communicate the new experiences "the people" have in common as a landless proletariat. However, because these solutions depend on artistic license, any tonal falseness undermines severely the massive artistic truthfulness the language is intended to present. So the overly editorial tone in several of the interchapters has a profoundly false linguistic ring, although the tonal lapse is limited and fairly trivial in itself.

The Joads are characterized further in comparison with four Okie types who refuse to know or are unable to gain the knowledge the family derives from its collective experience. They are the stubborn, the dead, the weak, and the backtrackers; they appear in the novel in that order.

Muley Graves is the stubborn man, as his punning name suggests. He reveals himself to Tom and Casy near the beginning of the novel. His refusal to leave Oklahoma is mere stubbornness; his isolation drives him somewhat mad. He is aware of a loss of reality, of "jus' wanderin' aroun' like a damn ol' graveyard ghos'," and his blind violence is rejected from the beginning by the strongest, who oppose his pessimism with an essential optimism.

Deaths of the aged and the unborn frame the novel. Grandpa and Grandma are torn up by the roots and die, incapable of absorbing a new, terrible experience. Rose of Sharon's baby, born dead at the end of the novel, is an index of the family's ordeal and a somewhat contrived symbol of the necessity to form the group.

The weak include two extremes within the Joad family. Noah Joad gives up the struggle to survive; he finds a private peace. His character is shadowy, and his choice is directed more clearly by Steinbeck than by any substance within him. Connie has plenty of substance. He is married to Rose of Sharon and deserts her because he had no faith in the family's struggle to reach California. His faith is absorbed in the values of "the Bank," in getting on, in money, in any abstract goal. He wishes to learn about technology in order to rise in the world. He does not admire technique for itself, as Al does. He is a sexual performer, but he loves no one. Finally, he wishes that he had stayed behind in Oklahoma and taken a job driving a tractor. In short, with Connie, Steinbeck chooses brilliantly to place a "Bank" viewpoint within the family. By doing so, he precludes a simplification of character and situation, and he endorses the complexity of real people in the real world. (*In Dubious Battle* is similarly free of schematic characterization.) In addition, the family's tough, humanistic values gain in credibility by their contrast with Connie's shallow, destructive modernity. The confused gas station owner and the pathetic one-eyed junkyard helper are embodied variations on Connie's kind of weakness. Al provides an important counterpoint. He wants to leave the family at last, like Connie, but duty and love force him to stay. His hard choice points the moral survival of the family and measures its human expense.

The Joads meet several backtrackers. The Wilsons go back because Mrs. Wilson is dying; the Joads do not stop, in spite of death. The ragged man's experience foreshadows what the Joads find in California; but they keep on. Some members of the Joad family think of leaving but do not, or they leave for specific reasons-a subtle variation on backtracking. Al and Uncle John wish deeply at times to leave, but they stay; Tom leaves (as Casy does) but to serve the larger, universal family of the group. Backtracking is a metaphor, then, a denial of life, but always a fact as well. The factual metaphor is deepened into complexity because the Joads sympathize with the backtrackers' failure to endure the hardships of the road and of California, in balance with where they started from the wasteland-while knowing they cannot accept that life-denying solution. All of these choices are the fruit of the family's experience.

A fifth group of owners and middle-class people are accorded no sympathetic comprehension, as contrasted with the Joads, and, as in *In Dubious Battle*, their simply and purely monstrous characterization is too abstract to be fully credible. The few exceptions occur in highly individualized scenes or episodes (chapter 15 is an example) in which middle-class "shitheels" are caricatures of the bad guys, limited to a broad contrast with the good guys (the truck drivers, the cook), who are in sympathy with a family of Okies. (Fifteen years later, Steinbeck detailed this technique in a witty article, "How to Tell Good Guys from Bad Guys," *The Reporter* 12 [March 10, 1955], 42–44. In that quite different, political context, Steinbeck demonstrates that he knows the technique is too bluntly black and white to permit any but the broadest cartoon characterization. There is every reason to think he knew as much in 1935 or 1939.) This limitation has the narrative advantage of highlighting the importance and vitality of the Okies to the extent that they seem by right to belong in the context of epic materials, but the disadvantage of shallow characterization is severe. Steinbeck can provide a convincing detailed background of the conditions of the time; he cannot similarly give a rounded, convincing characterization to an owner or a disagreeable middle-class person.

On the whole, then, fictive strength and conviction are inherent in the materials of *The Grapes of Wrath*. The noticeable flaws are probably irreducible aspects of the time context and of narrative shorthand, counterpointed by a complex recognition of human variety in language and behavior.

The ordering of the structure supports this conclusion. *The Grapes of Wrath* has three parts: Tom's return and his witnessing of events; the family's departure and experiences on the road; its arrival and experiences in California. The interchapters "locate" and generalize the narrative chapters, somewhat like stage directions. They supply, in a suitably dramatic or rhetorical style, information the Joads cannot possess, and they are involved more often than not in the narrative. (Because of that involvement, it is incorrect to think of the interchapters as choral. We see the difference in comparing the four detached interchapters in *Cup of Gold* with any interchapters in *The Grapes of Wrath*, and we see as well Steinbeck's artistic growth in the organic integration of chapter and interchapter in the later novel. The stylistic variety always suited to its content is further evidence of a conscious, intentional artistry.) This device provides for both precise detail and epic scope. The imagery fulfills the structural purpose of pitting life against death.

The first part contains ten chapters. The opening is a "location" interchapter. The dead land of the Dust Bowl in Oklahoma provides the imagery of a universal death, but at the close the women watch their men to see if they will break in the stress of that natural disaster. The men do not break; the scene is repeated in California at the close of the novel in a rising rhetoric. The objective imagistic frame sets life against death, and life endures in the will of the people to endure. The following nine chapters center on Tom's return from a kind of death-prison. With Casy, Tom is an external observer, witnessing with fresh eyes the dead land and the universal dispossession. Death seems to prevail. The turtle interchapter is recapitulated ironically in the narrative. Pa carries handbills that promise jobs in California, an analogue to the turtle carrying a head of oats; but the handbills falsely promise renewal; their intention is to cheapen the labor market. Later events prove the group concept is the genuine renewal, the true goal. Immediately, death is associated with "the Bank," an abstraction presented concretely in symbolic form as the tractor-the perfect tool of the abstract "Bank," which dehumanizes its driver and kills the fertility of the land.

When he sees the abandoned Joad home, Tom says, "Maybe they're all dead," but Muley Graves tells Tom the family is alive, with Uncle John, and about to leave without him for California. Tom is reborn or returned to life within the family, but its vital center has shifted (as represented in charged, frankly mystical terms) to a life-giving machine:

> The family met at the most important place, near the truck. The house was dead, and the fields were dead; but this truck was the active thing, the living principle.

The family's certainties develop from an ironically hopeful innocence, a failure to realize that a new basis for life has overtaken them, replacing family with group. The trek is an instinctive flight from death, but the economic system is more deadly than the drouth. The Joads accept the promise of the handbills, they are cheated when they sell their farm equipment, but they do not doubt that they will transplant themselves in California. The real certainty is the death of the past, as in the burning of relics by an unnamed woman in an interchapter, and by Ma herself, just before the trek begins.

All that is not dead is altered. Pa's loss of authority to Ma and Al's new authority (he knows automobiles) represent the shifts in value within the family. They retain a living coherence as farmers. They work as a unit when they kill and salt down the hogs in preparation for the trek. They are innocent of the disgusting techniques of close dealing in business, but Tom explains to Casy how the Joads can deal closely enough in their accustomed agrarian context. Their innocence, therefore, is touching, not comic, and their literal preparations support a symbolic preparation, a blindly hopeful striving to find life. Their journey is an expression, despite all shocks and changes, of the will to survive; hence, it has an epic dignity, echoing their retained, personal dignity.

In all the imagery of life and death, Steinbeck is consistent in that his symbols grow out of objective, literal facts. He thus achieves imagery in a more fully realized texture in this novel than in earlier work. This organically realized symbolism is maintained and developed in the seven chapters of the second section.

With the dead land behind them, the family carries the death of the past on its journey. Grandpa dies on the first night. Probably his stroke is caused, at least in part, by the "medicine" that Ma and Tom dope him with to take him away from the land-for the good of the family as a whole. An incipient group concept emerges in this overriding concern for the whole. Grandpa's death is offset by the meeting of the Joads and the Wilsons. At the beginning, Grandpa's illness and death join the two families in bonds of sympathy. There are other unifying forces; the language bar becomes senseless, and the two families help each other. Casy sees the emergence of the group, the whole absorbing the individual, in his sermon for Grandpa:

Casy said solemnly, "This here ol' man jus' lived a life an' jus' died out of it. I don't know whether he was good or bad, but that don't matter much. He was alive, an' that's what matters. An' now he's dead, an' that don't matter. Heard a fella tell a poem one time, an' he says, `All that lives is holy.'"

A modest dignity embodies the vitalistic dogma. As a further push from individual to group, the family decides to break the law by burying Grandpa secretly beside the road; a conventional funeral would eat up the money they need to reach California. Grandma's grisly, circumstantial death is delayed until the end of the section; it outweighs the achievement of reaching their destination and foreshadows the reality of California. True, the family can absorb death, even new kinds of death, into its experience. Ruthie and Winfield react most violently to the dog's death at the first stop on the road; they are less affected by Grandpa's death, still less by Grandma's. Late on the night of Grandpa's death after the Joads and Wilsons have agreed to join forces, Ma remarks: "Grandpa-it's like he's dead a year." Experience breeds a calm in the face of loss that fills in the past. Tom points this harshly realistic network of difference after Grandma's death:

"They was too old," he said. "They wouldn't of saw nothin' that's here. Grampa would a been a-seein' the Injuns an' the prairie country when he was a young fella. An' Granma would a remembered an' seen the first home she lived in. They was too ol'. Who's really seein' it is Ruthie and Winfiel'."

Life matters. The narrative context supports this fruit of the family's private experience. Between the deaths of Grandpa and Grandma, the Joads meet several symbolically dead people on the road. The gas station owner is incapable of learning the meaning of his own experience even when it is explained to him. The one-eyed junkyard helper lives in a prison of self, inside his ugly face and unclean body. Tom (who was in an actual prison) tries unsuccessfully to force him from his death into life. The several returning sharecroppers have come to accept a living death as the only reality. They have cut themselves off from the inchoate struggle to form a group, admittedly against severe odds, so they have no choice but to return to the dead, empty land.

But to outsiders, seeing only the surface, the Joads are not heroic lifebearers but stupidly ignorant, as in a dialogue between two service station boys when the family leaves on the final lap of the trek, the night trip across the Mojave Desert:

> "Jesus, I'd hate to start out in a jalopy like that." "Well, you and me got sense. Them goddamn Okies got no sense and no feeling. They ain't human. A human being wouldn't live like they do. A human being couldn't stand to be so dirty and miserable. They ain't a hell of a lot better than gorillas." "Just the same. I'm glad I ain't crossing the desert in no Hudson Super-Six...." "You know, they don't have much trouble. They're so goddamn dumb they don't know it's dangerous. And, Christ Almighty, they don't know any better than what they got. Why worry?"

The dialogue is exactly true, but the truth is ironic. The Joads do have the appearance of death, and ignorant, dirty, dispossessed yokels seem to be unlikely carriers of an affirmation of life. The ironic truth defines the heroism of the Joads. The family is aware of the dangers of the desert crossing, and Grandma dies during it, "for the fambly," as Ma says. In general the family is more aware than the boys at the service station are allowed to know. After meeting a second returning sharecropper, the Joads are even aware of the actual conditions in California; Uncle John, the family's weakest moral agent, voices the family's rejection of despair when he says, "We're a-goin' there, ain't we? None of this here talk gonna keep us from goin' there." The service station boys express, so we can dismiss, a superficially sentimental view of the Joads. The ironic truth is that the family goes ahead, knowing the dangers and aware that California may not be Eden. Their genuine heroism and nobility are all the more valid for being tested by irony.

Yet there is no suggestion that the Joads are merely deterministic formulae. They are pawns of circumstance up to a point. They react to events they do not understand fully, and no doubt partial ignorance and pure necessity keep them on the road and get them to California. But Ma and Tom undergo certain developments of character that exclude determinism. Ma's constantly increasing moral authority is her response to the forces that are tearing the family apart, but she acts out of love that is restricted to the family, that is not universalized until very near the end of the novel. Tom's role is more extensive and more complex. He begins by regarding himself as a creature of necessity-"I ruther jus'-lay one foot down in front a the other"-but his quietism relates to a prison experience he does not want to live "over an' over." His natural understanding of why and how people behave forces him into a moral concern that is larger but as intense as Ma's. His knowledge of people is established at the beginning of the novel, in his shrewd, unflattering understanding of the truck driver who gives him a lift, and it widens subsequently with experience on the road. His disdain for the gas station owner precedes his tough moral lecture to the one-eyed junkyard helper and an equally tough lecture to Al. That is to say, Tom is involved. His moral development follows Casy's, with the significant difference that his is the more difficult to achieve. Casy is a relatively simple character; he can express moral concern easily. Tom's emotional numbness following his time in prison does not permit meditation or cancel personality, so the awakening of his moral consciousness on the road is a more rigorous, more painful experience than Casy's time in the desert. Consequently, because of its special quality, Tom's growing awareness of good and evil is a highly credible mirror of the general experience that drives the family toward the group. The logic is paradoxical, but the artistic insight is realized deeply in Tom's circumstantial journey from moral quietism to moral concern for the group.

Enduring all the harsh experiences of their journey, the family gains moral stature and finds that it can function as a unit in the new environment of the road. Its survival in California is a result in part of its redefinition gained on the road.

The interchapters underscore and generalize these particulars. Chapter 14 states the growth of the group concept as a shift in the thinking of the migrants from *I* to *we*. The narrative context is Grandpa's death and the unity of the Joads and Wilsons. Chapter 15 suggests that the Joads' ordeal is a moral experience that affects society at large. Chapter 17 continues the theme that the road furthers the growth of the group concept:

> Every night relationships that make a world, established; every morning the world torn down like a circus. At first the families were timid in the building and tumbling worlds, but gradually the technique of building worlds became their technique. Then leaders emerged, then laws were made, then codes came into being. And as the worlds moved westward they were more complete and better furnished, for their builders were more experienced in building them.

The formation of a group is a "technique" with its basis in the older agrarian order. As with the Joads, the experience of building produces a new moral stature and a redefinition of the family.

In the relation of these events and changes, the narrative chapters and interchapters cohere in an organic unity. Their common theme is movement from and through death to a new life inherent in the group concept. The symbolic level extends the narrative level of movement on the road through time and space. The texture is fully realized. No generalization violates narrative particulars or exists apart from them. Steinbeck's work is careful, convincing, flawless.

The third part-the family's arrival and experience in California-marks an artistic decline. The materials alter and at times the structure is defective.

The chief difference in the materials is an absolute focus on man-made misery. In Oklahoma and on the road, survival can seem to be mainly a struggle against natural conditions. Drouth is the cause of the migration. "The Bank" dispossesses the Okies, but it is not the effective cause of the drouth. In California the struggle is almost entirely against men, and there is no possibility of an escape by further migration. The chief difference in structure stems from Steinbeck's need to begin to think of how to conclude the novel, which presents structural choices and manipulations not present in the first two parts of the novel. For a time the narrative thrust remains coherent, an organic unity disguising these changes.

Grandma's undignified burial establishes the pattern of the family's experience in California. Her pauper's funeral by the state contrasts with the full dignity and free will the family expressed in burying Grandpa. Landless poverty is a moral insult to family pride, and it affects their will to survive. For the moment, as their moral spokesman, Ma expresses a will to recover as quickly as possible for the sake of the future:

> "We got to git," she said. "We got to find a place to stay. We
> got to get to work an' settle down. No use a-lettin' the little fellas
> go hungry. That wasn't never Granma's way. She always et a good
> meal at a funeral."

The conserving lesson of the past is negated by the present economic reality. Ma's brave gesture fails as the family learns that California is a false goal. The imagery associated with California indicates these negations. Peter Lisca and Joseph Fontenrose have pointed to the major biblical parallels in *The Grapes of Wrath*, including those associating California and the Promised Land. The parallels are intensive, even more so than Lisca and Fontenrose suggest, and their function is ironic rather than associative. To begin with, California evokes images of plenty to eat and drink. The ironic fact is that California is the literal reverse of Canaan; there is little to eat and drink, at least for Okies; but California is the Promised Land so far as the family's experience there forces the full emergence of the group concept. Appropriately, the family enters California with a foreboding that runs counter to their expectations:

> Pa called, "We're here-we're in California!" They looked dully at the broken rock glaring under the sun, and across the river the terrible ramparts of Arizona.

They have crossed over, but the physical imagery foreshadows their actual human environment. The land is green across the river, but the biblical lists of landscape features are framed by the fact that they have been carrying Grandma's corpse. The human reality of California life is a living death, as the first camp, the Hooverville, suggests: "About the camp there hung a slovenly despair," everything is "grey" and "dirty," there is no work, no food, and no evident means of overcoming "despair." The deadly economic reality is explained by a young man in the Hooverville, when Tom asks why the police "shove along" the migrants:

> "Some say they don' want us to vote; keep us movin' so we can't vote. An' some says so we can't get on relief. An' some says if we set in one place we'd get organized."

That reply announces the political solution, the humanly possible way of countervailing power through organization. But the words are programmatic, not a revelation of character.

The difference in materials and in structure begins to appear at this point. The root of the matter is that Steinbeck is so compelled by the documentary facts that he permits their narration to take precedence over the central theme of the family's transformation into the group. And in moving the novel toward an affirmation of life in response to the facts, Steinbeck allows the Joads' experience in California to become a series of allegorical details within a panoramic structure. The narrowed scope of the materials and the schematic handling of the structure are visible in nearly every event in this part of the novel.

Casy's alternative to "despair," sacrificing himself for "the people," is almost wholly an allegorical solution. It is so abstractly schematic that at first none of the family understands its meaningful allegorical force-that loss of self leads to the group concept and thus to power to enforce the will of the group. Instead, the narrative is largely an account of the family's efforts to avoid starvation. The phrase "We got to eat" echoes through these concluding chapters. Ma's changing attitude toward hungry unknown children is ambiguous: "I dunno what to do. I can't rob the fambly. I got to feed the fambly." Ma grows more positive, later, when she is nagged by a storekeeper in the struck orchard:

> "Any reason you got to make fun? That help you any?" "A fella got to eat," he began; and then, belligerantly, "A fella got a right to eat." "What fella?" Ma asked.

Ma asserts finally that only "the poor" constitute a group that practices charity:

> "I'm learnin' one thing good," she said. "Learnin' it all a time, ever' day. If you're in trouble or hurt or need-go to poor people. They're the only ones that'll help-the only ones."

"The poor" are identified with "the people," who, in turn are the emerging group. Their purity is allegorical, and, in its limitation, incredible. Steinbeck's handling of "the poor" in *In Dubious Battle* is much less schematic, and therefore far more credible. In general, romanticizing "the poor" is more successful in an outright fantasy like *Tortilla Flat* but Steinbeck commits himself to a measure of realism in *The Grapes of Wrath* that does not sort well with the allegorical division of "good" from "evil."

Romanticizing "the poor" extends beyond Ma's insight to an idealization of the "folk law" that Tom envisions as the fruit of his own experience in California-at a great distance from the "building" experience on the road:

> "I been thinkin' how it was in that gov'ment camp, how our folks took care a theirselves, an' if they was a fight they fixed it theirself; an' they wasn't no cops wagglin' their guns, but they was better order than them cops ever give. I been a-wonderin' why we can't do that all over. Throw out the cops that ain't our people. All work together for our own thing-all farm our own lan'."

Presenting the reverse of Tom's beatific vision in an interchapter, Steinbeck draws on the imagery of the novel's title:

> This vineyard will belong to the bank. Only the great owners can survive.... Men who can graft the trees and make the seed fertile and big can find no way to let the hungry people eat their

produce.... In the souls of the people the grapes of wrath are filling and growing heavy, growing heavy for the vintage.

It is not vitally important that Steinbeck's prediction of some kind of agrarian revolt has turned out to be wrong. The important artistic fact is that "good," divided sharply, abstractly, from "evil," argues that Steinbeck is not interested in rendering the materials in any great depth. Consider the contrast between the people in the government camp and in the struck orchard. Point by point, the camp people are described as clean, friendly, joyful, and organized, while in the struck orchard they are dirty, suspicious, anxious, and disorganized by the police. Credibility gives way to neat opposites, which are less than convincing because Steinbeck's government camp is presented openly as a benevolent tyranny that averages out the will of "the people" to live in dignity and excludes people unable or unwilling to accept that average.

Neat opposites can gather fictive conviction if they are realized through individuals and in specific detail. There is something of that conviction in specific action against specific men, as when the camp leaders exclude troublemakers hired by business interests to break up the camp organization. There is more awkwardness in the exclusion of a small group of religious fanatics obsessed with sin. An important factor is that these people are genuinely Okies, not tools of the interests; another is that the exclusion is necessary, not realistic, if the secular values of the group concept are to prevail. Allowing for his selection and schematic treatment of these materials, Steinbeck does engineer his manipulated point with artistic skill. Fanaticism is considered a bad thing throughout the novel, both as a religious stance and as a social phenomenon. Tom's first meeting with Casy identifies "spirit" with emotional release, not a consciousness of sin, and Casy announces his own discovery, made during his time in the desert, of a social rather than an ethical connection between "spirit" and sexual excitement. Further, fanaticism is identified repeatedly with a coercive denial of life. Rose of Sharon is frightened, in the government camp, by a fanatic woman's argument that dancing is sinful, that it means Rose will lose her baby. The woman's ignorance is placed against the secular knowledge of the camp manager:

> "I think the manager, he took [another girl who danced] away to drop her baby. He don' believe in sin.... Says the sin is bein' hungry. Says the sin is bein' cold."

She compounds ignorance by telling Ma that true religion demands fixed economic classes:

> "[A preacher] says 'They's wicketness in that camp.' He says, 'The poor is tryin' to be rich.' He says, 'They's dancin' an' huggin' when they should be wailin' an' moanin' in sin.'"

These social and economic denials of life are rooted in ignorance, not in spiritual enlightenment, and they are countered by the materialistic humanism of the camp manager. So fanaticism is stripped of value and associated with business in its denial of life. The case is loaded further by the benevolent tyranny of the group. Fanatics are not punished for their opinions, or even for wrongdoing. They are merely excluded, or they exclude themselves.

A similar process is apparent in the group's control of social behavior, as when Ruthie behaves as a rugged individual in the course of a children's game:

> The children laid their mallets on the ground and trooped silently off the court.... Defiantly she hit the ball again.... She pretended to have a good time. And the children stood and watched.... For a moment she stared at them, and then she flung down the mallet and ran crying for home. The children walked back on the court. Pig-tails said to Winfield, "You can git in the nex' game." The watching lady warned them, "When she comes back an' wants to be decent, you let her. You was mean yourself, Amy."

The punishment is directive. The children are being trained to accept the group and to become willing parts of the group. The process is an expression of "folk law" on a primary level. There is no doubt that Ruthie learned her correct place in the social body by invoking a suitably social punishment.

Perhaps the ugliness implicit in the tyranny of the group has become more visible lately. Certainly recent students of the phenomenon of modern conformity could supply Steinbeck with very little essential insight. The real trouble is precisely there. The tyranny of the group is visible in all of Steinbeck's instances (its ambiguity is most evident in Ruthie's case), which argues for Steinbeck's artistic honesty in rendering the materials. But he fails to see deeply enough, to see ugliness and ambiguity, because he has predetermined the absolute "good" of group behavior-an abstraction that

precludes subtle technique and profound insight, on the order of Doc
Burton's reservations concerning group-man. The result is a felt
manipulation of values and a thinning of credibility.

Given this tendency, Steinbeck does not surprise us by dealing
abstractly with the problem of leadership in the government camp. Since
there is minimal narrative time in which to establish the moral purity of Jim
Rawley, the camp manager, or of Ezra Huston, the chairman of the Central
Committee, Steinbeck presents both men as allegorical figures. Particularly
Jim Rawley. His introduction suggests his allegorical role. He is named only
once, and thereafter he is called simply "the camp manager." His name is
absorbed in his role as God. He is dressed "all in white," but he is not a
remote God. "The frayed seams on his white coat" suggest his human
availability, and his "warm" voice matches his social qualities. Nevertheless,
there is no doubt that he is God visiting his charges:

> He put the cup on the box with the others, waved his hand, and
> walked down the line of tents. And Ma heard him speaking to the
> people as he went.

His identification with God is bulwarked when the fanatic woman calls him
the devil:

> "She says you was the devil," [says Rose of Sharon]. "I know
> she does. That's because I won't let her make people miserable....
> Don't you worry. She doesn't know."

What "she doesn't know" is everything the camp manager does know; and if
he is not the devil, he must be God. But his very human, secular divinity-he
can wish for an easier lot, and he is always tired from overwork-suggests the
self-sacrifice that is Casy's function. The two men are outwardly similar.
Both are clean and "lean as a picket," and the camp manager has "merry
eyes" like Casy's when Tom meets Casy again. These resemblances would be
trivial, except for a phrase that pulls them together and lends them
considerable weight. Ezra Huston has no character to speak of, beyond his
narrative function, except that when he has finished asking the men who try
to begin a riot in the camp why they betrayed "their own people," he adds:
"They don't know what they're doin'." This phrase foreshadows Casy's
words to his murderer just before he is killed in an effort to break the strike:
"You don't know what you're a-doin'." Just as these words associate Casy
with Christ, so they associate the leaders in the government camp with Casy.

Steinbeck's foreshortening indicates that, because Casy is established firmly as a "good" character, the leaders in the government camp must resemble Casy in that "good" identity.

The overall process is allegorical, permitting Steinbeck to assert that the camp manager and Ezra Huston are good men by definition and precluding the notion that leadership may be a corrupting role, as in *In Dubious Battle*. It follows that violence in the name of the group is "good," whereas it is "evil" in the name of business interests. The contrast is too neat, too sharp, to permit much final credibility in narrative or in characterization.

A still more extreme instance of Steinbeck's use of allegory is the process by which Tom Joad assumes the role of a leader. Tom's pastoral concept of the group is fully developed, and as the novel ends, Tom identifies himself through mystic insight with the group. Appropriately, Tom explains his insight to Ma because Tom's function is to act while Ma's function is to endure-in the name of the group. More closely, Ma's earlier phrase, "We're the people-we go on," is echoed directly in Tom's assurance when Ma fears for his life:

> "Well, maybe like Casy says, a fella ain't got a soul of his own, but on'y a piece of a big one-an' then-" "Then what, Tom?" "Then it don't matter. Then I'll be all aroun' in the dark. I'll be ever'where-wherever you look.... See? God, I'm talkin' like Casy. Comes of thinkin' about him so much. Seems like I can see him sometimes."

This anthropomorphic insight, borrowed from *To a God Unknown* and remotely from Emerson, is a serious idea, put seriously within the allegorical framework of the novel's close. Two structural difficulties result. First, Tom has learned more than Casy could have taught him-that identification with the group, rather than self-sacrifice *for* the group, is the truly effective way to kill the dehumanized "Bank." Here, it seems, the Christ/Casy, Saint Paul/Tom identifications were too interesting in themselves, for they limit Steinbeck's development of Tom's insight to a mechanical parallel, such as the suggestion that Tom's visions of Casy equate with Saint Paul's visions of Christ. Second, the connection between the good material life and Tom's mystical insight is missing. There is Steinbeck's close attention to Tom's political education and to his revival of belief in a moral world. But, in the specific instance, the only bridge is Tom's sudden feeling that mystical insight connects somehow with the good material life. More precisely, the bridge is

Steinbeck's own assertion, since Tom's mystical vision of pastoral bliss enters the narrative only as an abstract announcement on Steinbeck's part.

Characterization is, as might be assumed, affected by this abstracting tendency. Earlier, major characters such as Tom and Ma are "given" through actions in which they are involved, not through detached, abstract essays; increasingly, at the close, the method of presentation is the detached essay or the extended, abstract speech. Steinbeck's earlier, more realized presentation of Tom as a natural man measures the difference. Even a late event, Tom's instinctive killing of Casy's murderer, connects organically with Tom's previous "social" crimes-the murder in self-defense, for which Tom has finished serving a prison term when the novel begins, and the parole that Tom jumps to go with the family to California. In all of these crimes, Tom's lack of guilt or shame links with the idea that "the people" have a "natural" right to unused land-not to add life, liberty, and the pursuit of happiness-and that "the Bank" has nothing but an abstract, merely legal right to such land. Tom's mystical vision is something else; it is a narrative shock, not due to Tom's "natural" responses, but to the oversimplified type of the "good" man that Tom is made to represent in order to close the novel on a high and optimistic note. Tom is a rather complex man earlier on, and the thinning out of his character, in its absolute identification with the "good," is an inevitable result of allegorizing.

Style suffers also from these pressures. Tom's speech has been condemned, as Emerson's writing never is, for mawkishness, for maudlin lushness, for the soft, rotten blur of intellectual evasion. Style is a concomitant of structure; its decline is an effect, not a cause. Tom's thinking is embarrassing, not as thought, but as the stylistic measure of a process of manipulation that is necessary to close the novel on Steinbeck's terms.

The final scene, in which Rose of Sharon breastfeeds a sick man, has been regarded universally as the nadir of bad Steinbeck, yet the scene is no more or no less allegorical than earlier scenes in this final part. Purely in a formal sense, it parallels Tom's mystical union or identification with the group: it affirms that "life" has become more important than "family" in a specific action, and, as such, it denotes the emergence of the group concept. In that light, the scene is a technical accomplishment. Yet it is a disaster from the outset, not simply because it is sentimental; its execution, through the leading assumption, is incredible. Rose of Sharon is supposed to become Ma's alter ego by taking on her burden of moral insight, which, in turn, is similar to the insight that Tom reaches. There is no preparation for Rose of Sharon's transformation and no literary justification except a merely formal symmetry that makes it desirable, in spite of credibility, to devise a repetition.

Tom, like Ma, undergoes a long process of education; Rose of Sharon is characterized in detail throughout the novel as a protected, rather thoughtless, whining girl. Possibly her miscarriage produces an unmentioned, certainly mystical change in character. More likely the reader will notice the hand of the author, forcing Rose of Sharon into an unprepared and purely formalistic role.

Once given this degree of manipulation, direct sentimentality is no surprise. Worse, the imagistic shift from anger to sweetness, from the grapes of wrath to the milk of human kindness, allows the metaphor to be uplifted, but at the cost of its structural integrity. The novel is made to close with a forced image of optimism and brotherhood, with an audacious upbeat that cries out in the wilderness. I have no wish to deny the value or the real power of good men, optimism, or brotherhood. The point is that Steinbeck imposes an unsupported conclusion upon materials which themselves are thinned out and manipulated. The increasingly grotesque episodes (and their leading metaphors) prove that even thin and manipulated materials resist the conclusion that is drawn from them, for art visits that revenge on its mistaken practitioners.

To argue that no better conclusion was available at the time, granting the country's social and political immaturity and its economic innocence, simply switches the issue from art to politics. No artist is obliged to provide solutions to the problems of the socio-politico-economic order, however "engaged" his work may be. Flaubert did not present a socioeducational program to help other young women to avoid Emma Bovary's fate. The business of the artist is to present a situation. If he manipulates the materials or forces them to conclusions that violate credibility-especially if he has a visible design upon us-his work will thin, the full range of human possibility will not be available to him, and to that extent he will have failed as an artist.

We must not exclude the likelihood, not that Steinbeck had no other conclusion at hand, but that his predisposition was to see a resolution in the various allegorical and panoramic arrangements that close out *The Grapes of Wrath*; Steinbeck's earlier work argues for that likelihood.

Yet that is not all there is to John Steinbeck. If he becomes the willing victim of abstract, horrendously schematic manipulations as *The Grapes of Wrath* nears its close still he is capable of better things. He demonstrates these potentialities particularly in minor scenes dealing with minor characters, so the negative force of the imposed conclusion is lessened.

Consider the scene in which Ruthie and Winfield make their way (along with the family) from the flooded boxcar to the barn where Rose of Sharon will feed the sick man. The intention of the scene is programmatic:

the children's identification with the group concept. The overt content is the essentially undamaged survival of their sense of fun and of beauty. Significantly, the action makes no directly allegorical claim on the reader, unlike the rest of the concluding scenes.

Ruthie finds a flower along the road, "a scraggly geranium gone wild, and there was one rain-beaten blossom on it." The common flower, visualized, does not insist on the identity of the beaten but surviving beauty in pure nature with the uprooted, starved children of all the migrants. The scene is developed implicitly, in dramatic, imagistic terms. Ruthie and Winfield struggle to possess the petals for playthings, and Ma forces Ruthie to be kind:

> Winfield held his nose near to her. She wet a petal with her tongue and jabbed it cruelly on his nose. "You little son-of-a-bitch," she said softly. Winfield felt for the petal with his fingers, and pressed it down on his nose. They walked quickly after the others. Ruthie felt how the fun was gone. "Here," she said. "Here's some more. Stick some on your forehead."

The scene recapitulates the earlier scene on the playground of the government camp. Here, as there, Winfield is the innocent, and Ruthie's cruelty is changed by external pressure (the other children, Ma's threat) to an official kindness that transcends itself to become a genuine kindness when "the fun was gone." The observed basis of the present scene is the strained relationship, that usually exists between an older sister and a younger brother. There is no visible effort to make the scene "fit" a predetermined allegorical scheme. Ruthie's kind gesture leads into Rose of Sharon's, as child to adult, and both scenes project the affirmative values-the survival of optimism, brotherhood, kindliness, goodness-that are the substance of the group concept at the conclusion. The children's quarrel and reconciliation is a relatively unloaded action, an event in itself. Tom's affirmation is nondramatic, a long, deeply mystical speech to Ma. Rose of Sharon's affirmation is out of character and frankly incredible. Uncle John's symbolic action derives from his own guilt but expresses a universal anger.

As the scene between the children is exceptional, Steinbeck's development of the flood scene is typical. Allegorical intentions override narrative power: the family's struggle against the flood is intended to equate with its surviving will to struggle against hopelessness; Pa, Uncle John, and Al are exhausted but not beaten. Tom's insight precedes the flood; Rose of Sharon's agreement to breastfeed the sick man follows it. In the larger frame, neither extreme of drouth or flood can exhaust the will and the vitality of the people. The dense texture of these panoramic materials is impressive. They lie side by side, at different levels of the "willing suspension of disbelief," depending on whether they are convincing narrative actions or palpable links in an arranged allegory. Hence, there is no great sense of a concluding "knot," an organic fusion of parts; there is no more than a formulated ending, a pseudoclose that does not convince because its design is an a priori assertion of structure, not the supportive and necessary skeleton of a realized context. Here structure and materials fail to achieve a harmonious relationship.

These final scenes are not hackwork. We cannot apply to Steinbeck, even here, the slurring remark that F. Scott Fitzgerald aimed at Thomas Wolfe: "The stuff about the GREAT VITAL HEART OF AMERICA is just simply corny." Steinbeck's carefully interwoven strands of character, metaphor, and narrative argue a conscious, skillful intention, not a sudden lapse of material or of novelistic ability. Even in failure, Steinbeck is a formidable technician. His corn, here, if it exists, is not a signal of failed ability.

Steinbeck's feeling that *The Grapes of Wrath* must close on an intense level of sweetness, of optimism and affirmation, is not seriously in doubt. His ability to use the techniques of structure to this end is evident. The earlier novels demonstrate his able willingness to skillfully apply an external structure, to mold, or at least to mystify, somewhat recalcitrant materials. The letter withdrawing *L'Affaire Lettuceburg* suggests that Steinbeck is aware of having that willing skill-"just twisting this people out of shape"-and of having to resist its lures in this most serious work. So for the critic there is a certain horrid fascination in Steinbeck's consistent, enormously talented demonstration of aesthetic failure in the last quarter of *The Grapes of Wrath*.

The failure is not a matter of "sprawling asides and extravagances," or the more extreme motivational simplicities of naturalism, or a lapse in the remarkably sustained folk idiom and the representative epic scope. The failure lies in the means Steinbeck utilizes to achieve the end.

The first three quarters of the novel are masterful. Characters are presented through action; symbolism intensifies character and action; the central theme of transformation from self to group develops persuasively in a solid, realized documentary context. The final quarter of the novel presents a difference in every respect. Characters are fitted or forced into allegorical roles, heightened beyond the limits of credibility, to the point that they thin out or become frankly unbelievable. Scenes are developed almost solely as links in an allegorical pattern. Texture is reduced to documentation, and allegorical signs replace symbolism. The result is a hollowed rhetoric, a manipulated affirmation, a soft twist of insistent sentiment. These qualities deny the conceptual theme by simplifying it, by reducing the facts of human and social complexity to simple opposites.

The reduction is not inherent in the materials, which are rendered magnificently in earlier parts of the novel. The reduction is the consequence of a structural choice-to apply allegory to character, metaphor, and theme. In short, *The Grapes of Wrath* could conceivably have a sweetly positive conclusion without an absolute, unrestrained dependence on allegory. Yet the least subtle variety of that highly visible structural technique, with its objectionably simplified, manipulative ordering of materials, is precisely the element that prevails in the final part of *The Grapes of Wrath*.

Why? Steinbeck is aware of various technical options, and he is able to make use of them earlier in the novel. As we have seen in the previous novels, with the exception of *In Dubious Battle*, Steinbeck draws on allegory to stiffen or to heighten fictions that are too loose-too panoramic-to achieve the semblance of a dramatic structure purely by means of technique. Apparently Steinbeck was not offended aesthetically by the overwhelming artificiality that results from an extreme dependence on allegory. That the contemporary naturalistic or symbolic novel requires a less simple or rigid structure clearly escapes Steinbeck's attention.

On the contrary, Steinbeck is greatly attracted to some extreme kind of external control in much of the immediately preceding work and in much of the succeeding work. During the rest of his career, Steinbeck does not attempt seriously, on the massive scale of *The Grapes of Wrath*, to achieve a harmonious relationship between structure and materials. He prefers some version of the control that flaws the last quarter of *The Grapes of Wrath*.

This judgment offers a certain reasonableness in the otherwise wild shift from *The Grapes of Wrath* to the play-novelettes.

CHARLES MARZ

Dos Passos's *U.S.A.*:
Chronicle and Performance

John Dos Passos records and resists in *U.S.A.* the extinction of the private voice, the invasion of the private space, by the devastating forces of history. The landscapes of the text, like those of *Three Soldiers* and *Manhattan Transfer*, are strewn with that devastation's debris—the residue of character, the remains of narrative. Dos Passos chronicles in the trilogy the voices and the acts of residual men—the echoes, the fragments that compose America.

U.S.A. expands the themes and techniques of *Three Soldiers* and *Manhattan Transfer*. Structurally it is even more artificial and patterned. The usual criterion of realistic style, that it vanishes before the reality of the subject, does not apply to its pages. As in *Manhattan Transfer* Dos Passos deforms the voices of America, the bankrupt speech of anonymous men. *U.S.A.* is more than what Kenneth Lynn has described as "an anthology of the American idiom—of Texas drawl, Harvard broad 'a' and immigrant pidgin; of middle-class female twaddle and proletarian male coarseness; of popular songs, advertising slogans, and fragments from the yellow press," more than the ultimate extension of Twain's famous prefatory note to the *Adventures of Huckleberry Finn*. *U.S.A.* is not a recording of America. And it is not a story about America. Traditional novelistic unities of character and action are abandoned; beginnings and endings of persons and events are fortuitous. There is little progress, little growth, little development of character; there is no real concern with representation, illusion, or empathy.

From *American Fiction 1914 to 1945*, Harold Bloom, ed. Originally published under the title "U.S.A.: Chronicle and Performance," in *Modern Fiction Studies* 26, no. 3 (1980). © 1980 by the Purdue Research Foundation.

The trilogy is not held together by any chain of events or "story line"; it must be apprehended spatially and not sequentially. Sequence yields to a structure characterized by the juxtaposition of disconnected and, often incompatible word blocks. *U.S.A.* is a continent and a composition ruled by crisis and collision; it is fragmented, radically incomplete, and as amorphous and incoherent at times as its characters' lives.

The trilogy is a medley of juxtaposed and layered voices. Its meanings are generated by the thematic and structural tensions among its compositional blocks, by the complex and various juxtapositions of Camera Eyes, Newsreels, Narratives, and Biographies. Public and private lives and events constantly intersect; public and private voices collide. Dos Passos records the sound of the collisions, the noise of the public sphere and the silence of the private space during the first thirty crisis-ridden years of this century in America. But as he chronicles he resists the murderous forces of history, the triumph of the world. Neither the composition nor the country disintegrates. The performing voice of the novelist-historian, and his accomplice, the reader, survive the tale told as history and fiction of a world too much with us.

The conflict between the destructive chaos of public voices and the private voice that seeks survival in the world is manifested in the collisions of the Newsreel and the Camera Eye sections of *U.S.A.* The Camera Eye is the last preserve of the sensitive and embattled individual. It is the last remnant of the individual voice—the end product of Martin Howe, John Andrews, and Jimmy Herf—or perhaps the waste product. For the Camera Eye is a residual voice; it is what remains of the intense subjectivity of the early works.

The Camera Eye is not the autobiographical voice of John Dos Passos. It is not simply a method of smuggling chunks of personal "stream-of-memory" into an impersonal novel. It is not an autobiographical novel within a novel. It may be true that much of the material in the Camera Eye passages concurs with Ludington's, Cowley's, and Bernardin's accounts of Dos Passos's "hotel childhood," his love of Malory and Gibbon, his association with the Harvard Aesthetes, the Norton-Harjes Ambulance Service, and the Sacco and Vanzetti case. But the fact that the Camera Eye sections of *U.S.A.* might compose a partially autobiographical history of Dos Passos from the turn of the century to the early thirties is irrelevant to their use and meaning in the trilogy. Matching the life and text of the author is a critical game we need not play. *U.S.A.* is not a roman à clef.

The Camera Eye selections in *U.S.A.* contain both historical and fictional materials. They are representations and not samples of a private voice, and their meaning is not autobiographical. It is the manner more than the matter of the telling that is significant. The conversational expression, the direct address of the reader, the unfamiliar allusions, and the paratactic constructions create a sincere and private presence. It gives the appearance of real or natural speech and seems autobiographical, at times even confessional. It remains, however, essentially fictive discourse—the private voice of a fictive self speaking anonymously from the interior of the text. It is a portrait of a Self more than a self-portrait. And the speaker, as in the first Camera Eye, remains the embattled individual, often the stranger, the exile, "The Man Without A Country," the unknown soldier—always the sensitive observer isolated and buried by the world.

The Camera Eye of *The 42nd Parallel* is the protected "I" of youth. It is the most insulated voice, the most interior level of perception in the trilogy. In it the world is reduced to entirely personal (if not necessarily autobiographical) history; the camera eye is turned on the most private circumstances, the most intimate perceptions and sensory experiences of the autonomous and inviolate individual. In it the significant space of that individual is preserved; it is preserved, however, in isolation from the world and the text. It is the solitary space of the aesthete and solipsist; it is a cultivated voice under a bellglass, a powerless voice in retreat from the NOISE THAT GREETS THE NEW CENTURY. And it is the guilt-ridden voice of the spectator. The preservation of that private space, that highly rhetorical and complicitous voice, becomes in the trilogy an increasingly difficult, an increasingly irresponsible task. The World presses on the Camera Eye, and the bellglass is shattered by the central event of the trilogy—The Great War—the public NOISE that kills.

The voice of the Camera Eye in *Nineteen Nineteen* is familiar to the reader of *One Man's Initiation—1917* and *Three Soldiers*. It is the spectatorial voice of the ambulance driver, the voice of the gentleman-volunteer, and it exists at the margin of the War and the text. The voice of the gentleman-volunteer remains detached; it observes, describes, but does not protest the devastation; it is a passive voice, drained of moral content. The war becomes a modern museum of the grotesque, and the voice of the Camera Eye the voice of the spectator, the tourist. That aesthetic detachment becomes more difficult to maintain in a world rapidly filling with horrible exhibits. Retreat is no longer possible. The War and The City have become interchangeable landscapes, both debris-laden, both ruled by the slogans and lies of the public voice. Death is ubiquitous; the unknown soldier becomes the unknown citizen; both travel as strangers in strange lands, unrecognizable, faceless. Identities merge, blur and fade away like old photographs. The residual voice becomes difficult to locate and identify:

the poem I recited in a foreign language was not mine in fact it
was somebody else who was speaking it's not me in uniform in the
snapshot it's a lamentable error mistaken identity the service
record was lost the gentleman occupying the swivelchair wearing
the red carnation is somebody else than

(U.S.A. The Big Money)

The disembodied voice of the Camera Eye represents the slow dissolution of
a coherent, private individual. That dissolution is consistent with Philip
Fisher's notion of the changing territory of the self:

> Memories, secrets, feelings, and interior chatter of the mind—the
> whole realm of what we call "privacy" ... this residue was in the
> age of individualism what was meant by the self and was located
> inside the body ... Now, it is one of the most interesting facts
> about the representation of modern characters ... that this
> territory of the self within the body has vanished or declined in
> interest or investment.

The Camera Eye chronicles the disappearance, the gradual bankruptcy
of the self. It also resists that disappearance. The private voice of the Camera
Eye resists subordination—both syntactically and politically. It is expansive
and unpredictable; it rebels against order and form, history and society.
Violence (linguistic and political) is done to syntax and organization. The
world is deformed; it becomes asyntactical. The beginnings and endings that
constitute normal historical and narrative order—the "conspiracy" of history
we call "plot"—are resisted. And so finally are the echoes and clichés, the
headlines and slogans, the word-debris that buries the individual, the nose
that silences him. The private voice of the Camera Eye retreats from and
resists the world; it is a voice haunted by possible complicity, by the
deformations of word-slinging and slogan-mongering; it enlists the reader
(also complicitous in his aesthetic detachment) in the struggle to find an
authentic private voice—a voice that will successfully combat the public
noise.

The pressure of contemporary events increases in *The Big Money*. It
culminates in the trial and execution of Sacco and Vanzetti—symbolically the
last of America's embattled individuals. They are the victims of an oppressive
culture, and they have been betrayed by the word-slingers, destroyed by the
public voices. It is up to the speaker of the Camera Eye to renounce the lies
that kill. But our efforts are to no avail; the voice in the last Camera Eye of

U.S.A. has become collective; we are ultimately all complicitous. Sacco and Vanzetti die; the world triumphs; we stand looking into now familiar coffins:

> our work is over the scribbled phrases the nights typing releases the smell of the printshop the sharp reek of newsprinted leaflets the rush for Western Union stringing words into wires the search for stinging words to make you feel who are your oppressors America
>
> America our nation has been beaten by strangers who have turned our language inside out who have taken the clean words our fathers spoke and made them slimy and foul ...
>
> we line the curbs in the drizzling rain we crowd the wet sidewalks elbow to elbow silent pale looking with scared eyes at the coffins
>
> we stand defeated America
>
> *(The Big Money)*

The last Camera Eye of *U.S.A.* is an expression of defeat and an expression of shame. It is the voice of the spectator, the tourist, the gentleman-volunteer; it is the private voice of Martin Howe, John Andrews, and Jimmy Herf, and it has nothing to say to the prisoners of *U.S.A.*, nothing to express but the certainty of their destruction: "the men in jail shrug their shoulders smile thinly our eyes look in their eyes through the bars what can I say? ... what can we say to the jailed?" (*The Big Money*). The voice that survives is guilt-ridden; it is a residual and powerless voice; it is the voice of the reader.

> The public world with us has become the private world ... The single individual, whether he so wishes or not, has become part of a world which contains also Austria and Czechoslovakia and China and Spain ... What happens in his morning paper happens in his blood all day, and Madrid, Nanking, Prague are names as close to him as the names by which he counts his dearest losses.—Archibald MacLeish

The Newsreels of *U.S.A.* operate at several levels of meaning. Most obviously and, perhaps, least significantly, they mark time chronologically. The panoramic, historical aspect of *U.S.A.* is now a critical given. The Newsreels locate the historical background for the action of the trilogy; they provide its setting; they generate atmosphere; they indicate the passage of him in the world and in the text. It seems also given that the Newsreels may be linked to themes and actions in adjacent narrative, Camera Eye, and biographical passages; they date, comment on, and link the various persons and events in the trilogy. However, even if we could identify the historical source or referent for each of the Newsreel fragments, even if we could "plot" (as "conspiratorial" critics engaged in the "burial" of the text) the chronological progression of the trilogy from Newsreel I to Newsreel LXVIII, we would be no closer to explaining the power of *U.S.A.*, no closer to articulating the significance of the Newsreels. The trilogy must be understood dynamically. Its power and meanings come ultimately from vertical, atemporal, simultaneous events, and not from horizontal, biographical, successive actions. They are not generated by the historical exactness but by the random collisions of voices. The voices in the Newsreels collide with one another and with the rest of the text. These collisions generate grotesque ironies. It is not uncommon in a Newsreel to find juxtaposed celebrations and horrors of America, the dream and the nightmare. Dos Passos resists as he records the noise of history. Random collisions set off random explosions; the novelist is historian and saboteur.

The Newsreels chronicle the voices of the public sphere; they are the most banal, most impersonal, most mechanical registration of persons and events in the trilogy; they are the "nightmare of history," uncolored and uncontrolled by the private voice of the Camera Eye. Violence is objectively reported. The lies of the public voice reveal themselves in absurd and ironic incongruities. Death is reduced to statistical tabulation and the exalted rhetoric of the Great War; it is reported in the same manner and in the same space as a surge in the market. Devastations of vastly different magnitudes-though typographically and structurally equivalent collide:

> For there's <u>many a man</u> been <u>murdered</u> in <u>Luzon and Mindanao</u>
> <u>GAIETY GIRLS MOBBED</u> IN <u>NEW JERSEY</u>
>
> (*The 42nd Parallel*)

> <u>ARMY WIFE SLASHED</u> BY <u>ADMIRER</u>
> THREE <u>HUNDRED THOUSAND RUSSIAN NOBLES</u>
> <u>SLAIN</u> BY <u>BOLSHEVIKI</u>
>
> (*1919*)

Our sense of scale is annihilated; experience in the public sphere is reduced to the formula, cliché, echo of the headline; war and politics to the front page, love to the society page, and death to the obituary column. In a world in which private voices give way to the public noise, all private experience soon becomes public knowledge. The army wife slashed by her admirer and the death of three hundred thousand Russian nobles become equivalent public events. The most private destinies become public, and all men become—if only for a moment—celebrities.

As the noise of the world increases, the Newsreel demands economies of presentation, the brief notation of persons and events; it becomes an automated, dehumanized, faceless form of communication. There is neither the time nor the space in the public sphere for the continuous enactment of coherent, private lives. Narrative and voice contract, atrophy, and disappear. And all that remains in the Newsreels is the residue of voice, the debris of character, action, and experience. *U.S.A.*, like *Manhattan Transfer* before it, is a novel of physical and spiritual erosion. Dos Passos continues to catalogue the wreckage, the fragmentary form, the broken objects that invade and bury persons and landscapes. The Newsreels are composed of unintelligible and multiple verbal fragments in agitated motion. They surface, collide, and disappear much like the garbage in the Ferryslip section of *Manhattan Transfer*. Significance is drained from any single event by typographical uniformity, by the mechanical equivalence of the presentation:

PARIS SHOCKED AT LAST
TEDDY WIELDS BIG STICK

. . . .

MOB LYNCHES AFTER PRAYER
                    (*The 42nd Parallel*)

Each headline is a verbal snapshot, a mechanical recapitulation of some part of the world. Each snapshot is a short-lived event, incompletely defined at any particular moment, and limited by space-time constraints to verbal accidents or collisions. Persons and events are "shot" and the Newsreels preserve their remains: "SNAP CAMERA: ENDS LIFE" (*The 42nd Parallel*). Susan Sontag has noted that photography makes forgetting the world, escaping history's debris, increasingly difficult. The reader of the Newsreels, like the photographer, must passively receive and suffer the world and its debris. The world prints the image. Transitory meanings are occasionally available in the accidental configurations and collisions of fragments. But the wreckage and the noise increase, and it is not enough simply to chronicle the devastation. The collisions of public voices generate that devastation, the noise of history that creates Dos Passos's dilemma— perhaps the central dilemma of his time—how both to chronicle and resist a disintegrating world.

In the Camera Eye passage of *U.S.A.*, there is a refusal to abdicate personal control; the embattled individual stands at the center of the world, almost to the exclusion of it; there is an intense—though never transcendent or religious—residual individualism. In the Newsreels, however, the person exists nearer the periphery of the world. And the subject, the ever-present "I" and "you" of the Camera Eye, recedes. The public voices of the Newsreels are speakerless. They are voices over which men have no control. Individuals are not subordinated—they simply cease to exist. There are no coherent or continuous interior lives in the Newsreels. The space allotted to persons contracts. And the Newsreels become collages of torn spaces, broken and layered samplers of persons and events. The subjects of actions are often collective or absent. Occasional subjects may be public figures or anonymous individuals or groups. The Newsreels are spoken by anonymous public voices, spoken by the conspiratorial "they" of Camera Eyes 49 and 50. The world of the Newsreels is a lawless, violent world out of control, a world of personalities or celebrities and not characters, personalities whose lives are only as complete as the information available in the headlines. The speakerless world of the Newsreels is a constantly eroding world, a world without human responsibility or moral content. The dispassionate, technological voices of the Newsreels speak constant destruction and violence; they register the nightmare that is history. And in that nightmare the human scale is reduced; things become the locus and power of values. The individual is "heaped" by the world, slowly buried by its objects and its debris. Philip Fisher has noted that "for a man inside the city his self is not inside his body but around him, outside his body." And for a man in the *U.S.A.* that Dos Passos chronicles, his voice is not inside his body, but around him, outside his body in the verbal objects that engulf him—in the public space.

The Newsreels are ultimately verbal objects word and world debris. They are the residue of the natural world, divested of their original functions and contexts, wrenched from private and public occasions. In the trilogy they become ahistorical, non-contextual verbal acts, always possible but never actual verbal utterances. They are in many ways like "found poetry" in that their presentation invites a certain critical ingenuity, they are "the representation of a natural utterance in an implicit dramatic context, designed to invite and gratify the drawing of interpretive inferences"; they exist at the margins of discourse.

The borders between natural and fictive discourse, history and fiction, shift and dissolve in *U.S.A.* History is introjected and eroded in the text. And the Newsreels are the location of the debris. They are cemeteries and museums (both burial grounds of objects) of verbal artifacts. They preserve the afterlife of verbal objects—echoes and clichés. In them the world is dematerialized; scale is destroyed as persons and events are uniformly fragmented in space and in time. Those verbal fragments of the world are catalogued and displayed. The voice fragments exhibited become increasingly remote as one moves away from familiar historical persons and events. What may once have been most public, most accessible most immediately verifiable news becomes most strange. We are without access to reported historical circumstances. Contexts are ignored and unexplained; the most intriguing observations remain hermeneutically sealed. The reader is estranged from the text by the insufficiency and the incompleteness of information. An intimate relation with the text is denied. We must scan the text—as we must scan the world—as strangers, in search of recognizable characters and actions. And as the text and the world erode we must deal with their debris with the bits and pieces of lives and events—with the fragments of experience.

The meanings of the Newsreels are not located finally in the world of historical actions and consequences. Tracing the former lives of these artifacts is irrelevant. For they do not simply date the action of the trilogy; they do not simply provide atmosphere. They invade the text; they collide with the Camera Eye; scraps of reality, records of things, vestiges of the past set adrift, the wreckage of public voices buries the individual and silences him. Man is gradually replaced by his artifacts, by world and word debris, by the slowly and inevitably triumphant noise of history.

As the world becomes increasingly public, as private lives and voices atrophy, and as man is buried and silenced by the relics of history, the nature of the novel—traditionally a genre of and for private spaces—changes. Rather than insisting on the quality and interest of private lives (in the manner of Joyce, Proust, or Woolf), Dos Passos records in the Camera Eye the contractions of the private space, the dissolution of the private voice, and in the Newsreels the concurrent triumph of the world. In the narrative and biographical passages of *U.S.A.* the residual voice of the Camera Eye and the speakerless voice of the Newsreel give way to a voice of the "middle-distance," the performing voice of the chronicler-novelist. The performer and his complicitous audience, the reader, remove themselves from and resist the world by deforming it. Irony becomes the rhetorical strategy most useful in that deformation. It records as it deforms the public voice; it locates the disparity between word and thing; it demands the mutual participation and understanding of writer and reader; and it provides their necessary expiation. It is, after all, fundamental to an understanding of *The Great War* and *The Big*

Money. As Paul Fussell has recently noted, "there seems to be one dominating form of modern understanding; that it is essentially ironic; and that it originates largely in the application of mind and memory to the events of the Great War." Through ironic subversion, the world of public voices, of clichés and headlines, is mined by the writer as saboteur. The explosions that result from that subversion generate the energy of the text.

Survival becomes difficult in the noisy, debris-laden world of the Newsreel, a world constantly recorded, imaged, and fragmented. Persons are "shot," then their remains, their remnant images and voices, litter the landscape. Obliteration in the form of private or public apocalypse is imminent at every moment for the individual. Thus the cultural imagination seeks, creates, and clings to pseudo-heroes who survive that danger, personalities who derive their stature precisely through their ability to survive, if not to dominate, in the world. They remain visible if only as image. They remain audible if only as echo. They are the gods of a new pantheon; they are America's celebrities and newsmakers.

In the biographical passages of *U.S.A.* Dos Passos records the lives and voices of the public space. He chronicles the destruction of America's last heroes—embattled individuals who attempt to hollow out the expanding and consuming public space and preserve an authentic, private voice. And he chronicles and deforms the lives and voices of the survivors, the pseudo-heroes, the word-slingers who contribute to and sustain the public noise—the noise that kills.

Eugene Debs, Bill Haywood, John Reed, Randolph Bourne, Bob LaFollette, Thorstein Veblen, Joe Hill, and Wesley Everest—like Sacco and Vanzetti—are embattled individuals ultimately destroyed by the public noise. Debs is a threat to the power of the public voice; he resists the lies that kill. Big Bill Haywood campaigned for Debs for President in 1908; he spoke for cowboys and lumberjacks, harvesthands and miners, and participated in major strikes in Lawrence, Patterson, and Minnesota. He, like Debs, resists the public voice and is ultimately "buried" in Leavenworth. Debs, Haywood, Hill, and Everest are all men who refuse to submit to the conventional wisdom of public platitudes and clichés. Each of them is ultimately destroyed for his resistance, each is reduced to debris, "the mangled wreckage" of America: "As Wesley Everest lay stunned in the bottom of the car, a Centralia businessman cut his penis and testicles off with a razor.... They jammed the mangled wreckage into a packing box and buried it" (*1919*). Debs, Haywood, Everest, LaFollette, Veblen, Reed, and Bourne knew that the truth about America was grim. They identify the disparities between the way things are and the way they are reported by the public voice, by Mr.

Creel's bureau in Washington. They identify the real meanings of Wilson's empty phrases, the Lies of the public voice.

Dos Passos identifies the lies and points to the liars. Carnegie, Hearst, Morgan, and Wilson represent the survivors, the conspiratorial "they" of the Camera Eye. "They" are responsible for the destruction of the embattled individual, for the dissolution of the private voice, for the execution of Sacco and Vanzetti, for the defeat of Debs and Haywood and Hill and Everest and LaFollette and Veblen and Reed and Bourne. "They" are the "strangers who have turned our language inside out," the liars "who have bought the laws and fenced off the meadows and cut down the woods for pulp and turned our pleasant cities into slums and sweated the wealth out of our people and when they want to they hire the executioner to throw the switch" (*The Big Money*).

William Randolph Hearst controls the presses, the distribution of print and images. That "print" and those "images" invade the trilogy in the headlines of the Newsreels; it is the word-debris that litters the novel. Hearst, however, survives in splendor. The newspaper headline, after all, serves not to communicate information as much as to sell newspapers. It is an efficient if inauthentic mode of communication. With the Taylor Plan and Henry Ford's assembly line individual lives and voices give way to the demands of efficiency and public consumption. Men are reduced to cogs in the industrial machine. They are dehumanized; they become the voiceless debris of a beaten nation, used by the word-slingers and then discarded. They are the remains of the City and the War; they are the mechanical echoes, the hollow men, the citizens of *U.S.A.*

Survival demands submission to the public voice. Valentino spends his life in the public eye. Even the celebrity's death remains an entirely public affair. Dos Passos chronicles the funeral as if it has no existence other than that given it by the public voice of the *New York Times*: "The funeral train arrived in Hollywood on page 23 of the *N.Y. Times*." And survival demands submission to public values, to dehumanizing efficiency, to profit, even at the expense of life. It is that dedication to the dollar that Dos Passos detests in Carnegie and Morgan.

One survivor in the trilogy receives a more devastating treatment than any other. That man is the embodiment in Dos Passos's eyes of the Great War, the Big Money, the inauthentic public voice. "Meester Veelson" "lived in a universe of words," and his every action betrayed the meaning of those words. He takes the "clean words our Fathers spoke and makes them slimy and foul." Dos Passos suggests the Great War was fought for something other than "to make the world safe for democracy." The meaning, the power, the energy of the Biographies is generated by controlled, subversive collisions. In his biography of Wilson, Dos Passos locates the disparities between what Wilson said and what he did. Public expressions of "neutrality in thought and deed" and "too proud to fight" prove meaningless lies betrayed by actions. Wilsonian rhetoric is exploded by the writer as performer and saboteur. *U.S.A.* may be a chronicle of destruction, but it is also a subversive performance.

The lives and voices of the public space, of the Newsreels and Biographies, penetrate the trilogy. They invade and determine the world and the text in which the narrative characters act and speak. Historical and fictional lives collide. "Big Bill," for example, immediately precedes "Mac," a narrative section in which Big Bill Haywood speaks at a union meeting that Mac (Fenian MacCreary) attends in Goldfield, Nevada. The world and the text interpenetrate, history and fiction blur. Fictional lives, the habitual voices of average Americans, echo the recognizable historical gestures and voices of the public space. In the narrative passages of *U.S.A.*, Dos Passos chronicles the echoing voices and actions of hollow men. Characters are voiceless and nearly invisible; they are like Reginald Marsh's illustrations as described by William Steadman, "silhouettes of people ... whose features illustrate only too well the irreparable damage of time." They have no depth; their outlines are often broken; and there is no difference between the space of their interior and exterior lives.

The damage of the public space is inescapable; headlines—the word-debris that kills—stains the lives of the fictional characters: "A rancid smell of printer's ink came from it; the ink was still sticky and came off on her gloves. "DECLARATION OF WAR" (*1919*). Lives are stained and shaped by the daily papers. The propaganda of Mr. Creel's bureau in Washington becomes the material of characters' actions, thoughts, and values.

The embodiment of the inauthentic voice, the voice that purveys the lies of the Great War and the Big Money, the voice of salesmanship without moral content, the voice that is merely an echo, is the Public Relations Counsel J. Ward Moorehouse. He is a confidence man who betrays the meaning of words if it will make a profit; he reduces language to advertising clichés and lies in order to manipulate and deceive his audience, in order to mold the public mind. Moorehouse is the public voice, the publicity agent for America, Woodrow Wilson's advance man. He "does propaganda for the Morgans and the Rockefellers"; he is, as Jerry Burnham tells Eveline Hutchins, "nothing but a goddam megaphone ... a damn publicity agent." He has no interior life; his soul is hollow; his every activity is an echo. Moorehouse is incapable of feeling, incapable of expressing private sentiments—sentiments that originate with him and not his clients. He is an

American Success, much like Jay Gatsby or Citizen Kane as described by Robert Carringer:

> The chief misfortunes of the [three] men seem to stem not so much from an inability to keep public and private apart as from there being practically nothing private to separate. The defect seems to be ultimately traceable to their American personae. An all-consuming persona inevitably also consumes its wearer; the mask eventually becomes inseparable from the face.

Moorehouse's private self is sacrificed in pursuit of public images. Like Gatsby and Kane, he is incapable of interpersonal relationships, incapable of love. Moorehouse worries about divorce in much the same way that Charles Foster Kane worries about Susan leaving him—in terms of the harm it will do his public—not his private—life; divorce is simply bad business.

U.S.A. is ultimately an "economic novel of the self." That is not to say that it is simply a commentary or record of the American economy. It is a chronicle of inflated and officious sentiments (public voices), of counterfeit verbal transactions (echoes), of the loss of personal value (private space) in pursuit of the Big Money. *U.S.A.* is the record of the bankruptcy of the self. As one character remarks, "we hocked our manhood for a brass check about the time of the First World War." The Great War is an investment of human capital; losses are strictly financial, investments in the Big Money. In a society stripped of satisfactions other than financial the stock broker's office becomes a holy place. In that society interpersonal as well as religious relationships are reduced to economics, to sexual transactions. Marriages are seen as potentially profitable relationships. J. Ward Moorehouse suggests to Richard Savage that the consummation of their business relationship with Doc Bingham will be marrying him off to one of the Bingham girls. Sex is a commodity, marriage a negotiable contract, and divorce the dissolution of an unsuccessful business venture. Private lives must give way to the public space. Savage will not marry Daughter when he gets her pregnant because it stands in the way of his career with Moorehouse. Ben Compton and Helen Mauer will not have children because all of their strength must be devoted to the movement. And so Helen Mauer has an abortion. *U.S.A.* is replete with the debris of loveless relationships. Mary French, like Helen Mauer, has an abortion. Margo Dowling, raped by her stepfather, marries a Cuban homosexual and has a deformed child. Children are the residue of the private space, the reduplication of history's debris.

There are no love relationships in *U.S.A.* Women are bought, sold, and raped. Frenetic love (and business) affairs are abortive. Successful public men pursue public values during business hours. Their women serve as night deposit boxes—the pun captures the vulgarity, the sordid truth of the devalued, impersonal transactions.

The characters of *U.S.A.* drift through the narrative out of control, occasionally colliding and littering the landscape with their debris. They are not alienated; they are exhausted, invisible, and silent. Persons are subsumed by the public space, silenced by the public noise, the voices of the war and the exchange. They are purged of emotions, volitionless, and obedient. And they exist in a world without moral content or complication. Survival in that world demands the relinquishment of will, action and voice.

Dos Passos chronicles in the narratives of *U.S.A.* a society of stenographers, interior decorators, and advertising men, the counterfeit voices of a bankrupt society. In that society lives are conducted in relation to public values. Voices are conditioned by the invasion of the private space by the Newsreels and Biographies. Mac echoes Joe Hill and Wesley Everest, and Big Bill Haywood. Ben Compton and Mary French and Don Stevens are echoes of Eugene Debs. Margo Dowling is an echo of Isadora Duncan and Rudolph Valentino. And Charley Anderson is an echo of Henry Ford. Other characters are echoes of echoes, imitations of themselves. As Moorehouse is an echo of Wilson and Morgan so Janey Williams, his stenographer, and Richard Savage, his aide, are echoes of Moorehouse. Williams literally records his voice; Savage then repeats it.

Characters dissolve in the narrative passages of *U.S.A.*; they become transparent images of one another, echoing verbal structures. Private lives and voices disappear and history usurps the space of character. In narrative that becomes essentially iterative, lives become structurally identical and selves are erased. Futures remain uncertain in a world and text in which apocalypse is imminent at every moment, in a world and text in which men do not act out their own lives. Characters experience the world as oppressive; it is no longer the tangled predicament James experienced dramatically; men are no longer actors in the drama of life. Some 120 characters are introduced, interrupted, terminated, or forgotten in the narrative passages of *U.S.A.* None, however, is memorable. Characters in *U.S.A.* are not individually significant. Action and voice remain public. There are not the epiphanies or illuminations of Joyce, Woolf, or Lawrence. There are not the interesting interior lives of Proust or Dostoevsky. And there are not the dramatic portraits of human beings found in Dickens or James, for Dos Passos chronicles a world in which the psychological space disintegrates. The first person is indirect, occasional, and residual; characters are not flat; they are hollow.

The absence of interior life explains the physical intensity of Dos Passos—the strong sense of disintegrating animate and inanimate "things." As interior space disintegrates, so too does the space of representation. Characters in *U.S.A.* exist within a space as two-dimensional as the photographic landscapes of *Manhattan Transfer*. Characters are presented cinematically, as expanded Newsreel notations:

> All is as in a scene from the silent movies; the picture is flat, not always too clear; the movements of the characters are jerky as the movements of the machine which controls them ... On the screen two-dimensional Macs and Bens flicker and fade, reel after reel, to the dreary denouement of their lives ... Restless, synoptic, the telescoping action of the narrative sweeps back and forth across the country recording the triumph of the money-machine and the debasement of human life.

Characters survive in *U.S.A.* by adaptation to the "money-machine." They escape dissolution by constant reduplication of themselves, by the monotonous reaffirmation of public identities and voices. They simply repeat one another's actions and words. That repetition is grotesquely mechanical, the inhuman repetition of meaningless acts. And the narratives of the trilogy are ultimately chronicles of the bankrupt, the dehumanized, the habitual voice; they are cinematic chronicles of mechanical lives, of Taylor's American Plan.

The residual lives of the Narratives, the Biographies, the Newsreels, and the Camera Eyes meet and join in the young man at the beginning of each novel, in "Vag" and in "The Body of an American." In those passages history and fiction become indistinguishable. In the world and in the text, character is reduced to anonymity, to the vagrant and the unknown soldier. The road and the war become the dumping grounds for society's debris. The tramp and the soldier are rootless and mobile, in perpetual states of "vagabondage." They occasionally collide, but relationships on the bum and on the battlefield are always transitory. The content of their lives is determined by anonymous public voices. Advertising, radio, film, and Wall Street invade the consciousness of Vag: "ads promised speed, own your home, shine bigger than your neighbor, the radio-crooner whispered girls, ghosts of platinum girls coaxed from the screen, millions in winnings were chalked up on the boards in offices." And the brain of the unknown soldier has been charged with "savings print headlines":

Now is the time for all good men knocks but once at a young
man's door, It's a great life if Ish gebibbel, The first five years 'll be
the Safety First, Suppose a Hun tried to rape your country right
or wrong, Catch 'em young What he don't know won't treat 'em
rough, Tell 'em nothin',' He got what was coming to him he got
his, This is a white man's country, Kick the Bucket, Gone West.

Character in Dos Passos is bombarded by the public noise, by the buzz of
history. The continuous roar of the City (Vag) and the War (Body of an
American) is inescapable. The anonymous citizen is overwhelmed by the
remains of voices:

The young man walks by himself, fast but not fast enough, far but
not far enough (faces slide out of sight, talk trails into tattered
scraps ... the cars are caught tight, linked tight by the tendrils of
phrased words, the turn of a joke, the singsong of a story, the
gruff fall of a sentence, linking tendrils of speech twine through
the city blocks, spread over pavements, grow out along broad
parked avenues.

The world of *U.S.A.* is littered with the tattered scraps of voices. Its debris-
laden landscapes reek of the devastation of The City and The War. The
stench that lingers in the nostrils of Vag is the stench of the battlefield.
    The point to which all things descend in the world and in the text of *U.S.A.*
is "thememorialamphitheaterofthenational cemeteryatarlingtonvirginia." The
cemetery is the location of the remains of things, and the national cemetery is
the location of the remains of a nation. The anonymous debris of that nation,
"The Body of An American," is buried at the center of the world and the text. It
is the residue of a culture, of the nightmare of history, "history the billiondollar
speed up":

WhereastheCongressoftheunitedstatesbyaconcurrentresolution
adoptedonthe4thdayofmarchlastauthorizedtheSecretaryofwarto
causetobebroughttotheunitedstatesthebodyofanAmericanwho
wasamemberoftheamericanexpeditionaryforceineuropewholost
hislifeduringtheworldwarandwhoseidentityhasnotbeenestablished
forburialinthememorialamphitheaterofthenationalcemetery
atarlingtonvirginia

                                                                    (*1919*)

In "The Body of an American," Dos Passos explodes the solemn and official rhetoric of the public voice. He sabotages the empty ceremonial gestures that disguise and disfigure reality for the public's sake.

Dos Passos (and the reader) survive the devastation of the public noise. They do not retreat into anxiety-producing and complicitous aestheticism; they instead engage and resist the world; they participate in its ironic deformation. Dos Passos wires the ironies; the reader pushes the plunger.

The reduction of the human scale to the anonymity of the vagrant and the unknown soldier reminds us of our common humanity and warns us of our common fate. Dos Passos chronicles the disintegration of hollow men, but he does not unqualifiedly condemn them. For he, his characters, and his readers are linked in their susceptibility to reduction and anonymity. All are embedded in the echoing public space in the space of the text and the world. We, as readers, are in the same relation to the characters as they are to one another. We collide and know nothing of them but what we see and hear. We search for permanent, developing relationships, coherent and continuous lives, meaningful characters who mirror what we imagine to be our own human significance. We search, in short, for reassurance.

We are, however, like Vag, estranged from the world and the text. The continuity of our response to discontinuous lives is deliberately and continuously disrupted. As strangers we wander anonymously through the text (and the world). Our reduction to "The Body of An American," the waste product of *U.S.A.*, is the negative function of our estrangement. There is, however, a positive function of that estrangement, that tenuous connection to the world and the text. Dos Passos recognizes the subversive energy that often exists in society's outcasts. The stranger might escape "habit, piety, and precedent," the mechanical automatism that cultural patterns provide. The vagrant is both given off by and in search of a world. The young man of the text is bum and picaro, a culture's debris and its last best hope. The young man is driven by the world of echoes; he is driven, and he is in search of authentic voices: "he must catch the last subway, the streetcar, the bus, run up the gangplanks of all the steamboats, register at all the hotels, live in all the boardinghouses, sleep in all the beds." That young man and the reader travel *U.S.A.*, a catalogue of American debris, an exhaustive inventory of American people and places, in search of authenticity. Each stands in the midst of the great public noise, in the midst of a world too much with us.

Dos Passos refuses to relinquish his voice to the public space. He resists the invasions of history that determine and reduce lives, the public nightmares, the Newsreels. He resists voices that have become public, that demand conformity, that rest in cliché. He refuses to be silenced by the public voice, yet he does not retreat into solipsism. Silence and exile are not viable alternatives. There is only cunning. *U.S.A.* is a chronicle of word-debris, of language betrayals, of treasonous voices. It is also, however, a subversive performance. Its meanings lie neither in documentation (Newsreels), nor in conviction (Camera Eyes). They lie somewhere in between, in that frontier between history and fiction, in the ironic, performing voice of the author in concert with the reader, in their cunning resistance to the public voice, in our controlled deformation of the text and the world.

PHYLLIS ROSE

Modernism:
The Case of Willa Cather

In the 1950s David Daiches cannily predicted that literary historians would have difficulty placing Willa Cather. He did not foresee that Cather's work would be underrated because it was hard to place, but such may have been the case. It could be said that Cather has been ignored because she was a woman, but that would not explain why her rediscovery has taken ten years longer than Virginia Woolf's. Generally perceived as a traditionalist, Cather has been patronized. Many people read her for pleasure, but for the past twenty years few have taught her works or written about them. The novels seem curiously self-evident. They are defiantly smooth and elegant, lacking the rough edges that so often provide convenient starting points for literary analysis. To a critical tradition that has valued complexity, ambiguity, even obscurity, the hard-won simplicities of Cather's art seem merely simple. Her lucidity can be read as shallowness; her massive, abstract forms can be—and have been—viewed as naively traditional, the appropriate vehicle for an art essentially nostalgic and elegiac.

Although I am deeply distrustful of the way in which, for twentieth-century writers, the term "modernist" is not merely an honorific but the precondition of attention from literary critics and scholars, I will nonetheless try to show ways in which Willa Cather's work is allied to modernism. I do this by way of redressing a balance. Her public stance was so belligerently

From *American Fiction 1914 to 1945* edited by Harold Bloom. Originally published in *Modernism Reconsidered*. © 1983 by the President and Fellows of Harvard College. Harvard University Press, 1983.

reactionary (perhaps in order to mask the radically unacceptable nature of her private life) that she herself encouraged the flattening of her work into a glorification of the past, a lament for the shabbiness of the present, which has persisted for decades. The writer who titled a collection of essays *Not Under Forty* would have been the last person to feel congratulated at being called a modernist. But it is time to risk her wrath. In part because of her defensive self-presentation, in part because her fiction so perfectly embodies certain aesthetic ideals of modernism—monumentality, functionalism, anonymity— we have overlooked its innovative nature. To see its modernist elements is to readjust and enrich our response to her work—and also to widen our notions of modernism. If Cather is a modernist, she is a tempered, transitional modernist closer to Hardy than to Pound. Nonetheless, her work is moved in important ways by a modernist urge to simplify and to suggest the eternal through the particular. Because we have paid more attention to other aspects of literary modernism—the overtly experimental, the representation of subjectivity, the literary analogues of cubist collage—we react to Cather's novels as though we have stumbled across some giant work of nature, a boulder, something so massive that is seems inhuman, uncrafted. But I would suggest that what we have stumbled upon in fact is something like the literary equivalent of an Arp, a Brancusi, a Moore.

I would point first of all to her scale. I do not mean, of course, the size of her books, for they are conspicuously slender, little masterpieces of economy; I mean the size of the subjects to which her imagination responds. In her strongest work, the land is as much a presence as the human characters, and the landscapes that move her imagination are large and unbroken ones, the plains and fields of the American Midwest, the canyonlands and deserts of the Southwest. Reading *O Pioneers!*, *My Ántonia*, or *Death Comes for the Archbishop*, we experience the exhilarating potential of clear blank spaces. Few novels I can think of are less cluttered than these; they offer the breathing space of all outdoors, and one feels that Cather may be describing herself when she says of Alexandra Bergson, the Swedish immigrant farmer who is her first great female protagonist, that she was uncertain in her indoor tastes and expressed herself best in her fields, that properly speaking her house was the out-of-doors.

The vast Nebraska prairie, which Cather saw for the first time when she was ten, transplanted from the hill-enclosed perspectives of Virginia, determined—or answered to—her sense of scale. Whether it happened when she was ten, or, as seems more likely to me, when as a grown woman, a harried and successful magazine editor in New York, she turned her inner eye back to the landscape of her childhood, the landscape of her dreams, the impact of the prairie on her sense of self was probably such as her narrative stand-in, Jim Burden, describes in *My Ántonia*:

> There seemed to be nothing to see; no fences, creeks, or trees, no hills or fields. If there was a road, I could not make it out in the faint starlight. There was nothing but land: not a country at all, but the material out of which countries are made ... I had the feeling that the world was left behind, that we had got over the edge of it, and were outside men's jurisdiction. I had never before looked up at the sky when there was not a familiar mountain ridge against it. But this was the complete dome of heaven, all there was of it ... I don't think I was homesick. If we never arrived anywhere, it did not matter. Between that earth and that sky I felt erased, blotted out.

To feel "erased, blotted out" is not, from Cather's perspective, such a bad thing. The scale of the landscape erases trivialities of personality, and in one of the most beautiful passages in American literature Cather presents Jim at his happiest, most fully alive, when he has become a mere creature on the earth, sitting in his grandmother's garden, resting his back against a sun-warmed pumpkin, his individuality transcended. "I kept as still as I could. Nothing happened. I did not expect anything to happen. I was something that lay under the sun and felt it, like the pumpkins, and I did not want to be anything more. I was entirely happy. Perhaps we feel like that when we die and become part of something entire, whether it is sun and air, or goodness and knowledge. At any rate, that is happiness; to be dissolved into something complete and great."

Against the background of the plains, only the biggest stories stand out, only stories based on the largest, strongest, most elemental emotions. "There are only two or three human stories," Cather wrote in *O Pioneers!*, "and they go on repeating themselves as fiercely as if they had never happened before; like the larks in this country, that have been singing the same five notes over for thousands of years." If you approach *O Pioneers!* as a naturalistic account of the conquest of new land, four-fifths of the book is anticlimactic, even irrelevant, and you must wonder why the story of the adulterous love of Emil Bergson and Marie Shabata and their murder by her jealous husband is taking up so much space in a book about pioneers. In fact, the love of Emil and Marie, growing as inevitably as Frank's murderous jealousy, is the focus of the story, along with the autumnal attachment of Alexandra Bergson and Carl Lindstrum, Alexandra's ambition, and her fatigue. The rhythms of the seasons are matched by the natural growth of human emotions. Typically, Cather uses a metaphor of seed-corn to compare Emil's guilty passion for Marie with the happy love of his friend, Amédée: "From two ears that had grown up side by side, the grains of one shot joyfully into the light, projecting themselves into the future, and the grains from the other lay still in the earth and rotted; and nobody knew why." As in ballads, motivation is played down; motives in such oft-enacted human stories are assumed to speak for themselves. Amédée dies in the prime of life of a ruptured appendix; Emil dies from the gunshot blast of a man who is so enraged he hardly knows what he is doing and who is presented as acting with no conscious volition. In a curious way, both deaths seem equally natural in this novel which presents the life of man and the life of earth as concurrent, equivalent.

In the American Southwest, which Cather visited for the first time in 1912, she found not only another monumental landscape but the temporal equivalent for the vast spaces of the Midwest. For these were not, like the plains, uninhabited spaces whose history was just beginning. Here and there, tucked in the great half-dome caverns on the cliff-sides of canyons, were the remains of an ancient, civilized people. The cliff-dwelling Indians had lived, cultivated the land, and, in their weavings and pottery, produced art, long before Europeans had landed on American soil. The effect of Anasazi art and architecture on Cather's aesthetic was profound, but for the moment I want to concentrate merely on the imaginative impact of a long-inhabited, long-abandoned monumental landscape. It lengthened the past. If you included the Indians, American history, which had seemed so small and cramped a thing, suddenly became vast. When Thea Kronborg in *The Song of the Lark* and Tom Outland of *The Professor's House* encounter the canyonlands, the effect on their senses of themselves is like the effect of the prairie on Jim Burden: it obliterates the trivial and raises them, spiritually, to its own scale, uniting them to something larger than themselves.

Cather's imagination craved and fed on large scale, both in time and space, and her books repeatedly struggle to break outside the confines of town or city life and make their way, quite against the grain of the narrative, back to the wilderness. *The Song of the Lark* gets to Panther Canyon by way of the unlikely premise that Thea Kronborg, studying music in Chicago, needs the experience of exactly that locale to change her from a good artist into a great one. The relationship between Tom Outland's story of the discovery of the cliff-dweller ruins on the Blue Mesa (a version of the true story of the discovery of Mesa Verde by Richard Wetherill) bears an even more tenuous plot connection to the rest of *The Professor's House*, which concerns a transitional crisis in the life of a midwestern university professor. Thematic justification for the interpolated story may of course be found, but I find it more interesting to note how it does *not* fit into the rest of the novel. In the sudden, eccentric switch to the southwestern locale, we witness a Catherian compulsion. Explaining it, however, as an experiment in form (a tactic that would have been more persuasive had she not done something so similar in *The Song of the Lark*), Cather said she wanted to reproduce the effect of a square window opening onto a distant prospect set into a Dutch genre painting of a warmly furnished interior. She said she wanted the reader first to stifle amidst the trappings of American bourgeois domesticity, then to feel the clean air blowing in from the mesa. This suggests that the contrast between inside and outside worlds is essential to the power of both. But the effect of the massive dislocation within *The Professor's House* is less like the effect of Dutch genre painting, which carefully subordinates one scale to the other, than it is like the effect of surrealism, with its willful changes of scale and its reminders, within a canvas, of the artificiality of the canvas—Magritte's painting of a view out the window blocked by a painting of a view out the window, or Charles Sheeler's ironic *The Artist Looks at Nature* which depicts Sheeler out-of-doors, painting a kitchen interior. It is Cather herself who stifles in the housebound, small-town scenes, craves open air, and inserts the outdoors into the indoors as willfully as Sheeler's self-portrait does the reverse, justifying the change however she can. (The novel's epigraph, a quotation from itself, also seems a justification of the form: "A turquoise set in silver, wasn't it? ... Yes, a turquoise set in dull silver.") The first part of the novel seems to me strained—overly didactic, underlining all points, the dialogue forced—but when we move to the mesa, the writing achieves that effortless symbolic quality which is Cather's distinctive note and best achievement, in which everything seems radiant and significant, but in a way no one could precisely explain.

The pattern in *The Song of the Lark* and *The Professor's House* is repeated in her work as a whole. She alternates between two modes—a more conventional realism, which is evoked when she sets herself the task of describing people in groups, living in houses, and a more abstract and lyrical mode, evoked by people against a landscape. Writing about indoor people— Thea Kronborg, Bartley Alexander, Godfrey St. Peter—she writes in small strokes, with more circumstantial detail, with more accounts of what people think and say. Her first novel, *Alexander's Bridge*, was in this mode and has always reminded readers of the work of Henry James and Edith Wharton. Later, Cather preferred to think of *O Pioneers!* as her first novel, because it was the one in which she discovered the lyrical mode that she considered her authentic style. It is the mode in which her best books—*My Ántonia*, and *Death Comes for the Archbishop* as well as *O Pioneers!*—are written. Deeply associated with it, perhaps necessary to generate it, is the quality I have been calling scale.

I have already touched on the way in which scale determines an approach to character, but I would like to go into it more fully. The illusion of grandeur in her protagonists is another feature of Cather's most exhilarating work, and this illusion, I suggest, depends on simplification.

We are first introduced to Alexandra Bergson, for example, through the eyes of a traveling salesman who is never named, whose role is never developed, whose sole function is to provide a perspective on the heroine. And what does he think of her? That she is "a fine human creature" who makes him wish he was more of a man. That is, she makes an impact without individuation. Although Alexandra has a good deal of character—she is placid, firm, in some ways a visionary (about the future of the Divide), yet wholly unimaginative about other people's emotions—Cather's presentation of her consists of broad strokes. Alexandra is not clever in the manner of city-bred and well-educated people, such as the characters Cather had written about in *Alexander's Bridge*, and that absence of cleverness allowed—perhaps forced—Cather to treat character in a new way in *O Pioneers!* Alexandra cannot be an interesting "center of consciousness" in a Jamesian sense, because her consciousness is insufficiently complex. Nor is it the most important part of her. "Her personal life, her own realization of herself, was almost a subconscious existence; like an underground river that came to the surface only here and there, at intervals months apart, and then sank again to flow under her fields." Her conscious mind is a "white book, with clear writing about weather and beasts and growing things. Not many people would have cared to read it." So we do not explore her consciousness. We see her resolutely from the outside, and this, along with Cather's persistent contrast of her in terms of size to those around her ("'What a hopeless position you are in, Alexandra!' [Carl] exclaimed feverishly. 'It is your fate to be always surrounded by little men.'"), creates the illusion of grandeur which is a distinguishing trait of Cather's heroines, although they may be as different in background and personality as Ántonia Shimerda and Marian Forrester.

For Jamesian centers of consciousness, Cather substitutes objects of admiration. Her favorite narrator is the adoring young person, usually a man, creating out of some woman a creature with mythic resonance: Jim Burden and Ántonia, Niel Herbert and Marian Forrester in *A Lost Lady*, also Nellie Birdseye and Myra Henshawe in *My Mortal Enemy*. Ántonia provides the best example, for she is not so much characterized as mythicized from the opening—"This girl seemed to mean to us the country, the conditions, the whole adventure of our childhood"—to the conclusion: "She lent herself to immemorial attitudes which we recognize by instinct as universal and true ... She had only to stand in the orchard, to put her hand on a little crab tree and look up at the apples, to make you feel the goodness of planting and tending and harvesting at last ... She was a rich mine of life, like the founders of early races." Ántonia lingers in the mind more as a goddess of fertility than as an individuated woman; to Jim, certainly, she is archetypal woman, her face "the closest, realest face, under all the shadows of women's faces."

Cather shared the impatience with individuated character that she saw reflected in the way southwestern Indians spoke English or Spanish, dropping the definite articles: not "the mountain" but "mountain"; not "the woman" but "woman." She often presents her characters as conduits for a divine spirit, raised above human powers by some force above or below consciousness, approaching the condition of gods, goddesses, or saints. In her portrait of Archbishop Latour, who could so easily have been made to seem a cathedral-building executive, and managerial paragon, Cather goes out of her way to deemphasize willed activity. We see him first when he is lost in the desert, able to forget his own thirst through meditation on and identification with Christ's agony on the cross, and from then on, his "story" is largely a record of his finding or losing the spirit of God. Cather repeatedly chooses artists as subjects because she has an archaic sense of the way, in performing or creating, they are possessed by divine inspiration, a sacred breath that blows away consciousness of the petty circumstances of their lives, so that Thea Kronborg, for example, can look harried and fatigued in the afternoon, but that night, performing at the Met, she is the essence of youthful idealism.

Cather's art is peculiarly keen at registering surges of energy and at noting the presence or absence of spirit in an innocent girl like Lucy Gayheart or in an amoral woman like Marian Forrester, who resembles Lucy only in that she puts her whole heart into everything she does. Indeed, most of Cather's heroines—Lucy, Marian; Ántonia, and Alexandra—have the capacity, sometimes harmful to themselves, to live so intensely that they seem like powers more than people, and one sometimes feels that Cather has set herself the task of portraying pure spirit divorced from circumstance, that background and circumstance are merely accidents, and that in the earth-mother Ántonia as in the bitchy, bitter Myra Henshawe, what is essential is the vital breath. Although she would have been appalled by the terms "blood knowledge" and "head knowledge," Cather resembles Lawrence in her desire to bypass the conscious and intellectual elements in her characters in quest of the instinctual and unconscious. These elements she found most accessible in simple people like the farmers of the Divide, in the devout, like the Old World Catholics of her later books, or, in their ideal imagined form, Indians. (When Mabel Dodge married Tony Luhan, a Taos Indian, and many of her friends asked how she could do it, Willa Cather reportedly said, "How could she not?")

But if Cather and Lawrence were in some sense after the same thing in their characters, they went about it in very different ways, and she attacks him as a mere cataloguer of physical sensations and emotions in her most important critical statement, "The Novel Démeublé." Most of this essay is a rather predictable attack on the novel of physical realism which she calls "over-furnished," overly devoted to description and observation. Balzac serves as her example of misguided labor, as Bennett, Wells, and Galsworthy served in Virginia Woolf's comparable manifestos, "Modern Fiction" and "Mr. Bennett and Mrs. Brown." Balzac, says Cather, wanted to put the city of Paris on paper, with all its houses, upholstery, games of chance and pleasure, even its foods. This was a mistake, she believes. "The things by which he still lives, the types of greed and avarice and ambition and vanity and lost innocence of heart which he created—are as vital today as they were then. But their material surroundings, upon which he expended such labor and pains ... the eye glides over them." At this point Cather moves away from Woolf, who rejected physical realism in favor of psychological realism, outer for inner, including Lawrence in her camp, and moves instead toward an aesthetic of the archetypal, toward Jung rather than Freud. In a brilliant maneuver, she asserts that it is possible to be a materialistic enumerator about the inner life as well as the outer and offers Lawrence as her example. Cataloguing sensations, he robs the great stories of their intrinsic grandeur. "Can one imagine anything more terrible than the story of *Romeo and Juliet* rewritten in prose by D.H. Lawrence?" The minds of one's characters can be overfurnished, too, and in detailing the crockery and footstools of their interior life we can lose track of the distinctive forms of their humanity.

In her insistence on presenting her characters from the outside, in her refusal to explore their subjectivity, Cather seems to fly most conspicuously in the face of modernism, but that is because we have overidentified modernism in the novel with the techniques of interior monologue and stream of consciousness. Interior monologue and Cather's resolutely external treatment are equally reactions against traditional characterization. If we posit a traditional method of characterization in which the inner expresses itself in the outer—both action and physical surroundings in which character is compassable, knowable, and if we think of this as a middle-distance shot, then interior monologue may be thought of as a close-up, emphasizing uniqueness and individuality to the point of unknowability, and Cather's method of characterization as a kind of long shot, emphasizing the archetypal and eternally human, acknowledging individuality, perhaps, but not exploring it. Joyce tried to incorporate both the close-up and the long shot in his presentation of Leopold Bloom by suggesting that this highly individuated man was an avatar of Odysseus; Virginia Woolf seems to want to present eternal types in *The Waves* and to some extent in *Between the Acts*; and Lawrence likes to show his characters in the grip of cosmic forces, wrenched away from the personal. By abandoning the attempt to represent interior consciousness, by her resolute externality, Cather in her own way participated in the attempt to render the generally human as opposed to the individual. This is what I mean by the urge to abstraction in her handling of character (although "abstraction" is inevitably an imprecise and somewhat irritating word as applied to literature): her downplaying of individuality, her lack of interest in "personality" as opposed to essential force.

Heroic simplification is the essence of Cather's approach to character, and I will offer a visual analogy of this which Cather herself provides. In *My Ántonia*, Jim Burden and the Bohemian girls picnic on the banks of the river, and, as the sun begins to set, they notice a curious and striking phenomenon:

> Just as the lower edge of the red disk rested on the high fields against the horizon, a great black figure suddenly appeared on the face of the sun. We sprang to our feet, straining our eyes toward it. In a moment we realized what it was. On some upland farm, a plough had been left standing in the field. The sun was sinking just behind it. Magnified across the distance by the horizontal light, it stood out against the sun, was exactly contained within the circle of the disk; the handles, the tongue, the share black against the molten red. There it was, heroic in size, a picture writing against the sun.

When the sun goes down further, the plough sinks back into its own littleness somewhere on the prairie, but it is the moment of heroic magnification that intrigues Willa Cather.

Naïve readers responding to *O Pioneers!* or *My Ántonia* or *Death Comes for the Archbishop* have trouble seeing these works as novels. They appear to be collections of vignettes or sketches, and the connection between the parts is not always evident. This response is useful, reminding us how unconventional Cather's approach to form really is. Except in *The Song of the Lark*, her most traditional novel, Cather pays no more attention to plot than Woolf does in *To the Lighthouse* and looks for unity to mood. "It is hard now to realize how revolutionary in form *My Ántonia* was at that time in America," wrote Edith Lewis, Cather's companion. "It seemed to many people to have no form."

In the first part of *My Ántonia*, for example, one comes suddenly upon a story so powerful that it threatens to throw the novel off track: the story of Pavel and Peter, who, back in Russia, had been carrying a bride and groom home from their wedding in a sled over snow by moonlight, when the entire party was set upon by wolves. To lighten their load and make it to safety, Pavel and Peter throw the bride out of the sled to be devoured by the wolves. At first this violent, horrific story seems separate from the novel as a whole, but with time one's mind weaves it into the fabric. It serves as a prologue to the grim winter in which Mr. Shimerda, unable to endure longer the hostility of nature, shoots himself. And in the sacrifice of the bride so that Pavel and Peter may reach the safety of town, the story states, with the starkness of folktale, the theme of sexuality sacrificed to advancement which is the heart of the book. But the real power of the story, it seems to me, comes from our awareness that Pavel and Peter are ordinary men whose lives had once been suddenly shifted into the realm of elemental forces, then dropped back down again into the ordinary, men metaphorically struck by lightning who go back the next day—or the next month—to milking cows. Their detachment from their horrendous experience is what is so moving, precisely their failure to incorporate it into the texture of their lives. The narrative exemplifies the way in which Cather's fiction moves between the quotidian and the elemental, not forcing the former to render up its potential for transcendence, nor demanding that the latter be everywhere manifest, but acknowledging the abrupt transformations of the ordinary into the ghastly or elemental or transcendent.

Other writers, hardly modernists, have used inset stories—Cervantes and Dickens, for example. But in Cather the folktale material is not framed by the rest of the narrative; it penetrates it, bringing what might be read merely as naturalistic narrative into the realm of the mythic, so that, later in the novel, we are aesthetically prepared, though still surprised and shocked, when a tramp wanders in from the prairie, climbs onto a threshing machine, waves his hand gaily, and jumps head first into the blades. Why should a tramp be immune to despair? Heroic emotions are not just for heroes. Cather routinely works with mythic incident (Jim's killing of the giant rattlesnake, a dragon-slaying episode that proves his manhood, although the rattlesnake is definitely a rattlesnake at the same time as it is, psychically, a dragon), with folk material, and with dreams. Naturalism coexists with symbolism. Lena Lingard may be an upwardly mobile, sexy, independent dressmaker in Lincoln, Nebraska, when Jim is a student there, but she is at the same time what she appears to him in a dream: a woman in a wheat field with a scythe, both a symbol of harvest and a figure threatening death, the pleasant death of his will and ambition by surrender to her compelling sensuality. Lena, the Danish laundry girls, and the three Bohemian Marys are to Jim—and Cather—joyous evocative figures out of Virgilian rural life ("If there were no girls like them in the world, there would be no poetry"), and Jim, the student, is simultaneously Virgil ("For I shall be the first if I live to bring the Muse into my country").

With such an emphasis on the timeless, with the way in which human beings embody recurrent impulses and attitudes, with Swedish immigrant girls in Nebraska as avatars of Virgilian rustics, no wonder *My Ántonia* defies the traditional temporal organization of plot. Dorothy Van Ghent has noted how, out of homely American detail, Cather composes in *My Ántonia* "certain frieze-like entablatures that have the character of ancient ritual and sculpture." "The suffering of change, the sense of irreparable loss in time, is one polarity of the work; the other polarity is the timelessness of those images associated with Ántonia, with the grave of the suicide at the crossroads, with the mute fortitude of the hired men and the pastoral poetry of the hired girls, and most of all with the earth itself." In appreciating Cather's instinct for the timeless, Van Ghent begins to see the implications if formal terms of that instinct, the "frieze-like entablatures," the sculptural and abstract forms throughout Cather's work. "The boldest and most beautiful of Willa Cather's fictions are characterized by a sense of the past not as an irrecoverable quality of events, wasted in history, but as persistent human truths—salvaged, redeemed—by virtue of memory and art."

Most critics have noticed only the nostalgia, the "sense of irreparable loss in time" in Cather's work, a thematic emphasis that leads them to misperceive her art as traditional. This is like confounding Georgia O'Keeffe's skulls, crosses, and flowers with Landseer's dogs. Leon Edel, for example, demanding a representational three-dimensionality foreign to Cather's art, can only be dissatisfied with *The Professor's House* for offering, as he says repeatedly in his "psychoanalytic" reading of that novel, no explanation for the professor's depression. Forced to invent a narrative wholly outside the text, Edel offers an explanation, essentially that Cather herself was regressive, infantile, and so depressed when she was deprived of Isabelle McClung's maternal attention by her marriage to Jan Hambourg that she wrote her depression into Godfrey St. Peter without enough distinction between herself and her character to provide him with motivation. But Cather has her own notion of personal development, which is very well articulated in *The Professor's House*: she imagines childhood as a stage of pure being, divorced from accomplishment; in the middle years, from adolescence on, fueled by sexual energy, one asserts one's identity both through one's work and family life; old age is a return to a stage of pure being, a sadder or a richer childhood. The professor is at the end of the second stage of his life, his identity played out, his daughters grown and his work accomplished; his depression marks his transition to the third stage. In *Death Comes for the Archbishop* Cather would present her protagonist as having successfully performed the transition that was so difficult and painful for Professor St. Peter. The Archbishop "was soon to have done with calendared time, and it had already ceased to count for him. He sat in the middle of his own consciousness; none of his former states of mind were lost or outgrown. They were all within reach of his hand, and all comprehensible." Van Ghent, with her interest in primitive religion and myth, can understand what Cather is trying to do in her representation of old age. Edel, with his interest in Freudian analysis of a crude sort, insisting on the individual etiology of every "symptom," cannot even begin to understand. For him, *Death Comes for the Archbishop*, one of Cather's masterpieces, is an exercise in nostalgia, signaling Cather's final retreat into the past. That, indeed, is the way most critics of the forties and fifties—all dominated by a moralistic response to Cather, all disposed to condemn her for retreating into the past, all viewing her as a traditionalist saw that book.

In fact, from a formal point of view, *Death Comes for the Archbishop*, that extraordinary compilation of vivid scenes and great stories which ignores chronological time, is the most daring and innovative of Cather's works. It perfectly embodies the anti-illusionist aesthetic which many of her early books strove for. I will quote Cather's own excellent description of what she was trying to accomplish and, I believe, did accomplish:

> I had all my life wanted to do something in the style of legend, which is absolutely the reverse of dramatic treatment. Since I first saw the Puvis de Chavannes frescoes of the life of St. Genevieve in my student days, I have wished that I could try something a little like that in prose; something without accent, with none of the artificial elements of composition. In the Golden Legend the martyrdoms of the saints are no more dwelt upon than are the trivial incidents of their lives; it is as though all human

experiences, measured against one supreme spiritual experience, were of about the same importance. The essence of such writing is not to hold the note, not to use an incident for all there is in it—but to touch and pass on. I felt that such writing would be a discipline in these days when the "situation" is made to count for so much in writing, when the general tendency is to force things up. In this kind of writing the mood is the thing—all the little figures and stories are mere improvisations that come out of it.

Cather had begun her writing career imitating the "dramatic treatment" of Henry James. But what she had always been moving toward was what she calls here "legend." The distinctive note of modernism appears in her aspiration to do "something without accent," in her impatience with "artificial elements of composition," with traditional climaxes and resolutions ("not a single button sewn on as the Bond Street tailors would have it," said Virginia Woolf). Musically speaking, this lifelong lover of opera repudiates the operatic ("holding the note") as a model for fiction and turns instead—rather astonishingly—to jazz, with its emphasis on mood-generating "improvisations."

The attempt to write "something in the style of legend" involved the pursuit of another aesthetic quality: anonymity. This was hard for Cather to achieve. She had been a high school teacher; more important, she had suffered in her youth from the disapproval of her community, who regarded her nonconformity with distaste. She could never quite stop telling them off for it, and the theme of opposition between philistine materialism and artistic dedication too often evokes a marring didacticism in her work. The way she overcame the urge to preach was by complete submission to her material, which she said she learned from the example of Sarah Orne Jewett. And when she suppressed herself, she did it more completely than any writer I can think of.

The clarity and simplicity—the sheer absence of eccentricity—of Cather's prose style contributes to the effect of anonymity. She adheres to the traditional structure of the English sentence—subject, verb, object—as the surest way of suppressing individuality. Rarely does one find any complicated syntax. There are passages in Cather's writing that stop the heart with their beauty, but they are never purple passages in the usual sense. They tend, as in this passage, to depict moments of quiet, and they are signaled, if at all, by a toning down of the prose rather than a keying up:

> In stopping to take a breath, I happened to glance up at the canyon wall. I wish I could tell you what I saw there, just as I saw

it, on that first morning, through a veil of lightly falling snow. Far up above me, a thousand feet or so, set in a great cavern in the face of the cliff, I saw a little city of stone, asleep. It was as still as sculpture—and something like that. It all hung together, seemed to have a kind of composition: pale little houses of stone nestling close to one another, perched on top of each other, with flat roofs, narrow windows, straight walls, and in the middle of the group, a round tower ... It was red in colour, even on that grey day. In sunlight is was the colour of winter oak-leaves. A fringe of cedars grew along the edge of the cavern, like a garden. They were the only living things. Such silence and stillness and repose— immortal repose. That village sat looking down into the canyon with the calmness of eternity.

Although the moment Cather describes here is characteristic—the small and particular raised to the monumental, the once-busy seen in eternal repose— the force of this passage resides as much in its style, in the calm, methodical notation of colors and shapes, the note of awe suggested with no overtones of hysteria, as in its content. It insists on the sculptural qualities of its subject, as Cather tends to in her descriptions of prairie and sky as well. The prose is by no means flowery, but neither is it as stark as it might be, as Hemingway's is, for example. There is a softness about it which comes from Cather's willingness to offer neutral elaboration. "In the sunlight it was the colour of winter oak-leaves"—this is a nice detail but not hypercharged, as it might appear in Hemingway, where the excessively stripped-down quality of the prose makes everything seem almost too significant. Cather's range is more comfortable, and the effect is to reduce, symbolically, the glare. Georgia O'Keeffe comes to mind again, as opposed to Dali or Magritte.

O'Keeffe, Sheeler, and other visual artists allied, however loosely, with Precisionism in America offer a good example of aesthetic urges similar to Cather's, generated from analogous but different sources and worked out quite independently. The aim of the Precisionists was simplification of form, and this joined an impulse toward monumentalizing ordinary objects— Sheeler's "Totems in Steel," for example, a rendering of steel girders on a building project, or his eerie stairwells or imperious ladder-back chairs, or O'Keeffe's resonant adobe houses. Cather particularly recalls O'Keeffe in her response to the Southwest, in her homage to the scale of the American landscape, in her ability to monumentalize the ordinary, and in her gift for generating a sense of mystery out of simplified forms. Cather's sources of inspiration invite comparison with Sheeler's. Sheeler's formalism fed on a deeply native tradition which was not in itself modernist: he was a student of Shaker furniture and Shaker barns. Similarly, Cather took strength from what she saw as a native example of functionalism, the stories of Sarah Orne Jewett. In describing Jewett's work, Cather distinguished between two kinds of beauty: the beauty of the Chinese junk, which comes from ornamentation and embellishment, and the beauty of the racing yacht, in which every line is subsumed to purpose. The beauty of Jewett's prose, to Cather, was the sleek, functional, pared-down beauty of the yacht, and although it is possible to imagine a stripping down and functionalism that goes well beyond Cather's— Hemingway, again—that is certainly the beauty she aspired to herself.

Every great writer is an innovator, forging his or her own style in the face of the seductive force of the conventional. We must mean more than that when we use the term "modernist." Critics of the sixties tended to identify modernism in the novel with subjectivity, but newer accounts of modernism tend to emphasize art's awareness of its own artificial status. The modernists themselves, however, did not unanimously recognize that what they were producing was semiotically precocious fiction; nor were all of them effective theorists of their own positions. Joyce talked about the artist refined out of existence. Eliot talked about art as an escape from personality. Flaubert aspired to write a novel about nothing. Woolf talked about capturing the luminous halo of life. In this company, Cather, with her talk of the "novel démeublé," seems the least critically sophisticated, yet it is certainly in this company that she belongs. In modernist critical writings, including Cather's, certain themes recur: an urge to shake loose of clutter, a refusal to accept the mimetic function of art as previously defined, a feeling that a certain "spirit" was escaping the older forms, an urge toward anonymity. The vessel is emphasized rather than the content; art is imagined as a fragile container for the ineffable substance of life. Thea Kronborg speaks for Cather: "What was any art but an attempt to make a sheath, a mould in which to imprison for a moment the shining, elusive element which is life itself, life hurrying past us and running away, too strong to stop, too sweet to lose? The Indian women had held it in their jars." The modernists were aware of art as created artifact, not as a mirror reflecting reality or a camera eye absorbing and imprinting it. Nothing could be further from the modernist temper than Dreiser's boast about *Sister Carrie* that it was not intended as a piece of literary craftsmanship but as a picture of conditions. The modernists often, like Cather, looked to Flaubert as their Ur-aesthetician, with his emphasis on style, surface, disciplined craft; but the wittiest theorist of modernism was Oscar Wilde, whose assertion that life imitates art may be seen as the key to the modernist spirit.

If we describe the modernists as self-conscious artificers who rejected mimesis as their chief business, we risk overemphasizing the intellectual, game-playing, Nabokovian element in modernism. Not all experiment took place for the sake of experiment, but out of a conviction that the old forms did not capture something important in life, a "spirit," a force, a religious or spiritual dimension existing somewhere below or above consciousness but beyond the purviews of traditional fiction. Hence modernism's impatience with describing the here-and-now and its persistent urge to see the here-and-now in the light of, united to, all of human history: Eliot in *The Waste Land*, Pound in the *Cantos*, Joyce in *Ulysses*, and, I would suggest, Cather, in her continuing effort to tie contemporary life to a past that stretched back, in America, to the cliff dwellers and to see all human life in relation to the enduring earth.

An interest in the past and particularly in primitive cultures characterized the early twentieth century and was not just a piece of isolated nostalgia or conservatism on the part of Willa Cather. Gauguin had been impressed by Aztec sculpture at the Paris Exposition as early as 1889. Vlaminck began collecting African sculpture around 1903 and was followed in his enthusiasm for primitive art by Derain, Matisse, Modigliani, Brancusi, Moore, and Picasso, who, in 1907, incorporated renderings of African sculptures into *Les Desmoiselles d'Avignon*. Picasso had visited Altamira in 1902 to see the neolithic cave paintings. Lawrence left the Old World for the New in search of civilizations more ancient than the former could offer. The same impulse drove Cather to Walnut Canyon, Arizona, and later to Mesa Verde, where she found in the buildings and pottery of the Anasazi an objective correlative for aesthetic impulses she had felt in herself. Form in these cliff-dwellings followed function; the buildings blended with the landscape; towns were set inside natural caverns with the cliffs themselves providing protection from the elements. The pottery was elegantly functional, embellished only with abstract designs. No more in these designs than in Indian pictographs, no more than in the cave paintings of Altamira or in certain Greek vase painting, was there an attempt to imitate three-dimensionality on a flat surface. It is no surprise that a woman so moved by this art should also have responded strongly to the frescoes of Puvis de Chavannes, whose flat, almost frieze-like figures emphasize the picture plane and refuse to create the illusion of receding space. Although Puvis de Chavannes was not himself a modernist figure, he influenced Seurat, Gauguin, Matisse, and Picasso. Most modern painting has stemmed from a refusal like his to create the illusion of three-dimensional space, often encouraged by the example of primitive, non-Western, or pre-Renaissance art. Cather's antinaturalistic *Death Comes for the Archbishop*, a series of stories so arranged as to blur the distinction between the past and the present, the miraculous and the mundane, is, I would argue, a true even if somewhat surprising example in literature of the modernist aesthetic in art, and much of her early work should be seen as moving in that direction.

Visual analogues for Cather's modernism are many. The determining factor, as in so much modernist painting which exploded out of the confines of easel-sized canvases, is scale. One thinks of the wall-sized works of Picasso and Matisse, such as *Guernica* and *The Dance of Life*; one thinks of the giant canvases of Jackson Pollock and the vast areas, made to seem even vaster by their minimalist treatment, of works by Rothko, Frankenthaler, Barnett Newman; one thinks of the murals of Orozco and Thomas Hart Benton. To work on that scale involves simplification. The reduction to essential forms, which began in the visual arts with Cézanne, finds a literary analogue in Cather's insistence on there being only a few human stories which are told over and over. Her refusal to follow the twists and turns of her characters' individual thoughts, her insistence on seeing them as "human creatures," subject to an endlessly recurring cycle of emotions, recalls Cézanne's insistence that the cone, the circle, and the square are at the basis of everything we see. If her novels seem consequently simple, their simplicity has the same aim as Klee's figures, Matisse's late abstract cutouts, or Picasso's consciously childlike drawings. It is a simplicity that aims to capture the elemental and enduring and that requires the greatest art to produce.

However fragmented their initial impact, both *The Waste Land* in its relation to *The Golden Bough* and *Ulysses* in its relation to the *Odyssey* attempt to transcend the complexity of modern life by annexing the structural simplicities of myth. Embracing multiplicity but animated by an urge to abstraction, they attempt to search through the historical and accidental to the fundamental. The appropriate stance for the artist in the face of such mythic and archetypal material is anonymity. The appropriate style is no style. Joyce in *Ulysses* sought to approximate "no style" by parodying all styles. Gertrude Stein and Hemingway sought to produce an anonymous surface by means of prose styles of the utmost plainness, stripped of all ornament and connotation. But the lucid prose of Willa Cather makes even Hemingway's sentences look mannered. And as for Gertrude Stein, it is one of the many ironies of modernism that the pursuit of simplicity and anonymity produced works of such futile complexity and obtrusive personality. Like many other modernist artists, Cather sought to bypass consciousness and the circumstantial details with which it concerns itself and to produce an art that appealed to the most elemental layers of our minds.

Her enduring popularity with readers shows that she succeeded, and critics ought now to take account of her success.

BARBARA JOHNSON

Metaphor, Metonymy and Voice
in Zora Neale Hurston's
Their Eyes Were Watching God

Not so very long ago, metaphor and metonymy burst into prominence as the salt and pepper, the Laurel and Hardy, the Yin and Yang, and often the Scylla and Charybdis of literary theory. Then, just as quickly, this cosmic couple passed out of fashion again. How did it happen that such an arcane rhetorical opposition was able to acquire the brief but powerful privilege of dividing and naming the whole of human reality, from Mommy and Daddy or Symptom and Desire all the way to God and Country or Beautiful Lie and Sober Lucidity?

The contemporary sense of the opposition between metaphor and metonymy was first formulated by Roman Jakobson in an article entitled "Two Aspects of Language and Two Types of Aphasic Disturbances." That article, first published in English in 1956, derives much of its celebrity from the central place accorded by the French structuralists to the 1963 translation of a selection of Jakobson's work, entitled *Essais linguistiques*, which included the aphasia study. The words "metaphor" and "metonymy" are not, of course, of twentieth-century coinage: they are classical tropes traditionally defined as the substitution of a figurative expression for a literal or proper one. In metaphor, the substitution is based on resemblance or analogy; in metonymy, it is based on a relation or association other than that of similarity (cause and effect, container and contained, proper name and qualities or works associated with it, place and event or institution,

From *American Fiction 1914 to 1945*, Harold Bloom, ed. Originally published under the title "Metaphor, Metonymy and Voice in *Their Eyes Were Watching God*" in *Black Literature and Literary Theory*. © 1984 by Methuen, Inc.

instrument and user, etc.). The use of the name "Camelot" to refer to John Kennedy's Washington is thus an example of metaphor, since it implies an analogy between Kennedy's world and King Arthur's, while the use of the word "Watergate" to refer to the scandal that ended Richard Nixon's presidency is a metonymy, since it transfers the name of an arbitrary place of origin onto a whole sequence of subsequent events.

Jakobson's use of the two terms is an extension and polarization of their classical definitions. In studying patterns of aphasia (speech dysfunction), Jakobson found that they fell into two main categories: similarity disorders and contiguity disorders. In the former, grammatical contexture and lateral associations remain while synonymity drops out; in the latter, heaps of word substitutes are kept while grammar and connectedness vanish. Jakobson concludes:

> The development of a discourse may take place along two different semantic lines: one topic may lead to another either through their similarity or through their contiguity. The metaphoric way would be the most appropriate term for the first case and the metonymic way for the second, since they find their most condensed expression in metaphor and metonymy respectively. In aphasia one or the other of these two processes is restricted or totally blocked—an effect which makes the study of aphasia particularly illuminating for the linguist. In normal verbal behavior both processes are continually operative, but careful observation will reveal that under the influence of a cultural pattern, personality, and verbal style, preference is given to one of the two processes over the other.
>
> In a well-known psychological test, children are confronted with some noun and told to utter the first verbal response that comes into their heads. In this experiment two opposite linguistic predilections are invariably exhibited: the response is intended either as a substitute for, or as a complement to the stimulus. In the latter case the stimulus and the response together form a proper syntactic construction, most usually a sentence. These two types of reaction have been labeled substitutive and predicative.
>
> To the stimulus *hut* one response was *burnt out*; another, *is a poor little house*. Both reactions are predicative; but the first creates a purely narrative context, while in the second there is a double connection with the subject *hut*: on the one hand, a positional

(namely, syntactic) contiguity, and on the other a semantic similarity.

The same stimulus produced the following substitutive reactions: the tautology *hut*; the synonyms *cabin* and *hovel*; the antonym *palace*, and the metaphors *den* and *burrow*. The capacity of two words to replace one another is an instance of positional similarity, and, in addition, all these responses are linked to the stimulus by semantic similarity (or contrast). Metonymical responses to the same stimulus, such as *thatch*, *litter*, or *poverty*, combine and contrast the positional similarity with semantic contiguity.

In manipulating these two kinds of connection (similarity and contiguity) in both their aspects (positional and semantic)— selecting, combining, and ranking them—an individual exhibits his personal style, his verbal predilections and preferences.

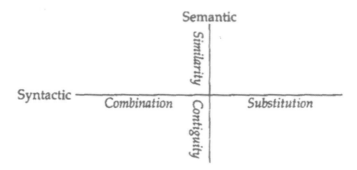

Figure 1

Two problems immediately arise that render the opposition between metaphor and metonymy at once more interesting and more problematic than at first appears. The first is that there are not two poles here but four: similarity, contiguity, semantic connection, and syntactic connection. A more adequate representation of these oppositions can be schematized as in Figure 1. Jakobson's contention that poetry is a syntactic extension of metaphor ("The poetic function projects the principle of equivalence from the axis of selection into the axis of combination"), while realist narrative is an extension of metonymy, can be added to the graph as in Figure 2.

The second problem that arises in any attempt to apply the metaphor/metonymy distinction is that it is often very hard to tell the two apart. In Ronsard's poem "*Mignonne, allons voir si la rose* ...," the speaker invites the lady to go for a walk with him (the walk being an example of contiguity) to see a rose which, once beautiful (like the lady), is now withered (as the lady will eventually be): the day must therefore be seized. The metonymic proximity to the flower is designed solely to reveal the metaphoric point of the poem: enjoy life while you still bloom. The tendency of contiguity to become overlaid by similarity and vice versa may be summed up in the proverb, "Birds of a feather flock together"—"Qui se ressemble s'assemble." One has only to think of the applicability of this proverb to the composition of neighborhoods in America to realize that the question of the separability of similarity from contiguity may have considerable political implications. The controversy surrounding the expression "legionnaires' disease" provides a more comical example: while the name of the disease

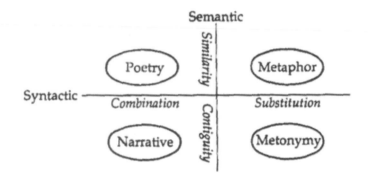

Figure 2

derives solely from the contingent fact that its first victims were at an American Legion Convention, and is thus a metonymy, the fear that it will take on a metaphoric color—that a belief in some natural connection or similarity may thereby be propagated between legionnaires and the disease— has led spokesmen for the legionnaires to attempt to have the malady renamed. And finally, in the sentence "The White House denied the charges," one might ask whether the place name is a purely contiguous metonymy for the presidency, or whether the whiteness of the house isn't somehow metaphorically connected to the whiteness of its inhabitant.

One final prefatory remark about the metaphor/metonymy distinction: far from being a neutral opposition between equals, these two tropes have always stood in hierarchical relation to each other. From Aristotle to George Lakoff, metaphor has always, in the Western tradition, had the privilege of revealing unexpected truth. As Aristotle puts it: "Midway between the unintelligible and the commonplace, it is a metaphor which most produces knowledge." Paul de Man summarizes the preference for metaphor over metonymy by aligning analogy with necessity and contiguity with chance: "The inference of identity and totality that is constitutive of metaphor is lacking in the purely relational metonymic contact: an element of truth is involved in taking Achilles for a lion but none in taking Mr Ford for a motor car." De Man then goes on to reveal this "element of truth" as the product of a purely rhetorical—and ultimately metonymical—sleight of hand, thus overturning the traditional hierarchy and deconstructing the very basis for the seductiveness and privilege of metaphor.

I should like now to turn to the work of an author acutely conscious of, and superbly skilled in, the seductiveness and complexity of metaphor as privileged trope and trope of privilege. Zora Neale Hurston, novelist, folklorist, essayist, anthropologist, and Harlem Renaissance personality, cut her teeth on figurative language during the tale-telling or "lying" sessions that took place on a store porch in the all-black town of Eatonville, Florida, where she was born around 1901. She devoted her life to the task of recording, preserving, novelizing, and analyzing the patterns of speech and thought of the rural black South and related cultures. At the same time, she deplored the appropriation, dilution, and commodification of black culture (through spirituals, jazz, etc.) by the pre-Depression white world, and she constantly tried to explain the difference between a reified "art" and a living culture in which the distinctions between spectator and spectacle, rehearsal and performance, experience and representation, are not fixed. "Folklore," she wrote, "is the arts of the people before they find out that there is such a thing as art."

> Folklore does not belong to any special area, time, nor people. It is a world and an ageless thing, so let us look at it from that viewpoint. It is the boiled down juice of human living and when one phase of it passes another begins which shall in turn give way before a successor.
>
> Culture is a forced march on the near and the obvious.... The intelligent mind uses up a great part of its lifespan trying to awaken its consciousness sufficiently to comprehend that which is plainly there before it. Every generation or so some individual with extra keen perception grasps something of the obvious about us and hitches the human race forward slightly by a new "law." Millions of things had been falling on men for thousands of years before the falling apple hit Newton on the head and he saw the law of gravity.

Through this strategic description of the folkloric heart of scientific law, Hurston dramatizes the predicament not only of the anthropologist but also of the novelist: both are caught between the (metaphorical) urge to universalize or totalize and the knowledge that it is precisely "the near and the obvious" that will never be grasped once and for all but will only be (metonymically) named and renamed, as different things successively strike different heads. I shall return to this problem of universality at the end of this essay, but first I should like to take a close look at some of the figurative operations at work in Hurston's best-known novel, *Their Eyes Were Watching God*.

The novel presents, in a combination of first- and third-person narration, the story of Janie Crawford and her three successive husbands. The first, Logan Killicks, is chosen by Janie's grandmother for his sixty acres and as a socially secure harbor for Janie's awakening sexuality. When Janie realizes that love does not automatically follow upon marriage and that Killicks completely lacks imagination, she decides to run off with ambitious, smart-talking, stylishly dressed Joe Starks, who is headed for a new all-black town where he hopes to become what he calls a "big voice." Later, as mayor and store owner of the town, he proudly raises Janie to a pedestal of property and propriety. Because this involves her submission to his idea of what a mayor's wife should be, Janie soon finds her pedestal to be a straitjacket, particularly when it involves her exclusion—both as speaker and as listener— from the tale-telling sessions on the store porch and at the mock funeral of a mule. Little by little, Janie begins to talk back to Joe, finally insulting him so profoundly that, in a sense, he dies of it. Some time later, into Janie's life walks Tea Cake Woods, whose first act is to teach Janie how to play checkers. "Somebody wanted her to play," says the text in free indirect discourse; "Somebody thought it natural for her to play." Thus begins a joyous liberation from the rigidities of status, image, and property—one of the most beautiful and convincing love stories in any literature. In a series of courtship dances, appearances, and disappearances, Tea Cake succeeds in fulfilling Janie's dream of "a bee for her blossom." Tea Cake, unlike Joe and Logan, regards money and work as worth only the amount of play and enjoyment they make possible. He gains and loses money unpredictably until he and Janie begin working side by side picking beans on "the muck" in the Florida Everglades. This idyll of pleasure, work, and equality ends dramatically with a hurricane during which Tea Cake, while saving Janie's life, is bitten by a rabid dog. When Tea Cake's subsequent hydrophobia transforms him into a wild and violent animal, Janie is forced to shoot him in self-defense. Acquitted of murder by an all-white jury, Janie returns to Eatonville, where she tells her story to her friend Phoebe Watson.

The passage on which I should like to concentrate both describes and dramatizes, in its figurative structure, a crucial turning point in Janie's relation to Joe and to herself. The passage follows an argument over what Janie has done with a bill of lading, during which Janie shouts, "You sho loves to tell me whut to do, but Ah can't tell you nothin' Ah see!"

"Dat's 'cause you need tellin'," he rejoined hotly. "It would be pitiful if Ah didn't. Somebody got to think for women and chillun and chickens and cows. I god, they sho don't think none theirselves."

"Ah knows uh few things, and womenfolks thinks sometimes too!"

"Aw naw they don't. They just think they's thinkin'. When Ah see one thing Ah understands ten. You see ten things and don't understand one."

Times and scenes like that put Janie to thinking about the inside state of her marriage. Time came when she fought back with her tongue as best she could, but it didn't do her any good. It just made Joe do more. He wanted her submission and he'd keep on fighting until he felt he had it.

So gradually, she pressed her teeth together and learned how to hush. The spirit of the marriage left the bedroom and took to living in the parlor. It was there to shake hands whenever company came to visit, but it never went back inside the bedroom again. So she put something in there to represent the spirit like a Virgin Mary image in a church. The bed was no longer a daisy-field for her and Joe to play in. It was a place where she went and laid down when she was sleepy and tired.

She wasn't petal-open anymore with him. She was twenty-four and seven years married when she knew. She found that out one day when he slapped her face in the kitchen. It happened over one of those dinners that chasten all women sometimes. They plan and they fix and they do, and then some kitchen-dwelling fiend slips a scrochy, soggy, tasteless mess into their pots and pans. Janie was a good cook, and Joe had looked forward to his dinner as a refuge from other things. So when the bread didn't rise and the fish wasn't quite done at the bone, and the rice was scorched, he slapped Janie until she had a ringing sound in her ears and told her about her brains before he stalked on back to the store.

Janie stood where he left her for unmeasured time and

thought. She stood there until something fell off the shelf inside
her. Then she went inside there to see what it was. It was her
image of Jody tumbled down and shattered. But looking at it she
saw that it never was the flesh and blood figure of her dreams.
Just something she had grabbed up to drape her dreams over. In
a way she turned her back upon the image where it lay and looked
further. She had no more blossomy openings dusting pollen over
her man, neither any glistening young fruit where the petals used
to be. She found that she had a host of thoughts she had never
expressed to him, and numerous emotions she had never let Jody
know about. Things packed up and put away in parts of her heart
where he could never find them. She was saving up feelings for
some man she had never seen. She had an inside and an outside
now and suddenly she knew how not to mix them.

This opposition between an inside and an outside is a standard way of
describing the nature of a rhetorical figure. The vehicle, or surface meaning,
is seen as enclosing an inner tenor, or figurative meaning. This relation can
be pictured somewhat facetiously as a gilded carriage—the vehicle—
containing Luciano Pavarotti, the tenor. Within the passage cited from *Their
Eyes Were Watching God*, I should like to concentrate on the two paragraphs
that begin respectively "So gradually" and "Janie stood where he left her." In
these two paragraphs Hurston plays a number of interesting variations on the
inside/outside opposition.

In both paragraphs, a relation is set up between an inner "image" and
outward, domestic space. The parlor, bedroom, and store full of shelves
already exist in the narrative space of the novel: they are figures drawn
metonymically from the familiar contiguous surroundings. Each of these
paragraphs recounts a little narrative of, and within, its own figurative terms.
In the first, the inner spirit of the marriage moves outward from the
bedroom to the parlor, cutting itself off from its proper place, and replacing
itself with an image of virginity, the antithesis of marriage. Although Joe is
constantly exclaiming, "I god, Janie," he will not be as successful as his
namesake in uniting with the Virgin Mary. Indeed, it is his godlike self-image
that forces Janie to retreat to virginity. The entire paragraph is an
externalization of Janie's feelings onto the outer surroundings in the form of
a narrative of movement from private to public space. While the whole of the
figure relates metaphorically, analogically, to the marital situation it is
designed to express, it reveals the marriage space to be metonymical, a
movement through a series of contiguous rooms. It is a narrative not of

union but of separation centered on an image not of conjugality but of virginity.

In the second passage, just after the slap, Janie is standing, thinking, until something "fell off the shelf inside her." Janie's "inside" is here represented as a store that she then goes in to inspect. While the former paragraph was an externalization of the inner, here we find an internalization of the outer: Janie's inner self resembles a store. The material for this metaphor is drawn from the narrative world of contiguity: the store is the place where Joe has set himself up as lord, master, and proprietor. But here Jody's image is broken, and reveals itself never to have been a metaphor but only a metonymy of Janie's dream: "looking at it she saw that it never was the flesh and blood figure of her dreams. Just something she had grabbed up to drape her dreams over."

What we find in juxtaposing these two figural mininarratives is a kind of chiasmus, or cross-over, in which the first paragraph presents an externalization of the inner, a metaphorically grounded metonymy, while the second paragraph presents an internalization of the outer, or a metonymically grounded metaphor. In both cases, the quotient of the operation is the revelation of a false or discordant "image." Janie's image, as Virgin Mary, acquires a new intactness, while Joe's lies shattered on the floor. The reversals operated by the chiasmus map out a reversal of the power relations between Janie and Joe. Henceforth, Janie will grow in power and resistance, while Joe deteriorates both in his body and in his public image.

The moral of these two figural tales is rich with implications: "She had an inside and an outside now and suddenly she knew how not to mix them." On the one hand, this means that she knew how to keep the inside and the outside separate without trying to blend or merge them into one unified identity. On the other hand it means that she has stepped irrevocably into the necessity of figurative language, where inside and outside are never the same. It is from this point on in the novel that Janie, paradoxically, begins to speak. And it is by means of a devastating figure—"You look like the change of life"—that she wounds Jody to the quick. Janie's acquisition of the power of voice thus grows not out of her identity but out of her division into inside and outside. Knowing how not to mix them is knowing that articulate language requires the co-presence of two distinct poles, not their collapse into oneness.

This, of course, is what Jakobson concludes in his discussion of metaphor and metonymy. For it must be remembered that what is at stake in the maintenance of both sides—metaphor and metonymy, inside and outside—is the very possibility of speaking at all. The reduction of a discourse to oneness, identity—in Janie's case, the reduction of woman to mayor's wife—has as its necessary consequence aphasia, silence, the loss of the ability to speak: "she pressed her teeth together and learned how to hush."

What has gone unnoticed in theoretical discussions of Jakobson's article is that behind the metaphor/metonymy distinction lies the much more serious distinction between speech and aphasia, between silence and the capacity to articulate one's own voice. To privilege *either* metaphor *or* metonymy is thus to run the risk of producing an increasingly aphasic *critical* discourse. If both, or all four, poles must be operative in order for speech to function fully, then the very notion of an "authentic voice" must be redefined. Far from being an expression of Janie's new wholeness or identity as a character, Janie's increasing ability to speak grows out of her ability not to mix inside with outside, not to pretend that there is no difference, but to assume and articulate the incompatible forces involved in her own division. The sign of an authentic voice is thus not self-identity but self-difference.

The search for wholeness, oneness, universality, and totalization can nevertheless never be put to rest. However rich, healthy, or lucid fragmentation and division may be, narrative seems to have trouble resting content with it, as though a story could not recognize its own end as anything other than a moment of totalization—even when what is totalized is loss. The ending of *Their Eyes Were Watching God* is no exception: "Of course [Tea Cake] wasn't dead. He could never be dead until she herself had finished feeling and thinking. The kiss of his memory made pictures of love and light against the wall. Here was peace. She pulled in her horizon like a great fish-net. Pulled it from around the waist of the world and draped it over her shoulder. So much of life in its meshes! She called in her soul to come and see." The horizon, with all of life caught in its meshes, is here pulled into the self as a gesture of total recuperation and peace. It is as though self-division could be healed over at last, but only at the cost of a radical loss of the other.

This hope for some ultimate unity and peace seems to structure the very sense of an ending as such, whether that of a novel or that of a work of literary criticism. At the opposite end of the "canonical" scale, one finds it, for example, in the last chapter of Erich Auerbach's *Mimesis*, perhaps the greatest of modern monuments to the European literary canon. That final chapter, entitled "The Brown Stocking" after the stocking that Virginia Woolf's Mrs Ramsay is knitting in *To the Lighthouse*, is a description of certain narrative tendencies in the modern novel: "multipersonal representation of consciousness, time strata, disintegration of the continuity of exterior events, shifting of narrative viewpoint," etc. "Let us begin with a tendency which is particularly striking in our text from Virginia Woolf. She holds to minor, unimpressive, random events: measuring the stocking, a fragment of a conversation with the maid, a telephone call. Great changes, exterior turning points, let alone catastrophes, do not occur." Auerbach concludes his discussion of the modernists' preoccupation with the minor, the trivial, and the marginal by saying:

> It is precisely the random moment which is comparatively independent of the controversial and unstable orders over which men fight and despair.... The more numerous, varied, and simple the people are who appear as subjects of such random moments, the more effectively must what they have in common shine forth.... So the complicated process of dissolution which led to fragmentation of the exterior action, to reflection of consciousness, and to stratification of time seems to be tending toward a very simple solution. Perhaps it will be too simple to please those who, despite all its dangers and catastrophes, admire and love our epoch for the sake of its abundance of life and the incomparable historical vantage point which it affords. But they are few in number, and probably they will not live to see much more than the first forewarnings of the approaching unification and simplification.

Never has the desire to transform fragmentation into unity been expressed so succinctly and authoritatively—indeed, almost prophetically. One cannot help but wonder, though, whether the force of this desire has not been provoked by the fact that the primary text it wishes to unify and simplify was written by a woman. What Auerbach calls "minor, unimpressive, random events"—measuring a stocking, conversing with the maid, answering the phone—can all be identified as conventional *women's* activities. "Great changes," "exterior turning points," and "catastrophes" have been the stuff of heroic *male* literature. Even plot itself—up until *Madame Bovary*, at least— has been conceived as the doings of those who do *not* stay at home, i.e., men. Auerbach's urge to unify and simplify is an urge to resubsume female difference under the category of the universal, which has always been unavowedly male. The random, the trivial, and the marginal will simply be added to the list of things all *men* have in common.

If "unification and simplification" is the privilege and province of the male, it is also, in America, the privilege and province of the white. If the woman's voice, to be authentic, must incorporate and articulate division and self-difference, so, too, has Afro-American literature always had to assume its double-voicedness. As Henry Louis Gates, Jr., puts it in "Criticism in the Jungle": "In the instance of the writer of African descent, her or his texts occupy spaces in at least two traditions—the individual's European or American literary tradition, and one of the three related but distinct black traditions. The 'heritage' of each black text written in a Western language, then, is a double heritage, two-toned, as it were.... Each utterance, then, is double-voiced." This is a reformulation of W.E.B. DuBois's famous image of the "veil" that divides the black American in two:

> The Negro is a sort of seventh son, born with a veil, and gifted with second sight in this American world,—a world which yields him no true self-consciousness, but only lets him see himself through the revelation of the other world. It is a peculiar sensation, this double-consciousness, this sense of always looking at one's self through the eyes of others, of measuring one's soul by the tape of a world that looks on in amused contempt and pity. One ever feels his twoness—an American, a Negro; two souls, two thoughts, two unreconciled strivings; two warring ideals in one dark body, whose dogged strength alone keeps it from being torn asunder.
>
> The history of the American Negro is the history of this strife,—this longing to attain self-conscious manhood, to merge his double self into a better and truer self.

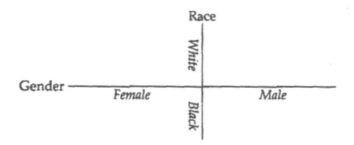

Figure 3

James Weldon Johnson, in his *Autobiography of an Ex-Colored Man*, puts it this way: "This is the dwarfing, warping, distorting influence which operates upon each and every colored man in the United States. He is forced to take his outlook on all things, not from the viewpoint of a citizen, or a man, or even a human being, but from the viewpoint of a *colored* man.... This gives to every colored man, in proportion to his intellectuality, a sort of dual personality." What is striking about the above two quotations is that they both assume without question that the black subject is male. The black woman is totally invisible in these descriptions of the black dilemma. Richard Wright, in his review of *Their Eyes Were Watching God*, makes it plain that for him, too, the black female experience is nonexistent. The novel, says Wright, lacks a basic idea or theme that lends itself to significant interpretation.... [Hurston's] dialogue manages to catch the psychological movements of the Negro folk-mind in their pure simplicity, but that's as far as it goes.... The sensory sweep of her novel carries no theme, no message, no thought.

No message, no theme, no thought: the full range of questions and experiences of Janie's life are as invisible to a mind steeped in maleness as Ellison's Invisible Man is to minds steeped in whiteness. If the black *man's* soul is divided in two, what can be said of the black woman's? Here again, what is constantly seen exclusively in terms of a binary opposition—black versus white, man versus woman—must be redrawn at least as a tetrapolar structure (see Figure 3). What happens in the case of a black woman is that the four quadrants are constantly being collapsed into two. Hurston's work is often called nonpolitical simply because readers of Afro-American literature tend to look for confrontational *racial* politics, not sexual politics. If the black woman voices opposition to male domination, she is often seen as a traitor to the cause of racial justice. But, if she sides with black men against white oppression, she often winds up having to accept her position within the Black Power movement as, in Stokely Carmichael's words, "prone." This impossible position between two oppositions is what I think Hurston intends when, at the end of the novel, she represents Janie as acquitted of the murder of Tea Cake by an all-white jury but condemned by her fellow blacks. This is not out of a "lack of bitterness toward whites," as one reader would have it, but rather out of a knowledge of the standards of male dominance that pervade both the black and the white worlds. The black crowd at the trial murmurs, "Tea Cake was a good boy. He had been good to that woman. No nigger woman ain't never been treated no better." As Janie's grandmother puts it early in the novel: "Honey, de white man is de ruler of everything as fur as Ah been able tuh find out. Maybe it's some place way off in de ocean where de black man is in power, but we don't know nothin' but what we see. So de white man throw down de load and tell de nigger man tuh pick it up. He pick it up because he have to, but he don't tote it. He hand it to his womenfolks. De nigger woman is de mule uh de world so fur as Ah can see."

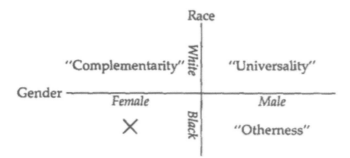

Figure 4

   In a very persuasive book on black women and feminism entitled *Ain't I a Woman*, Bell Hooks (Gloria Watkins) discusses the ways in which black women suffer from both sexism and racism within the very movements whose ostensible purpose is to set them free. Watkins argues that "black woman" has never been considered a separate, distinct category with a history and complexity of its own. When a president appoints a black woman to a cabinet post, for example, he does not feel he is appointing a person belonging to the category "black woman"; he is appointing a person who belongs *both* to the category "black" *and* to the category "woman," and is thus killing two birds with one stone. Watkins says of the analogy often drawn—particularly by white feminists—between blacks and women: "Since analogies derive their power, their appeal, and their very reason for being from the sense of two disparate phenomena having been brought closer together, for white women to acknowledge the overlap between the terms 'blacks' and 'women' (that is, the existence of black women) would render this analogy unnecessary. By continuously making this analogy, they unwittingly suggest that to them the term 'women' is synonymous with 'white women' and the term 'blacks' synonymous with 'black men'." The very existence of black women thus disappears from an analogical discourse designed to express the types of oppression from which black women have the most to suffer.
   In the current hierarchical view of things, this tetrapolar graph can be filled in as in Figure 4. The black woman is both invisible and ubiquitous: never seen in her own right but forever appropriated by the others for their own ends.
   Ultimately, though, this mapping of tetrapolar differences is itself a fantasy of universality. Are all the members of each quadrant the same? Where are the nations, the regions, the religions, the classes, the professions?

Where are the other races, the interracial subdivisions? How can the human world be totalized, even as a field of divisions? In the following quotation from Zora Neale Hurston's autobiography, we see that even the *same* black woman can express self-division in two completely different ways:

> Work was to be all of me, so I said.... I had finished that phase of research and was considering writing my first book, when I met the man who was really to lay me by the heels....
>
> He was tall, dark brown, magnificently built, with a beautifully modeled back head. His profile was strong and good. The nose and lips were especially good front and side. But his looks only drew my eyes in the beginning. I did not fall in love with him just for that. He had a fine mind and that intrigued me. When a man keeps beating me to the draw mentally, he begins to get glamorous.... His intellect got me first for I am the kind of woman that likes to move on mentally from point to point, and I like for my man to be there way ahead of me....
>
> His great desire was to do for me. *Please* let him be a *man*! ...
>
> That very manliness, sweet as it was, made us both suffer. My career balked the completeness of his ideal. I really wanted to conform, but it was impossible. To me there was no conflict. My work was one thing, and he was all the rest. But I could not make him see that. Nothing must be in my life but himself.... We could not leave each other alone, and we could not shield each other from hurt.... In the midst of this, I received my Guggenheim Fellowship. This was my chance to release him, and fight myself free from my obsession. He would get over me in a few months and go on to be a very big man. So I sailed off to Jamaica [and] pitched in to work hard on my research to smother my feelings. But the thing would not down. The plot was far from the circumstances, but I tried to embalm all the tenderness of my passion for him in *Their Eyes Were Watching God*.

The plot is indeed far from the circumstances, and, what is even more striking, it is lived by what seems to be a completely different woman. While Janie struggles to attain equal respect *within* a relation to a man, Zora readily submits to the pleasures of submission yet struggles to establish the legitimacy of a professional life *outside* the love relation. The female voice may be universally described as divided, but it must be recognized as divided in a multitude of ways.

There is no point of view from which the universal characteristics of the human, or of the woman, or of the black woman, or even of Zora Neale Hurston, can be selected and totalized. Unification and simplification are fantasies of domination, not understanding.

The task of the writer, then, would seem to be to narrate both the appeal and the injustice of universalization, in a voice that assumes and articulates its own, ever differing self-difference. In the opening pages of *Their Eyes Were Watching God* we find, indeed, a brilliant and subtle transition from the seduction of a universal language through a progressive de-universalization that ends in the exclusion of the very protagonist herself. The book begins:

> Ships at a distance have every man's wish on board. For some they come in with the tide. For others they sail forever on the horizon, never out of sight, never landing until the Watcher turns his eyes away in resignation, his dreams mocked to death by Time. That is the life of men.
>
> Now, women forget all those things they don't want to remember, and remember everything they don't want to forget. The dream is the truth. Then they act and do things accordingly.
>
> So the beginning of this was a woman, and she had come back from burying the dead. Not the dead of sick and ailing with friends at the pillow and the feet. She had come back from the sodden and the bloated; the sudden dead, their eyes flung wide open in judgment.
>
> The people all saw her come because it was sundown.

At this point Janie crosses center stage and goes out, while the people, the "bander log," pass judgment on her. The viewpoint has moved from "every man" to "men" to "women" to "a woman" to an absence commented on by "words without masters," the gossip of the front porch. When Janie begins to speak, even the universalizing category of "standard English" gives way to the careful representation of dialect. The narrative voice in this novel expresses its own self-division by shifts between first and third person, standard English, and dialect. This self-division culminates in the frequent use of free indirect discourse, in which, as Henry Louis Gates, Jr., points out, the inside/outside boundaries between narrator and character, between standard and individual, are both transgressed and preserved, making it impossible to identify and totalize either the subject or the nature of discourse. Narrative, it seems, is an endless fishing expedition with the horizon as both the net and the fish, the big one that always gets away. The meshes continually enclose and let escape, tear open, and mend up again. Mrs Ramsay never finishes the brown stocking. A woman's work is never done. Penelope's weaving is nightly re-unraveled. The porch never stops passing the world through its mouth. The process of de-universalization can never, universally, be completed.

MAX PUTZEL

De Profundis:
The Sound and the Fury I

If 1928 was indeed Faulkner's mysterious year par excellence, the heart of its mystery centers round the problems which found expression and perhaps partial resolution in the great book begun that spring in Oxford and finished in New York the first week in October. Certainly the crisis brought on by the rejection of "Flags in the Dust" was magnified by the presence in Oxford of the boyhood sweetheart he had once hoped to marry. It would take Estelle two years to get a divorce from Franklin. William Faulkner was thirty. For all the fascination with women evinced in his early writing, one is made insistently aware that unfulfilled sexual yearnings were becoming urgent. Almost inevitably they must have been attended by buried fears. The promise of young love gratified, then just as suddenly cut off by the untimely death of the lover, provides a kind of ground bass for so much of the early prose. Invariably the feelings elicited are those of immaturity, of adolescent dreams or of childhood and its unformulated, cloudy desires.

Whatever its nature Faulkner seems to have gone through an emotional crisis in the course of the spring and summer, yet with no diminution of his literary output. Estelle got him to recommend a novel of her own to Liveright and to collaborate in writing several stories, none successful. That autumn she persuaded him to take the unfinished manuscript of the novel he'd been working on to New York, as Ben Wasson

From Genius of Place: William Faulkner's Triumphant Beginnings by Max Putzel. © 1985 by Louisiana State University Press suggested. He did so even though it seemed most unlikely to find a publisher, being far more obscure than "Flags" or anything else he had attempted.

Yet the stay in New York proved invigorating and seems to have taken away the tensions that had beset him. Wasson proved a genial host and got him to see a good many friends—some of them transplanted southerners he was already acquainted with, others new admirers of his talent and promise. The most notable was Harrison Smith, the assistant editor at Harcourt. Brace who was responsible for the acceptance of "Flags" and its publication as *Sartoris*. Among the numerous friends from New Orleans days Faulkner encountered was William Spratling, who accompanied him on a visit to Horace Liveright that resulted in the termination of their contract. This left him free to commit himself to Smith, who remained his publisher through many changes of affiliation. It was to Hal Smith he entrusted the manuscript of *The Sound and the Fury* once he recovered from the total exhaustion and half-starved coma in which it left him.

Though he could hardly believe it, this fourth novel was published sooner than expected and found a small but perceptive circle of appreciative readers. It was not until years later, to be sure, that it was widely accepted. By now there is general agreement that it measures Faulkner's long stride from the passable competence of the early war novels to the monumentlike solidity on which the best of his work is grounded.

Cleanth Brooks calls it his first "great novel" and others far too numerous to enumerate agree. Richard P. Adams likens it felicitously to *The Scarlet Letter*, finding here "that charm very hard to express" (he is quoting from Henry James's *Hawthorne*), "which we find in an artist's work the first time he has touched his highest mark." In the most comprehensive monograph on the subject Andre Bleikasten declares that in this masterpiece "something happened to Faulkner that had never happened before and would never happen again."[1]

One might conclude that it is here if ever we should expect to witness the first amorous encounter between the poet and his Genius. One might see Quentin Compson as another self-mocking mask somewhat akin to the marble faun, but now smitten with love for a nymphet whose seeming innocence and trauma call up for her sad lover the bliss of their shared childhood in the lost Eden of a green new world. For Candace Compson has more in common with Lolita than with some golden nymph combing her "short blown hair" before taking a dive into some pool. (Leslie Fiedler suggests as much.)[2] Caddy is the tutelary nymph of the Compson domain, the New South, and perhaps of twentieth-century America—though not of Yoknapatawpha, for that county is yet to be invented.

While the underlying validity of these frivolous analogies is what I mean to demonstrate, they are clearly oversimplified, as are Faulkner's own. One might think mine like another of those plausible efforts *he* made more and more frequently in his late fifties to explain the miracle that had dawned in his thirtieth year. "It began with the picture of the little girl's muddy drawers, climbing that tree to look in the parlor window," he told students at the University of Virginia in the spring of 1957. Though that sounds like an afterthought, this account was one he had restated with remarkable consistency almost ever since the event. Five years or less after its miraculous conception, he wrote of his vision as "the only thing in literature that would ever move me very much"—Caddy Compson climbing that blooming pear tree to peek in at her grandmother's funeral, while her three brothers and their Negro companions "looked up at the muddy seat of her drawers."

The remark occurs in one of many drafts he made for an introduction to a new edition which never appeared. In another he summed up the experience in these touching words: "So I, who had never had a sister and was fated to lose my daughter in infancy, set out to make myself a beautiful and tragic little girl."[3] His statement has been accepted without skepticism, for though the infant the Faulkners mourned in 1931 could hardly have inspired the tragic little girl of 1928, the nostalgia for something painfully lost was genuine enough. It rang true.

That much-labored preface was one of several such efforts telling how he came to write the book, what he had thought about while writing it, and "what Benjy was trying to tell and why I let him tell it." The same handwritten draft confided in a burst of candor such as no writer must ever permit himself, "that any introduction to any book of fiction written by a fiction writer is likely to be about fifty per cent fiction itself."[4] Faulkner suppressed that admission, yet, as he told his agent in the letter of transmittal, he had worked on this preface during the summer of 1933 "like on a poem almost."[5] So although it cannot be received as eyewitness testimony, it does supply unique insight into the powerful feelings that begot the book. It tells also of some of the ties linking it to its native environs.

The longer of the two trial versions of the preface that have since been published begins with a garrulous comparison a la *Double Dealer,* between northern and southern attitudes toward art. The southerner, needing "to talk, to tell, since oratory is our heritage," is compelled either "to draw a savage indictment of the contemporary scene or to escape from it into a make-believe region of swords and magnolias and mockingbirds," each course being in reality an act of "violent partizanship, in which the writer unconsciously writes ... his violent despairs and rages and frustrations or his still more violent prophecies of still more violent hopes. I seem to have tried both of the courses," Faulkner continues. "I have tried to escape and I have tried to indict."[6]

While it is easy to see the impulse to indict the backward-looking society in which Faulkner had grown to manhood, I can only interpret this novel as escape literature by assuming that he had subconsciously acted out feelings of guilt and retribution and thus purged himself in recounting so intimately the private thoughts rushing through Quentin's mind on the day he spent preparing to kill himself. John T. Irwin puts it in more Freudian terms. "It is as if, in the character of Quentin, Faulkner embodied and perhaps tried to exercise, certain elements present in himself and in his need to be a writer. Certainly Quentin invokes that father-son struggle that a man inevitably has with his own literary progenitors when he attempts to become an "author." He evokes as well Faulkner's apparent sense of the act of writing as "a progressive dismemberment of the self in which parts of the living subject are cut off to become objectified in language.... drained, in that specific embodiment, of their obsessive emotional content."[7]

Faulkner could hardly have been drawing inspiration from Freud's *Papers in Applied Psycho-Analysis* (Englished in 1925), though it, too, bespeaks the *Zeitgeist*. It is merest coincidence that Faulkner's preface bears out so neatly those Freudian concepts Irwin first derives from the novel and at last confirms by alluding to the prefaces. In one Faulkner likens the book to "a vase like that which the old Roman kept at his bedside and wore the rim slowly away with kissing it." Speaking of the same vase in what appears to be a canceled version, Faulkner adds: "I knew that I could not live forever inside of it," Then, ambiguously, a few lines later: "It's fine to think that you will leave something behind when you die, but it's better to have made something you can die with." Irwin sees the vase as a womb image and goes on to explain that Quentin's desire to take incestuous possession of his sister ends by merging his corporal self with its mirror image in the Charles River—a symbolic reentry and "a supplanting of the father that amounts to the 'killing' of the father." Or as Bleikasten adds, "symbolically his death by drowning is indeed a *double* suicide."[8]

Just as Nabokov later described *Lolita* as a record of his love affair with the English language, so Faulkner told how *The Sound and the Fury* taught him "how to approach language, words." In a delightful, slyly insinuating, Humbert Humbertian metaphor Faulkner said he learned to treat them "with a kind of alert respect, as you approach dynamite; even with joy, as you approach women: perhaps with the same secretly unscrupulous intentions."[9]

Though neither the introductions he wrote nor the unusual

consistency of Faulkner's accounts of the novel's genesis are evidential, several sources of primary evidence do help explain the growth of its form, the pattern its symbolic structure obeys, and the inventive process that dictates its stylistic innovations. Its four parts called forth four separate styles, so that Maurice Coindreau likens the work to a symphony and assigns musical directions to its four "movements."[10]

The novel remains recondite, and we need all the sources of information available to deepen understanding. Of course our best guide is still the text printed (however imperfectly) in 1966. But there are also the manuscript and typed revisions, which provide an unusually clear record of the emotional as well as the stylistic process by which the artifact evolved. Then there are the recurrent archetypes and varying settings and images to be found in earlier fiction, some of it fumbling and primitive. At least these will teach us that the muse did not, like Athena, come popping out of her author's brow. She had to be long and humbly wooed before blazing forth. Taken together all these give testimony to the aesthetic stature of the immense work of art we are considering. While a sense of place certainly affects its growth and contributes to the richness of its design, it is not easy to see just how this can be true in a work in many ways so disembodied. For an explanation one has to draw on biographical evidence, for I can think of no other means to come at the source of those harmonic vibrations that animate its very core. So there are many ways in.

But for all its density of form and texture and that moral subtlety and penetrating humor likely to render it for years to come the most discussed of all Faulkner's novels, the book has a simple theme. It is a Christian tragedy about a once-great family and deals with the betrayal of innocence, the fall from grace, and the reality of hell. Like *Macbeth*, whence it takes its title, it is about damnation.[11] Its concern with time may derive from the artist's own Keatsian impulse to evade the clutch of death. Shakespeare too sought to embalm his love in a sonnet. Michel Gresset seems to feel this preoccupation with time had more to do with the fascination death itself held for Faulkner—its mystery. But it also has to do with a theological truism, namely that man can incur damnation only in this world but must suffer it in eternity, if only because the dead cannot repent.

Christian tragedy has seemed to some a contradiction in terms, and indeed it was in the same year the novel appeared that Joseph Wood Krutch in his essay "The Tragic Fallacy" declared tragedy itself to be out of keeping with the modern temper. Pathos or farce might express our world view "but it has not the dignity of tragedy." Lionel Trilling chose three novels as examples to refute this heresy, but compared Faulkner's unfavorably to

Hemingway's *A Farewell to Arms* and a novel by Edward Dahlberg which now seems just "rather murky violence." The critic objected to Faulkner's obscurity. The editor of the quarterly the *Symposium*, in which Trilling's rejoinder to Krutch appeared, disagreed. He took space in a later issue to publish an essay of his own declaring that of all living American novelists he would pick Faulkner as the most likely to penetrate the mysteries of existence.[12]

Sweeping the horizon of world literature since the Book of Job, Richard B. Sewall credits Faulkner with "restoring to fiction the true dialectic of tragedy." If he is correct, and he devotes a treatise to the tragic vision and a fine anthology to refuting Krutch, the restoration must have started with *The Sound and the Fury* rather than its successor *Absalom, Absalom!*[13]

Faulkner's first tragedy centers on two characters with whom we can all identify, the one through existential fear, the other through profound compassion. It is Quentin, his sensibility out of tune with his time, who like Hamlet peers into the vortex, bringing us face to face with its terrors. It is Caddy who inspires pity, less for herself than for mankind. Her loving nature is incompatible with the taboos of society, and she must defy them just as Antigone had to defy Creon for her brother's sake. While all the house of Compson suffer, it is these two whose ruin defines the catastrophe and voices its dialectic, raising it above the level of mere pathos.

The innocent Benjy, whose dark, scrambled recollections begin the tale and tell it in the voice of an idiot, and faithful Dilsey, who looms angelic over its ending—they both suffer. The design of the novel leads us from the dimness of a white man's world to the brightness and hope of a black woman's, making a deliberate paradox. But spotless and martyred as they may be, these two have no more power than a Greek chorus to stay the ineluctable march of events. Like that unmitigated devil, Jason, and those quaint souvenirs of decadence, Mr. and Mrs. Compson, the two innocents play roles subsidiary to the two damned souls they envy or adore.

Dilsey's husky voice dominates the coda, but only the flutelike soprano of Caddy's young daughter accompanies the echoes of her fated mother and uncle, a thin, forlorn, female note piping madly on that lonely prairie where ghosts abide and man awaits the ultimate drum-roll, the threat that menaces his very existence. Pitiful little Miss Quentin acts out her author's reiterated belief that the tragedy of tragedy is its repetition. Its everlasting repetition.

What makes it hard to identify Quentin and Caddy as the Polynices and Antigone of the piece is their absence throughout the ostensible dramatic present. Conversely, their home is more real to Quentin and Caddy as absence than as presence. For even if he manages to return twice during his nine months at Harvard and she, though officially banished, steals back to town several times after her brief, unhappy marriage, their home place was never paradise but always paradise lost. Hence the terrible ironic aptness of that hymn of John Keble's that echoes so annoyingly through Quentin's mind whenever its tune, set to the line "The voice that breathed o'er Eden," revives the horror of his sister's wedding day. Indeed it is the agonized, Dantean pang of homelessness, rather than any such pensive and graphic nostalgia as afflicted Wolfe, Joyce, or Nabokov, that dominates this book.

The source of our impressions in the completed text helps reveal the rationale of its otherwise baffling arrangement. What we see is garnered almost entirely from Benjy's and Quentin's recollections of the Compson children's unhomelike world. Its presentation in these two sections is remarkably similar to the process of psychoanalysis, which focuses on a recollection of some hidden, crucial, and emotion-charged event (usually in fact a nexus of superimposed events) and keeps returning to it for the light it may cast on a present dilemma.[14] Benjy's chaotic mind and random associations are triggered by names. The golfer's cry "Caddie!" recalls her ministrations on a bitter cold day just before Christmas around 1904. The phrase "one more time" recalls his given name, which had been Maury. Each recollection touches on a loss—the loss of his pasture, of his sister, of his testicles, of his name. Evidently it is that last, that seal on lost identity, his official effacement, that is the most painful of all. Toward the end of his thirty-third birthday it recurs to him more insistently than do his memories of Caddy, who left him behind, and Damuddy, who died.

The time of their grandmother's death had been one of the children's earliest rememberings—their first two encounters with death coming hard on one another. Nancy the mare broke her leg and had to be put down, in a ditch where she was left and the buzzards "undressed" her. Damuddy took sick about the same time in 1898, and Jason wondered if they would undress her, too. Until then Jason had been allowed to sleep with her. Now he seems to have sponged away her memory altogether.

It had been the day of her funeral that the children, sent off to play, had been naughty and splashed in the branch, muddying Caddy's drawers. That summer Quentin had been nine, Caddy seven, Jason five, and Benjy (still known as Maury) just three. Normal children seldom remember what occurs before they learn to talk, and Maury never did learn. Yet he seems to have been thought normal until two years later when his name was changed in deference to his feckless uncle Maury L. Bascomb; by then it was obvious to all that he was not. Lacking words of his own, this Benjamin, the favored youngest, the innocent, stores away those words he hears, most of them reproachful or jealous or querulous. Had these children ever known innocence, it was obliterated in all save him by the time they first met death. He had been sheltered not only by his mental defect but also by Caddy's innate loving kindness, the one pure force for good in their midst. Her consoling presence stood in sunny contrast to Quentin's glowering petulance and Jason's acid spite—both boys bitten by jealousy, endlessly contentious. At thirty-three Benjy remembers Jason tattling and Quentin knocking Caddy down in the stream, kicking T.P. at Caddy's wedding, and forcing wine on Benjy himself much as that monstrous king plied Poe's Hop-Frog. Benjy's mind is a scrap heap of painful memories. Quentin coming home after a fight at school. Quentin turning his face to the wall the night Damuddy died. Quentin himself being dead and gone, almost forgotten.

If in all his previous writing Faulkner had made concessions to the popular taste—daring allusions to sex, romantic appeals to war's comradeship and the glamorous past, sometimes banal essays into humor—this work was uncompromising. Its structure confounded every precept of expository correctness by plunging into deliberate obscurity and attempting an impossibility to unfold a tangled web of events through the yet more tangled mind of an idiot. Then to elucidate his tale through the subverbal or verbally chaotic associations of a young man in a frenzy to kill himself. Thirdly to go back and pick up what was omitted, in the jargon of a vulgarian. However defiant of convention this effort might be, it could only succeed if the reader were provoked into discovering some basis logic. For us today that effort seems justified. But it is the overall shape that informs us, not any such explication of the discourse as teachers commonly use to make this book an instrument of classroom torture.

Pointing toward the form of this tragedy is Fairchild's a perçu that genius is a "Passion Week of the heart." The book is framed by the last three days of the Passion of Our Lord, its Saturday being Benjy's birthday. The book seeks moreover to transcend what Fairchild called "the hackneyed accidents which make up this world" and to achieve in its closing lines an "instant of timeless beatitude." Hence, in his urgency to impart his own apperceptions of the mystery and terror of the human condition, Faulkner bypasses all the usual aesthetic criteria and seeks to voice a mystical revelation. Literally he is speaking in voices through the first three sections. He turns his world inside out, ransacking memory and imagination, betraying darkest secrets, stripping naked the most rooted of fears. Inevitably one is forced to overhear the personal voice that cries out. Yet we cannot translate its words, for here if ever Faulkner seeks to attain the ineffable, to make words say what words cannot.

Such an effort necessarily dispenses with exposition and explanation. It plunges us without preparation or coaching into the midst of life as it seems to a mindless natural. Having begun the story thus and descried its outlines, Faulkner takes it up once more as it rushes pell-mell through the tormented mind of Quentin, already destroyed by its events. Thus the first two movements of this *symphonie fantastique* ought not to be denominated moderato and adagio, as Coindreau suggests. The terms are appropriately musical, but both movements are molto agitato and both end (like Bach's *St. Matthew Passion*) in dissonance. Like Berlioz, Faulkner takes us into shadowy hinterlands where the imminence of death and the wrath of God are made manifest to a dreamer in an attic. The third movement crosses over into the deceptive glare of artificial light and common sense. Through Jason's eyes we see things as a practical man of affairs deludes himself into thinking them to be. And we share the fervor with which his niece and victim declares, "I'd rather be in hell than anywhere you are."[15]

But in the two opening sections cruelty and suffering, wickedness and pain are relieved again and again by one sustained leavening feature. It is the resilience of children and their sprightly flow of playful, mocking squabble. "'Jason going to be rich man.' Versh said. 'He holding his money all the time'" (43). Genteel white children vie with earthy black ones, interspersing the pathos and brightening the gloom with their constant jabber of parties and funerals, buzzards and snakes, and "where we have our measles": "'Where do you and T.P. have the measles, Frony.' 'Has them just wherever we is, I reckon.' Frony said" (45). Such lines echo *The Wishing Tree*, the little book Faulkner gave Estelle's daughter for her birthday.

Through the sickly honeysuckle-scented cloud cover outside and the mildewed interior of that neglected mansion resounds the children's homely interchange, the backstairs vernacular always in shrill contest with Mrs. Compson's stubborn propriety. Caddy has a way with Benjy, as her mother does not. "I like to take care of him. Don't I, Benjy."

> "Candace," Mother said. "I told you not to call him that. It was bad enough when your father insisted on calling you by that silly nickname, and I will not have him called by one. Nicknames are vulgar. Only common people use them Benjamin," she said.

The inevitable bellowing begins. Caddy tries to quiet Benjy, but their mother now grasps him in her arms and joins in, howling and hugging him, the two of them caterwauling together in a lugubrious duo. "'Hush, Mother.' Caddy said. 'You go upstairs and lay down so you can be sick. I'll go get Dilsey'" (49).

Though the Compson household is anything but cheerful, it does have its entertaining side, to which Mrs. Compson and Jason both contribute. Her resounding contralto woes are countered by the consoling staccato of Dilsey's forthright commands, irreverent responses to her masters, and ferocious threats to her young—or else punctuated by Jason's sarcastic asides. Similarly, Mr. Compson's protests are answered by the incessant crackle of children bickering.

One can forget the theme in the fascination of its orchestration; the precision of dialect and the individuation of voices alone is a source of all but musical delight. All these incidental effects help us through the agony and confusion which are the main burden of the first half of the book. But at this point there comes an abrupt division. It marks a sudden shift in the temporal frame of reference, the line of perspective, and the mutually contrasting attitudes of the first two narrators. By now we have accustomed ourselves to startling alterations of time sequence, but moving time present from a Saturday in 1928 back to the preceding Good Friday (via a day in 1910) and then forward to Easter Sunday—that gives the whole book a shape akin to some eccentric move in a game. Or perhaps it is as if someone telling a story had lost his place, forgotten how the story began, and then felt compelled to start over from an earlier beginning—as children do when we ask them what the show was about. Naturally Jason's monologue and the tale's resumption (in the fourth part) in the voice of a new narrator, this time a total outsider, implies that each of the four sections demands (as I said) a style of its own. Each produces a tone that is the product of that style.

In examining a text, Michel Gresset warns, one must resist the temptation to lug in biography or other extraneous matter. "The truth of Faulkner is in his manuscripts."[16] Yet here we are faced with a dilemma, for Faulkner not only knows more about Quentin than any other character, but clearly identifies with him in peculiar ways we can hardly overlook. Here is another despised twin hounded by a death wish. Like Bayard and the young poet in "Carcassonne," this one seems to be struggling with another self. Like the poet, the creative artist and romantic dreamer who craves eternal life longs to "perform something bold and tragical and austere." But fails. So it is of particular interest that while the earlier of the surviving typescripts of "Carcassonne" goes back to 1926 when Faulkner was busy with *Mosquitoes* and courting Helen Baird, the later copy, which contains relatively few alterations, could well have been typed in the spring of 1928. There are, in fact, striking evidences that it was.

The manuscript of *The Sound and the Fury* is extraordinarily revealing. It provides legible traces of the process of organic evolution that turned what began as the short story "Twilight" into the novel. If that is so, it must have occurred just about the time Faulkner retyped "Carcassonne" and decided to try it on a magazine editor, for unlike the earlier version, this seven-sheet typescript bears a return address. The earlier one does not. Moreover the second "Carcassonne" is *typed* on the same rarely used bond paper on which the original first seven sheets of the Quentin section are *penned*, the Benjy section of the manuscript being on another stock. (The balance of the novel manuscript is penned on the same onionskin used for the novel's carbon copy.)[17]

Looking more closely at the first sheet of the Benjy section we note that the date "April 7, 1928" is fairly centered over the text lines. The working title "Twilight" was presumably intended as the title of the short story Faulkner had set out to write, but it is away off-center to the left. Both appear to have been separately added after the sheet was drafted—perhaps after all thirty-three sheets of the Benjy section were. The date could even have been an afterthought, for its style differs from the one excised on the original opening sheet of the Quentin section.

I would conjecture on the basis of this evidence that about the time Faulkner finished the Benjy section he retyped "Carcassonne," and that he did so before beginning Quentin's. That section audibly echoes the prose poem and clearly anticipates its theme of a struggle between romantic aspiration and amorous desire for death. There is reason to believe, however, that "Carcassonne" was already in Faulkner's mind while he worked on the Benjy section, for as Gresset notes, there is a slip of the pen there when Faulkner uses the name Davy for the idiot and excises it in favor of Benjy. In the second "Carcassonne" typescript (much altered before publication in *These 13*), the young poet is called David. That, it will be recalled, was the name by which Sherwood Anderson referred to Faulkner in "A Meeting South," and Faulkner used it for other characters with whom he identified in his early fiction, including the narrator of "The Leg."

To be sure, these surface resemblances between documents hold far less interest than does their content. As originally conceived, the Quentin section was to *start* with a painful scene Benjy recalls near the *end* of *his* day: the scene of Caddy's humiliation when she arrives late for dinner and her mother denounces her before the family for her clandestine affair with Dalton Ames. That happened in 1909, but Benjy thinks of it when Dilsey announces supper in 1928. It is one of a series of torture scenes recalled to him by seeing Jason torment little Quentin and Luster, which prompts Luster to torture Benjy in turn. That the torture pattern is thematic and deliberate becomes clear in the published text, where Luster steals Benjy's birthday cake. For, as Emily Izsak points out, the cake is a detail not found in the manuscript.[18] Luster is only one in a parade of tormentors going back to Versh, who teased Benjy in 1900 for losing his name. "They making a bluegum out of you," and he tells of the beastly habits of bluegum children, cannibalistic little demons. All these associations summon up the dinner table scene so wretched for Caddy.

The family are seated at the table when she comes in "walking fast." Her mother stops her with the sharp command, "Candace." Despite Mr. Compson's feeble protest—"Hush Caroline. Let her alone"—the girl is sharply ordered back.

> Caddy came to the door and stood there, looking at Father and Mother. Her eyes flew at me, and away. I began to cry. It went loud and I got up. Caddy came in and stood with her back to the wall, looking at me.... She put her hands out but I pulled at her dress. Her eyes ran. (84)

Benjy follows the girl upstairs, where again she shrinks against the wall. When she tries to retreat into her bedroom, he pulls her by her dress toward the bathroom. "Then she put her arm across her face and I pushed her, crying." He seems to be asking her to wash the stain of tears and smeared makeup from her face. Benjy had always hated her cosmetics and the admirers they helped attract.

His recall of the accusation scene is brief and is not reverted to as the section ends with his final recollections of Dilsey and Father putting him and the other children to bed the night after their grandmother's funeral. These, incidentally, reveal a readily overlooked fact: that though Caddy alone witnessed the funeral, to her it remained an enigma. Only Quentin knew for certain of Damuddy's death.

In the original draft, the opening of Quentin's section takes up the same episode Benjy had found so traumatic, giving the dining room scene from the elder brother's point of vantage. As published, this constitutes the trancelike daydream Quentin lapses into while absently hearing Mrs. Bland, plumped beside her picnic hamper in the country near Cambridge, ramble on and on about her son Gerald's grandfather and his mint juleps.

> one minute she was standing there the next he was yelling and pulling at her dress they went into the hall and up the stairs to the bathroom door and stopped her back against the door and her arm across her face (185)

Moving as it is, this tableau as given in the manuscript is only a prelude to the train of misery that follows after Quentin pursues Caddy out of doors, running. He finds her lying in the branch flowing through Benjy's pasture, her head resting on a sand spit, her skirt moving in the current. Reluctantly she obeys his order and climbs the bank, but refuses to wring out her streaming garments, wanting to get sick. In the manuscript the passage is profoundly suggestive, even numinous.

"The branch sucked and gurgled across the sand spit and on in the dark among the willows. Across the shallow the water rippled and flapped like a piece of cloth, holding a little light as water does." Caddy might be some shy nymph or a Leda clasped in the wet embrace of a god, her spirit caught in the purling current; but she is also a most unhappy little girl. Here she starts to tell of her earthly lover, and the dialogue proceeds in straightforward language, the lover's name kept secret as in an aubade or a minnesong.

> "He's crossed all the oceans," she said. "All the way around the world." Then she talked about him. Her hands were clasped about her wet knees and her face was lifted so that the gray light fell on it, and the odor of honeysuckle. I could see the house, and the light in Mother's room, and Benjy's room, where Dilsey was putting him to bed. Then Caddy stopped talking, sitting there, clasping her knees, her face lifted in the gray light.
>
> "Do you love him?" I said. Her hand came out toward me. I didn't move. I watched it fumble along my arm and slip down and take my hand. She held it flat against her chest, and I could feel her heart thudding.
>
> "No," she said.
>
> "Did he make you, then?" I said. "He made you do it. He was stronger than you and he—tomorrow I'll kill him. I swear to. Father needn't know until afterwards, and then you and I— Nobody ever need know. We can take my school money; we can cancel my matriculation. Caddy! You hate him, don't you? Don't you?" ...
>
> She took my hand from her breast and held it against her throat. I could feel her heart hammering there.
>
> "Poor Quentin," she said. Her face was still lifted. The sky was so low that all the scents and sounds seemed to be crowded down, like under a slack bent. Especially the honeysuckle....
>
> "Yes," she said. "I hate him. I would die for him," she said. "I've already died for him. I die for him over and over again every

time this goes," she said, holding my hand against her thudding throat.[19]

The passage that follows makes clear that Caddy is not afraid to die, that she knows Quentin is a pitiful weakling and she feels sorry for him. For she knows a strong man and knows that her brother is none. So she surrenders calmly when he offers to kill her with his penknife and himself after her. But as he puts its point to her throat he thinks of Damuddy's funeral and (in a canceled passage) of "the muddy bottom of Caddy's drawers in the pear tree." Released from death, the girl casually asks what time it is, goes off to keep her rendezvous, and adds to his humiliation the indignity of introducing Quentin to her lover.

Poor Quentin, indeed. After all the self accusations, the waves of guilty passion, he confronts Dalton Ames next day, and when the lover who has brought about Caddy's disgrace hands over his pistol and offers to let him have his revenge, he faints like a girl. He only longs to be punished for the coward he is, and in the end only one punishment will match the enormity of his shame: death by drowning.

When the texts of manuscript and typescript are published there will doubtless be readers who agree with the early reviewer annoyed by the seemingly willful obscurity of the finished text. "One can imagine Mr. Faulkner inventing his stories in chronological order," Granville Hicks complained, "and then recasting them in some distorted form."[20]

Hicks of course altogether missed the rationale of the book. Faulkner did seek to demolish the orderly, neatly punctuated narrative of the manuscript but for the deliberate purpose of revealing first Benjy's and then Quentin's inner turmoil. And Quentin, whose daylong soliloquy shows Faulkner's virtuosity near its height, is the most intimately known and perfectly understood character Faulkner ever created. Though anything but a surrogate, he might be taken for another slanted portrait of "myself when young." But what a comparison of manuscript and printed text actually reveals is how artfully Faulkner had learned to deploy a form of stream-of-consciousness rhetoric as a means of illustrating a state of mind it would have been idle to render otherwise than through mimicry of its untrammeled flow under the stress of agonized emotions.

Contemporaries thought Faulkner was imitating Joyce, while better informed recent critics know he was battening on a vast literature that includes *Hamlet*, "The Waste Land," and myriad sources besides *Ulysses*. But the insights revealed through Quentin derive as little from Shakespeare as from Joyce or Freud; they come rather from keenly felt private needs of Faulkner's own. Here it is necessary to bring together a few biographical facts. While we shall never know the precise nature of the crisis that inspired Faulkner to write down Quentin's thoughts while plotting the course of his suicide, a review of some salient external events suggests its outlines.

Discussing the proposed translation of this book, Faulkner told Maurice-Edgar Coindreau it was written while he was "beset with personal problems." The translator sagely added a note to the effect that "profound emotional shocks" usually seemed to be a factor in the novelist's inspiration.[21] One of the cruelest must have been Estelle Oldham's decision to marry a more prosperous suitor after encouraging Faulkner to think she would marry him. Soon after leaving Oxford to avoid her wedding day, he volunteered for service as a combat pilot, with literary results we have already considered. A second romantic disappointment some commentators seem to consider as traumatic was Helen Baird's jilting him about the beginning of 1926. He wrote the lyrics *Helen: A Courtship* and the prose pastiche *Mayday* in her honor and kept his promise to dedicate *Mosquitoes* to her. A year later, when that novel was about to come out, Faulkner was back in Oxford for his usual Christmas visit when Estelle once more returned with her two children, leaving her husband to fend for himself in China. This time she told Faulkner she was filing for a divorce.

He promptly resumed his courtship, as evidenced by the handmade booklet entitled *The Wishing Tree*, which he made for her daughter's eighth birthday the very next month. He did not return to Spratling's apartment but settled down to work on his third novel, optimistic for its success even when reviews of *Mosquitoes* proved disappointing and sales more so. He now looked forward confidently to a best seller that would lift him out of the financial slough before Estelle's divorce decree could be handed down. The restrictions on their intimacy the two-year delay would involve would give Faulkner ample time to work up new anxieties and to indulge new fantasies of literary and marital conquest.

But that autumn came the profoundest shock of all: the "consternation and despair" after Liveright's rejection of "Flags." Four months later, still shaken, he informed the publisher he had put aside the novel on which he was then working in order to write some short stories. We might assume with some confidence that "Twilight" and "Carcassonne" (as revised) were among them and that their affinities were partly accounted for by all the detonations shaking their author's career. That during this period Faulkner was also living close to parents who opposed his marriage plans—a father who despised his novels and a mother who, if she could understand, could hardly approve of them—these circumstances might also have affected work in progress, turning him in upon himself and confirming the feeling that he was unlikely ever to be understood.

While it is fruitless to speculate further on the precise nature of the external stresses that seemed to Coindreau to aid Faulkner's inspiration, we are on more solid ground when we plot the recurrence of imagery distinguishing this masterpiece. What we find are not just a set of image clusters or recurrent symbols, though these are tangible, audible, and pungent; there are also persons and places belonging to the writer's recollections of childhood. Among the first that come to mind are the models for Dilsey and Benjy.

The Oldham and Faulkner children had once used to play together in summery, tree-shaded backyards under the watchful eye of Caroline Barr Clark. A former slave, who had joined the Falkners when they first moved to Oxford, old Callie remained in the writer's household until death overtook her in her hundredth year and he read her funeral eulogy in his parlor. Certainly she supplied the original on whom Dilsey was modeled.

Faulkner's boyhood friend John Cullen recalls those scenes, the children playing beside Callie: he remembers the boys building a possum cage. Nearby lived a doctor's son, an idiot boy who wore dresses until he was twelve, was kept behind a high fence, and "chased little girls and frightened them." As well he might, for while the boys were busy building their cage, this unfortunate "played with his testicles all the time."[22] Undoubtedly the model for Benjy, he lived past the age of thirty and is vividly depicted in one of the *Times-Picayune* sketches, "The Kingdom of God." There he is seen clutching a broken flower stalk and bellowing until it is repaired with a splint—a detail reused in the novel (393).

In drawing his portrait of Benjy, Faulkner would seem to have gone through a process resembling the Stanislavski method so popular among. American actors in that time. In "creating" a part one must live it, much as the Jesuit mystic practices composition of place in recreating a biblical happening. Faulkner seems to have been able to do that most successfully— to live himself into a role—only when he was *in* his hometown as well as writing about it. Thus his slip of the pen while writing "Flags" when he substituted "Oxford" for "Jefferson"; and thus his misnomer when he calls Benjy "Davy."

But if he identified not only with Quentin but even with Benjy, he seemingly dissociated himself as vehemently from that devil Jason, who, as Bleikasten says, now "assumes the role of storyteller with almost histrionic glee."[23] That Jason is representative of a long dramatic and fictional tradition and is more complex than the melodramatic villain he at first might seem, is a point well taken. But Bleikasten also uses James Dahl's interviews with Faulkner's mother as the source of a chain of insights that bear out my conviction that the impulse to "indict" his home place and its inhabitants was one of the salient factors that account for the success of the novel.

"Now, Jason, in *The Sound and the Fury*," Mrs. Falkner told Dahl, "—he talks just like my husband did. My husband had a hardware store uptown at one time. His way of talking was just like Jason's, same words and same style."[24] Here one might note that, where Quentin's name doubtless derives from a romantic hero out of Sir Walter Scott, Jason is named for his own father.

Bleikasten remarks that Carvel Collins once called Jason a fictional embodiment of the superego. "It is interesting to know that his voice is perhaps quite literally the voice of the father," Bleikasten adds, with the facetious suggestion that the third section might be an "oedipal setting of accounts."[25] He goes on to consider the possibility that Jason is another instance of self-recognition. Here I would add that, if so, he is also another example of the Hawthorne syndrome: a son finds a haunting likeness of himself in a murdered father, or a father actually kills his son to atone for his own deficiencies.

Quentin and Jason are unsuccessful players of opposing roles. When Quentin is sarcastically referred to by his sister's wooers as a half-baked Galahad, a young Lochinvar, a champion of dames, all these insulting epithets fit. He is a failure as Caddy's knight, as the protector of chastity. Richard Ellmann once likened him to Faulkner playing the role of Count No- count—a Don Quixote seeking to restore purity to a lost world.[26] He is a loser like Elmer Hodge, but so is Jason. What a sorry businessman *he* is, the failed speculator, the merest bungler even as a thieving cheat. Not only little Quentin but the sheriff and the town are on to his absurd skullduggery. It is notorious that he loses far more of the girl's money than she finds in his strong-box. Jason is successful only as a character in fiction, a comic. A runner-up to his neurotic mother, he is an artistic triumph to rival any in Dickens. Hence we can enjoy the privilege of watching his utter defeat and confusion as we enjoy Mrs. Compson's incomprehension of everything happening around her. Or can we?

The complementarity of the brothers entails our empathy with them all. Bleikasten remarks the extent to which Jason's defeat and loneliness elicit a final gesture of compassion from his maker. Faulkner confers on Jason at last "that respect mingled with pity that [he] had grace enough to grant to each of his creatures at the moment of extreme solitude or impending death." The same last-minute benediction had been conferred on Bayard Sartoris, it will be remembered. There too, brotherly resemblance stamped each side of the coin with the same image of his creator—their Creator. [27]

If we look at the structure of the sections wherein each brother, from Benjy on, is given a crowded day to speak his lines, we realize that each is more complex than his predecessor. Apart from vocal differences, the significant distinction is the span of time covered by their various accounts. Benjy and Quentin relive events going back to the turn of the century, where Jason recalls nothing earlier than the breakup of Caddy's forced marriage, which cheated him, as he thinks, of that job in her husband's bank. From that time forward he can think of a vast number of moments that deserve his bitterness, but each one circles back to the same grudge. His powers of concentration on a vengeance he takes out on all around him—blacks, rednecks, "jews," parents, siblings, niece, and fellow townspeople—are as much to be admired as those of Satan in Milton's epic of the fall.

It would not be difficult to chart the shifts in Jason's pattern of action and memory as I have charted Benjy's for Appendix 2. His day, Good Friday, is as motile in its action, as dizzying in the shuttling course of its recollections of the cause of an *idée fixe*, as is Quentin's. But while Benjy's day ends on the eve of little Quentin's revenge, Jason's leads up to the night before Ben's day begins. Thus it creates a suspense that would be lost on us if we knew the significance of what Ben and Luster see shaking the pear tree before Easter Sunday morning, when Jason discovers that Miss Quentin has departed with what is left of the money he had robbed her of. At least that would be the case if *The Sound and the Fury* could possibly be read as straightforward narrative. But clearly that is not its nature. Nor can we discuss it sequentially.

Like or *Ulysses* or "Notes Toward a Supreme Fiction" or the *Cantos* of Ezra Pound, this book must be assimilated by retrospective reading, for that is how it was written. Its backward and forward motion in time brings us to realize and accept the fact that in Faulkner (as in Sir Thomas Browne) diuturnity is a dream and folly of expectation. Yet the unwavering theme of the first three books is damnation. Quentin and Jason are idol worshipers ethically of the same stripe. The one's care for honor like the other's care for respectability are alike mere vanity

One hesitates to single out the most poignant irony buried in Jason's unquenchable flow of sarcasm, but I seem to revert most frequently to his reflection on leaving the Memphis whorehouse and Lorraine. He thinks of a man "right here in Jefferson made a lot of money selling rotten goods to niggers, lived in a room over the store about the size of a pigpen." Yet, frightened of death, this man "joined the church and bought himself a

Chinese missionary, five thousand dollars a year." Jason's syntax, his anacoluthons, his shuffling of tense and mood, are as revealing of the inner demon as Macbeth's, who'd jump the life to come. "I often think how mad he'll be if he was to die and find out there's not any heaven, when he thinks about that five thousand dollars a year. Like I say, he'd better go on and die now and save money" (241). For Faulkner as for Wallace Stevens, money is a kind of poetry, too.

NOTES

1. Cleanth Brooks, *William Faulkner; The Yoknapatawpha Country* (New Haven, 1978), 325; Adams, *Myth and Motion*, 215. One authoritative reviewer (Mrs. Broughton) has characterized Bleikasten's *The Most Splendid Failure: Faulkner's "The Sound and the Fury"* (Bloomington, 1976) as too heavy on psychological factors to give due weight to theological ones. While I have here sought to remedy this omission I do so with humility, considering that Bleikasten's command of both text and commentary far surpasses all forerunners. I quote here from opening of his second chapter, "Caddy; or, The Quest for Eurydice."

2. Leslie Fiedler, *Love and Death in the American Novel* (New York, 1960), 309–27.

3. Meriwether has edited two of the drafts of this Introduction found in the Rowan Oak Papers. See *New York Times Book Review*, November 5, 1972, pp. 6–7, and *Southern Review*, n.s., VIII (1972), 705–10. See also Meriwether, (ed.), *Faulkner Miscellany*, 156–61. Blotner, *Biography*, I, 810–13, and *Selected Letters*, 74. My quotation is from the *Southern Review* version.

4. Found with various drafts and fragments of drafts for the preface is a single holograph sheet I take to be either a memorandum for his own guidance or a draft for a letter containing the lines quoted by Blotner (*Biography*, I, 810), who omits some memorable remarks on the nature of fiction questioning "the logical economy of cause and effect" which some believe exists "outside of fiction." Faulkner says he has come to doubt their existence.

5. *Selected Letters*, 74.

6. Meriwether (ed.), *Faulkner Miscellany*, 158.

7. Irwin, *Doubling and Incest*, 158–159

8. Bleikasten, *The Most Splendid Failure*, 118.

9. Meriwether (ed.), Draft of an Introduction for *The Sound and the Fury (Southern Review)*, 708.

10. Maurice-Edgar Coindreau, Translator's Preface to Faulkner, *Le Bruit et La fureur* (Paris, 1938). George McMillan Reeves translated the preface, and it appeared in *Mississippi Quarterly*, XVI (1966), and was reprinted in Coindreau, *The Time of William Faulkner: Essays*, trans. Reeves (Columbia, S.C., 1971), 41–50.

11. The play ... is about damnation," writes Kenneth Muir in his Introduction to the New Arden *Macbeth* (Rev. ed., London, 1953), li. An avid reader of Faulkner, Muir has helped me with several enlightening comments.

12. Lionel Trilling. "Tragedy and Three Novels," *Symposium*, I (January, 1930),106–14 James Burnham was the editor, and as Gresset notes, had been a student of Coindreau's at

Princeton. His essay "Trying to Say," appeared in *Symposium*, II (1931), 51–59. Gresset emphasizes the acuteness of his observation that the structure of the book describes a progressive clarification of initial obscurity. *Œuvres romanesques* I 1253.

13. Richard B. Sewall, *The Vision of Tragedy* (New Haven, 1959), Chaps, 12, 13, esp. p. 118. See also Sewall and Laurence Michel (eds.) *Tragedy: Modern Essays in Criticism* (Englewood Cliffs, N.J., 1963) *passim*, esp. Michel's essay, "The Possibility of Christian Tragedy," 210–33.

14. Sigmund Freud, "A Childhood Recollection from *Dichtung and Wahrheil*," in Benjamin Nelson (ed.), On *Creativity and the Unconscious* (New York, 1958), 111–21.

15. *The Sound and the Fury* (New York: Random House, 1956). 147, hereinafter cited parenthetically in the text.

16. Gresset, Avant-propos, in *Œuvres romanesques* I, xvii.

17. "The Sound and the Fury" (MS, in Alderman Library, University of Virginia); "Carcassonne." See Annotated Bibliography.

18. Emily K. lzsak. "The Manuscript of *The Sound and the Fury:* The Revisions in the First Section," *Studies in Bibliography*, XX (1967), 189–201.

19. "The Sound and the Fury," sheets 70–71.

20. Granville Hicks, "The Past and the Future of William Faulkner," *Bookmart*. LXXIV (September, 1929), 17–23.

21. Coindreau, Translator's Preface to *Le Bruit et la fureur*.

22. Cullen and Watkins, *Old Times*, 78–80.

23. Bleikasten. *The Most Splendid Failure*, 146.

24. *Ibid.*, 49, *Cf.* "A Faulkner Reminiscence," *Journal of Modern Literature*, 111 (1974). 1028.

25. Bleikasten, *The Most Splendid failure*, 150.

26. Richard Ellmann, "Faulkner as The Count," *Dimension* (Evanston, III.), LXXXIII (May 27, 1963), 304.

27. Bleikasten, *The Most Splendid Failure* 167. This part of Bleikasten's discussion seems to me to put the question raised by Panthea Broughton itself in question. For regardless of his choice of emphasis. Bleikasten shows himself to be aware of Jason's moral and theological function as well as his literary function as a double.

TOM QUIRK

Fitzgerald and Cather:
The Great Gatsby

I

Shortly after *The Great Gatsby* was published in 1925, F. Scott Fitzgerald received a letter from Willa Cather complimenting him on his achievement.[1] Fitzgerald was understandably excited about the letter, so much so that he woke up Christian Gausse and his wife at one o'clock in the morning to celebrate.[2] His behavior was extravagant, for Gausse was a Dean at Princeton and much Fitzgerald's senior, but extravagant behavior was not unusual for Fitzgerald. Nevertheless, there is reason to suppose that the excitement Cather's letter generated in the young author was authentic and that it somehow verified his own ambitions for his new novel. For he had consciously striven to emulate Cather's literary technique; but, more importantly, she had exerted a greater influence upon him than even he seems to have realized, in matters of incident and story as well as style and technique.

Maxwell Geismar, in his book *The Last of the Provincials*, was the first to suggest the influence of Cather upon *The Great Gatsby*. He perceived a similarity of theme and tone in the concluding passages of My *Ántonia* and *Gatsby*. The novels bear a special similarity as well, he argued, in their first person narrators, Jim Burden and Nick Carraway, both of whom possess a remembered association with someone unique and unexampled yet who

From *American Literature*, Volume 54, Number 4, December 1982. © 1982 by Duke University Press.

embodied something precious, if lost, "like the founders of the early races," as Cather had phrased it.[3]

James E. Miller augmented and fortified the Cather/Fitzgerald connection considerably in his *The Fictional Technique of F. Scott Fitzgerald.* He suggested the possibility that Fitzgerald might have been acquainted with Cather's essay "The Novel Démeublé," in which Cather urged novelists to throw all of the furniture of fiction out the window; and, in contrast to Geismar, Miller speculated that Fitzgerald might have learned more about literary form from reading *A Lost Lady* (another first person narrative) than from *My Ántonia* because the first is more compact, less "furnished." At any rate, Miller is surely correct in arguing that *Gatsby* represents Fitzgerald's movement away from the heavily furnished novel of "saturation," which swarms with detail, and toward the unfurnished, refined novel of "selection." And *A Lost Lady* does display greater artistic restraint than *My Ántonia.* Miller further identified the nature of Cather's influence on Fitzgerald as essentially one of technique, and especially that Fitzgerald learned from her a great deal about "point of view and about form and unity."[4]

Henry Dan Piper went even further in arguing Cather's influence on Fitzgerald when he contended that she was "almost as important as" Conrad in contributing inspiration to Fitzgerald's developing literary craftsmanship. And he additionally speculated that the young author may have responded to Edmund Wilson's review of *A Lost Lady* in January, 1924, in the *Dial.* There, Wilson had argued that that novel achieved its dramatic intensity through the skillful management of its first-person point of view. This review, Piper suggested, "may even have had something to do with Fitzgerald's decision three months later to abandon the third-person approach to his story.[5] But I would argue that Cather's influence upon Fitzgerald was not restricted to matters of technique alone and that his affinity with her was even more extensive than Geismar, Miller, and Piper have suggested.

There is no doubt that Fitzgerald thought highly of Cather's achievements (he identified himself in a letter to her as one of her "greatest admirers"), and her work was in his mind during and after the composition of *The Great Gatsby.* He was familiar enough with *A Lost Lady* (though he consistently misremembered the title as "*The Lost Lady*") to recognize that he had written a paragraph in *Gatsby* that "strangely paralleled" a paragraph in that book and conscientious enough to write Cather directly before the publication of his novel and inform her of this accidental plagiarism.[6] Additionally, in a letter to Charles C. Baldwin, again before the completion of *Gatsby,* he proudly announced that his book would be an "attempt at form," an attempt "to convey the feel of scenes, places and people directly—

as Conrad does, as few Americans (notably Willa Cather) are already trying to do."[7] After the publication of his novel, however, despite his conscious ambitions to write a novel of form rather than a rambling chronicle of the jazz age, Fitzgerald confessed to H.L. Mencken that his book was a "failure" compared to *My Ántonia* and *A Lost Lady*.[8] This may or may not have been false modesty on Fitzgerald's part; he had often bragged about his accomplishment in *Gatsby* and felt this book made him a novelist to be reckoned with. In fact, simply in terms of what he had attempted, a novel of form, he was probably correct in the comparison. Artistically, *A Lost Lady* is no doubt the better book—it is quiet and sure; its tone is steadier; its narrative persona more consistently drawn; it seldom yields to excitable variations of mood and tempo.

But, be that as it may, we know as well that Fitzgerald, while he recognized Cather as a fellow artist, equally recognized her as a fellow mid-Westerner. Somewhat mistakenly, however, he thought of her as a mid-Western novelist whose pioneers were exclusively "Swedes."[9] He may have had Cather in mind, in fact, and was distinguishing his experience from hers, when he had Nick recall his return trips with fellow students from Eastern schools at Christmas-time. When they saw and breathed once again the snow in the air, Nick recalls, we became "unutterably aware of our identity with this country for one strange hour, before we melted indistinguishably into it again." "That's my Middle West—," says Nick, "not the wheat or the prairies or the lost Swede towns, but the thrilling returning trains of my youth, and the street lamps and sleigh bells in the frosty dark and the shadows of holly wreaths thrown by lighted windows on the snow. I am part of that." It is this reverie in the final chapter which triggers the recognition that his story has been a mid-Western one: "I see now that this has been a story of the West, after all—Tom and Gatsby, Daisy, Jordan and I were all Westerners, and perhaps we possessed some deficiency in common which made us subtly unadaptable to Eastern life."[10] And it is the "El Greco-like" "distortions" (pp. 177–78) he perceives in Eastern life which justify his return home after Gatsby's death.

Although *My Ántonia* and *A Lost Lady* are the only Cather novels Fitzgerald mentions in his letters, he showed a special respect for one of her short stories, "Paul's Case," when he wrote that that story alone was worth more than anything Dorothy Canfield had to say in her fiction and had claimed in his letter to Cather herself that it was one of his favorites.[11] His mention of this story is suggestive because of certain similarities it has to *Gatsby* and its thematic similarity to one of Fitzgerald's own stories, "Absolution," which had been originally intended as a prologue to *The Great*

Gatsby and which would fill in details about Gatsby's early life. Cather's story, as its subtitle, "A Study in Temperament," suggests, is clearly a case study.

It is the story of a young man living in Pittsburgh who leads two lives— a cramped, conventional one symbolized by the pictures of George Washington and John Calvin and the motto "Feed the Lambs" which hang above his bed, and the life of his romantic imagination which thrives when he is at work as an usher at Carnegie Hall. Paul takes his courage to deal with the first from his romantic convictions about the second. He dresses flamboyantly and is disdainful of the conventional expectations placed upon him by his father and his school. In one episode, Paul follows the theater performers to their hotel after the performance and allows his imagination to play upon the exotic possibilities that lay within. As he stood in the gravel drive in the rain, he looked up at "the orange glow of the windows above him. There it was, what he wanted—tangibly before him, like a fairy world of a Christmas pantomime"; but mocking spirits stood guard at the doors, and, as the rain beat in his face, "Paul wondered whether he were destined always to shiver in the black night outside, looking up at it."[12]

In a bold gesture, he steals three thousand dollars and travels to New York and lives in romantic splendor for a fortnight. His resources depleted and aware that his father is in New York looking for him, he opts to end his life rather than return to his home on Cordelia Street. Paul commits suicide by throwing himself in front of an onrushing train, and he drops back into the "immense design of things." Reminiscent as "Paul's Case" is of certain elements in *Gatsby*—Gatsby's flamboyant dress, his romantic imagination, and his sacred, late night vigil in Chapter VII standing in a gravel drive in a pink rag of a suit, looking up at lighted windows—the emotional complex of boyhood, the imagined life which gives Paul courage, is closer to Fitzgerald's story of Rudolph Miller, which he called "Absolution."[13]

"Absolution," too, deals with a young man caught between the conventional expectations of him and his own romantic imagination, represented by his undaunted double, who neither observes convention nor is fearful of the consequences of his disregard. For Rudolph Miller, the imagined double has a name, Blatchford Sarnemington. Blatchford lives in "great, sweeping triumphs," but Rudolph is gnawed by conscience. And when he goes to his priest to admit that he had lied in confession, he is taken aback by Father Schwartz's rhapsodic speech about the seductive attractions of a gay world. The priest advises Rudolph to go to an amusement park, where "everything will twinkle." For Father Schwartz, like Rudolph, is attracted to the romantic world where "things go glimmering."

He eventually removed this episode from his novel and sold it separately as a short story, and in the novel he changed Rudolph's name to Jimmie Gatz and his alter ego's to Jay Gatsby, but the double life of his newly named character persisted. More than "Paul's Case," however, Cather's first novel, *Alexander's Bridge*, seems to have exerted the most suggestive influence upon Fitzgerald. The novel was serialized in *McClure's* under the title *Alexander's Masquerade* in 1912 and published as a book by Houghton Mifflin later the same year. It was well received and was reissued with an author's preface in 1922, at a time when Fitzgerald was contemplating the novel which would become *The Great Gatsby*.

As a first novel, *Alexander's Bridge* is understandably an apprentice piece in many ways—Cather herself was to claim her second novel, *O Pioneers!* (1913), her first spiritually and to confess that at the time of writing *Alexander's Bridge* she was too fascinated by the unfamiliar and unmindful of the richness of the subject matter closest to her—her native Nebraska.[14]

In any event, *Alexander's Bridge* is the story of a middle-aged engineer named Bartley Alexander whose worldly success and marital happiness are vaguely insufficient for him. Living in Boston, his supervision of the construction of a cantilever bridge in Canada requires him to travel to London periodically to reacquaint himself with British building codes. It is in London that he attends a play in which Hilda Burgoyne, his first love of several years before, stars. He re-kindles the flame against his better judgment, all the while recognizing that his marriage is the more valuable and durable relationship. But Bartley is not actually in love with Hilda so much as he is in love with a more youthful and vital image of himself which he perceives to be slipping away from him and which he seeks to recapture through her. Repeatedly he resolves to put an end to the affair, but he is so obsessed with this idea of himself that his resolution weakens and he travels to London to be with her.

Toward the end of the novel, Hilda's troupe travels to New York and they meet in an apartment which he keeps for business purposes. It is the distraction of Hilda which prevents Alexander from attending to a telegram from Canada concerning a structural problem with the bridge. A second telegram reaches him and he rushes to the construction site. The lower beams are showing strain, and Bartley immediately orders the workers off the bridge. But his commands come too late; the bridge collapses and Alexander drowns along with dozens of workers.

The novel is principally interesting in that it reveals Cather's persistent concern with the doubleness of personality, though with the Catherian technique as yet unrefined. In particular, her symbolism is too obvious and heavy-handed. The cantilever bridge is a conspicuous analogue for Bartley's mental state—just as Bartley's personality is described as possessing a "weak spot" where some day strain would tell,"[15] so is there a structural defect in the bridge he is building. The strain is tested, of course, in his maintenance of two lives, the secure domestic one with his wife and the youthful, romantic one with Hilda. Bartley longs for the days when he had a "single purpose and a single heart" (p. 101), but in pursuing that dream in middle age he develops a "another nature," as if "a second man has been grafted into me," and "he is fighting for his life at the cost of mine" (p. 102). The cantilever bridge, stretched half-way across the river, is explicitly identified as symbolic of Alexander's passion, and the river beneath as "death, the only other thing as strong as love. Under the moon, under the cold, splendid stars, there were only those two things awake and sleepless; death and love, the rushing river and his burning heart" (p. 118).

The angles of this love triangle are roughly congruent with those in *Gatsby,* but the most suggestive similarities exist in a single passage which identifies Alexander's background and his developing desire to retrieve himself from the past through his passion for Hilda. He recognizes that he is afraid of the "dead calm of middle life which confronted him" (p. 38) and longs for the days when he felt his own "wild light-heartedness":

> Such hours were the only ones in which he could feel his own continuous identity—feel the boy he had been in the rough days of the old West, feel the youth who had worked his way across the ocean on a cattle-ship and gone to study in Paris without a dollar in his pocket. The man who sat in his offices in Boston was only a powerful machine. Under the activities of that machine the person who, in such moments as this, he felt to be himself, was fading and dying. He remembered how, when he was a little boy and his father called him in the morning, he used to leap from his bed into the full consciousness of himself. That consciousness was Life itself. Whatever took its place, action, reflection, the power of concentrated thought, were only functions of a mechanism useful to society; things that could be bought in the market. There was only one thing that had an absolute value for each individual, and it was just that original impulse, that internal heat, that feeling of one's self in one's own breast.
>
> When Alexander walked back to his hotel, the red and green lights were blinking along the docks on the farther shore, and the soft white stars were shining in the wide sky above the river. (pp. 39–40)

The parallels between the lives of Gatsby and Alexander as they are revealed in this passage are rather obvious. Both characters come from provincial Western or mid-Western homes and had worked aboard ships. Both studied abroad—Alexander in Paris, Gatsby for a few months at Oxford. And both observe green lights across the water, which serve as emblems of that image of themselves which they attempt to retrieve through reviving a lost love. This last parallel is the most significant because it is the green light at the end of Daisy's dock in East Egg which becomes the dominant symbol of Gatsby's emotional complex. At the conclusion of Chapter I, Nick returns home in the evening and observes his mysterious neighbor "regarding the silver pepper of the stars." He decides to call to him, but checks himself when he realizes Gatsby is content to be alone—"he stretched out his arms toward the dark water in a curious way, and, far as I was from him, I could have sworn he was trembling. Involuntarily I glanced seaward—and distinguished nothing except a single green light" (pp. 21–22). And Fitzgerald returns to this image in the lyrical conclusion of the book when he has Nick sum up Gatsby's motivation: "Gatsby believed in the green light, the orgiastic future that year by year by year recedes before us" (p. 182).

The green light did not always occupy so central a position in the novel. Originally there were two lights at the end of Daisy's dock and were meant simply to convey a certain romantic intimacy, for they were introduced in Chapter V when Daisy and Gatsby were reunited.[16] Through revision, Fitzgerald made the image central to his novel. He made it the dominant image of the concluding paragraphs and introduced it into the final paragraph of Chapter I. It became a symbol to which Gatsby devoted the last ounce of his "romantic readiness," "his extraordinary gift for hope." Fitzgerald's appropriation of this image and his transformation of it into a forceful symbol invites further speculation about how extensive the influence of *Alexander's Bridge* was upon the author.

Gatsby enacts his own masquerade and, like Alexander, at odd moments the strain of his dual-life tells. Despite his "resourcefulness of movement," Nick notices that Gatsby was "never quite still; there was always a tapping foot somewhere or the impatient opening and closing of a hand" (p. 64). There is also a fascinating division between Gatsby's public personality and his private, sinister business dealings which Fitzgerald wisely decided to keep mysterious. Jay Gatsby, as opposed to Jimmie Gatz, is an invention which Nick says, "sprang from his Platonic conception of himself" (p. 99), and to this immutable conception, we are told, Gatsby was faithful to the end. His extravagant and obsessive designs to recapture Daisy's love are vain attempts to "repeat the past," an ambition to which Gatsby devotes all his energies.

Like Bartley Alexander, Gatsby pursues his own lost vitality and youth; Alexander is in his mid-forties, but Gatsby is much younger. He is, according to Nick, an "elegant young roughneck, a year or two over thirty" (p. 48). Yet when Maxwell Perkins, Fitzgerald's editor, wrote the author after reading the manuscript, that Gatsby seemed to be a much "older man," Fitzgerald replied: "It seems of almost mystical significance to me that you thought he was older—the man I had in mind, half-unconsciously, *was* older."[17] This discrepancy is not one of detail—what we know of Gatsby's background numerically tallies with his actual age—; it is rather a matter of the emotional quality of Gatsby's character. He is not so old as to possess Meyer Wolfsheim's tired sentimentality, who excuses himself at the restaurant because he belongs to "another generation" (p. 73). But Gatsby is well into that "menacing" decade which Nick imagines for himself on his thirtieth birthday: "Thirty—the promise of a decade of loneliness, a thinning list of single men to know, a thinning briefcase of enthusiasm, thinning hair" (p. 136). Gatsby's enthusiasms already have thinned to one, his enthusiasm for Daisy.

Gatsby's obsessions are, as Nick speculates, with "some idea of himself": "He talked a lot about the past, and I gathered that he wanted to recover something, some idea of himself perhaps, that had gone into loving Daisy. His life had been confused and disordered since then, but if he could once return to a certain starting place and go over it all slowly, he could find out what that thing was" (pp. 111–12). That "thing," in fact, probably never existed for Gatsby (or for Jimmie Gatz for that matter). For Nick renders Gatsby's recollections of his love for Daisy five years before in such romantic and distorted detail that we immediately recognize the futility of his dreams. The moonlit "blocks of the sidewalk" in Daisy's hometown really formed a ladder to a "secret place above the trees" where, once climbed, Gatsby could "gulp down the incomparable milk of wonder" (p. 112). As he kissed Daisy that autumn evening in Louisville, he listened "for a moment longer to the tuning-fork that had been struck upon a star. Then he kissed her. At his lips' touch she blossomed for him like a flower and the incarnation was complete" (p. 112).

The "incarnation" of which Nick speaks, and which is unbelievable precisely to the degree that it is poetic, is that particularized moment, as it is sustained by memory, when Gatsby believed his own Platonic self had for an instant touched the earth; and it is that identity, which never actually existed, that he seeks and which is symbolized by the green light across the water. It is Gatsby's futile dream which Fitzgerald explicitly identifies with the American Dream in the conclusion of the novel and which thus makes a mythical figure of his character:

> I became aware of the old island here that flowered once for Dutch sailors' eyes—a fresh, green breast of the new world. Its vanished trees, the trees that had made way for Gatsby's house, had once pandered in whispers to the last and greatest of all human dreams; for a transitory enchanted moment man must have held his breath in the presence of this continent, compelled into an aesthetic contemplation he neither understood nor desired, face to face for the last time in history with something commensurate to his capacity for wonder. (p. 182)

This is the age-old dream Gatsby seeks, but it is a vain striving: "He had come a long way to this blue lawn, and his dream must have seemed so close that he could hardly fail to grasp it. He did not know that it was already behind him, somewhere back in the vast obscurity beyond the city, where the dark fields of the republic rolled on under the night" (p. 182).

These famous concluding passages of *The Great Gatsby* not only bear the weight of the novel and, in fact, transport Gatsby's story into the realm of myth, but they had informed it as well. The final paragraphs grew out of a single lyrical sentence which Fitzgerald had originally used to conclude the first chapter. He crossed that sentence out, worked up the paragraphs, and placed them at the conclusion. In doing so, he introduced the green light which had before been confined to Chapter V, and then worked it into the concluding paragraph of Chapter I as well. Thus, he gave Gatsby's yearnings a single and dramatic focus, for this green light, as symbol, is inextricably wed to Gatsby's consciousness of it. Through revision, he made his small town boy from North Dakota a jaded and mysteriously sinister figure, for whom the world at large does not go "glimmering," as it had in "Absolution," but for whom a single and resolute purpose, existing in the free solution of his own imagined memory, of a possession five years past, is palpably located and symbolized in the green light at the end of Daisy's dock.

Fitzgerald's creative imagination, as Arthur Mizener has pointed out, was an instinctive rather than a calculating one. Despite his claims that he was attempting to write a novel of form, the author's relation to his material in *Gatsby* was probably felt rather than discerned. Surely Maxwell Perkins must have been dismayed by the reply he received after he had written Fitzgerald commending him on his achievement with this novel and making a few suggestions: "You once told me you were not a *natural* writer," he wrote, "—my God! You have plainly mastered the craft, of course; but you needed far more than craftsmanship for this."[18] Fitzgerald's response included a curious remark: "My first instinct after your letter was to let [Gatsby] go and have Tom Buchanan dominate the book ... but Gatsby sticks in my heart."[19] If we imagine what a small and trivial book his novel might have been with Tom Buchanan as the dominant character, we must realize how much we have to thank for Fitzgerald's "heart." But more than that, we can understand how, in his meticulous attention to individual sentences, his "craftsmanship," he was somehow blind to the larger successes of his novel except in the most instinctive way. This may help to explain why he might recognize a paragraph that "strangely paralleled" one of Cather's in *A Lost Lady* and, at the same time, to have failed to remember the title of that novel or to recognize the ultimately larger influences which "Paul's Case" and *Alexander's Bridge* had exerted upon him.

II

Willa Cather had written Fitzgerald of her admiration of *Gatsby* in the spring of 1925; the next fall she would begin to write what she ultimately considered her finest novel, *Death Comes for the Archbishop* (1927). It would be written, she would recall a few years later, in "the style of legend," the essence of which is to lightly "touch and pass on." Such a creative method would be a "kind of discipline," she wrote, "in these days when the 'situation' is made to count for so much in writing."[20] It was this sort of artistic detachment which Cather had cultivated since the beginning of her career and which gave rise to some of her finest work. In part, her disparagement of *Alexander's Bridge* in the preface to the 1922 edition of the novel proceeded from her belated recognition that she had relied too much upon "interesting" material and had tried to capitalize upon a situation. But, unlike Cather, the imaginative coherence Fitzgerald achieved in *The Great Gatsby* appears to have derived not from his detachment from but his involvement with his material. However much Fitzgerald may have learned from Cather about the writer's craft, however much *Alexander's Bridge* may or may not have contributed to his plot, one suspects that the real achievement of *Gatsby* had its sources in an intense emotional identification with both his main character and his narrator in a way that was but half-conscious. If Fitzgerald responded to *My Ántonia* and *A Lost Lady* professionally, he probably responded to *Alexander's Bridge* personally, for it identified an emotional complex he found sympathetic, one indeed that may have tallied with his own.

In the opening chapter of *The Great Gatsby*, Nick Carraway confesses to his burgeoning expectations for his new career in the East: I was going to "become again that most limited of all specialists, the 'well-rounded man.' This isn't just an epigram—life is much more successfully looked at from a single window, after all" (p. 4). His single window ambitions prove untenable, however; soon after his arrival in New York his life becomes entangled with the careless, careening lives of others. Dragged to a New York City apartment by Tom Buchanan, Nick, Tom, Myrtle Wilson, and the rest drink, argue, and lament through the afternoon and into twilight, and Nick reflects upon his unwilling association with this crowd: "Yet high over the city our line of yellow windows must have contributed their share of human secrecy to the casual watcher in the darkening streets, and I was him too, looking up and wondering. I was within and without, simultaneously enchanted and repelled by the inexhaustible variety of life" (p. 36).

Casual observer and reluctant participant, Nick brings a double vision to the story he tells, at once diffuse and exact. It is a simultaneous vision which, much like a stereopticon, lifts its figures from the page precisely because the images don't quite jibe, but are, instead, flat and lifeless without this discrepancy. How close this sort of double consciousness is to Fitzgerald's very sane assessment of his own "crack up" in an essay by the same name. "The test of a first-rate intelligence," he wrote a decade after the publication of *Gatsby*, "is the ability to hold two opposed ideas in the mind at the same time, and still retain the ability to function."[21] Fitzgerald's quiet and lucid self-diagnosis is a complaint not of the loss of his intelligence but of his ability to function, his artistic edge.

While he was writing *The Great Gatsby*, however, he retained the ability to function though he divided himself by identifying with both the jaded and obsessive Gatsby and the dazzled Nick, full of "interior rules" yet awestruck by the variety of life. Thus divided, he would divide his sympathies. Fitzgerald had of course identified with Gatsby; he wrote John Peale Bishop that that character "started out as one man I knew and then changed into myself—the amalgam was never complete in my mind."[22] But he was Nick Carraway, too. For he could well remember his own first reactions to New York as being one "up from the country gaping at the trained bears ... I had come only to stare at the show ... I took the style and glitter of New York even above its own valuation."[23]

In nearly every line of the book there is a certain divided quality, not yet a "crack up" but a slight fissure that yields a pervasive emotional tension, a tension where someday strain would tell. "I had no girl whose disembodied face floated along the dark cornices and blinding signs" (p. 81), says Nick; and lacking Gatsby's obsession, he is left simply with dark cornices and blinding signs for which his "interior rules" are sorry equipment. The world goes "glimmering" for Nick, but it lacks focus. This paragraph is representative of such a tension, I think: "Again at eight o'clock, when the dark lanes of the Forties were five deep with throbbing taxicabs bound for the theater district, I felt a sinking in my heart. Forms leaned together in the taxis as they waited, and voices sang, and there was laughter from unheard jokes, and lighted cigarettes outlined unintelligible gestures inside. Imagining that I, too, was hurrying toward gayety and sharing their intimate excitement, I wished them well" (p. 57–58). Nick's despair and provincial magnanimity punctuate his description of this haunted scene of faceless forms—irregularly lighted and half heard—throbbing with excitement but stalled in traffic.

This is typical of the El Greco-like distortion that permeates the novel, "at once conventional and grotesque" (p. 178). And we find it everywhere in the book. In the photograph of Myrtle Wilson's mother that "hovered like an ectoplasm on the wall" (p. 30); in the invisible object Jordan Baker balances upon her chin; in Nick's simultaneous fascination and repulsion by the idea that one man could fix the World Series; in the tramp who sells dogs on the street and yet looks all the world like John D. Rockefeller; in the tragic eyes and short upper lips of eastern European faces in a funeral train; in the city itself, "rising up across the river in white heaps and sugar lumps all built with a wish" (p. 69). And we find it in Nick's reaction to Gatsby himself, at once "gorgeous" and representative of "everything for which I have an unaffected scorn" (p. 2).

How much of this was the result of sheer "craftsmanship" and how much represented a heavy investment of the author himself in his material is unknown. But we do know that Fitzgerald continued his inventory of losses in a sequel to "The Crack-Up" which looks back to that time: "For a check-up of my spiritual liabilities indicated that I had no particular head to be bowed or unbowed. Once I had had a heart but that was all I was sure of."[24] His perception of the grotesqueries of life had once been tempered by sympathy and sustained by an enormous vitality. But these qualities had played out; he had developed a "sad attitude toward sadness, a melancholy attitude toward melancholy and a tragic attitude toward tragedy."[25] He had become identified with the objects of his "horror and compassion," and he was paralyzed by his own perceptions. "Life, ten years ago," he wrote, "was largely a personal matter. I must hold in balance the sense of the futility of effort and the sense of the necessity to struggle.... If I could do this through the common ills—domestic, professional and personal—then the ego would continue as an arrow shot from nothingness to nothingness with such force that only gravity would bring it to earth at last."[26] This passage has the ring of truth, but it stands as a statement of philosophical conviction rather than a felt reaction to life. But there seems to have been a time when life, indeed, was a "personal matter" for Fitzgerald, when Gatsby, when all vain human striving, "stuck in his heart."

The search for a lost vitality and a lost self which characterized the strivings of Bartley Alexander and Jay Gatsby was too familiar to Fitzgerald by the time he came to write "The Crack-Up." If at one time he had sympathized with their middle-aged dream of youth, now he shared it. In the end, Fitzgerald suffered from that very condition he had himself once so compassionately dramatized:

> It was back into the mind of the young man with cardboard soles who had walked the streets of New York. I was him again—for an instant I had the good fortune to share his dreams, I who had no more dreams of my own. And there are still times I creep up on him, surprise him on an autumn morning in New York or a spring night in Carolina when it is so quiet that you can hear a dog barking in the next county. But never again as during that all too short period when he and I were one person, when the fulfilled future and the wistful past were mingled in a single gorgeous moment—when life was literally a dream.[27]

NOTES

1. This letter is in "Scrapbook IV (The Great Gatsby)," p. 21, in the Firestone Library, Princeton University, and is dated 28 April 1925. Cather's letter was actually written in response to a letter from Fitzgerald in which he confessed to writing a passage in *Gatsby* that he thought reminiscent of a passage from *A Lost Lady*. Fitzgerald's letter is reprinted in Matthew Bruccoli's "'An Instance of Apparent Plagiarism': F. Scott Fitzgerald, Willa Cather, and the First *Gatsby* Manuscript," *Princeton University Library Chronicle* 39 (1978), 171–78; stipulations in Cather's will prohibit quotation from her letter.

2. Reported in Arthur Mizener's *The Far Side of Paradise: A Biography of F. Scott Fitzgerald* (Boston: Houghton Mifflin Co., 1965), p. 202.

3. *The Last of the Provincials: The American Novel, 1915–1925* (Boston: Houghton Mifflin Co., 1943), p.166.

4. James E. Miller Jr., *The Fictional Technique of Scott Fitzgerald* (The Hague: Martinus Nijhoff, 1957), p. 78; rev. ed. as *F. Scott Fitzgerald: His Art and His Technique* (New York: New York Univ. Press, 1964).

5. Henry Dan Piper, *F. Scott Fitzgerald: A Critical Portrait* (New York: Holt, Rinehart, and Winston, 1965), pp. 133–34.

6. *The Letters of F. Scott Fitzgerald*, Andrew Turnbull, ed. (New York: Charles Scribner's Sons, 1963), p. 507. Hereafter cited as *Letters*.

7. Quoted in Miller, pp. 73–74.

8. Letter to H.L. Mencken, 4 May 1925 *Letters*, pp. 480–81.

9. Letter to Perkins, C. I June 1925. *Letters*, pp. 183–88. Fitzgerald provided Perkins with a "History of the Simple Inarticulate Farmer and His Hired Man Christy" in this letter. In his entry for 1918, he wrote: "Willa Cather turns him [the simple farmer] Swede." 1918 is the year of publication of *My Ántonia*, which does not deal with Swedes but Bohemians. Fitzgerald was probably thinking of *O Pioneers!* (1913), which does deal with Swedish farmers.

10. *The Great Gatsby* (New York: Scribner's Sons, 1925), p. 177. Hereafter cited parenthetically in the text.

11. Letter to Dayton Kohler, 4 March 1938. *Letters*, pp. 571–72.

12. "Paul's Case," in *Youth and the Bright Medusa* (New York: Random House, 1975), p.189. "Paul's Case" was first published in *McClure's* and later collected in *The Troll Garden* (1905) and *Youth and the Bright Medusa* (1920). Since Fitzgerald mentions "Paul's Case" and "Seduction," both of which are included in *Youth and the Bright Medusa*, in his letter to Cather as being his favorite stories by her, it is likely that he read the story in this last collection.

13. "Absolution" was first published in the *American Mercury* in June, 1924, pp. 136–51; it is reprinted in *Fitzgerald's The Great Gatsby: The Novel, the Critics, the Background*, Henry Dan Piper, ed. (New York: Charles Scribner's Sons, 1970), pp. 83–92.

14. "My First Novels: There Were Two," Part 6 of The Colophon, 1931; rpt. in *Willa Cather on Writing: Critical Studies on Writing as an Art* (New York: Alfred A. Knopf, 1949), pp. 89–97.

15. *Alexander's Bridge* (Lincoln: Univ. of Nebraska Press, 1982), p. 12. Hereafter cited parenthetically in the text.

16. Information concerning the composition of *The Great Gatsby* is primarily based on Kenneth Eble's "The Craft of Revision: *The Great Gatsby*," *American Literature, 36* (Autumn 1964), 315–26; and supplemented by Piper, pp. 138–54, and Matthew Brucolli's *Some Sort of Epic Grandeur: The Life of F. Scott Fitzgerald* (New York: Harcourt Brace Jovanovich, 1981), pp. 195–219.

17. Letter to Maxwell Perkins, c. 20 Dec. 1924. *Letters*, pp. 171–75.

18. Letter to Fitzgerald, 20 Nov. 1924, *Editor to Author: The Letters of Maxwell E. Perkins*, John Hall Wheelock, ed. (New York: Charles Scribner's Sons, 1950), pp. 38–41.

19. Letter to Perkins, c. 20 Dec. 1924. *Letters*, pp. 171–75.

20. "On *Death Comes for the Archbishop*," an open letter to the editor of *The Commonweal*, 23 Nov. 1927; rpt. in *Willa Cather on Writing*, pp. 3–13.

21. "The Crack-Up." in *The Crack-Up*, Edmund Wilson, ed. (New York: New Directions Publishing Corp., 1945). p. 69: this article originally appeared in *Esquire* Feb., 1936.

22. Letter to John Peale Bishop, 9 Aug. 1925. *Letters*, p. 358.

23. "My Lost City," in *The Crack-Up*, p. 24.

24. "Pasting It Together," in *The Crack-Up*, p. 80; this article originally appeared in *Esquire* April, 1936.

25. Ibid, p. 80–81.

26. "The Crack-Up," p. 70.

27. "Early Success," in *The Crack-Up*, p. 90; this article originally appeared in *American Cavalcade* Oct., 1937.

RANDA DUBNICK

Clarity Returns:
Ida and *The Geographical History of America*

Around the 1930s Stein approached intelligibility again by combining elements of both obscure styles and allowing both selection and combination to become fully operative again.[1] In works such as *Ida* and *The Geographical History of America*, language is both discursive and arbitrary, and the boundaries between poetry and prose blur, a tendency that Steiner noticed in Stein's work of this period in general.[2] Stein's writing does not return to clarity unchanged. From the influence of cubist painters, she retains a playful awareness of the artist's power to produce a nonmimetic work that exists on its own terms rather than as a representation of the world as it is.

The publication of *The Autobiography of Alice B. Toklas* in 1933[3] marks not only an important milestone in Stein's literary fortunes, but also the flowering of a new trend in her stylistic development. Bridgman says of that work's composition, "After twenty years of enigmatic utterances, Gertrude Stein at last chose to speak in a voice of singular clarity. She was fifty-eight years old."[4] Relative clarity emerges in much of Stein's writing of the thirties, most notably with the *Autobiography* written in 1932.[5] This trend appears in her theoretical writings and lectures, *Lectures in America* (1934); *What Are Masterpieces and Why Are There So Few of Them* (1935); her so-called philosophical meditations, such as *The Geographical History of America; or, The Relation of Human Nature to the Human Mind* (1935); her writing about

From *The Structure of Obscurity: Gertrude Stein, Language, and Cubism* by Randa Dubnick. © 1984 by the Board of Trustees of the University of Illinois herself, *Everybody's Autobiography* (1936), *Wars I Have seen* (1942), and about *Picasso* (1938). But even more significantly, this new impulse toward clarity is seen even in some of her creative work, such as *Ida: A Novel* (1940) *The World Is Round* (1938), and *Mrs. Reynolds: A Novel* (1940). Bridgman proposes biographical explanations for the appearance of this clearly written work; among them are "heightened fame, a creative slump, and the hope of pleasing Alice."[6] He even raises the question of whether Toklas had a hand in writing the book. Bridgman said of the *Autobiography:*

> Its ironic precision was utterly foreign to Gertrude Stein, and therefore it is natural to wonder if her companion was in any way responsible for the drastic stylistic metamorphosis.
>
> One possiblity is sufficiently heretical that no one has dared advance it directly; but there have been hints that Alice Toklas composed her own autobiography.[7]

But one need not speculate so broadly about Stein's new clarity. It is more fruitful to examine her stylistic escape from deepest obscurity as she allows both axes of language to become fully operative again.

Up to this point Stein's obscurity had been manifested in several styles. First there was the earliest obscure style of her pre-1912 portraits and of the latter portions of *The Making of Americans*, which emphasized syntax and suppressed vocabulary: "He was knowing some who were being ones at the end of the beginning of being living when he was at the end of the beginning being living. In a way he was one with them, in many ways he was not one with them. He was one with them in being one being one of them, in being one completely understanding something." (*The Making of Americans*, p. 874.) Then there was the second obscure style, represented by *Tender Buttons* as well as by the poems and portraits written after 1912, which extended vocabulary and suppressed syntax:

APPLE

Apple plum, carpet steak, seed clam, colored wine, calm seen, cold cream, best shake, potato, potato and no no gold work with pet, a green seen is called bake and change sweet is bready, a little piece a little piece please.

A little piece please. Cane again to the presupposed and ready eucalyptus tree, count out sherry and ripe plates and little corners of a kind of ham. This is use. [*Tender Buttons*, p. 48.]

Another extreme outgrowth of this second kind of obscurity is the lists and a vertical format, as syntax, sentences, and paragraphs are all eliminated as in "Study Nature" (1918):

> I do.
> Victim.
> Sales
> Met
> Wipe
> Her
> Less.[8]

This phenomenon began about the same time as the *Tender Buttons* style in 1912. This style, in some ways an extension of the second obscurity that Stein classified as poetry, often occurs in combination with paragraphs, as poetry is expressed in both vertical and horizontal formats. But in both cases, the operation of selection (vertical axis) is stressed. Up to this point none of these obscure styles or variations of styles had been *conventionally* comprehensible. Only when syntax and vocabulary, selection and combination are simultaneously allowed to come within a normal range of development does Stein's writing begin to "make sense," as in the following passage from *Ida* (1940): "It was a nice time then. Instead of working or having his money Arthur just listened to anybody. It made him sleepy and he was never more than half awake and in his sleep he had a way of talking about sugar and cooking. He also used to talk about medicine glasses."[9] Although the events described seem fantastic, the passage is certainly understandable. In *The Geographical History of America* (p. 199), Stein incorporates similar poetic passages expressed both in paragraphs and in columns:

> And human nature is what everybody knows and time and identity is what everybody knows and they are not master-pieces and yet everybody knows that master-pieces say what they do say about human nature and time and identity, and what is the use, there is no abuse in what is the use, there is no use. Why not.
> Now listen. What is conversation.
> Conversation is only interesting if nobody hears.
> Hear hear.
> Masterpieces are second to none.
> One and one.

Although both of these passages are a bit eccentric and the second is a bit hard to read because punctuation is lacking, they are certainly clearer than much of Stein's writing since the relatively conventional prose narratives in *Three Lives* (1905–6).

Although some critics, who consider Stein's early conventional prose (*Three Lives, Things as They Are*) her best writing, see her obscurity as a loss, her later return to intelligibility in the thirties does not imply that her work evolved toward this as a goal or that her later work is better or more interesting than *The Making of Americans* or *Tender Buttons* because it is clearer. In fact, her more obscure work is more innovative, and on that account it is more interesting and more important. Much of her later work merely repeats or modifies the earlier stylistic innovations.

This reemerging clarity may have been just a response to Stein's relatively late awareness of audience, which began to grow during the early thirties,[10] and a new desire to make herself clear to that audience. In fact, this awareness of audience raised questions of identity that became key concerns in both *Ida* and the *Geographical History*. Brinnin writes that "Identity, in particular the identity of genius, was the main subject" of *The Geographical History of America*.[11] The theme of identity and audience comes up often in passages like the following (pp. 112–13): "I am I because my little dog knows me[12] ... and yet the little dog knowing me does not really make me be I no not really because after all being I I am I has really nothing to do with the little dog knowing me, he is my audience, but an audience never does prove to you that you are you." Brinnin also points out that in *Ida*, Stein tried to examine and resolve "the problem of identity that had obsessed her ever since she had become famous,"[13] and which was partially responsible for a creative slump. In *Everybody's Autobiography* Stein discusses this problem, which she experienced after *The Autobiography of Alice B. Toklas* was published: "All this time I did no writing. I had written and was writing nothing. Nothing inside me needed to be written.... And I was not writing. I began to worry about identity. I had always been I because I had words that had to be written inside me.... I am I because my little dog knows me. But was I I when I had no written word inside me."[14]

The fact that Stein's writing becomes more comprehensible does not mean that she renounced her earlier obscurities. In fact, she incorporated elements of both of her obscure styles into the works that followed. The resulting increase in clarity is no more than one would expect, given Jakobson's observation that suppression of either combination or selection causes serious disintegration in the comprehensibility of language. A look at the novel *Ida* and *The Geographical History of America*, a nonfiction philosophical meditation, shows how Stein combines elements of her first obscure style, which emphasized the horizontal axis of language, with elements of her second obscure style, which emphasized the vertical axis.

In "And Now," printed in *Vanity Fair* in 1934 during her U.S. tour, Stein said, "I write the way I used to write in *The Making of Americans*."[15] This is not strictly true. In these later works she no longer restricts vocabulary or emphasizes the present participle as in *The Making of Americans*. Although she had been producing works emphasizing the vertical format and the list for some time and continued to do so until her death, the paragraph reappears more frequently during the 1930s. And although one can still occasionally find fragments and fused sentences in these works, the predominant syntax approaches a normal range, as in at least some of her writing she turned away from the almost exclusive use of isolated words and phrases. But the use of the sentence and paragraph is not the sole basis for distinguishing prose from poetry in Stein's work. *Tender Buttons* is written in paragraphs and looks like conventional prose, but Stein classifies it as poetry because of its emphasis on the word. Even though written in paragraphs, other works, such as "The Portrait of Mabel Dodge" (1912) and *Lucy Church Amiably* (1927), would be classified as poetry according to Stein's criteria.

In the reemerging clarity of her later works, not only does syntax approach (but not reach) orthodoxy, but sentence length is more conventional than either the long sentences of *The Making of Americans* or the short phrases of *Tender Buttons* and works written in columns. Here is an example taken from *The Geographical History of America* (p. 80):

> Are there any customs and habits in America there is geography and what what is the human mind. The human mind is there because they write and they do not forget or remember and they do not go away and come back again. That is what the human mind does not human nature but the human mind. Listen to the human-mind.
>
> I will tell a story about the human mind what is the story.
>
> It is the story of Bennett.
>
> Bennett has an uncle who is as young as he is that is to say he is about the same age and age has nothing to do with the human-mind.
>
> When a great many hear you that is an audience and if a great many hear you what difference does it make.
>
> Bennett and his uncle do not know anything about that.

And why not. Because that has nothing to do with the human mind.

Although there are a few run-on sentences in the above passage, most sentences are correctly constructed in terms of grammar, although the lack of punctuation makes them hard to follow (as in *The Making of Americans*). Here, most individual sentences are understandable, despite vague pronoun references in the first paragraph (another vestige of the first obscure style). Most of the difficulty in the passage comes from Stein's digressions and from the separations of several lines between related statements about a particular topic.

As in much of Stein's writing of the thirties and forties, this passage has more semantic meaning than works of the *Tender Buttons* style. The syntax is more conventional and also has more specific content than the "abstract" style of the late *The Making of Americans* and the early portraits, and the vocabulary is not so stringently restricted and limited to general words:

> One day it was not Tuesday, two people came to see her great-aunt. They came in very carefully. They did not come in together. First one came and then the other one. One of them had some orange blossoms in her hand. That made Ida feel funny. Who were they? She did not know.... A third one came along, this one was a man and he had orange blossoms in his hat brim. He took off his hat and said to himself here I am, I wish to speak to myself. Here I am. Then he went on in the house. [*Ida*, p. 9.]

Stein's statements are sometimes disconcerting, but they do make sense. The subject and verb are no longer semantically disjunctive as in *Tender Buttons*. The passage also conveys enough concrete information to communicate an idea. In *Ida* Stein combines elements of both earlier styles, producing comprehensible writing, at least on the level of the individual sentence.

However, one can also see traces of the kind of obscurity found in *The Making of Americans*. Although the characters in *Ida* are given names rather than just pronouns (as in the extremes of Stein's first obscure style), Ida resembles that style in presenting only very general information about the characters' external qualities. Most characters are identified only by first names, and "biographical" information is most superficial. For example, one of Ida's many husbands is introduced to the reader as follows (p. 35):

> Ida married Frank Arthur.
> Arthur had been born right in the middle of a big country.

He knew when he was a tiny boy that the earth was round so it never was a surprise to him. He knew that trees had green leaves and that there was snow when time for snow came and rain when time for rain came. He knew a lot.

Action in *Ida* may also be presented very generally, even though there are more verbs expressing action than in the early portraits or the end of *The Making of Americans*. The reader is not given a detailed description that shows the action, but merely a generalized summary of the event (p. 77):

> And so Ida was in Washington.
> One day, it happened again and again some one said something to her, they said Oh Ida, did you see me. Oh yes she said. Ida never did not see anybody, she always saw everybody and said she saw them. She made no changes about seeing them.
> So he said to her Ida, your name is Ida isn't it, yes she said, and he said I thought your name was Ida, I thought you were Ida and I thought your name is Ida.
> It is, she said.
> They sat down.

This passage presents only a general picture of the event. Its location is no more specific than Washington. Where did they sit down? Ida's interlocutor is not identified by gender in the first paragraph but is referred to only as someone, although *he* is used in the next paragraph. (His name is eventually supplied on that page, however.) Other general words, such as *something*, *anybody*, *everybody*, and *them*, are reminiscent of *The Making of Americans*, as is the repetition.

Ida is also abstract in another sense, in the same sense that *Tender Buttons* is abstract. Although the vocabulary of *Ida* is more concrete than that of *The Making of Americans*, the work as a whole resembles *Tender Buttons*—not in syntax or semantic content, both of which are much more orthodox—but in its freedom from fidelity to the external world as referent. Although Stein has returned to prose, the discoveries made while writing the "poetry" of *Tender Buttons* have had their influence. The prose of *The Making of Americans* and similar works was tied to representation of the referent (capturing a person's basic nature, creating a history of all human possibilities), however generalized and eccentric that representation was. But now, in this new kind of prose, language is used arbitrarily, not only in fiction, but also in Stein's critical, philosophical, and autobiographical writing.

While much of the language in this new prose conveys information and discursive thought, Stein also includes in it elements of her "poetic" style. In the second lecture of *Narration*, she said:

> In the beginning there really was no difference between poetry and prose.... How could there be ... since the name of anything was then as important as anything ... that could be said about anything....
>
> [T]he Old Testament did this thing there was not really any difference between prose and poetry then....[16]
>
> Well and now, now that we have been realizing that anything having a beginning and middle and ending is not what is making anything anything, and now that everything is so completely moving in the name of anything is not really anything to interest any one about anything, now it is coming that once again nobody can be certain that narrative is existing that prose and poetry have different meanings.[17]

Once Stein discovered "poetry" while writing *Tender Buttons*, she did not separate it from the rest of her work. Many of her plays contain some poetry, and it also crops up in her prose works, both fiction and nonfiction. For one thing, many of her prose works contain what Copeland calls Stein's "treatment of language as if it were an autotelic rather than a representational entity."[18] That is, Stein pays attention to the word itself and to its qualities as a signifier, which is what she considered the essence of poetry to be in *Tender Buttons* and similar works *Ida: A Novel* is often interrupted by passages just as poetic, by Stein's definition, as anything in *Tender Buttons* or in Stein's long poem "Before the Flowers of Friendship Faded Friendship Faded." One way in which poetry manifests itself in *Ida* is in whimsical wordplay. Among its many puns is, for example, Ida's dog named Love, who was born blind, a pun on an old cliché (p. 10). Ida tells this dog, "Later on they will call me a suicide blonde because my twin will have dyed her hair" (p. 11), another pun.

Stein also uses rhyme within her prose. Sometimes the essentially linear, though often discontinuous, narrative line is interrupted by passages of rhyme that may be only one line long. Stein's rhyme often functions as a closural device at the end of a discursive statement or paragraph: "Anybody likes to know about then and now, Ida was one and it is easy to have one sister and be a twin too and be a triplet three and be a quartet and four and be a quintuplet it is easy to have four but that just about does shut the door" (*Ida*, p. 42). Not only rhyme, but wordplay also is characteristic of the poetic

Tender Buttons style. Besides the jingle at the end of the above passage, there is also a pun on the word *too*. *Quartet* is substituted for the similar word *quadruplet*. Thus Stein plays games with the reader's expectations and demands attention to words qua words.

Stein occasionally even interrupts the prose narrative of *Ida* with a little poem arranged vertically (p. 116).

> For a four.
> She shut the door.
> They dropped in.
> And drank gin.
> I'd like a conversation with Ida.

Here vestiges of the poetic style include not only rhyme but also truncation of the sentence into fragments. Sometimes poetic digressions are much longer. Whole paragraphs bounce along in sing-song rhythm, with several rhymes within the line. The following passage (pp. 122–23) is probably the longest poetic digression in *Ida:*

> Listen to me I, I am a spider, you must not mistake me for the sky, the sky red at night is a sailor's delight, the sky red in the morning is a sailor's warning, you must not mistake me for the sky, I am I, I am a spider and in the morning any morning I bring sadness and mourning and at night if they see me at night I bring them delight, do not mistake me for the sky, not I, do not mistake me for a dog who howls at night and causes no delight, a dog says the bright moonlight makes him go mad with desire to bring sorrow to any one sorrow and sadness, the dog says the night the bright moonlight brings madness and grief, but says the spider I, I am a spider, a big spider or a little spider, it is all alike, a spider green or gray, there is nothing else to say, I am a spider and I know and I always tell everybody so, to see me at night brings them delight, to see me in the morning brings mourning, and if you see me at night, and I am a sight, because I am dead having died up by night, even so dead at night I still cause delight, I dead bring delight to anyone who sees me at night, and so every one can see me sleep tight who has seen me at night.

Here characteristics of *The Making of Americans* and *Tender Buttons* are combined. As in *The Making of Americans*, Stein has created a paragraph-length sentence, sometimes linked by conjunctions and sometimes by clauses run together. The repetition is also characteristic of the earlier prose style. "I am a spider" is repeated four times; "you must not mistake me for the sky" is repeated three times, and so forth. However, the participles and genderless pronouns have been dropped, making the work easier to understand.

But although the syntax of the quoted sentence is stretched unmercifully, characteristics of Stein's poetic style dominate. Rhyme and rhythm are used here more than in *Tender Buttons*. The quality of the word, rather than its semantic content, predominates. Many phrases are apparently generated for the sake of the rhythm and/or rhyme. Many more adjectives and nouns appear here than in Stein's first obscure style. The words *spider* and *mourning* are associated, evoking the idea of a black widow spider through the association of *mourning* and *widow*. These associations all function along the vertical axis of language and are based on similarity. (In fact, the subject of the entire passage is superstition, the positing of a causal relationship based on the observation of similar patterns of events.)

Although much of the language in *Ida* functions to carry the narrative forward, some of the language (both in the digressions and the narrative) is used plastically as in the *Tender Buttons* style. Yet this use of language is juxtaposed with language that moves toward abstraction in much the same way as did *The Making of Americans*, as in the passage discussed above (ch. 1, pp. 9–10).

However, despite the lyrical passages, *Ida* is predominately a return to prose and, in some ways, a return to the traditions of prose fiction. In her transatlantic interview with Robert Bartlett Hass, Stein said that after she wrote *Four Saints in Three Acts* in 1932, she "went back to the form of narration."[19] In *Ida*, once again a central character is followed throughout the narrative as in the earlier stories of *Three Lives*, "Melanctha." "The Good Anna," and "The Gentle Lena." But Stein's return to the prose narrative has been greatly influenced by the discovery made in the course of writing *Tender Buttons* that language can be used arbitrarily. In *Ida* Stein extends the artist's arbitrary power over language to the very structure of the narrative. The action in *Ida* is not only episodic and temporally noncontiguous, as in *The Making of Americans*; it is also alogical. As a story *Ida* makes no sense in causal terms. The logic is the logic of the fantasy. *Ida* makes the kind of sense *Alice in Wonderland* does.

Although the novel tells a story, the plot seems to be what Copeland would call self-generative. For example, many characters are apparently introduced only because they bear the names of U.S. presidents, e.g., Andrew, Abraham, and George. The narrative grows out of the language and is very often subordinated to it, rather than vice versa. The logic of *Ida* arbitrarily suspends laws of causality and chronology; Ida's description of her dog Polybe (p. 103), for example, seems almost as fantastic as Lewis Carroll's description of the Cheshire cat:

> Polybe was not a small dog he was a hound and he had stripes red and black like only a zebra's stripes are white and black but Polybe's stripes were as regular as that and his front legs were long, all his family could kill a rabbit with a blow of their front paw, that is really why they danced in the moonlight, they thought they were chasing rabbits, any shadow was a rabbit to them and there are lots of shadows on a hillside in the summer under a bright moon.

Events don't develop as logical consequences of other events, but occur suddenly and arbitrarily, with no motive or explanation supplied: "Ida was married again this time he came from Boston, she remembered his name. She was good friends with all her husbands" (p. 62); or: "Ida never saw Arthur again. She just did not" (p. 40).

The constraints of temporal contiguity are often rejected along with assumptions of logic and causality in prose, assumptions that are basically diachronic and associated with the horizontal axis of language:

> Narrative has been the telling of anything because there has been always a feeling that something followed another thing that there was succession in happening.... What has made the Old Testament such permanently good reading is that ... in the Old Testament writing there really was not ... any succession of anything.... In the Old Testament writing there is really no actual conclusion that anything is progressing that one thing is succeeding happening is a narrative of anything ... but most writing has been a real narrative writing a telling of the story of anything in the way that the thing has been happening and now everything is not that thing there is at present not a sense of anything being successively happening, moving is in every direction beginning and ending is not really exciting ... and this has come to be a natural thing in a perfectly natural way that the narrative of today is not a narrative of succession as all the writing for a good many hundreds of years has been.[20]

Stein doubted the interest of traditional narrative for modern readers, who see and hear of so many events in the media, yet see little action in their own lives. Stein's observation that modern Americans spend most of their time standing around doing nothing is reflected in *Ida*. The protagonist spends a lot of time just resting. "Ida led a very easy life, that is she got up and sat up and went in and came out and rested and went to bed" (p. 68). This deemphasis of action obviously makes the time of the adventure irrelevant to the order of the novel. When the action presented is undramatic, mundane, or inconsequential, chronology becomes irrelevant. Quotidian events are by definition repeated actions. In *Ida* Stein shows the irrelevance of chronological time to an inconsequential life:

> One day did not come after another day to Ida. Ida never took on yesterday or tomorrow, she did not take on months either nor did she take on years. Why should she when she had always been the same, what ever happened there she was ... resting and everything happening. Sometimes something did happen, she knew to whom she had been married but that was not anything happening, she knew about clothes and resting but that was not anything happening. [*Ida*, p. 135]

As action is suppressed in favor of mental processes, the mental time of perception displaces chronological order in Stein's writing. Despite the roughly chronological order of events, time in *Ida* has less to do with chronological or diachronic (horizontal) time than with mythological or synchronic (vertical) time. Sutherland sees *Ida* as a legend and a myth; Ida's activities are recounted out of time: "In a vague way, *Ida* is about the Duchess of Windsor, but it is really the story of what Gertrude Stein called a 'publicity saint,' that is a person who neither does anything nor is connected with anything but who by sheer force of existence in being there holds the public attention and becomes a legend."[21] Events occur for no reason and out of time, as in the presentation of one of Ida's marriages (p. 75 above). As in myth the particulars are less important than the essential structure of the event. Sutherland classifies many of Stein's late works, such as *Ida* (1940). *Picasso* (1938), *Brewsie and Willie* (1945), as legends.[22] Stein, always faithful to present tense, could deal with the past by making it into a legend, which is eternally present. The legend solves the problem of time in the narrative, as Sutherland implies:

> Narrative cannot possibly go on living by its truth to the

historical facts or to the psychological or moral facts, or by
having one thing lead to another, it now has to go on the
conviction that sheer happening in the immediate present, and
above all in the immediate written present, is the final reality. In
short the business of the narrative artist is now ... the creation of
legend.[23]

Stein also tries to conquer the traditionally chronological and linear
organization of the novel. She uses associative time, as events narrated evoke
similar events associated with it in the narrator's mind, though there may be
no chronological connection. For example, *Ida* contains a very long
digression (pp. 96–106), absolutely extraneous to the action, in which the
protagonist catalogs and comments on all the dogs she has ever owned. The
only apparent reason for the sudden appearance of this digression is that the
subject happened to come to Ida or to Stein's mind: "So Ida was left alone,
and she began to sit again. And sitting she thought about her life with dogs
and this was it" (p. 96). Within the six-page digression that follows this
passage, the movement of thought is largely associative. Although Ida at first
seems to describe her dogs in the chronological order in which she owned
them, she soon digresses and makes links on the basis of similarities: "That
was all. Then there were a lot of dogs but none of them interesting. Then
there was a little dog, a black and tan and he hung himself on a string when
somebody left him. He had not been so interesting, but the way he died made
him very interesting" (p. 97).

Stein used this digressive associative time in *The Making of Americans*,
but her use of it in *Ida* is different in two ways. First, the digressions in *The
Making of Americans* are still prose and of the same style as the narrative that
is being interrupted, while in *Ida* they are very often poetic by Stein's criteria.
Secondly, in *The Making of Americans* Stein conveyed a sense of the duration
of both external and internal processes (partially through the participle as
well as through long, tortuous sentences). Both her early portraits and *Tender
Buttons* are static and timeless because they have no narrative per se. But in
Ida Stein tries to tell a story without creating a sense of duration. The passage
of time is announced but is not shown or described for the reader, as in the
following account of Ida's childhood (p. 14):

Ida gradually was a little older and every time she was a little
older some one else took care of her. She liked the change of
address because in that way she never had to remember what her
address was and she did not like having to remember. It was so

easy to forget the last address and soon she really forgot to guess
what the next address was.

Little by little she knew how to read and write and really she
said and she was right it was not necessary for her to know
anything else. And so quite gradually little by little she grew
older.

We aren't shown Ida's development over time, but are merely told that she
"was gradually a little older," "gradually little by little she grew older," and
learned to read and write "little by little." The gradual passage of time is just
announced. This is certainly not a detailed description that captures a feeling
of duration. But it does convey the transience and probably loneliness of Ida's
upbringing (she can't remember her last address), as well as the shallowness
of her education ("it was not necessary for her to know anything else").[24]
Evident here is Stein's desire to capture the essence of a person or action
without directly describing either.

Representing the chronology of passing time during an event does not
concern Stein. She does not care about the order or duration of Ida's
adventures. Instead she represents the duration and order of the narrator's
subjective mental time. In this novel the time of the telling is more important
than the time of the vague, episodic action. Although Stein was interested in
this kind of time throughout her career, the portrayal of the circuitous
workings of mental time is not her invention. It is at least as old as *Tristram
Shandy*, but as new as Robbe-Grillet's *Project for a Revolution in New York*.

Stein's *The Geographical History of America: or, The Relation of Human
Nature to the Human Mind* and similar nonfiction works also combine goals
and elements of Stein's prose and poetic styles. *The Geographical History of
America*, a kind of philosophical meditation, is more sober than *Ida*. One goal
of the work is ostensibly to explore simple ideas with some degree of clarity.
On the very first page, Stein announces: "These are ordinary ideas. If you
please these are ordinary ideas" (p. 53). Much of what she writes here can be
classified as discursive, expository prose. The following passage is a straightforward and clear observation. "I used to wonder when I saw boys who had
just been boys and they went into an office to work and they came out with
a handful of papers and I said to them how since you never had anything to
do with papers before these business papers were given to you how do you
know what to do with them. They just did. They knew what to do with
them" (p. 133). Although sometimes vague and hard to follow, this book is
still relatively clear because its vocabulary and syntax both approach normal
usage. Yet one finds traces of both obscure styles in this work.

Many observations about the style of *Ida* are also true of *The Geographical History of America*. The work contains some very long sentences, some as long as an average paragraph. Their construction is much like that of the long sentences in *The Making of Americans*. But, as in *Ida*, the participles are gone and the vocabulary is less radically limited. The syntax of the following sentence-paragraph resembles that of *The Making of Americans*:

> I know so well the relation of a simple center and a continuous design to the land as one looks down on it, a wandering line as one looks down on it, a quarter section as one looks down on it, the shadows of each tree on the snow and the woods on each side and the land higher up between it and I know so well how in spite of the fact that the human mind has not looked at it the human mind has it to know that it is there like that, notwithstanding that the human mind has liked what it has which has not been like that. [*The Geographical History of America*, p. 85].

This sentence is roughly one hundred words long and contains at least nine clauses. There is some repetition resembling both the style of *The Making of Americans* and the repetition of rhythmic phrases ("as one looks down on it") with words arbitrarily inserted as in *Tender Buttons*. The syntax is definitely that of *The Making of Americans*. On the whole, the vocabulary is still relatively small and simple. Some key terms, e.g., *human mind, human nature, and identity*, are repeated. Although mainly discursive, this prose work is also often interrupted by snatches of Stein's poetry, wordplay, passages that bounce along in singsong rhythm and rhyme within the line, and the occasional use of vertical structures. Alongside the extended sentences in *The Geographical History of America* are many fragments in passages that emphasize the vertical axis of language.

When a "play" is introduced into *The Geographical History of America*, as in the following passage (p. 161), one can see Stein's use of fragments, puns, vertical format, and other devices characteristic of her second "poetic" style.

Part I

I am not confused in mind because I have a human mind.

Part II

Yes which is.

Part I

Romance and money one by one.

Part II

Lolo.

Part II

Care fully for me.
As often as carefully.
Each one of these words has to do with nothing that is not
romance and money.

Part III

Romance has nothing to do with human nature.

Part III

Neither has money.

Despite the truncated sentences and wordplay, some of her statements are perfectly orthodox declarative propositions, such as the next to last sentence above, "Romance has nothing to do with human nature." Such statements are also interspersed with labels (Part II) that parody the conventional linear division of a book into chapters and parts. As in *Ida, Thee Geographical History of America* challenges the linear organization of the book by playing with the order of chapters, as on page 141 where chapter 91 immediately precedes chapter 2. Stein also comments: "There is no reason why chapters should succeed each other since nothing succeeds another, not now any more. In the old novels yes but not now any more" (p. 90); and she announces, "I could have begun with Chapter I but anybody even I have had enough of that" (p. 95).

The obscurity that remains in the grammatically orthodox sentences of *The Geographical History of America* comes partly from failure to define or describe terms adequately, as in the following passage (p. 53): "Now the relationship of human nature to the human mind is this. / Human nature does not know this. / Human nature cannot know this." The next few lines clarify, but at this point the reader is already confused:

What is it that human nature does not know. Human nature
does not know that if every one did not die there would be no
room for those who live now.

Human nature can not know this.

Now the relationship of human nature to the human mind is this.

Human nature cannot know this.

But the human mind can. It can know this.

Although one can follow the above passages, Stein is still leaping suddenly from one proposition to another without any intermediate steps, rather than following a sequence of logical development. In *The Geographical History of America*, she still uses pronouns without clearly designated antecedents, as she did in *The Making of Americans*. In the above passage, *this* refers to both what human nature can know and the relationship of human nature to the human mind, and that pronoun is used for three lines before any antecedent is mentioned at all.

Stein's philosophical musings are juxtaposed with internal rhymes that occur frequently enough to create the impression of a jingle. Passages similar to the following (p. 54) occur throughout the work: "After all would do we like to live to have lived, then if we do then everybody else has had to die and we have to cry because we too one day will have to die otherwise the others who will like to live could not come by." Stein also occasionally indulges in wordplay characteristic of *Tender Buttons*: "Money is interesting and romanticism not human nature and sadism. Make it another thing if you like sad is and sadism" (*The Geographical History of America*, p. 189). Some passages evoke a series of colorful images that Stein might classify as poetic:

> Tears of pleasure numbers have such pretty names. They have something to do with money and with trees and flat land, not with mountains or lakes, yes with blades of grass, not much a little but not much with flowers, some with birds not much with dogs.... They have nothing to do with dogs and human nature but have they anything to do with the human mind, they ought to have something to do with the human mind because they are so pretty and they can bring forth tears of pleasure [p. 115].

Discursive passages that emphasize the words as *signifieds* are juxtaposed with and interrupted by passages that emphasize poetic concerns, that is, the words as signifiers. In the latter the concern is with language as an entity in its own right, free to be used arbitrarily, not only as a carrier of meaning. And in the above passage, one can see language used both discursively and poetically.

In this combination of Stein's two obscure and most extreme styles, the distinctions blur between prose and poetry, lyricism and narrative, prosody and philosophy. In Thornton Wilder's introduction to *The Geographical History of America*, he says:

> Metaphysics is difficult enough; metaphysics by an artist is still more difficult; but metaphysics by an artist in a mood of gaity is most difficult of all. The subject matter of this book is grave, indeed.... But Miss Stein has always placed much emphasis on the spirit of play in an artist's work. The reward of difficult thinking is an inner exhilaration. Here is delight in words and in the virtuosity of using them exactly: Here is wit; here is mockery at the predecessors who approached these matters with so cumbrous a solemnity.[25]

The heaviness of philosophical prose is countered by the light and playful spirit and the "delight in words." The combination of poet and metaphysician is not altogether unheard of, as Wilder points out. "When the metaphysician is combined with the poet we get such unusual modes of expression as the myths of Plato, the prophetic books of Blake, and the difficult highly figured phrases in Keats' letters."[26]

In works like *Ida* and *The Geographical History of America*, which resist categorization as either prose or poetry, Stein seems to deny the clear separation of these two genres as self-contained and inviolate. Wendell Wilcox, in "A Note on Stein and Abstractionism," noted the blurring of Stein's own distinctions between prose and poetry and observed that in

> much of her prose you meet recurrence to and calling and re-calling upon a single person or thing, and the prose style which she invented for her use, being patterned and rhythmic not in the sense of set patterns and meters, but in the sense of the play and movement between the words themselves, has in it tone and a quality which comes close to poetry.
>
> Whitman years before had brought poetry as close to the boundary line of prose as poetry could come without becoming prose. In Stein we find that prose has been brought across the line which he left, and I rather think that in her own mind the distinction was lost, or to speak more accurately, abandoned.[27]

In both *Ida* and *The Geographical History of America*, Stein combines prose with poetry, and she returns to the temporal discontinuity of *The Making of Americans*. She is again interested in mental time, the time of telling, with its repetitions and digressions. But in these later works, digressions are likely to be poetic or even dramatic rather than just discursive prose. So use of the vertical axis of language found in Stein's second obscure style and developed further in the vertical format of her plays is combined with the essentially horizontal orientation of prose. This suggests that associative structures, the basis of poetry (those vertical systems of selection or sets of words associated in absentia by similarity), operate beneath the surface of the ongoing discursive chain of speech or stream of thought (a horizontal structure linking words in *praesentia* through combination). However logical the chain of speech, those associative structures—more or less conscious, more or less rational—are always there. By letting them surface and interrupt the linear flow of her narrative or discursive writing, Stein represents the thought process, which is in reality similarly interrupted, even though most authors censor such digressions and diversions before thought becomes speech or writing.

One can see, then, why it is so disconcerting to have a nonfiction prose work such as *The Geographical History of America* interrupted by bits of play or jungles, or to have banal rhymes interrupt a novel or even an autobiographical account of World War II, as in *Wars I Have Seen*. Stein questions not only the conventional Aristotelian divisions of the genre, but also some basic assumptions about the logical, rational, and exclusively discursive nature of conscious thought processes. She demonstrates that the underlying mental activities and operations of prose and poetry really always coexist in the writer's mind. Although the writer usually suppresses one mental process or the other, this is an artificial convention and a conscious effort that Stein apparently felt was unnecessary.

Stein's mixture of genres may seem disconcerting to many. Bridgman implies that this sort of thing occurs because of Stein's supposed inability to carry a project through:

> The actual contents of *The Geographical History of America or The Relation of Human Nature to The Human Mind* reverse the title and subtitle. Relatively little attention is devoted to the "geographical history," while the two psychological conditions of "human nature" and "human mind" preempt the book. Possessed of one of those dualities that invariably stimulated her imagination, Gertrude Stein opened with some sixty strong and coherent pages of distinctions. But then her prose grew increasingly prolix until

at last the expositional fabric unraveled altogether and concluded on a wavering note. "I am not sure that this is not the end."[28]

But this disintegration of expository prose and the mixture of prose and poetry is an outgrowth of some of Stein's major concerns. Stein's self-appointed role as innovator often led her to redefine the genre along non-Aristotelian lines of poetry and prose in "Poetry and Grammar":

> Prose is the balance the emotional balance that makes the reality of paragraphs and the unemotional balance that makes the reality of sentences and ... prose can be the essential balance that is made inside something that combines the sentence and the paragraph....
>
> Now if that is what prose is ... you can see that prose real prose really great written prose is bound to be made up more of verbs adverbs prepositions prepositional clauses and conjunctions than nouns.[29]

The follc ving is her definition of poetry:

> Poetry is I say essentially a vocabulary just as prose is essentially not.
>
> And what is the vocabulary of which poetry absolutely is. It is a vocabulary entirely based on the noun just as prose is essentially and determinately and vigorously not based on the noun.
>
> Poetry is concerned with using with abusing, with losing with wanting, with denying with avoiding with adoring with replacing the noun.[30]

Stein also tended to jettison literary labels for artistic ones—*portraits, still lifes, landscapes*. But an even more basic concept in her work remains, which precludes any definition of genre from dominating absolutely in her work. Her one enduring concern was fidelity to the present moment of creation. For her whatever was happening in the conscious mind at the moment of creation was admissible as part of the work. William Gass, in his introduction to *The Geographical History of America*, calls it "the stylized presentation of the process of meditation itself, with many critical asides."[31] Gass explains that some of the difficulties in the book stem from the fact that it portrays the mind at work:

We not only repeat when we see, stand, communicate; we repent when we think. There's no other way to hold a thought long enough to examine it except to say its words over and over, and the advance of our mind from one notion to another is similarly filled with backs and forths, erasures and crossings-out. The style of *The Geographical History of America* is often a reflection of this mental condition.[32]

As in most of Stein's work, the referent to which she is ultimately faithful is the "stream of consciousness." so she lets the reader see when the mind is distracted from discursive thought or narrative flow by bursts of lyricism, wordplay, rhyme, and poetic language. She even lets what is happening around her interrupt her train of thought. Wilder says: "One of the aspects of play that most upsets some readers is what might be called 'the irruption of the daily life' into the texture of the work.... She weaves into the book the very remarks let fall in her vicinity during the act of writing."[33] This desire to maintain the integrity of the present moment accounts for the inclusion of digressions about her work, her dogs, her plans for the next paragraph. It follows, then, that if Stein begins to rhyme words while writing a novel, as in *Ida*, the poetry produced should be included. If she is thinking in terms of drama in the midst of philosophical musings, she will include that digression in that form. (This is really not such a radical departure: the dramatic presentation of philosophical content is as old as Plato.)

In spite of critics who imply that Stein's tendency to wander from her established purpose or to abandon her plans for a work in the middle of a chapter shows confusion or lack of character, this is Stein's way of dramatizing the problem of the artist who tries to work only in the present tense, without memory. The preconceived plan of the artist has to be remembered to be carried out, and Stein rejected remembering as confusing. Perhaps it is a sign of her integrity that Stein subordinates that preconceived purpose to the continuing activity in her conscious mind and has no fear of changing her mind if her mind has indeed already changed. She even shows the reader the process of the artist's own interest in a project waning. Admittedly, to witness such a process can be intensely annoying if one has a mind used to categorization and consistency and a character that insists on carrying out projects, however foolishly conceived. But if one can put aside one's own habits of mind, it can be interesting to watch the human mind at work, which is what Stein most directly presents, not only in *The Geographical History of America*, but throughout her writing.

NOTES

1. Steiner (p. 117) notes this tendency toward increased clarity beginning in some of the portraits written between 1926–46. "Some are as difficult as the 1913 portraits, although differently so, while others are as close to straight expository prose as anything in Stein's writing (they are certainly precursors of *The Autobiography of Alice B. Toklas*)." It is interesting that Fry (p. 35) dates the return of "expressive intensity ... which had so long been suppressed or sublimated" In Picasso's work as beginning in 1925.

2. Steiner, p. 181.

3. Bridgman, p. 363.

4. Ibid., p. 206.

5. Ibid., p. 380.

6. Ibid., p. 206.

7. Ibid., p. 209.

8. Stein, "Study Nature," p. 181.

9. Gertrude Stein, *Ida: A Novel* (New York: Random House, 1941), p. 38. The date of composition supplied by Bridgman (p. 384) is 1940. Subsequent references to this work will appear within the text.

10. Bridgman, p. 205.

11. Brinnin. p. 350.

12. Rogers, p. 114, identifies the source of this phrase as Mother Goose.

13. Brinnin, p. 367.

14. Gertrude Stein, *Everybody's Autobiography* (1937; reprint, New York: Random House, 1973). p. 64.

15. Gertrude Stein, "And Now," *Vanity Fair* 19 (September 1934): 65.

16. Gertrude Stein, "Lecture Two," in *Narration* (Chicago: University of Chicago Press, 1935), p. 27.

17. Ibid., p. 28.

18. Copeland, p. 74.

19. Stein, quoted in "A Transatlantic Interview 1946," p. 19.

20. Stein, "Lecture Two," pp. 18–19.

21. Sutherland, *Gertrude Stein*, p. 154.

22. Ibid., pp. 160–66.

23. Ibid., p. 160.

24. It is interesting that *Ida* has also been seen as a female *Bildungsroman*. See, for example, Cynthia Secor, "*Ida*: Great American Novel," *Twentieth Century Literature* 24 (Spring 1979):97, for a discussion of the content of this novel as feminist.

25. Thornton Wilder, introduction to *The Geographical History of America*, p. 47.

26. Ibid., p. 45.

27. Wendell Wilcox, "A Note on Stein and Abstraction," *Poetry* 55 (February 1940):254.

28. Bridgman, p. 261.

29. Stein, "Poetry and Grammar," pp. 229–30.

30. Ibid., p. 231.

31. William H. Gass, introduction to *The Geographical History of America*, p. 23. This introduction is copyrighted 1973.

32. Ibid., p. 33.

33. Wilder, introduction to *The Geographical History of America*, p. 48.

ROBERT A. MARTIN

The Expatriate Predicament in
The Sun Also Rises

Why is *The Sun Also Rises*, which takes place in Paris and Spain, called an "American" novel, other than the obvious fact of the nationality of its author? How can it be read as "American," and what does this term mean? Can it mean anything in Hemingway's work? "America" is presented in this novel by its conspicuous absence. For how else can it be better understood than by stepping outside of it as a place—a sort of literary displacement? The idea of "American" exists through three characters who have, to varying degrees, left America behind but who do not (or cannot) entirely forsake their internalized American values: Robert Cohn, Bill Gorton, and Jake Barnes.

How they interact and clash with one another, with other Americans in Europe, and as "expatriates" and "foreigners" among the French and Spanish show the limits and the possibilities of American experience and existence. As Gerald Nelson comments in his analysis of Jake Barnes,

> All over the world after the war, one found the disenfranchised and the disenchanted, English, American, French, and German, wandering their different ways, occasionally crossing paths, sharing a common motivation—the world they wanted was a different one from the one in which they were supposed to live.... they were escaping a totally new type of oppression. They just

From *French Connections: Hemingway and Fitzgerald Abroad*, J. Gerald Kennedy and Jackson R. Bryer, ed. © 1998 by J. Gerald Kennedy and Jackson R. Bryer.

didn't like where they'd been; they could have stayed, but they
didn't want to. (30)

Among these self-induced exiles were those "who did not wish to go to
Europe as much as they wanted to get out of the United States" (Nelson 30).
Robert Cohn is in this category. He is most closely connected with America
through an account of his background there. He appears to have achieved the
American dream: prestigious Jewish family, Princeton graduate, magazine
editor and publisher, successful published writer, and European traveler. Yet
his seemingly high status is undercut with ironic and pitiful (to use Bill
Gorton's phrase) contradictions: His Jewish background gives him outsider
status. "I never met anyone of his class [at Princeton] who remembered him,"
Jake remarks (*Sun* 3). Both his wife and his lover exploit him (5), and his
success in American culture comes, Jake says, through "a very poor novel" (6)
that has been rewarded materialistically by money and women who "put
themselves out to be nice to him" (8).

Cohn's success in America has tantalized him with the sight of new
"horizons": "He's decided he hasn't lived enough. I knew it would happen
when he went to New York," Francis Clyne comments (47). Yet his horizons
are rooted in America, which provides security and identity for him: "[L]ike
many people living in Europe, he would rather have been in America," Jake
remarks (5). He wants to continue to travel, he tells Jake, because he is "sick
of Paris," and "sick of the Quarter" (12). Cohn believes he is adventurously
directing his quest not toward America but toward an exotic image of South
America. In Paris his horizon shifts upon meeting Brett, whom he looks at as
if looking at "the promised land.... he had that look of eager, deserving
expectation" (22). Brett is Cohn's Daisy Buchanan; she has become the
repository of his Romantic illusions of true love, fidelity, and chivalric honor,
which have been stimulated by his success in American culture. She provides
a reason for Cohn to assert himself at last, to defend something he believes
has value and meaning: "until he fell in love with Brett, I never heard him
make one remark that would, in any way, detach him from other people,"
Jake comments (45).

Amused, Harvey Stone refers to Cohn as "a case of arrested
development" (44). As we see later, Cohn is unable to play by the rules of the
game, to "behave himself" among Jake, Brett, Bill, and Mike. His hopeless
pursuit of Brett and his Gatsby-like naïveté do not suit him for survival in
this new world of the lost generation in Europe, especially among the Paris
expatriates. He belongs to an earlier generation that represents the ideals of
the old America, an America whose development is perhaps also "arrested"

in its need for an impossible happy ending. Jake mocks, "He was so sure that Brett loved him. He was going to stay and true love would conquer all" (199). Nelson describes American expatriates such as Cohn:

> ... they brought with them their own versions of the peculiar Puritan American vitality to a world where it just wouldn't work. They had left home and said, sincerely, that they never wanted to go back. But they missed it.... The American ego is quite different from that of any other nation. It is one American product that is not exportable. The American hopes to hell he's right and even if he isn't he will triumph. (32)

Cohn's conceit, vanity, and naïveté go hand in hand with his inability to appreciate the sense of beauty in Paris and in Spain and the passion and camaraderie of the fiesta at Pamplona. While driving through the Spanish countryside, he is asleep (93); while drinking with the Basques, Cohn has passed out and is left in the dark (158); he does not speak Spanish and, thus, makes no attempt to communicate with the Spanish people[1], at the bullfight he is "afraid [he] may be bored" (162). Cohn is a classic outsider whose horizon is limited to the position of "the Other," here labeled "American." Cohn is so entrapped within his perspective that he is unconscious of it and thus does not attempt to overcome it. When he asks Bill in Pamplona, "Where are the foreigners?" he must be told "We're the foreigners" (154). His false sense of personal and cultural "superiority" blinds Cohn to the truth of his own meager existence; while Pedro Romero actually risks his life in the bullring, Cohn is supposedly "ready to do battle for his lady love" (178). Cohn's demeaning and vainglorious American values seem weak when compared to the values of self-dependence, pride, and passion embodied by Romero: "Because he did not look up to ask if it pleased he did it all for himself inside, and it strengthened him, and yet he did it for her, too. But he did not do it for her at any loss to himself. He gained by it ... " (216).

Cohn can retaliate only physically against Romero, he cannot spiritually match or overcome his strength: "The fight with Cohn had not touched his [Romero's] spirit ... " (219). Aware of his spiritual shallowness, Brett says of Cohn in reference to their affair, "He can't believe it didn't mean anything" (181); and later, "I hate his damned suffering" (182). Cohn suffers for something that was never more than an image in his own mind, spurred by an American belief in just desserts and heroic honor: "Cohn is madly futile, trying to make dreams reality in a society where the nightmare is the accepted norm" (Nelson 42). By suffering for self-created false ideals, he indulges in an egotistical self-pity. Unlike Brett and Jake, Cohn cannot comprehend the pain of love without fulfillment, a pain that Brett and Jake refuse to indulge in (Spilka 82).

When Cohn seeks forgiveness and understanding from Jake, Jake observes that he is wearing the kind of shirt he'd worn at Princeton (194), the attachment of Cohn's identity to the idyllic past, to America, reasserts itself. Cohn's superficial and melodramatic sentimentality is not a basis for but a deterrent to the mutual friendship and love shared by Jake with Brett, with Montoya, and with Bill.

Jake's friendship with Bill Gorton, as opposed to Cohn, is built on a qualitative difference. Bill knows who he is and has real values. That he is reticent about his friendship with Jake stems from his acculturation in America. Finally, in another country, Bill is able to express his admiration and friendship for Jake: "You're a hell of a good guy, and I'm fonder of you than anybody on earth. I couldn't tell you that in New York. It'd mean I was a faggot" (116). Bill recognizes that his Americanness, however deplorable, is an inescapable part of his identity. When shaving, he says to Jake, "Go west with this face and grow up with the country."[2] He then looks in the mirror, a classic metaphor for internal reflection, and says, "My God! Isn't it an awful face? (102). The irony is that, even as the American philosophy tells him to escape, he is unable to escape the ugly mask of the "American."

Although Bill is sometimes viewed as the in-house humorist in the novel (Donaldson 27–28; Hinkle 85–86, 88–89), he also serves as an antithetical character to Robert Cohn as a writer and human being. Bill does not bait Romero, or Brett, or Cohn, or Mike. When he arrives in Paris in Chapter VIII, we learn that he has been traveling around Europe. Jake says Bill "was very cheerful and said the States were wonderful. New York was wonderful.... Bill was very happy" (*Sun* 69–70). Opposed to Robert Cohn who says he is "sick of Paris" and the Quarter and who, in fact, seems dissatisfied with everything, Bill expresses his fondness for Paris as he and Jake are crossing over to the Left Bank from the Quai de Bethune on a wooden footbridge. They stop and look "down the river at Notre Dame." "It's pretty grand,' Bill said, 'God, I love to get back'" (77). Bill had also "made a lot of money on his last book, and was going to make a lot more" (70), suggesting that Bill, unlike Robert Cohn, is a successful writer who has written more than one book and one whom Jake admires. Viewed from this perspective, Bill is everything that Cohn is not. Although Cohn has achieved some degree of literary success in America, Jake does not hesitate to tell us that Cohn has written "a very poor novel" and that his "mother had settled an allowance on him, about three hundred dollars a month" (5–6). When they meet in Paris, Brett takes an instant liking to Bill when they have a drink at the Closerie des Lilas, and tells Jake to bring Bill along with him when they meet later that night: "Mind you're at the Select around ten. Make him [Bill] come" (74–75).

In Bayonne, Jake and Bill meet Cohn at the station on their way to the fishing trip. In the cab to the hotel, Cohn tells Bill, "I'm awfully glad to meet you.... I've heard so much about you from Jake and I've read your books" (89). Cohn, in effect, acknowledges Bill's professional identity and achievement, at least suggesting that he knows who Bill is from his books. In Pamplona, Bill easily merges with the Paris crowd while Cohn antagonizes nearly everyone. Bill is a summer visitor with an expatriate's manner and attitude, which is why he fits in and Cohn does not. Bill also appreciates the ritual of the bullfights and enjoys seeing the bulls as Cohn does not.

During the days just before the fiesta begins, Jake tells us that he sometimes took a walk in the mornings and that "Sometimes Bill went along. Sometimes he wrote in his room" (150). But in the next sentence he says that Cohn "spent the mornings studying Spanish or trying to get a shave at the barbershop," thus reenforcing the notion that Bill is a serious and professional writer who works when he has an opportunity while Cohn is a dilettante and completely undisciplined in his craft. After Cohn has hit Mike and Jake and beaten Romero badly, it is only Bill who has any compassion for Cohn's bad behavior at the fiesta:

> "I feel sorry about Cohn," Bill said. "He had an awful time."
> "Oh, to hell with Cohn," I said.
> "Where do you suppose he went?"
> "Up to Paris."
> "What do you suppose he'll do?"
> "Oh, the hell with him" [Jake replies]. (222)

In Hemingway's dichotomous portrait, however, most Americans are shown traveling in groups, or herds. While Jake has considered the possibility of escaping himself, these people are unable or unwilling to escape each other. Unlike Jake and his friends, they have no desire for either the close intimacy Jake enjoys with Bill and Harris in Burguete or the temporary seclusion that Jake uses in San Sebastian as an opportunity to rejuvenate himself. Madame Lecomte's "quaint restaurant on the Paris quais" is crowded with Americans hoping to find a place "as yet untouched by Americans" (76). The train Jake and Bill take to their fishing trip is filled with Americans on a pilgrimage to Biarritz and Lourdes. As Bill says, "So, that's what they are, Pilgrims. Goddamn Puritans" (86). Unlike their predecessors, however, their promised land is not America. The Americans in Jake and Bill's compartment decide to pass themselves off as pilgrims in order to get a meal, Jake refuses to assume this identity even temporarily, despite the fact that he is Catholic. He is antagonistic to their assumed superiority and their exclusionary attitudes, which defy any religious ideal of brotherhood. As one of the tourists remarks,

> "It certainly shows you the power of the Catholic Church. It's a pity you boys ain't Catholics. You could get a meal, then, all right."
> "I am," I said. "That's what makes me so sore." (87)

At the fiesta, Hemingway similarly describes tourists as watching and observing from a distance, rather than engaging with the Spanish: "Some of the women stared at the people going by with lorgnons" (179-80), as if it were a performance put on for their benefit. Neither are they able to be emotional participants of the bullfight, like Cohn, these tourists understand neither the reality and danger of death nor the art of courage and endurance. Instead, they impose their own ignorant interpretation on the events unfolding before them: "The Biarritz crowd did not like it. They thought Romero was afraid, and that was why he gave that little sidestep each time as he transferred the bull's charge from his own body to the flannel" (217–18).

Jake is typical of a character who is defined to a large extent by loss. Yet his losses—of his "masculinity," in one sense, and of his country—have allowed him to know himself without any encumbrances and to pass through the world semidetached, without need of permanent attachments and meanings. He is an "expatriate," which means that his status in the world is defined by his oppositionary relationship to his original country. Thus, though he is external to America, he is still inescapably connected to it.[3] Jake warns Cohn: "You can't get away from yourself by moving from one place to another" (11). "Place" is differentiated and detached from "self," yet it is difficult to read this comment in the sense of radical individualism to mean that place, community, and society had no part in shaping identity. Jake's expatriate status does not so much denote a physical quest as an inward quest for self-knowledge or, more likely, simply coming to terms with the burden of oneself. In *Imagining Paris*, J. Gerald Kennedy discusses a basic "contradiction" in Jake:

> If his relation to Paris thus holds the key to book one, his
> problem goes beyond a mechanical balancing of public and
> private attitudes. His troubled relation to the city derives from his
> simultaneous association with and antagonism for the expatriate
> group, as well as his perverse identification with the
> Montparnasse quarter, which he detests. Ultimately, Jake's
> complex attachment to Paris and the "Quarter" reveals a
> contradiction within the narrator himself: his perceptions of
> locale disclose an agonizing personal conflict. (99)

The fact that Jake has left America and lives permanently in Paris
signifies his attempt to leave his American existence and social identity
behind because it interferes in some manner with his quest. Why is this
abandonment of America desirable? It is not because of a mere attraction to
its opposite, Europe, rather, he is one of those Americans "who did not wish
to go to Europe as much as they wanted to get out of the United States"
(Nelson 30).[4] America in the 1920s was not the comfortable environment for
artists and intellectuals that Paris was and is. Jake makes clear that the desire
of tourists to "see" Europe is the legacy of the old American desire to "go
West," to explore new frontiers and enact new dreams. There is perhaps
nowhere left in America "commensurate with [man's] capacity for wonder,"
as Fitzgerald wrote in *The Great Gatsby* (189), so Europe, or an image of what
Europe should be, has become the object. These American tourists do not
escape themselves (as Jake warns), but bring along their American naïveté
and wealth. These encumbrances act as a screen through which they view
what they believe is an exotic, "virgin" land, but they are guilty of self-
deception. The scene of Jake's American acquaintances meeting the
prostitute Georgette, whom Jake passes off as his fiancée, illustrates the
expatriate's tendency to see what their idealized vision presents rather than
the facts. Georgette is a novelty for them; she becomes an "Other" to the
Americans by which they conceitedly "prove" their ability to speak a
"foreign" language and their cultural appreciation:

> "Oh, Mademoiselle Hobin," Frances Clyne called, speaking
> French very rapidly and not seeming so proud and astonished as
> Mrs. Braddocks at its coming out really French. "Have you been in
> Paris long? Do you like it here? You love Paris, do you not?"
> "Who's she?" Georgette turned to me. "Do I have to talk to
> her? ... No, I don't like Paris. It's expensive and dirty." (*Sun* 18–19)[5]

The distinction between Jake and his "compatriots" "lies in the 'tourist-phonies' not having the right sense of values: not being in the know or not recognizing the importance of what they observe" (Peterson 30).

Regardless of Jake's cynicism and disregard for "Americans," his own "American-ness" is not extractable. It is only displaceable, in that it does not serve as a barrier to his enjoyment and understanding of the experiences that form his existence. But the freedom he has to move from place to place also holds him at a certain distance from the inhabitants who "belong" to the place, for he is, like Cohn, defined in relation to them as a "foreigner"—he can never really "belong" either in France or in Spain. An advantage of the displaced American expatriate-hero is his increased existential freedom: "One can be merely an observer or spectator if he doesn't like what is happening around him. 'In another country' the hero is not really involved unless he chooses to be" (Peterson 194).

The loss, or blurring, of Jake's sexual identity is signified at the same time by the loss of a national identity: "'You, a foreigner, and Englishman' (any foreigner was an Englishman) 'have given more than your life'" (*Sun* 31). Just as Jake must reconcile the loss of sex with his desire for Brett, so must he reconcile the loss of his country with his desire for fellowship. The journey that Jake is on has a far less superficial goal than the quest of his fellow Americans, though he shares the motivation: the need to go beyond the known and the well traveled, to push frontiers. In microcosm, Jake's quest parallels American history. As Philip Young has commented, "Once we were fully discovered, established, and unified we began to rediscover the world, and this adventure resulted in our defining ourselves in the light of people who did not seem, to us or to them, quite like us" (185).

The mentorlike figure of Count Mippipopoulos, who is accepted as "one of us" by Brett, states the philosophy of the expatriate: "You see, Mr. Barnes, it is because I have lived very much that now I can enjoy everything so well.... That is the secret. You must get to know the values" (*Sun* 60). The key is the plural "values"—many, not one. Unlike Cohn, Jake is not fixated on one ideal or value or philosophy. Conscious of his expatriate, or nonbelonging, status, Jake is thus able to act as a "bridge" between ever-changing places and times. He experiences many horizons and values, without ever having a permanent commitment to any: "Perhaps as you went along you did learn something. I did not care what it was all about. All I wanted to know was how to live in it. Maybe if you found out how to live in it you learned from that what it was all about" (148). This freedom is "enviable," for "he cannot be blamed much for rejecting foreign values which he dislikes; on the other hand, he is ennobled when he imposes foreign values on himself because he believes in them" (Peterson 194).

The way Jake formulates what he has experienced and how he has learned "the values," even while he is showing that the values of America have become unnecessary, shows that his American-ness provides a foundation to his "bridge." Even in Paris—"the city of light" and the center of the expatriate movement—as a way of explaining his current philosophy of living, he uses metaphors of paying and exchange that smack of American capitalism, where "value" takes on the double meaning of moral and material standards: "No idea of retribution or punishment. Just exchange of values. You gave up something and got something else.... You paid some way for everything that was any good.... Enjoying living was learning to get your money's worth and knowing when you had it.... The world was a good place to buy in" (*Sun* 148). To some extent, Jake is still following the American "myths" of escape and fulfillment. Cornellier argues: "Hemingway's expatriates in *The Sun Also Rises* each seek out ways to escape, to find a form of fulfillment the war and society has left void in them.... they find themselves victims again not only of the war but the materialistic wasteland which has emerged to replace it" (15). While he is praying in the cathedral, Jake prays not only for his friends and for the bullfighters but for money. He then becomes "ashamed, and regretted that I was such a rotten Catholic, but realized there was nothing I could do about it ... and I only wished I felt religious" (*Sun* 97). The Catholicism he learned in America has been corrupted with materialism; it cannot provide him with that spiritual sustenance he experiences through fishing, bullfighting, and companionship.

On the bus ride with the Basques, Jake and Bill almost become one of them, learning from them, sharing their wine, and talking in their language. One of the Basques identifies them as Americans and speaks in English, thus singling them out. When the Basque speaks of his trip to America, Jake and Bill ask: "Why did you leave?" and "Why did you come back here?" (107), showing their implicit belief that America is a place to go to, not away from—a destiny. As Nelson has noted, "America had always been the place people went, not the place they left, especially not dissatisfied. The whole idea behind the American Dream was that there was room to do anything you wanted anywhere you wanted" (30).[6] The Americans' questions are now more appropriately directed to themselves.

The materialism of America is shown by the Basque's comments about the wine, the sharing of which betokens the friendship among the men. When asked if they can get the wine in America, the Americans reply "There's plenty if you can pay for it" (107). Hemingway implies that

American friendship, or fellowship, is not shared but bought. The American Dream has been sold, as Bill cynically observes to Jake: "You ought to dream. All our biggest businessmen have been dreamers" (124).

Better than dreams, Hemingway suggests, is Jake's possession of *aficion*, which "it was taken for granted that an American could not have." Like Cohn's devotion to Brett, "he might simulate it or confuse it with excitement, but he could not really have it" (132). Jake's dual existence as American and aficionado gives him power, for he has knowledge that threatens the values and faith of *aficion*. Montoya seeks his advice concerning the American ambassador's invitation to Pedro Romero, for Jake is an American. Jake confirms his opinion that Americans, foreigners, are a corrupting influence. Montoya replies: "People take a boy like that. They don't know what he's worth. They don't know what he means. Any foreigner can flatter him" (172). In a foreboding line, Jake warns, "There's one American woman down here now that collects bull-fighters" (172). While Cohn and Mike are crude, envious, and self-deprecatory toward Romero, Jake is able to communicate with him on several levels, in the languages of Spanish, English, and bullfighting. His opinion is respected by Romero who, to Jake, is a model of honor, strength, and courage.

Ultimately and tragically, this ideal does not succeed in filling the vacancy of a lost American dream, for Jake's "foreignness," his inescapable American identity—personified in its worst form in Cohn—has brought violence to Romero through Brett. Jake has betrayed the "very special secret" shared between Montoya and himself by exposing it to "outsiders" who do not "understand" it (131) and who were under his protective responsibility. Romero's physical pain is paralleled in Jake by a feeling of physical dislocation inflicted by memory after Cohn knocks him out.

> Walking across the square to the hotel everything looked new and changed.... I felt as I felt once coming home from an out-of-town football game.... I walked up the street from the station in the town I had lived in all my life and it was all new.... my feet seemed to be a long way off, and everything seemed to come from a long way off, and I could hear my feet walking a great distance away. I had been kicked in the head early in the game. It was like that crossing the square. (192–93)

In the guilt of betraying and losing his ideal, Jake is sent back, in his memory, to the origin of his innocent identity in America. The pain he seeks to cure has made him an outsider. He has again been confronted by Young's paradigm of "violence, an essential experience of the frontier, and also in our time—which is a wartime—of the American in Europe. And there is nothing triumphant about the beating which innocence takes, or about what happens to it after it is beaten" (186). As a wanderer, an expatriate, he has already understood that for him America cannot provide a sense of rootedness and belonging. But Jake always has Paris, and he will return there—and that is quite possibly more than enough for any American expatriate.[7]

By using Cohn, Jake, and Bill as representative Americans in Paris during the expatriate period, Hemingway portrayed the best and worst qualities of Americans abroad. His scathing portrait of American tourists leaves little doubt about his feelings for the huge number of summer visitors who flocked into Paris from 1920 on. As the narrator, Jake tells us "how it was," and we feel pity for him and his difficult situation. But *The Sun Also Rises* is not just a sad tale of frustrated lives and bad endings. Jake is a survivor and searches for some value to give meaning to his present existence. Cohn embodies the values and attitude of a time long past. He cannot merge gracefully into the world of the expatriates because he has all the wrong assumptions about life, about love, and about himself. His is a world long gone and he will never become "one of us," as Brett says of the count (60). Bill, on the other hand, is the American who merges into a different culture with ease because he does not hold on to the romanticized past. He enjoys life and appreciates its intensity and variety. *The Sun Also Rises* remains as a historical view of the expatriates with permanent value for those of us in the contemporary world. Hemingway's Paris and Pamplona and the expatriate life are no longer possible in quite the same way that they were for his time. But *The Sun Also Rises* lives on as a reminder of the good times in the good place. "Isn't it pretty to think so?" Jake comments to Brett at the end of the book. To that slightly ambiguous remark we might respond "yes" and reflect on our own lives and loves.

NOTES

1. Reynolds, in "*The Sun Also Rises*," observes that "Most Americans spoke little or no French; there was no need, for they seldom engaged natives in any real conversation. Except to provide services, few native French or Spanish appear in *The Sun Also Rises*" (1).

2. Readers may recognize Bill's remark as based on a phrase mistakenly attributed to Horace Greeley in his *New York Tribune* editorial of about 1851 or 1852. The phrase was originally used by John Babsone Lane Soule in an article in the *Terre Haute* (IN) *Express* in 1851. As the saying became widespread and popular, Greeley reprinted Soule's article, to show that it was not original with him (cited in *Bartlett's Familiar Quotations*, 13th edition, under "Soule, John Babsonc Lane" [585a]. Indexed under "West go, young man").

3. John W. Aldridge, however, argues that the expatriates in Europe possessed "an intellectual arrogance, a disdain for bourgeois society," that caused them to become "cosmopolitan provincials abroad; they learned to judge America by essentially elitist standards; and of course, they found America provincial. But since they were themselves provincial, their attitudes retained a dimension of ambivalence that helped to humanize their satire and finally made it seem an expression more of regret than of contempt" (116).

4. For an extensive analysis and reliable background of the expatriate milieu, see Kennedy, Reynolds, *Hemingway*, and Cowley. The collection *In Transition; A Paris Anthology* contains a special section entitled "Why do Americans live in Europe?" with responses to a survey by, among others, Robert McAlmon, Kay Boyle, Gertrude Stein, and Kathleen Cannell (217–27).

5. See Reynolds, *"The Sun Also Rises"* 75–76, on Georgette's "sickness" and the prostitute world of Paris in the 1920s.

6. For a more detailed commentary, see Cowley 36–47.

7. Although not cited herein, I am greatly indebted to the following for enlarging my understanding of the expatriate period: Roger Asselineau, Professor Emeritus of American Literature at the Sorbonne, for his work and for many conversations in the United States and France over many years; Sheri Benstock, *Women of the Left Bank: Paris, 1900–1940* (Austin: U of Texas P, 1986); Humphrey Carpenter, *Geniuses Together: American Writers in Paris in the 1920s* (Boston: Houghton Mifflin, 1988); Noel Riley Fitch, *Sylvia Beach and the Lost Generation* (New York: Norton, 1983), Jean Méral, *Paris in American Literature* (Chapel Hill: U of North Carolina P, 1989); Brian N. Morton, *Americans in Paris* (New York: Morrow, 1986); and George Wickes, *Americans in Paris* (Garden City, NY: Doubleday, 1969).

WORKS CITED

Aldridge, John W. "Afterthoughts on the Twenties and *The Sun Also Rises*." *New Essays on "The Sun Also Rises."* Ed. Linda Wagner-Martin. New York: Cambridge UP, 1987. 109–29.

Cornellier, Thomas. "The Myth of Escape and Fulfillment in *The Sun Also Rises* and *The Great Gatsby*." *Society for the Study of Midwestern Literature Newsletter* 15.1 (1985): 15–21.

Cowley, Malcolm. *Exile's Return*. 1951. New York: Penguin, 1979.

Donaldson, Scott. "Humor in *The Sun Also Rises*." *New Essays on "The Sun Also Rises."* Ed. Linda Wagner-Martin. New York: Cambridge UP, 1987. 19–41.

Fitzgerald, F. Scott. *The Great Gatsby*. 1925. The Authorized Text. Ed. Matthew J. Bruccoli. New York: Scribners, 1992.

Hemingway, Ernest. *The Sun Also Rises*. 1926. New York: Scribners, 1970.

Hinkle, James. "What's Funny in *The Sun Also Rises*." *Ernest Hemingway: Six Decades of Criticism*. Ed. Linda W. Wagner. East Lansing: Michigan State UP, 1987. 77–92.

In Transition: A Paris Anthology. Introduction by Noel Riley Fitch. New York: Doubleday (Anchor Books), 1990.

Kennedy, J. Gerald. *Imagining Paris: Exile, Writing, and American Identity*. New Haven, CT: Yale UP, 1993.

Nelson, Gerald. *Ten Versions of America*. New York: Knopf, 1972.

Peterson, Richard K. *Direct and Oblique*. Paris: Mouton, 1969.

Reynolds, Michael. *Hemingway: The Paris Years*. Cambridge, MA: Blackwell, 1989.

———. *"The Sun Also Rises": A Novel of the Twenties*. Boston: G.K. Hall, 1988.

Spilka, Mark. "The Death of Love in *The Sun Also Rises*." *Hemingway and His Critics*. Ed. Carlos Baker. New York: Hill and Wang, 1961. 80–92.

Young, Philip. "Ernest Hemingway." *Seven Modern American Novelists*. Ed. William Van O'Connor. Minneapolis: U of Minnesota P, 1964. 153–88.

D.G. KEHL

Writing the Long Desire:
The Function of *Sehnsucht* in *The Great Gatsby* and *Look Homeward, Angel*

A pervasive quality of modern American literature, but one which has received hardly a critical nod, is longing, homesickness, nostalgia. "Our literature is stamped with a quality of longing and unrest," Carson McCullers wrote in 1940,[1] referring specifically to Thomas Wolfe as being "maddened by unfocused longing."[2] More than simple longing or nostalgia, however, and lacking a sufficiently expressive English term, this quality can best be characterized by the German term *Sehnsucht* (a compound of the verb *sehnen*, "to long for," and the noun *sucht*, "addiction"), an intense addiction of and to longing. Deeply rooted in German Romanticism (note, for example, Goethe's "*Selige Sehnsucht*," Schiller's "*Sehnsucht*," Eichendorff's "*Sehnsucht*," and Novalis' *Hymns to the Night*), it cuts across literary movements, geographical regions, ethnicity, and gender. *Sehnsucht* plays a major role in modern American fiction, ranging from the work of Kate Chopin, at the cusp of the twentieth century, to that of contemporary writers, such as Marge Piercy, Gail Godwin, Anne Tyler, and Ann Beattie, and from Theodore Dreiser and Sinclair Lewis to Vladimir Nabokov, Walker Percy, and Saul Bellow.[3] One of few critics to discuss nostalgia, Wright Morris, in his essay on Scott Fitzgerald, entitled "The Function of Nostalgia," concludes that the "subject" of Wolfe, Hemingway, and Faulkner, however diverse their backgrounds and styles, is nostalgia, but that it was left to Fitzgerald to carry the subject to its logical conclusion and

From the *Journal of Modern Literature*, vol. 24, no. 2 (winter 2000/2001), pp. 309–319. © 2001 by Indiana University Press.

become "the aesthete of nostalgia."[4] Further, in his essay on Wolfe, entitled "the Function of Appetite," Morris concludes, without qualification, and erroneously, I believe, that "an insatiable hunger, like an insatiable desire, is not the sign of life, but of impotence,"[5] "impotence [being], indeed, ... part of the romantic agony."[6] What has not been recognized is that neither in the case of Fitzgerald nor in the case of Wolfe is this simply nostalgia, desire, or hunger but something much deeper and more significant: *Sehnsucht.*

Some have considered this quality to be endemic in American culture. This "curious emotion," McCullers writes, "[is w]ith Americans ... a national trait, as native to us as the roller coaster or the jukebox.... It is no simple longing for the home town or the country of our birth.... As often as not, we are homesick most for the places we have never known." McCullers further ties homesickness to loneliness as a peculiarly American quality: "All men are lonely. But sometimes it seems to me that we Americans are the loneliest of all. Our hunger for foreign places and new ways has been with us almost like a national disease."[7]

Nine years later, in her essay "Loneliness ... An American Malady," McCullers further argues that "the aloneness of many Americans who live in cities is an involuntary and fearful thing. It has been said that loneliness is the great American malady."[8] Wolfe himself makes much the same comment when, in a 1930 letter to Maxwell Perkins, he reports on his first visit with Fitzgerald in Paris: "I said we were a homesick people, and belong to the earth and land we came from...."[9]

Perhaps a variety of factors in confluence have made *Sehnsucht* seem most pronounced in American culture. One such factor is the pluralism and cultural diversity created by immigration, often resulting in emotional incertitude, isolation, and homesickness for the old country. "The European, secure in his family ties and rigid class loyalties," McCullers argues, "knows little of the moral loneliness that is native to us Americans."[10] This loneliness, she suggested, is essentially "a quest for identity,"[11] that is, a consciousness of self keenly and realistically aware of the relation between oneself and one's environment. Further, the dominant American individualism often tends to create the isolation and loneliness that foster *Sehnsucht.* American restlessness and nervous energy, leading to mobility and uprootedness, if not anomie, perhaps do so as well. It has often been said that Americans, perhaps more than other nationalities, have always been dissatisfied, unhappy with who they are. Indeed, the American Dream's promise of freedom, of limitless potentiality, of the attainability of supereminent expectations—"I can achieve what I wish, possess what I want, be what I will"—"as surely played a major role in prompting the voice which

Bellow's Eugene Henderson hears every afternoon: "*I want, I want, I want!*"[12] An increasingly more materialistic society proffered, like an electric carrot, ever more "things" for Americans to (think they) want, as in the case of Dreiser's Sister Carrie, who "longed and longed and longed. It was now for the old cottage room in Columbia City, now the mansion upon the Shore Drive, now the fine dress of some lady, now the elegance of some scene."[13]

Although especially prominent in modern American culture and literature, *Sehnsucht* is surely universal, common to all humankind. In "The Message in the Bottle," Walker Percy depicts every person as a castaway on an island, longing and searching for messages in bottles washed up by the waves. Something is wrong; something is missing, but he does not know what. "He might say that he was homesick except that the island is his home and he has spent his life making himself at home there. He knows only that his sickness cannot be cured by island knowledge or by island news."[14] This yearning and the malaise which often accompanies it, well dramatized by such characters as Binx Bowling in Percy's *The Moviegoer*, may be universal, but Percy also suggests that perhaps they are more evidenced not only at certain times (Sunday afternoons in Binx' case) but also in certain places: America, the South, the Gulf Coast.

Fitzgerald and Wolfe, perhaps more than any other American Modernist writers, seem to share, in their lives and in their fiction, a wistful longing to return in thought, if not in fact, to a former time or place, a pervasive yearning for something long ago and far away,[15] which is, of course, one denotation of *nostalgia* (from the Greek *nostos*, "return home," plus *algos*, "pain"), originally a medical term coined in 1688 by the Swiss scholar, J. Hofer, to translate the German *heimweh*, "homesickness."[16] Although Fitzgerald reportedly denied Wolfe's assessment of their Paris visit, in another letter to Maxwell Perkins, Fitzgerald compares himself to Wolfe and Hemingway for what seem on the surface to be nostalgic similarities: "What family resemblance there is between we three [sic] as writers is the attempt that crops up in our fiction from time to time to recapture the exact feel of a moment in time and space ... , an attempt at a mature memory of a deep experience."[17] The attempt "to recapture the exact feel of a moment in time and space," which Fitzgerald identifies as especially Wordsworthian, and the Proustian "attempt at a mature memory of a deep experience," do in fact place Fitzgerald and Wolfe in a singular brotherhood, not under the aegis of Sisyphus, the archetypal absurdist, but more accurately under that of a frustrated Nestor (literally "one who returns"), the only survivor when Hercules killed his twelve brothers, who returned to Troy as wise old counselor relating sagacious tales of his adventures.

Taken out of context, many of Fitzgerald's Nestor–statements might easily be attributed to Wolfe, as in the conclusion of "My Lost City": "All is lost save memory ... For the moment I can only cry out that I have lost my splendid mirage. Come back, come back, O glittering and white!"[18] echoing Wolfe's epigraph: "O lost, and by the wind grieved, ghost, come back again." Or note this statement from "Pasting It Together," which could have been written by Wolfe and spoken by Eugene: "My own happiness in the past often approached such an ecstasy that I could not share it even with the person dearest to me but had to walk it away in quiet streets and lanes with only fragments of it to distil into little lines in books...."[19] Similarly, note the poignancy of the assertion in "'Show Mr. and Mrs. F. to Number—'" "... [I]t is sadder to find the past again and find it inadequate to the present than it is to have it elude you and remain forever a harmonious conception of memory."[20] The fiction of both writers would seem to indicate that perhaps each possibility is equally sad. Jay Gatsby does find fragments of the past, but, like Eugene, he finds it inadequate because it is changed, lost, impossible to be relived; further, the past eludes both characters and, merged with the green-lit orgastic future, it yields no stone upon the hills, no leaf in the forest, no open door in East Egg.

Fitzgerald devotes an entire page in his *Notebooks* to what he called "Nostalgia or the Flight of the Heart," consisting of a list of some forty places or locations that apparently evoked nostalgia for him. Wolfe and Eugene would have especially appreciated the entry, "Old Boarding house or summer hotel."[21] In 1931, Fitzgerald openly declared that he already looked back to the Jazz Age with nostalgia, lamenting that when he left Princeton on a March afternoon, he "lost every single thing [he] wanted";[22] he regretted that he had "lost somewhere, and lost forever" all the symbols of his city.[23]

But even then, when the city and its symbols seemed irrevocably lost, he saw, for one fleeting moment, its future as it lay "wrapped cool in its mystery and promise."[24] Although he assuredly realized that the past was dead—or had "ceased to exist," it was not necessarily this awareness that robbed the present of its future. A superficial, reactionary nostalgia, mired in a dead past, may, in fact, be a "snare and delusion" or "a limbo land leading nowhere," but the wistful longing which pervades *The Great Gatsby* and *Look Homeward, Angel*, respectively, is neither superficial nor reactionary, and is not, in fact, simply nostalgia.[25] To insist that nostalgia is all there is in Fitzgerald and Wolfe is to miss a major subtext in each novel.[26]

Gatsby's frustrated longing to "repeat the past,"[27] his "incorruptible dream" (162) to reclaim Daisy, and Eugene's "deep desire burn[ing] inextinguishably,"[28] his "vast, strange hunger for life," are no mere velleities, are more than simple yens. Evidence that the pervasive yearning in the two novels is, in fact, *Sehnsucht*—an addiction of longing and to longing—is substantial. For example; both novels provide considerable linguistic evidence of *Sehnsucht* despite the authors' difference of opinion about the so—called "novel of selected incidents" and the "leaver–outer" vs. "putter–inner" philosophies as expressed in their famous exchange of letters in 1937. The most pertinent, recurring term in Wolfe's novel is "lost," appearing about one hundred sixty times—not surprising in view of the original title *O Lost: A Story of the Buried Life.*[29] Irrevocably lost and lamented are ghosts of the departed or the "dead lost faces" as well as one's own lost ghost, the "great lost legion of himself" (*Angel*, p. 559), the "faun lost in the thickets" of self (p. 562), "the lost and secret adyts[30] of childhood" (p. 496); lost forever are the years, the farer's way, the world, land, seas, cities, home, freedom, sensuous delight or "dead lusts," love, joy, hope. But most significantly, it is the loss of things indefinable, as Eugene tells Ben's ghost: "There is something I have lost and have forgotten. I can't remember, Ben" (p. 559).

Nick Carraway experiences a similar frustration over indefinable and irretrievable loss when, after Gatsby has talked "a lot about the past ... [as if] he wanted to recover something" (*Gatsby* p. 117), Nick is "reminded of something—an elusive rhythm, a fragment of lost words, that [he] had heard somewhere a long time ago," but the words do not come, and "what [he] had almost remembered was uncommunicable forever" (p. 118), a loss reminiscent of the "incommunicable past" of Jim Burden in Cather's *My Antonia*.[31] "'Can't repeat the past?'" Gatsby had just asked Nick incredulously. In *Trimalchio*, the earlier version of the novel, Fitzgerald had elucidated both Gatsby's insistence that Daisy inform Tom that she never loved him and, at least in part, his deep sense of loss and longing. Nick remarks that "he seemed to feel that Daisy should make some sort of atonement that would give her love the value that it had before.... [H]e wanted this to have an element of fate about it, of inevitability—the resumption of an interrupted dance. And first Daisy must purify herself by a renunciation of the years between."[32]

Both writers indicate that not only can the past not be repeated or relived, it cannot essentially be communicated, for according to Wolfe, there are not only "fragments of lost epics upon a broken shard of Gnossic pottery" (*Angel*, p. 560) but also "lost meaning" (p. 544) and "lost communications of eternity" (p. 74). During the confrontation between Gatsby and Tom Buchanan at the hotel near Central Park, Nick, in another passage added to the revisions in the galley proofs, describes "the dead dream" [fighting] on as the afternoon slipped away" and Daisy's "lost voice across the room" (*Gatsby*, p. 142). Later, he describes in flashback Gatsby's "miserable but irresistible journey" (p. 160) to Louisville after Tom and Daisy's wedding, much like Eugene's journey to Norfolk to seek out the married Laura James. As Gatsby's train pulled away, " ... [h]e stretched out his hand desperately as if to snatch only a wisp of air, to save a fragment of the spot that she had made lovely for him..., [but] he knew that he had lost that part of it, the freshest and the best, forever" (160–61).[33]

Fitzgerald's musings about the possible relation of art to loss are suggested by a Notebook entry in which he describes a "story" as "a hole or bag in which someone finds all the things he's ever lost."[34] Southern literature, almost from its inception, has been preoccupied with loss. As a recent example, Maggie Moran, in Anne Tyler's *Breathing Lessons*, contemplates an old man in her nursing home who believes that in heaven "all he had lost in his lifetime would be given back to him ... in a gunnysack"—not just such intangibles as "youthful energy ... or that ability young people have to get swept away and impassioned" but concrete objects such as "the little red sweater his mother had knit him just before she died, that he had left on a bus in fourth grade and missed with all his heart ever since. The special pocketknife his older brother had flung into a cornfield out of spite. The diamond ring his first sweetheart had failed to return to him when she broke off their engagement and ran away with the minister's son."[35] For Gatsby and Eugene, however, there is no expectation of celestial recompence of lost objects and desires. Eugene, like his father, W.O. Gant, must seek "the lost lane–end into heaven" (p. 7) and the more secular "sad comfort of unfulfilled Arcadias" (301), whereas Gatsby seeks a Platonic kingdom of heaven and a Jacob's–ladder mounting to "a secret place above the trees" (p. 117). As Gatsby "found that he had committed himself to the following of a grail" (p. 156), so, too, "young Galahad–Eugene ... had gone a-Grailing" (p. 316).

Other key terms suggesting *Sehnsucht* in *Look Homeward, Angel*, in descending order of recurrence, are: *hunger/hungry, desire, stranger/strange/strangeness, loneliness/lonely, mystery/mysteriousness, passion/passionate, alone, departure/ departing, lust, sad/sadness, longing/yearning/craving, exile, home,* and *wistful.* Those in *The Great Gatsby* are: *sad/saddening, last, mystery, stranger/strange, alone and solitary, desire/desired, repeat/recover, and loneliness.* Significantly, both protagonists are depicted as strangers in a strange land, a phrase Wolfe apparently borrowed from Exodus 2:22, perhaps by way of Sophocles' *Oedipus at Colonus* ("stranger in a strange country"). But the alien plight of the yearning soul is perhaps best described by another Southern writer, Walker Percy: he is "a stranger, a castaway, who despite a lifetime of striving to be at home on the island is as homeless now as he was the first day he found himself cast up on the beach."[36]

It is important to note that *Sehnsucht* is distinguished from just any longing by at least four distinct characteristics. First, *Sehnsucht* is characterized by its great intensity, a word which Nick uses several times to describe Gatsby's yearning. "... [H]e was consumed with wonder at [Daisy's] presence," he says when Gatsby shows Daisy his mansion; "he had been full of the idea so long, dreamed it right through to the end, waited with his teeth set, so to speak, at an inconceivable pitch of intensity" (p. 97). Later, he sees the two as being "possessed by intense life" (p. 102), just as Daisy's house had possessed "an air of breathless intensity" (p. 155) for Gatsby simply because Daisy lived there. Further evidence of Fitzgerald's wish to stress Gatsby's intensity of longing for Daisy are various additions he made to the ur–novel *Trimalchio*. One such passage appears in Chapter VIII, in which Nick suspects "some intensity in [Gatsby's] conception of the affair that couldn't be measured" (*Gatsby*, p. 160).[37] Gatsby had "an extraordinary gift for hope," "a romantic readiness such as [Nick had] never found in any other person and which [he thought] it [was] unlikely [he would] ever find again," "a heightened sensitivity to the promises of life" (*Gatsby*, p. 6) and a rare "capacity for wonder" (p. 189).

Like Gatsby, Eugene is consumed by "his young goat–cry of desire and hunger" (526), devoured by "a vast, strange hunger for life" (p. 537). His "lonely ache" (p. 62) has all the intensity of *Sehnsucht*, as suggested, for example, by Wolfe's reference, in the extensively intertextual Chapter 24, to Goethe's *Wilhelm Meister's Apprenticeship*. Wilhelm, recovering from his wounds, lapses into "a state of dreamy longing"[38] for the delightful countess and noble Amazon, as Mignon and the Harper sing a free duet expressing his very feeling: "*Nur wer die Sehnsucht kennt, weiss was Ich leide*" (*Angel*, p. 311)— "Only the one who yearns,/ Knows what I suffer!" or "Only they know my pain/ Who know my yearning!"[39] Wolfe, fond as he was of the German language and culture, was obviously well–acquainted with the German term and its referent. In a real sense, this is the subtext message of his novel: Only the reader who knows *Sehnsucht*—and who has not experienced it?—will understand what I and my characters—Americans, indeed all humans—suffer from irrevocable loss.

A second distinctive characteristic of *Sehnsucht* is its inexplicability, its mysterious object. As with *angst*, "there is a peculiar mystery about the object of this Desire," and "every one of [the] supposed *objects* for the Desire is inadequate to it."[40] Some of the supposed "objects" and attempted means of fulfillment are: the "faroff hillside" of childhood and its idealized associations, past events, distant places, mystery and beauty, nature, exotic travels and adventure, romantic tales, a craving for knowledge, and, of course, "the perfect beloved." Eugene quests for all of these, seeking fulfillment of his "undefinable desire" (p. 87), whereas Gatsby concentrates primarily on "the perfect beloved" and the past which she had so enchanted. But, like Nabokov's Lolita, Humbert's idealized recreation of Dolores Haze, the gum–chewing, bubble–blowing adolescent with unkempt armpits, Daisy is the epitome of Gatsby's deeper yearning for that which he himself cannot identify. But Nick, just after Gatsby's first reunion with Daisy, ponders his impression that "a faint doubt had occurred to [Gatsby] as to the quality of his present happiness" (p. 101), highlighting Fitzgerald's subsequent statement in *The Crack-Up* : "... The natural state of the sentient adult is a qualified unhappiness ... [and] the desire to be finer in grain than you are ... only adds to this unhappiness in the end—that end that comes to our youth and hope."[41] The "qualified unhappiness" seems to come, in large part, from yearning intensely for something both unidentifiable and elusive.[42]

That Daisy is essentially a representation of Gatsby's deeper yearnings is suggested in Nick's further musings: "There must have been moments even that afternoon when Daisy tumbled short of his dreams—not through her own fault but because of the colossal vitality of his illusion. It had gone beyond her, beyond everything" (p. 101). Perhaps, as Owen Barfield had said of C.S. Lewis' use of *Sehnsucht*, "true longing is never fulfilled by anything in the earthly life, but ... it's always a disguised longing for God."[43] Indeed, as Lewis writes: "It appeared to me ... that if a man dilgently followed this desire, pursuing the false objects until their falsity appeared and then resolutely abandoning them, he must come out at last into the clear knowledge that the human soul was made to enjoy some object that is never fully given—nay, cannot even be imagined as given—in our present mode of subjective and spatio–temporal experience."[44] Conversely, the *persona* of Schiller's poem "*Sehnsucht*" notes that "Gods ne'er lend a helping hand" and concludes that it is "by magic alone/ Thou canst reach the magic land!"[45]

A third characteristic of *Sehnsucht* is the irony of an unfulfilled longing which, as Barfield notes, "is itself its own fulfillment."[46] "There is no cnd to hunger" (p. 561), Ben's ghost tells Eugene, for, as Eugene experienced earlier in Norfolk, "there was a hunger and thirst in him that could not be fed" (p. 463). Earlier, for Eugene, as a new student at the university in Pulpit Hill, "the old hunger returned—the terrible and obscure hunger that haunts and hurts Americans, and that makes us exiles at home and strangers wherever we go" (p. 382). Perhaps neither Eugene nor Gatsby takes what Barfield has called "the further step"—that is, "discovering for oneself that the very presence of the desire is its own fulfillment; that 'what we really wanted' all the time was, not any one of the many successive objects to which the desire deludes us by appearing to point, but the desire itself, or an essential quality in it,"[47] although each seems to take a preliminary step of divestiture in at least coming to realize that the objects of their quest are powerless to satisfy their wistful yearnings.

A fourth characteristic that distinguishes *Sehnsucht* from other longings is its oxymoronic bittersweetness: "Though the sense of want is acute and even painful, yet the mere wanting is felt to be somehow a delight. Other desires are felt as pleasures only if satisfaction is expected in the near future: hunger is pleasant only while we know (or believe) that we are going to eat. But this desire, even when there is no hope of possible satisfaction, continues to be prized, and even to be preferred to anything else in the world, by those who have once felt it. This hunger is better than any other fullness; this poverty better than all other wealth."[48] Accordingly, both novels seem at once to evoke the pleasantry of the "magnificent summer night" in Eichendorff's poem "*Sehnsucht*"[49] and to dramatize the ambivalence of the *persona* in Goethe's poem "*Sehnsucht*": "What stirs in my heart so?/ What lures me from home?/ What forces me outwards,/ And onwards to roam?"[50] Eugene's "ecstasy of a thousand unspoken desires" is characterized by oxymoronic feelings of "delightful loneliness" and "delicious sadness" (p. 542), whereas Gatsby, having "paid a high price for living too long with a single dream," must have realized the paradox of "what a grotesque thing a rose is and how raw the sunlight was upon the scarcely created grass" (p. 169).

Sehnsucht, then, performs, in varying degrees, at least three significant functions in the two novels. First, it adds greater breadth by moving the underlying motif of wistful yearning beyond stereotype to archetype, performing what Ralph Ellison identified as one of the major challenges of the writer, that is, to "redeem" the stereotypes, to "reveal the archetypical truth hidden within the stereotype."[51] Dead–end nostalgia is transformed into what Hermann Hesse called "humanity's innate, unavoidable longing,"[52] part of the "mystery" of the human condition (a term which both Wolfe and Fitzgerald use extensively). The archetype of *Sehnsucht* in the two novels is corroborated further by particular sensory images—for example, the auditory (the melancholy train whistles—fifteen just in *Look Homeward, Angel*—and the music motif in both novels), the visual (the green light in one case, the misty mountains rimming Altamont in the other), and the olfactory (for example, Altamont's seasonal "nostalgic odors," *Angel*, p. 62).

A second function is to provide greater depth of meaning, what Fitzgerald himself called "a mature memory of a deep experience."[53] One might argue that the yearning hungers of both Eugene and Gatsby haunt them like the numinous Hound of Heaven in Francis Thompson's 1891 poem, transforming them into pursued–pursuers. "I fled Him, down the nights and down the days," the persona says; "I fled Him, down the arches of the years;/ I fled Him, down the labyrinthine ways/ Of my own mind," and, when caught, he hears the Voice say: "'Ah fondest, blindest, weakest,/ I am He whom thou seekest! / Thou dravest love from thee, who dravest Me.'"

In her essay on Dreiser's *Sister Carrie*, Blanche Gelfant asks, "What more can Carrie want?"[54] a question one could ask as well of Eugene and Jay, whose desires are also "illimitable" but whose "objects of desire are different." But perhaps the something more that Carrie wants is the same as what Eugene and Jay want: numinous transcendence and wholeness (in the dual sense of completeness and holiness, *whole* and *holy* being cognates), or "longing for Paradise" as "an image of Unitary Reality," to use Mario Jacoby's phrase.[55] The point that Walter Benn Michaels makes in his perceptive discussion of Carrie applies as well to Eugene and Jay: Dreiser "identifies [character] with desire, an involvement with the world so central to one's sense of self that the distinction between what one is and what one wants tends to disappear."[56]

A third function of *Sehnsucht* in the two novels is to provide greater scope, becoming an aesthetic means of escape from the labyrinth and its youth–consuming Minotaur. Or, to change the metaphor to Fitzgerald's own, art serves as the bag in which one recovers objects lost. As Lawrence Lerner notes, "Longing is what makes art possible...."[57] Accordingly, Dreiser's Robert Ames, in the original, uncut edition, instructs Carrie that the reason "we have great musicians, great painters, great writers, and actors" is that "they have the ability to express the world's sorrows and longings...."[58] *Sehnsucht* is thus at once both cause and effect of art, both provocateur and *raison d'etre*. "The task of the artist," Hermann Hesse said, "is ... above all to awaken Sehnsucht."[59] The artist, driven by his/her own yearnings, expresses the world's yearnings and awakens still others. The insatiable hunger, the *Sehnsucht*, of Gatsby and Gant is not a sign of impotence, although each is impotent to fulfill it, but rather a sign of life and creativity. *Sehnsucht* is central to all creativity, as expressed in the poem "*Sehnsucht*," by Anna Wickham, friend of D.H. Lawrence, Dylan Thomas, and Malcolm Lowry:

Because of the body's hunger are we born
And by continuing hunger are we fed;

Because of hunger is our work well done,
As so are songs well sung, and things well said.
        Desire and longing are the whips of God.
God save us all from death when we are fed.[60]

Because of hunger—that of Wolfe and Fitzgerald themselves as well as that of their characters and their readers, whether American or any other nationality—are these works well done, these songs well sung, these comments well said.

NOTES

1. Carson McCullers, *The Mortgaged Heart*, ed. Margarita G. Smith, (Bantam, 1972), p. 235.

2. McCullers, p. 239.

3. Arguably, other major American writers might be included (among them Hemingway, whose ritualistic depiction of eating and drinking often suggests a hunger and thirst for more than mere food and spirits), but the criteria must be the four distinguishing characteristics of *Sehnsucht* to be discussed below, along with ample linguistic reference to longing or synonymous expressions.

4. Wright Morris, *The Territory Ahead: Critical Interpretations in American Literature*, (Atheneum, 1963). pp. 157, 160.
D.G. Kehl, "Writing the Long Desire: The Function of *Sehnsucht* in *The Great Gatsby* and *Look Homeward, Angel*," *Journal of Modern Literature*, XXIV, 2 (Winter, 2000–20001), pp. 309–319. ©Indiana University Press, 2001.

5. Note George Santayana's "Homesickness for the World," in which Avicenna tells the Stranger: "... [T]o live in time, to dwell in a body, to thirst, to love, and to grieve are forms of impotence and self-deception. If we knew all we could not live." But note also his subsequent conclusion: "But it is precisely this cajolery, this vivid and terrible blindness of life, which Allah cannot share, in which his creatures shine" (*Dialogues in Limbo*, University of Michigan Press, 1957, p. 221).

6. Morris, p. 155.

7. McCullers, p. 235.

8. McCullers, p. 293.

9. Elizabeth Nowell, ed. *The Letters of Thomas Wolfe* (Charles Scribner's Sons, 1956), pp. 237–238. Note also *My Other Loneliness: Letters of Thomas Wolfe and Aline Bernstein*, ed. Suzanne Stutman (University of North Carolina Press, 1983).

10. McCullers, p. 294.

11. McCullers, p. 293.

12. Saul Bellow, *Henderson the Rain King* (Fawcett Crest, 1965), p. 24.

13. Theodore Dreiser, *Sister Carrie* (Bantam, 1982), p. 93.

14. Walker Percy, *The Message in the Bottle* (Farrar, Straus and Giroux, 1976), p. 143.

15. Note Frederick Buechner's comments in *The Longing for Home: Recollections and Reflections*. "The word *longing* comes from the same root word *long* in the sense of length in either time or space and also the word *belong*, so that in its full richness to *long* suggests

to yearn for a long time for something that is a long way off and something that we feel we belong to and that belongs to us" (HarperCollins, 1996, pp. 18–19)

16. The unique term *Sehnsucht* and its archetypal concept have been sparingly treated in English and not at all in relation to American literature. *Sehnsucht* is, of course, a unifying motif in the works of C.S. Lewis, who sometimes translated the term as "longing" and "joy." For a psychological treatment, see Mario Jacoby's *Longing for Paradise: Psychological Perspectives on an Archetype*. transl. Myron B. Gubitz, Sigo Press, 1985).

17. John Kuehl and Jackson R. Bryer. eds. *Dear Scott/Dear Max: The Fitzgerald-Perkins Correspondence* (Charles Scribner's Sons, 1971), pp. 203–04.

18. F. Scott Fitzgerald, *The Crack-Up*, ed. Edmund Wilson (New Directions, 1956), p. 33.

19. Fitzgerald, *The Crack-Up*, p. 84.

20. Fitzgerald, *The Crack-Up*, p. 50.

21. Fitzgerald, *The Notebooks of F. Scott Fitzgerald*, ed. Matthew J. Bruccoli (Harcourt Brace Jovanovich, 1980), p. 241.

22. Fitzgerald, "Handle with Care," *The Crack-Up*, p. 76.

23. Fitzgerald, "My Lost City," *The Crack-Up*, p. 23.

24. Fitzgerald, *The Crack-Up*, p. 31.

25. For further development of this argument, see the two essays by Wright Morris mentioned above.

26. For a helpful discussion of nostalgia in pastoral poetry from Virgil, Spenser, and Milton to Baudelaire, Proust, and Dylan Thomas, see Laurence Lerner's *The Uses of Nostalgia: Studies in Pastoral Poetry* (London: Chatto and Windus, 1972).

27. F. Scott Fitzgerald, *The Great Gatsby* (Simon and Schuster, 1995), p. 116. Subsequent quotations from the novel are from this edition and are noted parenthetically as *Gatsby*.

28. Thomas Wolfe, *Look Homeward, Angel* (Macmillan Collier, 1957), p. 134. Subsequent quotations from the novel are from this edition and are noted parenthetically as *Angel*.

29. See the original, uncut version published on the centenary of Wolfe's birth, Arlyn and Matthew J. Bruccoli, eds. (University of South Carolina Press. 2000).

30. Wolfe's choice of the term is significant (although the plural form of *adytum* is *adyta*). Dating from the seventeenth century, an adytum is literally a place not to be entered, a sacred inner shrine which the public is forbidden to enter. In Wolfe's use of the term, childhood is that private sanctum, forbidden now, lost even to the one who knew it in earlier days.

31. Willa Cather, *My Antonia* (Houghton Mifflin, 1977), p. 238.

32. F. Scott Fitzgerald, *Trimalchio: An Early Version of The Great Gatsby*, ed. James L.W. West III (Cambridge University Press, 2000), p. 90.

33 At the conclusion of Chapter VI of *Trimalchio*, when one of Gatsby's parties is ending, it is Daisy who provides the ritualistic tableau in stretching our her hand toward Gatsby: "As the car moved off a flush of apprehension made her stretch out her hand, trying to touch his once more" (87). In the revision, Fitzgerald played down Daisy's longing and emphasized Gatsby's.

34. Fitzgerald, *Notebooks*, p. 300.

35. Anne Tyler, *Breathing Lessons* (Alfred A. Knopf, 1988). p. 316.

36. Walker Percy. *The Message in the Bottle*, p. 143.

37. See James L.W. West III's all–too–brief Introduction to *Trimalchio* and his observation that "in a novel as intricately patterned and skillfully written as this one, all of these differences matter," p. xix.

38. Johann Wolfgang von Goethe, *Wilhelm Meister's Apprenticeship*, ed. and trans. by Eric A. Blackall and Victor Lange (Princeton University Press, 1995), p. 142.

39. Goethe, pp. 376, 142.

40. C.S. Lewis. *The Pilgrim's Regress* (Bantam, 1981), pp. x–xi.

41. Fitzgerald, *The Crack-Up* (New Directions, 1956), p. 84.

42. Santayana's Stranger provides a suitable gloss on this passage when he tells Avicenna. "... What survives of you here is the very happiness of your life, realized in the intellect, as alone happiness can be realized; and if this happiness is imperfect, that is not because it is past, but because its elements were too impetuous to be reduced to harmony. This imperfect happiness of yours is all the more intelligible and comforting to me on account of its discords unresolved; they bring me nearer to my day and to its troubles.... They seem to me pure music in contrast to the optimism which simpers daily in a wretched world" ("Homesickness for the World," *Dialogues in Limbo*, p. 228).

43. Owen Barfield, *Owen Barfield on C.S. Lewis*, ed. G.B. Tennyson (Wesleyan University Press, 1989), p. 132.

44. Lewis. *The Pilgrim's Regress*, p. xii.

45. Friedrich Schiller, *The Poems of Schiller*, trans. Edgar A. Bowring. (G. Bell and Sons, Ltd., 1916), pp. 102–03.

46. Barfield, p. 132

47. Barfield, p. 56.

48. Lewis, pp. ix–x.

49. Quoted in Theodor W. Adorno, *Notes to Literature*, transl. Shierry Weber Nicholsen (Columbia University Press, 1991), pp. 70–71.

50. Johann Wolfgang von Goethe, *The Works of J. W. von Goethe*, transl. by John Storer Cobb (Wyman–Fogg Company, 1902). p. 56. Cf. the version in *The Poems of Goethe*, transl. Edgar Bowring (Union School Publ., 1874), pp. 61–62, and his poem "*Selige Sehnsucht.*"

51. Ralph Ellison. *Going to the Territory* (Random House, 1986), p. 284.

52. Hermann Hesse. *Mit Hermann Hesse durch das Jahr* (Suhrkamp, 1976). p. 64.

53. John Kuehl and Jackson R. Bryer, eds. *Dear Scott/Dear Max: The Fitzgerald/Perkins Correspondence.* pp. 203–04.

54. Blanche H. Gelfant, "What More Can Carrie Want? Naturalistic Ways of Consuming Women," in *The Cambridge Companion to American Realism and Naturalism*, ed. Donald Pizer (Cambridge University Press, 1995), p. 178.

55. Jacoby writes: "... Every form of longing is for the experience of one's own fulfillment, salvation, harmony-whatever you chance to call it-even though the manifest object of the longing may be the mother, the loved one, a tropical landscape. Holy-India, bygone days, or what–have–you: In the best sense, the longing experience expresses a desire to overcome one's own self-alienation, to achieve consonance with one's own wholeness" (*The Longing for Paradise: Psychological Perspectives on an Archetype*, transl. Myron B. Gubitz (Sigo Press, 1985), p. 9.

56. Walter Benn Michaels. *The Gold Standard and the Logic of Naturalism* (University of California Press, 1987), p. 41.

57. Lawrence Lerner, *The Uses of Nostalgia: Studies in Pastoral Poetry* (Chatto and Windus, 1972), p. 52.

58. Theodore Dreiser, *Sister Carrie*, Unexpurgated Edition (Penguin, 1981), p. 485.

59. Hermann Hesse, p. 52.

60. Anna Wickham. *The Writings of Anna Wickham: Free Woman and Poet*, ed. R.D. Smith (Virago Press, 1984). p. 185.

R O N A L D   B E R M A N

Order and Will in
A Farewell to Arms

The first half-dozen chapters of *A Farewell to Arms* pose certain questions. Frederic Henry has not been to a battle like the Somme, and Caporetto has not yet occurred. Yet he is suffering from something, although it is not battle fatigue. Possibly it is from the other war that Rinaldi describes as "nothing but frostbites, chilblains, jaundice, gonorrhea, self-inflicted wounds, pneumonia and hard and soft chancres" (12).[1] Such things eventually force even the relentlessly scientific Rinaldi to break down, whereas Henry seems able to live through them unmoved. Self-control is a stoic virtue—but why is Henry silent, without will, without much feeling or any fellow-feeling? Does his emotional and moral passivity—really paralysis—derive from the shock of war at all, or is it a condition drawn from the period between the time of the novel, 1917, and its writing more than a decade later? Finally, does the text recall only the Great War, or does it superimpose other things on that experience?

It is not about shell-shock or, as Michael Reynolds has pointed out, about battlefield experience at the sites described. The text depicts Frederic Henry's withdrawn consciousness, which devolves into silence and even entropy; and it seems aware of what Freud had at the beginning of the war identified as the form that "disillusionment" was bound to take, namely, rejection of conventional personal values.[2] *A Farewell to Arms* is also a farewell to previous beliefs, social and political. Its language of existential and moral insentience will often make points argued by philosophy. Frederic

From *Fitzgerald, Hemingway, and the Twenties* by Ronald Berman. © 2001 by The University of Alabama Press.

Henry has for a long time felt very little about anything, including the
following subject:

> "Have you ever loved any one?"
> "No," I said. (19).

It is always possible that this statement is a sexual tactic, not true. Ironies
aside, Frederic Henry is in some ways even more "scientific" than Rinaldi, a
perceiving machine seeing everything while feeling nothing.

The novel deploys known ideas about subjectivity; about emotional
and intellectual inertia; about failure at what is now in a febrile way called
"communication." These concepts had been debated for a generation. They
took different form and used different terminologies, but they were about
the work of the will and the capacity to relate the self to people and ideas. It
will be best to start just before the publication of *A Farewell to Arms*, with the
prescient Edmund Wilson thinking over in a letter to Maxwell Perkins the
way that literature was losing its will to be material, moral, and public. The
letter is about the book that was to become *Axel's Castle*. Wilson describes a
strange new climate of "resignationism" or the "discouragement of the will."
The phrases are loaded with references to the disintegrating heritage of
American idealism and Idealism. Here is Wilson's account of the literary
situation as the year 1929 approached:

> We have now arrived ... just about where they were with
> Romanticism a hundred years ago.... The generation since the
> war go in for introspection: they study themselves, not other
> people: all the treasures, from their point of view, are to be found
> in solitary contemplation, not in any effort to grapple with the
> problems of the general life.... [Subjectivity] has led to a kind of
> resignationism in regard to the world at large, in fact, to that
> discouragement of the will of which Yeats is always talking.... The
> heroes of these writers never act on their fellows, their thoughts
> never pass into action.
>
> This is partly, I believe, the effect of the war, either acting
> directly on the writers themselves or acting on the literary
> public.... This raises general political and social questions [about
> the paralysis of] the will....[3]

Particular phrases and ideas allow us to place this passage: Although
resolutely a modern, Wilson retained an older mental vocabulary of

subjectivity, solitariness, and especially of "the will"—that phrase made famous by the Public Philosophy of James and Lippmann. What he refers to bears on *A Farewell to Arms* because, in that book, Hemingway silently introduces issues more extensive than the experience of war.

Those issues raised by Wilson had been long argued, but in a somewhat different language. In the most influential psychology text before Freud, James had stated his own anxieties about the problem of modern character and "the closed individuality of each personal consciousness." He centered these problems, as Wilson does in the cited passage, on the will. He believed that one of the great problems of American life was our weakened relationship to things and beings outside ourselves. Modernity encouraged isolation and emotional indifference. For James, the ideal was to be "like trees in the forest," independently alive—yet with out roots commingled "in the darkness underground."[4] It is a splendid psychic passage, but James knew the difficulty of our being "continuous" with one another. It may seem like lèse majesté to intrude the name of Fitzgerald's Josephine Perry among those of Edmund Wilson, William James, and Hemingway, but she does seem in "Emotional Bankruptcy" (1931) to belong there. If the following from that aptly named story were listed along with lines from *A Farewell to Arms*, few readers might detect its origin: "I don't feel anything at all."[5] At the turn of century William James and others worried about the diminishing modern capacity to feel anything; by the end of the twenties, Wilson, Hemingway, and Fitzgerald were to depict the issue in their fiction. When Frederic Henry says, in the brief passage I have cited, that he has never loved anyone, irony is not intended; nor is there an indirect allusion to the emotionally crippling effect of the war. Both question and answer reverberate in Hemingway's writing of the twenties. In two stories of 1924 they are premonitory: "The End of Something" has Nick tell Marjorie "No" to the question of love; and "Soldier's Home" frames the same "No" to the same question. In the latter, Krebs, remarks, "I don't love anybody," cutting off even the possibility.[6]

There are different explanations, listed in ascending order of persuasive power: Kenneth Lynn states that Krebs enacts Hemingway's own escape from the suffocation of motherly love; Michael Reynolds states that Krebs has been affected by the overpowering fear of trench warfare; and James R. Mellow states that sexual experience in Europe after the war has made it impossible for Krebs ever again to be sentimental.[7] The prolonged unconsciousness that Krebs learns to desire, punctuated by occasional sexual pleasure, does not require relationship. It is unlikely that this realization has been caused by war, although war may have been a catalyst. Krebs simply wants a life that is not—Hemingway's phrasing is instructive—"complicated"

by otherness. Clear-sighted, without religion, he is also without will, another
useless imperative from the past.

The opening chapters of *A Farewell to Arms* describe life behind the
lines in 1917 but are concerned with the way that a *contemporary* American
mind reacts to that life. As in "The Short Happy Life of Francis Macomber"
Hemingway uses an exotic scene to open up a familiar subject. He had many
sources of contemporary ideas about denatured Americans to draw upon, and
one point of the novel is its reactivity. What, for example, are we intended to
think of some pointed references in the text, like the following: "That night
at the mess I sat next to the priest and he was disappointed and suddenly hurt
that I had not gone to the Abruzzi.... I myself felt as badly as he did and could
not understand why I had not gone. It was what I had wanted to do." Or, in
continuation, "I explained, winefully, how we did not do the things we
wanted to do; we never did such things" (13). In these passages, the language
of Jamesian psychology has been borrowed and calls attention to itself. The
subject is meant to be reflexively familiar. Frederic Henry understands not
only the distance between ideal behavior and real behavior but also the
distance between will and act described by Wilson. That distance had been
measured for over a generation.

In "The Obstructed Will," a central part of his major work on
psychology, William James had combined mind, morals, and literature. It
was to become a familiar combination in his essays. He states here, "in such
characters as Rousseau and Restif it would seem as if the lower motives had
all the impulsive efficacy in their hands. Like trains with the right of way,
they retain exclusive possession of the track. The more ideal motives exist
alongside of them in profusion, but they never get switched on." In a striking
premonition of both Conrad and Eliot he added, such "inert" characters
have "the consciousness of inward hollowness." He drew a sharp distinction
between the pursuit of pleasure and the avoidance of pain: inert character
does not seek pleasure but unconsciousness. Character is its own adversary.
In one of his best-known passages James had stated, "I have put the thing in
this ultra-simple way because I want more than anything else to emphasize
the fact that volition is primarily a relation, not between our Self and extra-
mental matter (as many philosophers still maintain), but between our Self
and our own states of mind."[8] Was that any longer useful?

This Jamesian belief remained influential; in the case of Fitzgerald, it
was intellectually dominant, and in that of Edmund Wilson, powerfully
reminiscent. Like James, Wilson thought of "normal existence" as the realm
of "non-thinking and non-feeling, the laziness of bodily processes inertly
fulfilling their functions, of the consciousness inertly drifting."[9] The issue of

will may account for Hemingway saying ironically as late as 1941 that *A Farewell to Arms* was "an immoral book." It was not immoral for the reasons usually adduced—drinking, whoring, blasphemy, lying and idleness. Nor was it immoral because of language and depiction.[10] It was immoral because it depicted a modernist sensibility indifferent to abstractions about human nature, otherwise sensed as values.

Argument on the moral sensibility of Americans had begun well before the war. In 1904, William James had warned that "I seem to read the signs of a great unsettlement," concluding that our national lives might easily be confused with an aggregate of solipsisms. He suggested that the new radical empiricism, with its intense rejection of any ideals or universals, might speak for a new generation. Life might become understood solely through "a philosophy of pure experience."[11] That would necessarily make "an immoral book," much harder for Americans to take than contempt for public phrases in common use like "sacred, glorious, and sacrifice and the expression in vain."

The "immorality" goes deeper. James posited a kind of theater of the self in which a highly dramatic encounter occurs between desires and conscience. "The cooling advice which we get from others" leads actually to internal debate between sexual passion and "reasonable ideas." Consciousness is engaged, and the passions have to come to terms with their interlocutors. Reason in James even has some (deeply Victorian) lines to deliver: "Halt! give up! leave off!"[12] Sexual and other passions become abashed or at least they become consciously acknowledged. Not in Hemingway, however, who sets up the issue in the opening chapters of *A Farewell to Arms*, draws attention to the psychological and moral basis of the dialogue—even combines James with Freud by naming a "priest" within that dialogue—and neutralizes it. Frederic Henry is reminded of the good life in a good place, but instead, "I had gone to no such place but to the smoke of cafés and nights when the room whirled and you needed to look at the wall to make it stop, nights in bed, drunk, when you knew that that was all there was" (13). This is not, however, entirely a moral issue, because we know by 1929 that the unreasonable matters at least as much as the reasonable, and what is reasonable in any case no longer has the power of conviction. The dialogue of will is there, carefully restated, but now has a different and more naturalistic conclusion.

Long before anything has happened we begin to understand the various aspects of the problem. The following is not simply descriptive but in some ways diagnostic: "I came back the next afternoon from our first mountain post and stopped the car at the *smistimento* where the wounded and sick were sorted by their papers and the papers marked for the different hospitals. I had been driving and I sat in the car and the driver took the papers in. It was a hot day and the sky was very bright and blue and the road was white and dusty. I sat in the high seat of the Fiat and thought about nothing" (33). These lines coexist with others depicting intense subjectivity, distancing from perceived objects, passivity, the refusal to impose values (derived from now-ineffective idealism) upon experience. They are about the solitary condition.[13] Of this, both James and Dewey had much to say. In "The Moral Philosopher and the Moral Life" James in fact discussed the condition he called "moral solitude." As he put the issue, if a thinker is not consciously responsive to impulse then he may as well think he is a god, detached from human connections. His only problem will be "the consistency of his own several ideals with one another." James adds that some of these will conflict with the rest, and may even "return to haunt him"; and yet, "beyond the facts of his own subjectivity there is nothing moral in the world."[14] Frederic Henry plays out this dilemma. His own experience has been projected against the explanations provided by prewar orthodoxy.

Here is a summary of the later work of Dewey on the failure of the solitary mind: "experience is meaningful: communication pervades experience, events become objects with meaning, experience is 'funded.' The relations and consequences of an object ... can become the very meaning (both referential and immanent) of the thing itself."[15] That is to say, whether among Romantics or Idealists or, as Dewey hoped, among an educated citizenry, experiences can be experienced only when conveyed, or when shared. We want to remember that phrase "objects with meaning." Very little experience has been funded in this novel, and few objects have any meaning at all.

The first two chapters of *A Farewell to Arms* are precise when they depict the passage of time over a landscape perceived. It might be difficult even for photography to duplicate their restrained factuality: "I saw a cloud coming over the mountain. It came very fast and the sun went a dull yellow and then everything was gray and the sky was covered and the cloud came on down the mountain and suddenly we were in it and it was snow. The snow slanted across the wind, the bare ground was covered, the stumps of trees projected, there was snow on the guns and there were paths in the snow going back to the latrines behind trenches" (6). But there are no "relations and consequences." Hemingway has described absolute subjectivity rendered through absolute objectivity. Nothing perceived has an effect on the mind perceiving it. Perception is enhanced (it is very nearly perfect), but feeling is so delimited as to enforce the idea or sensation that there are no connections between what is seen and the eye seeing it. After many such passages, the refusal to value essences may be, after all, too radically empirical. Nothing here means anything, and that itself is a statement of considerable purpose. Put another way, what we see is disconnected from what we are. Hemingway is not solitary because he is alone; he is solitary in a way no Romantic could possibly comprehend, because his being recognizes no tangencies with being outside itself.

When the writings of William James on subjectivity without will rebound throughout the lifetime of Hemingway; when in 1926 John Dewey wonders aloud in one of his most famous essays about the declining power of idealization for established institutions, *stating that the words "sacred" and "holy" can't really be used about national purposes anymore;* when in 1928 Edmund Wilson writes about our literature of "exhaustion;" when in 1930 he despairs about its ability to deal with "large political, social, moral, and aesthetic questions"; and when in 1929–30 Freud states the limits of the pleasure principle—"against the suffering which may come upon one from human relationships the readiest safeguard is voluntary isolation, keeping oneself aloof from other people ... turning away"[16]—then certain conclusions begin to impose themselves. *A Farewell to Arms* has many echoes. It illustrates at least two problems. The first was the winding-down of American character, its increasing passivity, alienation, and self-concern. The second and related problem was the failure of norms in the face of reality.

In 1931, in the book that became *Axel's Castle*, Wilson began his study of modernism by applying some of the ideas of A.N. Whitehead to the subject of landscape:

> There is no real dualism, says Whitehead, between external lakes and hills, on the one hand, and personal feelings, on the other: human feelings and inanimate objects are interdependent and developing together in some fashion of which our traditional notions of laws of cause and effect, of dualities of mind and matter or of body and soul, can give us no true idea. The Romantic poet, then, with his turbid or opalescent language, his sympathies and passions which cause him to seem to merge with his surroundings, is the prophet of a new insight into nature: he is describing things as they really are; and a revolution in the imagery of poetry is in reality a revolution in metaphysics. Whitehead drops the story at this point; but he has provided the key to what follows.[17]

Against this contemporary view should be set the scientific and anti-Romantic ideas of the great modernists, who believed that the primary purpose of late nineteenth-century art was *not* "to communicate the emotional excitement of the artist ... [so that] the recording of nature is secondary."[18] The landscape of *A Farewell to Arms* is decidedly objective but in its own way full of meaning and with an entirely different set of emotions and impressionistic ideas. It might be said that emotions are so delimited as to force a different sense of their own definition:

> The trunks of the trees too were dusty and the leaves fell early that year and we saw the troops marching along the road and the dust rising and leaves, stirred by the breeze, falling and the soldiers marching and afterward the road bare and white except for the leaves. (3)
>
> There was fighting for that mountain too, but it was not successful, and in the fall when the rains came the leaves all fell from the chestnut trees and the branches were bare and the trunks black with rain. The vineyards were thin and bare-branched too and all the country wet and brown and dead with the autumn. (4)

These are intellectually large passages, and they begin with the beginning:

> ... why ask of my generation?
> As is the generation of leaves, so is that of humanity.
> The wind scatters the leaves on the ground, but the live
>   timber
> burgeons with leaves again in the season of spring
>   returning.
> So one generation of men will grow while another
>   dies.[19]

Hemingway's practice was often to reroute passages from the past, and to compare himself, not invidiously, with Tolstoy or Turgeniev. He is very much up to comparing his writing with Homer. But a dialogue with certain dynamics has been turned into a meditation, and the cycle of life has been negated. As Wilson implies, landscape and humanity are intertwined. But (and this sounds as if Wilson had Hemingway's language in mind) things have been described "as they really are"; and if that is the way they really are at the moment of their description, the old connections have failed to hold. I am not speaking of any duty that Hemingway has to be faithful to Homer, only about his refusal to engage in Wilson's enterprise of making sense out of communicated perception. Life and death move into each other so silently as the language develops; and so little value is wasted on this, that the studied neutrality of description becomes an almost impossible neutrality of feeling and conception. Throughout this novel Hemingway wants to tell us about humanity in landscape and also about the deadened feelings that his narrator has about his perceptions. This goes beyond the studied objectivity of modernism. We are meant to understand that Henry is himself alone. This, however, is itself a problem. Both James and Dewey, unavoidable figures in the history of American thought, had endowed the present with doubts about anyone being himself alone.

Their thought was philosophically but not existentially persuasive. The isolation of Frederic Henry is, I think, the central problem of *A Farewell to Arms*. Edmund Wilson got his ideas about the solitary imagination from Whitehead, whose *Science and the Modern World* observes that it is clearly a by-product of modernity—a form of moral "relativity." Whitehead adds, "Of course, with the exception of those who are content with themselves as forming the entire universe, solitary amid nothing, everyone wants to struggle back to some sort of objectivist position. I do not understand how a common world of thought can be established in the absence of a common world of sense."[20] Whitehead's conclusion depends on a sense of things now lost.

Before Frederic Henry's psychology can be debated, his solipsistic, honest philosophy needs outlining. It certainly is true that Henry invites psychological explanation. One notes that our language of psychological explanation has changed drastically. Kenneth Lynn's 1987 biography of Hemingway makes its point in terms of current terminology: "the portrait of Frederic Henry is a study in affective disorder, and retreat and desertion are functions of a larger disengagement from life."[21] A variety of diagnostic choices have been posed by Hemingway scholarship between "Bergsonian intuitionism, which deprecates mind as an unfortunate limiting agent; pragmatism, which has its locus in action and the results of action; the once popular crude Watsonian behaviorism and its more refined replacement, positivism; phenomenology, with its abdication of all interpretation and evaluation; and existentialism, with its concern for certain emotional states."[22] Nevertheless, one of the most useful combinations of ideas for psychology in fiction had been long provided. In terms of Jamesian psychology and Lippmann's sociology, Frederic Henry is perfectly capable of functioning; he is the last of the great figures of the decade of the twenties whose lives exemplify "drift" rather than navigation.

The term "drift," a trademark of William James, was, as I have noted, redeveloped by Lippmann and Dewey, and it is referenced by Fitzgerald in *The Great Gatsby*. The *locus classicus* is in James, who wrote that without our own adversarial consciousness all thought "would slip away." As he put it, our "spontaneous drift is towards repose," and we have a natural tendency to evade responsibility, consciousness, and action, a tendency which must be fought by the exertion of will. Frederic Henry is particularly opposed to what James had called "simultaneous possibilities," the comparison, selection, and even suppression of which identified a mature mind.[23]

John Dewey updated (and moralized) the point in his "Search for the Great Community" of 1926, stating that "There is a social pathology which.... manifests itself in a thousand ways ... in impotent drifting, in uneasy snatching at distractions ... in riotous glorification of things 'as they are,' ... ways which depress and dissipate thought." It led, he thought, to an ungoverned life composed principally of "rationalizations."[24] It cuts close to the bone of contemporary fiction. Hemingway found the idea of drift useful—and also, as Dewey intended, psychologically compelling. He certainly understands the meaning of "will," but he understands also the *necessity* of its failure in a real world.

Jamesian psychology states, "the cognitive faculty, where it appears to exist at all, appears but as one element in an organic mental whole, and as a minister to higher mental powers—the powers of will."[25] James and Dewey may seem morally over-determined (Kenneth Lynn may be quite right in his more clinical diagnosis), but we need them to get at Hemingway. The problem of Frederic Henry is will, which he has himself already described: "We did not do the things we wanted to do; we never did such things" (13). Cognitively, he has no superior in fiction; however, he has no faith in will ("I did not care what I was getting into" [30]), which is the point for ethics in the first quarter of our century. He is in that condition of "moral solitude" foretold by James and remarked by Edmund Wilson. In a passage full of subtle refractions of meaning, it is also directly implied by Rinaldi. In this case, Rinaldi does not act as a scientist:

> He stood up and sat down on the bed. "The knee itself is a good job." He was through with the knee. "Tell me all about everything."
> "There's nothing to tell," I said. "I've led a quiet life."
> "You act like a married man," he said. "What's the matter with you?"

"Nothing," I said, "What's the matter with you?"

"This war is killing me," Rinaldi said, "I am very depressed by it." He folded his hands over his knee.

"Oh," I said.

"What's the matter? Can't I even have human impulses?" (167)

When Rinaldi states that last phrase he implicitly leaves Henry out of it. And when Henry talks about "nothing" and the meaning of "nothing" he may well mean it. The difference between what Henry has experienced and what he has communicated illuminates Dewey's test case about experience becoming real only when objectified through language. But, Hemingway implies, who cares if Dewey is right? "A quiet life" of absolute subjectivity may be the only possible life and silence the only possible attitude.

Can a case be made *for* Frederic Henry? Is there something in his self-examining honesty that is intellectually valuable if not redemptive? On another part of the Italian front, Ludwig Wittgenstein wrote of the difference between his state of self-consciousness in 1916 and 1918. "I am now *slightly* more decent. By this, I only mean that I am slightly clearer in my own mind about my lack of decency." He adds, it makes no sense whatsoever "to theorize about myself."[26] This suggests the ways in which the *Tractatus* may well be considered a war book. In a previous world, ideals would have been better than actuality; in this one, honesty is better than ideals and silence the condition for honesty. Much remains to be said about the language of silence.

Rinaldi is "depressed" by the war, but the same expression was to be used for its surcease. In 1918, Beatrice Webb wrote about the coming post-war world:

There is little or no elation among the general body of citizens about the coming peace.... What are the social ideals germinating in the minds of the five millions who will presently return from the battlefields and battle seas? What is the outlook of the millions of men and women who have been earning high wages and working long hours at the war trades and will presently find themselves seeking work? What are the sympathies of the eight millions of new women voters? The Bolsheviks grin at us from a ruined Russia and their creed, like the plague of influenza, seems to be spreading westwards from one country to another. Will famine become chronic again over whole stretches of Europe, and will some deadly pestilence be generated out of famine to scourge even those races who have a sufficiency of food? Will Western Europe flare up in the flames of anarchic revolution? Individuals brood over these questions and wonder what will have happened this time next year. Hence the depressed and distracted air of the strange medly of soldiers and civilians who throng the thoroughfares of the capital of the victorious Empire.[27]

Webb had a strange political life, and her reputation is now low, but this passage bears comparison to the ending of the first part of *Democracy in America*. Everything in it from Weimar to fascism seems to have come true. Hemingway had the benefit of ten years of historical experience before predating his version of the above.

Frederic Henry may or may not be "depressed" as Rinaldi is, but he labors under the burden of omniscience. Hemingway knows for him and for the reader that the ideals of 1918 will have become politically extinct. Before the shell lands to inflict that fatal wound on the auto-ambulance crew and on American literary criticism, a dialogue has ensued that may be equally damaging. Frederic Henry is arguing tactically against the Socialist idealism of Gavuzzi, Manera, and Passini. But it can be said that both Henry and Hemingway are arguing against any form of political idealism:

> "I believe we should get the war over," I said. "It would not finish it if one side stopped fighting. It would only be worse if we stopped fighting."
>
> "It could not be worse," Passini said respectfully. "There is nothing worse than war."
>
> "Defeat is worse."
>
> "I do not believe it," Passini said still respectfully. "What is defeat? You go home."
>
> "They come after you. They take your home. They take your sisters."
>
> "I don't believe it," Passini said. "They can't do that to everybody. Let everybody defend his home. Let them keep their sisters in the house."
>
> "They hang you. They come and make you be a soldier again. Not in the auto-ambulance, in the infantry."
>
> "They can't hang every one."
>
> "An outside nation can't make you be a soldier," Manera said. "At the first battle you all run."
>
> "Like the Tchecos."

"I think you do not know anything about being conquered and
so you think it is not bad." (49–50)

This implies the history of Europe from 1920 on, much as Beatrice Webb
thought it might be and as Hemingway thought it had turned out. The
unspoken answer to the assertion is that they *can* hang everyone. The novel
prefigures the police state with its social breakdown, its constant danger of
informers, its militarization. Most of all, it implies the end of civilized
expectations: this passage is full of our post-war awareness of the violation of
taboos and the unimagined violation of limits on power. Unthinkable before,
they are now, Hemingway recognizes, part of the assumptions of reality. And
this book is above all realistic.

The conditions have been set for fascism. With great political insight
Hemingway has weighted the development of fascism against the decline of
idealism. The auto-ambulance crew thinks in terms of pre-1914 possibilities.
We know where Passini has gotten his ideas—as he puts it, "We think. We
read. We are not peasants" (51). He is, in other words, a victim of ideas in
circulation. Every assertion that Passini makes comes from the armory of
Socialism; every response by Frederic Henry comes from Hemingway's
skeptical experience of the twenties in Italy. Fixated on social justice (itself a
major irony), the crew is oblivious to reality. Henry is politically astute, but
the impact of this exchange is a consequence of the infusion of fact and
feeling from the end of the decade. That verifies Henry's *realpolitik*.

Throughout the story men believe that if they stop fighting—if they
throw away their rifles—then peace will arrive. More important, if the war is
stopped, then life can resume its norms. That life would proceed, as Bertrand
Russell described, in a way foretold by late-Victorian idealism: "There was to
be ordered progress throughout the world, no revolutions, a gradual
cessation of war, and an extension of parliamentary government."[28] It is the
issue that Hemingway's omniscience best allows him to unveil. We ought to
ask whether, along with the experience of war and of love denied, the novel
makes other points, political and even metaphysical. Throughout, men have
believed in some kind of public and personal order, and they have developed
ideas that William James called remedies for the world of facts. Nearly every
one of these remedies turns out to be wrong. Everywhere we see logical but
unreal expectations: preparation means victory, victory means peace, peace
means order. Throughout, there are dialogues on the impending world after
the war—although Catherine, who also has a sense of military history, tells
Henry, when he is thinking too far ahead, "Don't worry, darling. We may
have several babies before the war is over" (155).

The effect of the war on Catherine Barkley, after her loss at the Battle of the Somme, and on Frederic Henry, after his wound, leads us naturally to conclude that it should be understood in terms of trauma. But Henry has been wounded before the *Minnenwerfer*. In 1915, in the essay that I have previously cited, Freud made his own contribution to the subject. He argued that a new kind of disillusionment would force a new relationship between men, women, and states. Until now, there had been a universal premise: If we lived lives of productive repression, if we accepted "much renunciation of instinctual gratification," then the state also would operate within certain limits. Its own public conscience would tacitly confirm private morals. Our individual lives, in other words, would be reflected, sanctioned, made fully intelligible. The first thing the war proved, however, was that states themselves no longer believed in the denial of aggressive impulses; and if *that* was true, why curb ours? We were bound to have become "disillusioned" because there was no longer any *point* to "high standards of accepted custom for the individual."[29] Public morality led only to war, private morality only to unhappiness. In *A Farewell to Arms* the exercise of the will and the force of conscience do not lead to anything. Toward the end of the novel (327) Hemingway actually invokes the concept of "rules" of life but states that we never have the time to learn them. There is a strong implication that even obeying the "rules" guarantees nothing. That is to say, there is no connection between will, act, and fate. Those are some of the issues on Frederic Henry's mind. He is in some obvious ways a victim of the experience of war, but he is more centrally aware—has from the beginning been aware—that the war has exposed the illusion of order. He knows that the world of James has become that of Freud.

Henry is set apart from most others in this story who fail to recognize that order is both a historical and a philosophical illusion, an idea whose time has gone. Many are looking for an overarching explanation of life through the schemata of religion, science, or politics, but none of these systems holds up. The reason why Hemingway ends this novel in chaos, disorder, and accident is that when these are elevated to the status of principles they make as much sense as their opposites. The novel's antiphilosophy is set against the system-building of the moment, not all of it Fascist. About one system, Hemingway was to put the issue this way: "It isn't all in Marx nor in Engels.... A lot of things have happened since then." Political fantasies of the era 1914–29 are answered by this story of personal and of ideological *defeat*. The utopian versions of *hope* in the twenties—Progressive, Socialist, Communist—dictated a Wellsian "perfected future"; however, as Eric Hobsbawm has observed, the twenties finished off the Age of Liberalism, destroying one after another those institutions of democracy that Bertrand Russell among many others took for granted.[30]

A Farewell to Arms is not entirely a war book but a post-war book. We might liken it to Isaiah Berlin's famous analysis of political realism versus idealism: the belief that we can discover *any* "correct, objectively valid solution to the question of how men should live," may, Berlin stated, itself be in "principle not true." So the pursuit of order, whether through science, religion, or politics, is futile by definition.[31] Philosophically and psychologically, Hemingway found nothing that might make imperfect life endurable, and there were no remedies for facts.

NOTES

1. All citations are to *A Farewell to Arms* (1929; reprint, New York: Charles Scribner's Sons, 1957).

2. See Michael Reynolds, *Hemingway's First War* (Oxford: Basil Blackwell, 1987), 5–7, see Sigmund Freud, "Reflections Upon War and Death," from *Character and Culture*, in *Collected Papers*, ed. Philip Rieff (New York: Collier, 1963), 107–33.

3. Edmund Wilson to Maxwell Perkins, n.d. [probably September 1928], in Wilson, *Letters On Literature and Politics*, 149–51.

4. James, *Principles of Psychology*, 1:xxxi–xxxiii.

5. *The Short Stories of F. Scott Fitzgerald*, 560.

6. *The Short Stories of Ernest Hemingway*, III, 152.

7. Lynn, *Hemingway*, 260; Reynolds, *Hemingway: The Paris Years*, 189—90; James R. Mellow, *Hemingway: A Life without Consequences* (Boston: Houghton Mifflin, 1992), 122–25. Mellow takes his subtitle (*A Life without Consequences*) from lines in this story. All of these interpretations have weight, but I have relied on his.

8. James, *Principles of Psychology*, 2:1154; ibid., 1172. See the critique of Jamesian thought in H.O. Mounce, *The Two Pragmatisms* (London: Routledge, 1997), 84–87.

9. Edmond Wilson, *I Thought of Daisy* (1929; reprint, Baltimore: Penguin Books, 1963), 125.

10. See the elegant explanation by Scott Donaldson, *By Force of Will* (New York: Viking, 1977), 151–52; and see Reynolds, *Hemingway's First War*, 82–3.

11. William James, "A World of Pure Experience," in *William James: Writings, 1902–1910*, 1159, 1160, 1182.

12. James, *Principles of Psychology*, 2:1167–68.

13. The solitary condition was once intensely valued, but note Dewey's scepticism: "no mind was ever emancipated merely by being left alone." From Dewey, "Search for the Great Community," 2:340.

14. James, *The Will to Believe*, 146.

15. John Dewey, *Classical American Philosophy*, ed. John J. Stuhr (New York: Oxford University Press, 1987), 331.

16. Dewey, "Search for the Great Community," 2:341; Wilson, *Letters on Literature and Politics*, 193; Sigmund Freud, *Civilization and Its Discontents*, ed. James Strachey (New York: W.W. Norton, 1961), 24.

17. Edmund Wilson, *Axel's Castle* (1931; reprint, New York: Charles Scribner's Sons, 1954), 5–6.

18. From "Impressionism," in *The Oxford Companion to Art*, ed. Harold Osborne (Oxford: Clarendon Press, 1970), 563.

19. From the sixth book of *The Iliad*, ed. Richmond Lattimore (Chicago: University of Chicago Press, 1951). 157.

20. This passage from *Science and the Modern World* is from *Alfred North Whitehead: An Anthology*, ed. F.S.C. Northrop and Mason W. Gross (New York: Macmillan, 1953), 445.

21. Lynn, *Hemingway*, 386.

22. Robert Evans, "Hemingway and the Pale Cast of Thought," in *Ernest Hemingway*, ed. Arthur Waldhorn (New York: McGraw-Hill, 1973), 113.

23. James, *Principles of Psychology*, 2:1167–70; William James, "Are We Automata?" in *Essays in Psychology*, 51.

24. Dewey. *The Later Works*, 2:341–42.

25. William James, "Reflex Action and Theism," in *The Will to Believe*, 110.

26. This citation from Wittgenstein's correspondence is in Marjorie Perloff, *Wittgenstein's Ladder* (Chicago: University of Chicago Press, 1996), 31. See the extensive treatment of this letter to Paul Engelmann in Ray Monk's *Ludwig Wittgenstein: The Duty of Genius* (New York: Penguin, 1991), 152–53: "If you tell me now I have no faith, you are *perfectly right*, only I did not have it before either.... in fact I shall either remain a swine or else I shall improve, and that's that! Only let's cut out the transcendental twaddle."

27. Cited by Samuel Hynes in *A War Imagined* (New York: Atheneum, 1991), 265.

28. *The Basic Writings of Bertrand Russell*, 1903–1959, ed. Robert E. Egner and Lester E. Denonn (New York: Simon and Schuster, 1961), 51–2.

29. See Freud, "Reflections Upon War and Death," 109; ibid, 108. According to Edith Wharton, one consequence of the war was that presumably "unalterable rules of conduct" came to be seen "as quaintly arbitrary as the domestic rites of the Pharaohs." She cites Walter Lippmann's theory "of the country's present moral impoverishment," i.e., its severance from the imperatives of the past. In "A Backward Glance," in *Novellas and Other Writings* (1934; reprint, New York: Library of America, 1990), 780–81.

30. Cited by Carlos Baker in *Hemingway: The Writer as Artist* (Princeton: Princeton University Press, 1972), 198. Baker also describes Hemingway's reaction to postwar dictatorship in Italy and elsewhere. Regarding a Wellsian future, see Fass, *The Damned and the Beautiful*, 33. Eric Hobsbawm, *The Age of Extremes* (New York: Vintage, 1996), 109–15.

31. Isaiah Berlin, *Against the Current* (New York: Viking, 1980), 66–67.

LISA KERR

Lost Gods:
Pan, Milton, and the Pastoral Tradition
in Thomas Wolfe's *O Lost*

Critics have long debated whether Wolfe was most influenced by Milton or Wordsworth and Coleridge. This debate has been centered around the final chapter of *Look Homeward, Angel* in which Eugene encounters the "ghost" of his brother Ben in the town square. Those who have argued for a Wordsworth/Coleridge influence note that Wolfe's "motto" for the novel— "a stone, a leaf, a door"—is modeled on Wordsworth's "Prelude" (III, 163) and that Wolfe's favorite writer was Coleridge. Proponents of the Milton theory point to the title, which is taken from Milton's "Lycidas." To date, neither theory has been strong enough to discount the other.

Previously, the argument for "Lycidas" as guiding framework has been undercut by the fact that *Look Homeward, Angel* was not Wolfe's original choice for a title.[1] However, a close study of the manuscript *O Lost* reveals that Milton is all-important to understanding Wolfe's use of the pastoral mode to frame Eugene Gant's coming of age as an artist. This revelation is explicit in Wolfe's motif of the god Pan, which permeates the novel but which has never been touched upon by any critic.

The Pan motif appears in Wolfe's 1925 notebooks among the first notes he made for the autobiographical novel he was planning to write. While traveling to Italy, he sketched these two lines on a writing tablet: "Death hath run upon him and riven his life away./Heard horns blown far off in a dark wood (forest)" (*Notebooks* 52). Read without any context, this

From *The Thomas Wolfe Review*, vol. 26, nos. 1 & 2. © 2002 by the Thomas Wolfe Society.

passage could appear to have no specific significance. However, when combined with evidence of strategically placed allusions to Pan in the novel, the passage suggests that Wolfe conceived of the Pan motif from the beginning. Before tracing this motif in *O Lost*, it is important to understand the god Pan's symbolic significance in mythology and in the literary tradition and, specifically, in Milton's own work.

Generally, Pan (Faunus), whose name is interpreted as meaning both "He Who Feeds" and "All," is regarded in classical Roman and Greek mythology as the god of woodlands, pastures, and shepherds; however, his identity is much more complex. Pan, whom Socrates called the "double-natured son of Hermes," represents both artistic achievement and sexual lasciviousness. Pan is a composite character: He has the head and torso of a man, the hindquarters of a goat, and accompanying goat-like horns on his head. Like the goat, Pan is a symbol of lust and fertility, and his carnal desires bind him to earthly delights. Robert Graves notes in volume one of *The Greek Myths* that Pan was said to have coupled with every one of Dionysus' maenads and rivaled Dionysus in his tendency toward playful, promiscuous behavior (101). In fact, Pan was favored by Dionysus/Bacchus—when he was born, "all the immortals were glad in heart and Bacchie Dionysus in especial"—and became associated with bacchic behavior (Homeric "Hymn to Pan," XIX 11.1–26).

Pan is also associated with the Capricorn sign in astrology, the sea-goat or goat-fish. This association is derived from the myth about the war between the Titans and the younger gods, which included Zeus and his contemporaries, for control of the Cosmos. Gaia, "Mother Earth," created a monster, Typhon, to destroy the younger gods; in an attempt to escape, Pan transformed the lower half of his body into a fish. Therefore, Pan is viewed as a figure of transformation—this is not unrelated to the role he plays in the pastoral tradition.

Despite his connection to all things lustful and carnal, Pan is also closely tied to the world of aesthetics. Pan's home is the paradise of Arcadia, making him first and foremost an Arcadian god of nature and the pastoral. He is viewed also as the god of artistic inspiration, a god who instructs students in the ways of the panpipe (also called reeds, oatenstop, pan-horn). Although Pan is drawn to wild, earthy places, his greatest love is for his homeland. His laughter, which can inspire fear or "panic" in the hearts of travelers, is also said to be at times as sweet as the nightingale's song; his pipe playing is said to have the power to transform the mundane into the magical.

Pan was traditionally the greatest figure of the pastoral; writers such as Ovid, Virgil, and Theocritus portrayed him as the inventor of the pastoral song. This tradition has been largely lost to modern readers, but would have been familiar to Wolfe, having been passed down to him through the poetry of Milton, Spenser, and Ben Jonson, perhaps even Oscar Wilde, Robert Frost, and Robert and Elizabeth Barrett Browning. The tradition has its origins in the story of Pan and the nymph Syrinx.

The story of Pan and Syrinx is most important to this study. In brief, Pan was "lustful and enjoyed cavorting with nymphs" (Bentley 103). One of the nymphs he pursued was Syrinx, who tried to escape his unwanted passes by having herself transformed into a bed of reeds (there are several theories on who actually aided in her transformation). Finding her transformed, Pan fastened several of her reeds together to produce a new musical instrument. Thus, Pan's act of creation is two-sided: He creates, yet he does so in isolation, and his creation has its origins in loss. This myth suggests that the artist's role is one of sacrifice and potential loneliness, a pervasive theme in Wolfe.

Thomas K. Hubbard has written that the "initiation of Pan" is an "initiation into the arts." Certain stories of Pan that have circulated suggest that Apollo stole the idea of creating his own musical instrument from Pan and passed it off as his own. It is Pan, though, not Apollo, who is considered the "archetypal teacher of pastoral tradition" (Hubbard 244). He is the symbol "of an imagined originary past ... to whom all subsequent imitations ... are by definition inferior" (209). Various writers have altered the story of Pan to fit their needs, but Pan is consistently portrayed not only as creator but as teacher. In Virgil, his creation of the panpipe is motivated by a desire to teach and pass on his talent. In a sculpture dating back to the second century A.D., Pan casts his arm around Daphnis—a central pastoral figure from Theocritus—as he instructs him to play the syrinx (Boardman 36). In other works of art, Pan is often figured blowing a horn, calling artists to create (Boardman 12, 23, 34). Because Pan is known as a great teacher, his pipe became the symbol for the pastoral tradition, and the inheritance of the pipe became the method by which the pastoral tradition was passed on. Theocritus figures himself as the Syracusan shepherd, who inherits the pipe from Pan; Virgil depicts the Mantuan Tityrus who inherits the pipe from Theocritus; when Virgil is done, he hangs the pipe in a sacred pine tree so that it may be appropriated by others (Hubbard 260).

As the text of *O Lost* illustrates, Wolfe was well read in the pastoral tradition: He mentions Virgil, Herodotus, Ovid, and Theocritus by name. Yet, it is more precise to say that the pastoral tradition he inherits is filtered to him through Milton. Milton connects his collection to the pastoral tradition by using an epigraph from Virgil. Wolfe connects his novel to

Milton through the title, *Look Homeward, Angel*, taken from "Lycidas" (1637). The movement of Wolfe's novel and Eugene's progression toward his artistic vocation follow a similar pattern from "innocence to its loss," figured by Wolfe as Eugene's experience of Ben's death and his encounter with Ben's ghost in the final scene of the novel. One of the central motifs that Wolfe uses to chart this process is that of Pan. In the end, Wolfe places his novel squarely in the tradition of the pastoral, which is from its origins a "vehicle of transition from the past to the future" (Hubbard 350).

Wolfe had most certainly read of the tradition of Pan not only through Milton but through various sources of poetry; textual evidence reveals that he read many of the poets who were themselves influenced and inspired by the figure of Pan. Pan appears in Virgil's *Georgics* as well as in Ovid's *Metamorphoses* and works by Pindar, Homer, Plato, and Socrates—all writers with whom Wolfe was familiar and whom he cites by name in *O Lost*. In Ben Jonson's "Pan's Anniversary," Pan is "our All, by him we breathe, we live" (167). In Shelley's "Hymn of Pan," the goat-god sings of his own musical prowess, claiming that his ability surpasses the ability of the god of arts and letters himself, Apollo. The final stanza of Shelley's poem might have provided an ample epigraph for *O Lost*:

> I sang of the dancing stars,
> I sang of the daedal Earth,
> And of Heaven—and the giant wars
> And Love and Death, and Birth. (264)

Robert Browning retells the myth of "Pan and Luna." Elizabeth Barrett Browning's poem "A Musical Instrument" revisits the story of Pan playing his reed pipes by the river in order to express the "cruel isolation of poetical genius." The last stanza of the poem conveys her theme:

> Yet half a beast is the great god Pan,
> To laugh as he sits by the river,
> Making a poet out of a man:
> The true gods sigh for the cost and pain,—
> For the reed which grows nevermore again
> As a reed with the reeds in the river. (44)

Like Elizabeth Browning, Wolfe returns again and again to the isolation of the artist. Also, Browning portrays Pan sitting by the river; in *O Lost* Wolfe makes reference to "riverhaunting Pan" (205); this reference was cut when Wolfe revised his original manuscript to create *Look Homeward, Angel*, but its appearance in the early notebooks of Wolfe supports the theory that Wolfe had conceived of using the Pan figure early on.

Robert Frost's 1913 "Pan with Us" is one of the last works by a major poet in which the theme of Pan as artistic teacher is evident. Yet, Frost's poem points to the place of Pan in the modern world:

> He tossed his pipes, too hard to teach
> A new-world song, far out of reach
> ... Times were changed from what they were:
> Such pipes kept less of power to stir
> ... They were pipes of pagan mirth,
> And the world had found new terms of worth. (33)

Frost's portrayal of Pan as a god who has lost his power in the modern world reveals that Pan, as a god of artistic inspiration, was being forgotten.

Oscar Wilde also wrote of the modern world's loss of Pan in his poem "Pan: Double Villanelle." The poet calls to Pan, "This modern world hath need of thee" and begs the pastoral god to "blow some trumpet loud and free,/And give thine oaten pipe away,/Ah, leave the hills of Arcady!" (802-03). Wilde even cites Milton as predecessor and connects Milton to the tradition of Pan: "This is the land of liberty/Lit grave-browed Milton on his way,/This modern world hath need of thee!" (803).

These modern poets' predictions that Pan would be lost in the modern world were correct; ignorance of Pan as a central figure of the pastoral tradition has kept readers from understanding Wolfe's full vision of the artist-in-the-making process and his placement of his novel into the pastoral tradition. The section on Judge Webster Sondley and his demonology studies originally contained the one direct reference to "riverhaunting Pan," but the section was trimmed during Wolfe's and Perkins's revisions, and Pan's name was removed. However, the Sondley section of *O Lost* is not peripheral. It provides an indication of Wolfe's view of the modern world's loss of gods such as Pan.

Sondley has not only sketched a god resembling Pan, "growing out of earth, the thighs emerging in hairy flanks," but also includes Pan in a list of gods who have been "Beaten, beaten, beaten" and transformed by societies into "Demons and Devils" (205). Wolfe's narrator expounds on the value of these lost gods: "But to follow a God who is forever beaten—to endure hunger, exhaustion, battle, and death ... to stand at length against the final cliffs and hear his horn—and go again to death—how fine a thing would that be!" (205). Here, Wolfe expresses his esteem not only for forgotten gods such as Pan but also for those who have the courage to follow them. In the case of Pan, following him would be to endure the "hunger, exhaustion, battle, and death" that come with the territory of artistic apprenticeship.

In addition to the one direct reference, the figure of Pan and Pan-related topics are alluded to thirteen times in *O Lost*. Five times Eugene is referred to as goat-like. Wolfe mentions the reed pipes four times, at central moments in the novel. He calls the golden world Eugene searches for Arcadia and Parnassus, Pan's native land and the land in which he has a sacred Cave of Corycian. He portrays Margaret Leonard as a Syrinx figure. These allusions will be explored in depth in the following section.

There are several general trends in *O Lost* that point to the Pan motif that should be noted before moving on to specific textual references. First of all, Wolfe's concept of the artist's ability to transform the mundane to the magical through art may be derived from the myth of Pan's musical abilities; it was believed that when Pan played his pipes, he had the ability to transform the mundane into the extraordinary. Wolfe's task in *O Lost* was to create "new magic in a dusty world" by transforming the ordinary into the epic.

Second, like Pan, Eugene is portrayed as semidivine—caught between the aesthetic divinity of poetry and the base humanity of bodily urges such as lust and hunger. Jennifer Larson writes in *Greek Nymphs*, "Pan's symbolic power lay in his evocation of an imagined primitive past, a period of protocivilization that, while harsh and savage, was also in some sense an idealized golden age.... Pan, the sacred cave dweller, is both beast and god" (97–98). Eugene's great love of food and alcohol—as discussed, for example, in chapter 3 of *O Lost*—and his insatiable libido are all linked to his artistic ability and demonstrate the close connection Eugene draws between the passions and the intellect.

Eugene is not the only character whom Wolfe describes as partly divine. Eugene's love interests and other young women in *O Lost* are referred to and/or depicted as nymphs, maenads, and dryads—mythological figures closely linked to the god Pan as well as to his mentor Bacchus/Dionysus. Like Pan and Dionysus, nymphs were connected to nature; they lived by mountains and rivers, slept in sacred caves, and were connected to both the natural and the musical—they represented the "presence of the supernatural in everyday life" (Larson 98).

In particular, Eugene's love affair with Laura James is depicted in pastoral terms: In the primary love scene between Eugene and Laura, she is described as a nymph/maenad:

He kissed her on her splendid eyes; he grew into her young maenad's body, his heart numbed deliciously against the pressure of her narrow breasts. She was as lithe and yielding to his sustaining hand as a willow rod—she was bird-swift, more elusive in repose than the dancing water motes upon her face. He held her tightly lest she grow into the tree again or be gone among the wood like smoke. (487)

Wolfe does not infer that Laura is one single nymph; in Eugene's mind, her identity is conflated with that of several nymphs: Or rather, she takes on general qualities associated with nymphs: she is described in terms of flight and is likened to water and trees that somehow he cannot fully possess. She threatens to transform before his eyes so that he will be left alone. The story of the nymph's transformation is common: Syrinx was transformed into reeds; Daphne was transformed into a tree; Echo was torn limb from limb until she was only a voice. In different stories, these nymphs were all pursued by lovers and transformed themselves in order to escape. Pan was often figured as one of the pursuers, as in the Echo and Syrinx stories.

Not only is Laura portrayed as a nymph, but also the grove in which the interlude takes place is a pastoral setting like those sacred to the nymphs and to Pan. In "Structure, Theme, and Metaphor in *Look Homeward, Angel,*" John Hagan claims that the garden Laura and Eugene enter is an Eden (129). However, in *O Lost*, Eugene and Laura *do not stop* in this garden; they *pass through* it, pass the "rich many acres" of Judge Webster Sondley's home, and go deeper into a wooded area (484). The fact that the lovers' secret grove is located near Sondley's place is too interesting to ignore. The reader is reminded of Sondley's association with the pre-Christian era and its gods, and when Eugene and Laura pass through the Christian Eden only to re-enter another woods, they are figuratively entering a pre-Christian pastoral world themselves. Moreover, Wolfe's description of the place at which they finally stop is reminiscent of places sacred to nymphs and to the god Pan, which are "characterized by abundant water, shade, and vegetation ... a grove set apart by a low wall as a sacred area" (Larson 9–10). Eugene and Laura's spot is "an island of tender grass, by a little brook that fell down from the green hill along a rocky fern bed in bright cascades" (485). It is a natural setting, but also a setting characterized by a sense of the musical: "All of that magic world—flower and field and sky and hill, and all the sweet woodland cries, sound and sight and odor—grew into him, one voice in his heart, one tongue in his brain, harmonious, radiant, and whole—a single passionate lyrical noise" (485). Eugene is not only in this pastoral place; he is described as being in union with both his surroundings and with Laura. He feels both of them "grow into" him; they become a part of him, and he is transformed.

Like his predecessors in the pastoral tradition, Wolfe uses art as a form of expressing both innocence and the loss of it. At the same moment that Eugene is celebrating his love with Laura, he is transported into the future and his/Wolfe's voice begins already to mourn the loss of the experience, crying, "Come up into the hills, O my young love: return.... Where is the day that melted into one rich noise?" (487). Even as Eugene experiences a pastoral moment, he predicts that he will lose it.

The most compelling evidence of Wolfe's use of Pan as a symbol of the transition from pastoral to epic lies in the specific references and allusions to Pan that appear in the text of *O Lost*. Wolfe uses Pan as an analog for Eugene Gant and buries his references to the god deep in the text. These allusions culminate in the final scene between Eugene and Ben's ghost. To understand Wolfe's method of incorporating Pan, a close study of each scene in which a reference or allusion appears and of the progression of these allusions as a reflection of Eugene's own progression is necessary.

In addition to these general resemblances, Wolfe carefully weaves the pattern of Pan references into his narrative structure. At first, his references apply generally to his vision of mankind as lost. As the narrative continues and Eugene journeys closer to his final epiphany in chapter 41, the references become more specific to Eugene as artist-in-the-making. Wolfe's first allusion to the lusty animal-god is in chapter 6. He implies that all young boys' desires are heightened by the coming of spring: "the young gods loiter: they hear the reed, the oatenstop, the running goathooves in the spongy wood, here, there, everywhere" (107). Here, Eugene and his peers are drawn to what Pan represents: free, lustful cavorting. The sound of his reed and oaten-stop inspire in them the "panic" or excitement Pan traditionally causes. He calls them to frolic; he also calls them home, to "their one fixed home" of Arcadia. But, Wolfe suggests, the young boys have no means by which to locate him or the lost, golden world: "they dawdle, listen, fleetest when they wait, go vaguely on ... because the earth is full of ancient rumor and they cannot find the way. All of the gods have lost the way" (107).

The next allusion to Pan appears in chapter 12. Wolfe prefaces his reference to Pan and Arcadia by writing, "Quod potui perfeci ["I have done what I could"]. By this fusion, perhaps, men like men" (203). These lines suggest that humankind are linked by their common efforts to get through life as best they can. But in the next lines, Wolfe seems to offer an alternative: "By the river the reed pipes, the muse's temple, the sacred wood again. Why not? As in this cove. I, too, have lived in Arcadia" (203). The alternative is to reclaim or return to some golden world from which man has become lost, a pastoral paradise where an artist finds true inspiration in the music of Pan's pipes and the muses. *Why not?* Wolfe seems to ask for Eugene. Why isn't it possible that a place such as this exists? He stakes a claim for Eugene, who feels his origins, like Pan's, are in Arcadia, a pastoral paradise.

In the next reference, the myth of Pan becomes more personal for Eugene. Wolfe uses it to show that Eugene is acquiring the tools by which to become an artist. In chapter 21, he not only shows Eugene beginning to actively play with language, but also shows Margaret Leonard to be the source of both inspiration and the means by which he gains access to the tools he will need to create. Wolfe writes of Margaret Leonard:

> She was like a voice that God seeks. She was the reed of demonic ecstasy. She was possessed, she knew not how, but she knew the moment of her possession. The singing tongues of all the world were wakened into life again under the incantation of her voice. She was inhabited. She was spent. (335–36)

Margaret Leonard is portrayed here as a Syrinx figure. Her body, which will become the reed by which Pan fashions his pipe, is "the voice" that Pan seeks. Wolfe makes the allusion clear by calling her "the reed." She is possessed by artistic inspiration, which Pan represents, and she is the force or vehicle by which artistic lives will be further inspired.

For Eugene, Margaret Leonard awakens desire not only to learn but also to create, for soon after Eugene acknowledges Margaret Leonard as a principal inspiration, he enters a new stage of artistic development. In chapter 23, the form of the novel is affected by the content of Eugene's changing artistic character. Freed from the classroom, which has become his after-school prison, Eugene takes his book knowledge into the world and applies his knowledge of literature to the everyday people, objects, and situations around him. Wolfe's weaving of unidentified literary quotes in this famous section of the novel is important not because its contents reveal Wolfe as a well-read man but because its form demonstrates that Eugene Gant has passed into a more active stage in his apprenticeship. It is also key that it is Wolfe the man, who has already become an artist, who *writes* the lines into the novel; Eugene the boy-protagonist only *imagines* them. He has been inspired to a new level of apprenticeship by his Syrinx, yet he does not move into the final stages of self-awareness or state his artistic manifesto until his encounter with Ben's ghost.

In *Look Homeward, Angel,* the section in which Margaret Leonard is figured as Syrinx is in chapter 23 and the scene of the boys walking home from school appears in chapter 24. In *O Lost*, however, the Margaret Leonard scene appears in chapter 21, and the boys do not walk home until chapter 23. In between lies chapter 22, which contains an important vignette centered around the character of Roy Brock. Roy Brock is important because, with his attitude toward life and literature, he acts as a foil to Eugene, spurring Eugene to make an important conclusion about the role of a poet/writer.

Wolfe posits Roy Brock as the anti-pastoral figure. He is a stranger to the South, "a false Yankee realist," who "had already hardened into the American city dweller's mold of infantile cynicism" (347). In Roy Brock's world. "Everyone was guilty until proved innocent, and then everyone was guilty" (347). Wolfe says of people such as Brock, "The proud clangor of poetry is not for them; they have no reverence" (348). Specifically, it is the innocent, rustic pastoral world to which Brock does not belong. Eugene, by contrast, is placed squarely in the pastoral tradition—he believes in innocence, beauty, and the miraculous. He has yet to be touched by the cynicism that Brock has.

Importantly, in this section, Wolfe asks, "Is it for such as these that Homer sang of gods and men upon the Argive coast? Is it for such as these that blind Milton rolled his sightless orbs inwards upon the luminous effulgences of his God-governed spirit?" (348). The specific naming of Milton here, at a central turning point in the novel, calls attention to the importance of what Milton represents. The three authors referenced in this line of questioning are all connected to the poetic, pastoral tradition rather than to a romantic tradition. In fact, Wolfe frowns upon the "bad Southern romantics" who were Brock's companions (347), consciously asserting Eugene's connection to the pastoral tradition.

As the world of possibility opens to Eugene, he feels both an increasing sense of expectation and of dread. In *Look Homeward, Angel*, in lines that were added during revisions and don't appear in *O Lost*, Eugene looks around himself at the town of Altamont. He fears that he will never achieve the dreams of a full, mysterious life before he dies: "Shall these eyes, drenched with visions yet unseen, stored with the viscous and interminable seas at dawn, with the sad comfort of unfulfilled Arcadias, seal up their cold dead dreams upon a tick, as this, in time, in some hot village of the plains?" (333–34). Wolfe's addition of these lines suggests that, as he revised, he felt it important to preserve the theme of Arcadia.

Other sections of *Look Homeward, Angel* illustrate this as well. In *O Lost* and *Look Homeward, Angel*, Eugene does escape when he goes to school, but only to another part of North Carolina. At college, his newfound freedom leads him to view himself again as a Pan figure—both full of lust for life and, as an emerging artist, isolated. In *Look Homeward, Angel*, when Eugene rushes out in pursuit of women at night, he does so with a "goat-cry of desire and hunger" (584). Yet no woman can fully satiate his hunger, for his true hunger is for self-knowledge. Although he is temporarily satisfied with being a popular man on campus, he resents his reputation as a strange character. He longs to find a way to be understood, but as a Pan figure, in the Elizabeth Barrett Browning tradition, he must pace the streets, alone and lonely. His freedom has come at a price.

In *O Lost*, Eugene chants "goatcries below the moon" (620), desiring to escape *into* the fullness of life. His dream of Arcadia is persistent; he always feels sure things would be better elsewhere. His art will come at an even higher price. Eugene's focus is always outward. His eyes are turned on vast, distant lands he knows of through myth. As the not-yet-enlightened artist, Eugene touches on the role his art will play, but he does not understand the true meaning of the fact that his fantasies find extensions in reality. Eugene is still very much a boy at play, recreating fantasies as he did when he played Bruce-Eugene as a child.

Finally, it is Ben's death that acts as the central catalyst to Eugene's emergence as an artist. In the final chapter of *O Lost*, where Eugene meets with the "ghost" of his brother Ben, a final reference to Pan appears, solidifying the symbol of Pan as artistic inspiration. After Ben's ghost leads Eugene to conclude that the one true journey he must take is into himself, Eugene calls to the "sudden and impalpable faun, lost in the thickets of [myself]," saying, "I will hunt you down until you cease to haunt my eyes with hunger" (662). Wolfe suggests that this faun is not only a part of Eugene's inner self but also a symbol associated with Arcadia: "I shall save one land unvisited, said Eugene. Et ego in Arcadia" (661). Eugene's ultimate realization is that he must search out the artist within, that within himself he will find both Pan and Arcadia.

The reader's experience of Pan in *O Lost* reflects Eugene Gant's experience with the forgotten god. He is there and not there at once. We have glimpses of him as goat and faun; we hear his far-forested horn note but are not sure who he is, what purpose he is to serve. Yet the evidence suggests that Wolfe knew exactly what role Pan was to play, what symbolism he would hold. The symbol of Pan reinforces the themes of artistic initiation in *O Lost* and solidifies Wolfe's relationship to the pastoral tradition.[2]

NOTES

1. See John S. Hill's "Eugene Gant and the Ghost of Ben." Also see *The Notebooks of Thomas Wolfe* 330, which includes the note, "Put into final scene of book: 'Look

Homeward, Angel, now, and melt with ruth.'" Although the footnote claims that Wolfe never did work this idea into the final scene of the book, the appearance of the note indicates that he did conceive that the last chapter would be somehow related to Milton's "Lycidas."

2. For a more detailed study of Wolfe's relationship to Milton and his inheritance of the pastoral tradition see "An American Pastoral Elegy: The Death of Ben and the Birth of the Artist" in "Climbing Parnassus: Thomas Wolfe's *O Lost* as Kunstler-roman" by Lisa Kerr (Ph.D. diss., University of South Carolina, 2002). This essay is an excerpt from that dissertation.

WORKS CITED

Bentley, Peter, ed. *Dictionary of World Mythology.* New York: Facts on File, 1995

Boardman, John. *The Great God Pan: The Survival of an Image.* New York: Thames and Hudson, 1997.

Browning, Elizabeth Barrett. "A Musical Instrument." *The Complete Works of Elizabeth Barrett Browning.* Vol. 6. Ed. Charlotte Porter and Helen A. Clarke. New York: Crowell, 1900. 44.

Frost, Robert. "Pan with Us." *Complete Poems of Robert Frost.* New York: Holt, Rinehart and Winston, 1949. 33.

Frye, Northrop. "Literature as Context: Milton's 'Lycidas.'" *Milton's "Lycidas": The Tradition and the Poem.* Ed. C.A. Patrides. Columbia: University of Missouri Press, 1983.

Graves, Robert. *The Greek Myths.* Vol. 1. London: Penguin, 1955.

Hagan, John. "Structure, Theme, and Metaphor in *Look Homeward, Angel.*" *American Literature* 53 (1981): 266–85. Rpt. in *Modern Critical Views: Thomas Wolfe.* Ed. Harold Bloom. New York: Chelsea House, 1987. 123–39.

Hill, John S. "Eugene Gant and the Ghost of Ben." *Modern Fiction Studies* 11:3 (Autumn 1965): 245–49.

Homer. "The Hymn to Pan." *The Homeric Hymns.* Trans. Charles Boer. Chicago: Swallow Press, 1970. 67–71.

Hubbard, Thomas K. *The Pipes of Pan: Intertextuality and Literary Filiation in The Pastoral Tradition from Theocritus to Milton.* Ann Arbor: University of Michigan Press, 1998.

Jonson, Ben. "Pan's Anniversary; or The Sheperd's Holyday." *English Masques.* Ed. Herbert Arthur Evans. London: Blackie & Son, 1897. 161–70.

Larson, Jennifer. *Greek Nymphs: Myth, Cult, Lore.* New York: Oxford University Press, 2001.

Merivale, P. *Pan the Goat God: His Myth in Modern Times.* Cambridge: Harvard University Press, 1969.

Osgood, Charles Grosvenor. *The Classical Mythology of Milton's English Poems.* New York: Holt, 1900.

Patrides, C.A., ed. *Milton's "Lycidas": The Tradition and the Poem.* Columbia: University of Missouri Press, 1983.

Revard, Stella. *Milton and the Tangles of Neara's Hair: The Making of the 1645 Poems.* Columbia: University of Missouri Press, 1997.

Shawcross, John T., ed. *The Complete Poetry of John Milton.* New York: Doubleday, 1971.

Shelley, Percy Bysshe. "Hymn of Pan." *The Poetical Works of Percy Bysshe Shelley.* Ed. Mary

Wollstonecraft Shelley. London: Ward, Lock, 1889. 264.

Wilde, Oscar. "Pan: Double Villanelle." *The Works of Oscar Wilde.* Ed. G.F. Maine. New York: Scribner's, 1954.

Wolfe, Thomas. *Look Homeward, Angel.* New York: Scribner's, 1929.

————. *The Notebooks of Thomas Wolfe.* Ed. Richard S. Kennedy and Paschal Reeves. Vol. 1. Chapel Hill: University of North Carolina Press, 1970.

————. *O Lost.* Ed. Arlyn Bruccoli and Matthew J. Bruccoli. Columbia: University of South Carolina Press, 2000.

Wordsworth, William. "The Prelude; Or, Growth of a Poet's Mind: An Autobiographal Poem." *The Complete Poetical Works of Wordsworth.* Boston: Houghton Mifflin, 1932.

KIRK CURNUTT

Youth Culture and the Spectacle of Waste:
This Side of Paradise and *The Beautiful and Damned*

I don't want you to see me growing old and ugly....
We'll just *have* to die when we're thirty.
    —Zelda Sayre to F. Scott Fitzgerald, Spring 1919 (Milford 49)

"About the Fitzgerald youth," Woodward Boyd wrote in 1922 as she set out
to "shoot a few arrows" through the celebrated image of the author as
"disillusioned, cynical, and so young"; "He is young, certainly, but not so
young as to look absurd in long trousers." As she points out, when *This Side
of Paradise* was published in 1920, Fitzgerald was Dickens's age when he
completed *The Pickwick Papers*, only a little younger than Keats when his final
poems were written, and actually older than John Dos Passos when *Three
Soldiers* first appeared. "Yet Keats, Dickens, Dos Passos, and hundreds of
others who wrote things before they were 25 are not judged as 'infant
phenomenons' while Scott Fitzgerald, in spite of the fact that he is only two
years younger than Ben Hecht, whom no one ever dreams of calling childish,
still suffers under this absurd handicap," Boyd observed (Bruccoli and Bryer
340). She makes what seems an obvious point here: while neither the
youngest nor the first writer to chronicle the temperament of his generation,
Fitzgerald identified with the theme of youth more intently than his
contemporaries did—so much so, in fact, that when Dorothy Parker set out
a year after Boyd's essay to skewer the media fascination with the era's

From *F. Scott Fitzgerald in the Twenty-first Century*, Jackson R. Bryer, Ruth Prigozy, and Milton
R. Stern, ed. © 2003 by the University of Alabama Press.

287

flappers and philosophers, she focused her satire on Fitzgerald's reputation as a "special correspondent from the front line of the younger generation" who bravely "broadcasts the grim warning that conditions are getting no better rapidly and that decadence, as those outside the younger generation know of it, is still in its infancy." As the author of such shocking tomes as *Anabelle Takes to Heroin, Gloria's Neckings,* and *Suzanne Sobers Up,* Tommy Clegg, Parker's fictionalized Fitzgerald figure, specializes in exposés of the "scandalous doings of modern youth" that excite parental anxiety while earning their author a pretty penny. While Boyd claims not to understand why Fitzgerald defines himself as an enfant terrible, Parker *does,* for by "cashing in" on the youth craze, "Tommy and his little playmates don't regard being young as just one of those things that are likely to happen to anybody. They make a business of it" (156).

At first glance, Boyd and Parker seem to arrive at disparate conclusions regarding Fitzgerald's relationship with youth. For the former, the popular image of him as "frightfully disillusioned in the younger manner [is] really laughable," since his work glows with an optimism and enthusiasm that suggests "he believes anything and everything and is enchanted and ecstatic because there are so many interesting things to believe" (339).[1] For Parker, by contrast, his "lurid" tales of "debauched doings" evince entrepreneurial opportunism, for this "commercial genius who began the grand work of selling this younger generation to the public" (156) secured an enviable profit by capitalizing upon an erupting fad. Yet in the end, these essays disagree less than an initial reading suggests, for both authors acknowledge that Fitzgerald would never have achieved notoriety had a mass audience not been eager for insight into how the twentieth century's first generation, its "heirs of progress," was shaped by the emergence of modernity.

One would think that Fitzgerald's contribution to the image of the youth of the 1920s as ambassadors of "unchanneled and potentially disruptive energies" (Fass 21) would constitute a central line of scholarly inquiry. Yet, except for the obligatory admission that *This Side of Paradise* inaugurated a brief vogue for novels and films about "bright young things," the question of how his thematic obsession with youth relates to his modernist milieu is largely neglected.[2] The reason can be inferred from Theodore Roethke's comment that Fitzgerald was "born, and died a Princeton sophomore" (249). At worst, his age-consciousness strikes detractors as endemic of the immaturity of his interests; at best, it seems a romantic indulgence whose glitter and gilt distract from the professionalism of his craft. Even ardent admirers like John O'Hara find it necessary to remove Fitzgerald from his era to redeem his artistry. Although he recalled in *The Portable Fitzgerald* (1945) his intense adolescent affection for *Paradise*. O'Hara elsewhere insisted that "one of the worst things that ever happened to Fitzgerald was the simultaneous popularity of John Held's drawings," the cartoons of frolicking flappers that often adorned the covers of Fitzgerald's books: "Who would ever want to take Fitzgerald seriously if all they ever knew about him was that he wrote about those John Held girls?" (18).[3] Scholars are equally anxious about seriousness. As Matthew J. Bruccoli pointedly told an Associated Press reporter during the 1996 Fitzgerald centennial celebrations, the lost-youth legend surrounding Fitzgerald is frivolous and "detracts attention from what's important.... And what's important is little black marks on pieces of paper" (Thompson).

Unfortunately, such judgments overlook the deep sociohistorical importance invested in youth in this century. The phrase "youth culture" may bring to mind a never-ending cycle of teen fads, fashions, and fascinations, but its significance transcends the oversimplified images of generational identity that have stereotyped each decade's adolescents, from the 1920s' slicker to today's slacker. As Patricia Meyer Spacks has noted, American culture mythologizes youth as a time of "exploration, becoming growth pain" and thus, by implication, dismisses aging as a time of "stodginess, inertia, stasis," and "absence of feeling" (4). As such the term has become a multivalent measure of everyday life, evoking not just a demographic constituency of adolescents but a standard of psychic well-being achievable by anyone of any age with the correct salutary regard for life. As Lawrence Grossberg puts it, youth is at once a category of "chronology, sociology, ideology, experience, style, [and] attitude" (171). When referring to young people, it most often functions as an index of social change, becoming, in Grossberg's words, a "battlefield" upon which teens and adults fight "for control of its meanings, investments and powers, [as both groups attempt] to articulate and thereby construct its experiences, identities, practices, discourses and social differences" (183). Yet in its broader usage, youth is celebrated as a universal remedy for the encroachments of senescence. As advertisers incessantly inform us, we can *feel* young even if we can no longer credibly claim to *be* young—as long as we purchase their particular wares.

Given the prevalence of interest in youth, acknowledging the ways in which Fitzgerald's early writing reflects its valorization in no way devalues it as Hemingway did when he dismissed his friend's fictional corpus as a "little children's, immature, misunderstood, whining for lost youth death-dance" (Bruccoli, *Some Sort of Epic Grandeur* 374). Rather, *This Side of Paradise* and *The Beautiful and Damned* vividly record evolving ideas on youth that today are the norm. Not only do these novels critique outmoded Victorian ideals of maturation, but they explore the ambiguous power that flagrant displays of youth styles afford young people. Most intriguingly, these works reflect the anxiety of a burgeoning age-consciousness that encouraged the young to maximize their youth before losing it to middle age. As Lois tells her brother in the early short story "Benediction," "Youth shouldn't be sacrificed to age" (*Flappers and Philosophers* 141). But while Fitzgerald—long before Abbie Hoffman or Jerry Rubin—insisted that anyone over thirty was corrupt in morals and imagination, his work acknowledges the impossibility of staying young forever. The result is a fascinating tension: though these early novels idealize youth, they also recognize its imminent passing and thus illustrate the desire throughout American culture to segregate youth from age.

An obvious way that Fitzgerald's work reflects emerging attitudes toward youth is its rejection of the Victorian myth of adolescence, a critique most apparent in the structure of *This Side of Paradise*. When Scribner's declined Fitzgerald's first effort at a novel, "The Romantic Egotist," in August 1918, the austere publishing firm singled our the story's inconclusiveness as its major flaw: "Neither the hero's career nor his character are shown to be brought to any stage which justifies an ending," the rejection letter noted, adding, "This may be intentional on your part for it is certainly not untrue to life: but it leaves the reader distinctly disappointed and dissatisfied since he has expected him to arrive somewhere ... perhaps in a psychological [sense] by 'finding himself' as for instance Pendennis is brought to do" (Bruccoli and Duggan 31).[4] By offering Thackeray's 1848 novel as a model, Scribner's was encouraging Fitzgerald to subscribe to a bildungsroman formula that dictated the protagonist's entry into an adulthood governed by genteel notions of humility, duty, and self-sacrifice. But as Fitzgerald later confessed in a preface to *This Side of Paradise* which he wrote in August 1919 but never published, he was uncertain "how [he] could intrigue the hero into a 'philosophy of life' when [his] own ideas were in much the state of Alice's after the hatter's tea-party" (394).[5] Not yet twenty-two, he knew *he* hadn't yet "arrived" at the vague "somewhere" that signaled the end of his own adolescent uncertainties. As a result, when he repaired to his parents' home in St. Paul, Minnesota, the following summer to redraft the book, eventually reinventing it as *This Side of Paradise*, he again grappled with the conclusion. While "The Romantic Egotist" ended with Stephen Palms declaring his intention to write his autobiography, his new protagonist, Amory Blaine, would finish his education brokenhearted and disillusioned, questioning the value of life's lessons. Alone among the spires and towers of the Princeton campus, Amory stretches his arms to the sky and announces, "I know myself ... but that is all —" (260).[6] As Fitzgerald decided, "Whether [the] hero really 'gets anywhere'" would be "for the reader to decide" (*This Side of Paradise 395*).

While critics have debated the dramatic merits of the ending of *This Side of Paradise*, Fitzgerald was in fact acknowledging the newfound indeterminacy of the adolescent experience. Victorian pedagogy insisted that maturation was a fixed period in the life cycle in which youth learned "the physical and moral regimen appropriate for success" and the proper "conduct required in the world of affairs" (Kett 167). As in Thackeray's novel, this script formed the plot of dozens of popular young–adult books. According to W. Tasker Witham, "sentimental dramas" like Compton Mackenzie's *Sinister Street*, Owen Johnson's *Stover at Yale*, and Booth Tarkington's *Seventeen* portrayed growing up as a series of moral challenges. Because their heroes inevitably triumph through their character and resolve, their message was that youth's problems will disappear in time and should not be taken seriously"(10–11).

But while these narratives popularized a teleological view of adolescence, early-twentieth-century social scientists like G. Stanley Hall rejected the determinism of "stages of life" theories of development and questioned instead the cultural prerogative to assume adult roles. In *Adolescence and its Psychology and Its Relations to Physiology, Anthropology, Sociology, Sex, Crime, Religion, and Education* (1994)—a mammoth study often credited with establishing youth as a viable field of academic study—Hall argued that the "storm and stress" of maturation arose from an effort to reconcile the "hot life of feeling" that "has its prime in youth" with the "prematurely old and too often senile" temper of adulthood (2:59). Unlike other Victorian psychologists, Hall insisted that the young should not capitulate to this process without a fight. Artists and "gifted people," he noted, "seem to conserve their youth and to be all the more children, and perhaps especially all the more intensely adolescent, because of their gifts, and it is certainly one of the marks of genius that the plasticity and spontaneity of adolescence persists into maturity. Sometimes even its passions, reveries and hoydenish freaks continue" (1:547). Growing up, in other words, should not mean growing old. While Victorians insisted that youth was a liability. Hall and other influential social theorists defined it as an important cultural resource that needed to be preserved. The result was an increasing divergence between the idea of adolescence as a set period in the life cycle and the idea of youth as a romantic attitude or instinct symbolizing one's essential humanism. While Fitzgerald was probably unaware of Hall's work, at least one reviewer did make the connection.

According to the *San Francisco Chronicle, This Side of Paradise* read like "an additional chapter to G. Stanley Hall's 'Adolescence' or a psychopathological case record" (Bryer, *Fitzgerald: The Critical Reception 29*).

The tension between Victorian and modern definitions of adolescence is prevalent throughout *This Side of Paradise*, lending dramatic coherence to the novel's otherwise episodic structure. At first, Amory's adolescence is guided by a sense of divine purpose. Fueled by the "aristocratic egotism" imparted to him by both his mother, Beatrice, and Monsignor Darcy, he approaches his youth as a series of preparatory adventures for his eventual emergence as a personage able to "see clearer than the great crowd of people ... [to] decide firmly ... to influence and follow his own will" (88). For Amory, growing up means disciplining the natural "energy" of youth as he "tr[ies] to orient [it] with progress"(121). Books provide convenient models for achieving this end: not surprisingly, many of the titles cited in this "romance and reading list" (*Notebooks* 158) are Victorian expositions on children's proper moral education. As a preadolescent, Amory reads Alcott's *Little Women*, R.H. Barbour's *For the Honor of the School*, and Annie Fellows Johnston's *Mary Ware,*, among other didactic fictions (23). At eighteen, he devours Tarkington's *The Gentleman from Indiana* and Johnson's *Stover at Yale*, the latter becoming "somewhat of a textbook" (38) for him. Later, during his junior year at Princeton, he notes his fondness for what he calls "'quest' books" like Robert Hugh Benson's *None Other Gods* or Mackenzie's *Sinister Street*, in which heroes "set off in life armed with the best weapons ... avowedly intending to use them as such weapons are usually used, to push their possessors ahead as selfishly and blindly as possible" (115). The books teach Amory what David Bakan calls the "promise of adolescence," the social contract which guarantees that "if a young person does all the things he is 'supposed to do' during his [maturation], he will then realize success, status, income, power" (989). By dramatizing growth as a simple process of applying set moral lessons to ethical quandaries, Amory's texts impose upon adolescence a linear structure that encourages him to think of youth as a time of "going forward in a direct determined line" (129).

Yet a series of events conspires slowly to erode his belief in the bildungsroman formula; his romance with Isabelle Borgé goes awry, he fails a crucial exam chat prevents him from assuming the chairmanship of *The Princetonian*, and his family's financial setbacks diminish his privileged sense of noblesse oblige. Most importantly, Amory loses Rosalind Connage to the wealthy dullard Dawson Ryder, who can more ably finance her luxurious frivolity. As his "philosophy of success" tumbles down around him, Amory finds himself haunted suddenly by a "purposeless[ness]" and a "general uncertainty on every subject" (104). Stripped of the certainty of its entelechy, the energy of youth threatens to stagnate into ennui, the "ambitionless normality" of being "très old and très bored" (197). Continually stimulating himself through drink and minor forms of debauchery, Amory attempts to stimulate the feeling of motion and purpose, yet he remains painfully aware that "life had changed from an even progress along a road stretching ever in sight ... into a succession of quick, unrelated scenes.... It was all like a banquet where he sat for this half-hour of his youth and tried to enjoy brilliant epicurean courses" (215–16). Accordingly, the stories that embodied the ideals of adolescent achievement lose their allure: "Mackenzie, Chesterton, Galsworthy, Bennett, had sunk in his appreciation from sagacious, life-saturated geniuses to merely diverting contemporaries" (195).

Recognizing the inefficacy of Victorian models of maturation, Amory indulges in various "experiments in convalescence" to assuage his newfound indirection and uncertainty. He gets drunk at the Knickerbocker Bar, hoping to tumble into a "merciful coma" to avoid dealing with his disappointments (185); he quits his job at Bascome and Barlow's advertising agency, telling his employer he couldn't care less "whether Harebell's flour was any better than anyone else's" (191); he even manages to get himself pummeled by "some waiters and a couple of sailors and a few stray pedestrians" (192–93). As he tells his Princeton pal and roommate Torn D'Invilliers, the beating "was bound to come sooner or later and I wouldn't have missed it for anything.... It's the strangest feeling. You ought to get beaten up just for the experience of it" (192–93).

Such moments typify the disaffection of youth when the promises of adult culture seem most illusory. As Dick Hebdige writes, young people voice their dissatisfaction with the world they are inheriting "by going 'out of bounds,' by resisting through rituals, dressing strangely, striking bizarre attitudes, breaking rules, breaking bottles, windows, heads, issuing rhetorical challenges to the law." Through such acts, they invoke "the only power at their disposal: the power to discomfit. The power, that is, to pose—to pose a threat" (17–18). Youth poses this threat by utilizing the power of display; rejecting the obligations of good citizenship and economic productivity before these ideals fail *them*, young people enact what Charles Acland calls the "spectacle of wasted youth"—in effect, a symbolic theater through which they act out their status as "lost" and encourage "the adult world [to crowd] around the accident scene of contemporary youth ... jostling and stretching to see the carnage" (132). By indulging in an "arabesque nightmare of [a] three weeks' spree," Amory externalizes the "dramatic tragedy" of his failure at Princeton *and* his loss of Rosalind. This intention is realized in the bizarre scene at Shanley's, when Amory announces to a table of casual strangers his decision to commit suicide: "This provoked discussion. One man said that he got so depressed, sometimes, that he seriously considered it. Another agreed that there was nothing to live for.... Amory's suggestion was that they should each order a Bronx, mix broken glass in it and drink it off" (189–90)—a plan foiled only when Amory passes out.

As he admits to himself when Prohibition "put[s] a sudden stop to the submerging of [his] sorrows," Amory's debauchery is the "most violent, if the weakest, method to shield himself from the stabs of memory, and while it was not a course he would have prescribed for others he found in the end that it had done its business: he was over the first flush of pain" (194). The passage is deceptive, however, for when the Eighteenth Amendment ends his public drunkenness, Amory finds other ways in which to dramatize his dissatisfaction. He assumes blame for the underage girl in his friend Alec's hotel room and flusters the house detective by boasting of his indifference to the corrupt old man's threats of prosecution under the Mann Act (230–33). He shocks Mr. Ferrenby and his supercilious assistant by posing as a socialist when the businessmen insist on lecturing him on the benevolence of capitalism (246–57). Nor is the audience for these supposedly shocking admissions of disdain for adult norms necessarily adults. Even by himself, Amory likes to "congraculat[e] Poe for drinking himself to death in that atmosphere of smiling complacency" (207).

The oft-disparaged "Young Irony" interlude—derided by James L.W. West III as *This Side of Paradise's* "weakest chapter" for "introduc[ing] new inconsistencies into Amory's character" (*The Making of "This Side of Paradise"* 70)[7]—serves as the novel's most extended examination of the power that self-wastage promises youth. As Hebdige writes, part of the intrigue of ostentatious displays of youth discontent is their ambiguity: while drinking, promiscuity, and other rituals of disaffection constitute a "declaration of independence, of otherness, of alien intent, a refusal of anonymity, of subordinate status," they are also "a confirmation of powerlessness, a celebration of [the] impotence" inflicted by their alienation. "Both a play for attention and a refusal, once attention has been granted, to be read according to the Book" (35), displays like Amory's insist that youth's exile from society's promise locates them outside the norms of comprehension. *If we can't belong,* the message is, *we can't be known.* Throughout "Young Irony," Amory and Eleanor Savage revel in this ambiguity as they try to trump each other's "Bohemian naughtiness." For her, Amory's resemblance to Rupert Brooke is enough to fuel her romantic rebelliousness and prolong her entry into the prescriptive sex roles of wife and mother; for him, Eleanor represents the allure of unconventionality that proved illusory in Rosalind. If his former love needed Dawson Ryder to support her petulant immaturity, Eleanor seems entirely self-sufficient in "the artificialities of the temperamental teens" (217). That is, Amory knows she will never demand he grow up. Indeed, immaturity for Eleanor is vital because it allows her to avoid boarding "the sinking ship of future matrimony," which she knows is her inevitable future. "If I were born a hundred years from now, well and good, but *now* what's in store for me—I have to marry, that goes without saying" (219).

On a horseback ride during their last night together, Amory and Eleanor test each other's commitment to their nihilism. Infuriated by Amory's insistence that she is not the atheist she pretends to be, Eleanor declares, "If there's a God let him strike me—strike me!" (220), and to authenticate her Byronism, she charges toward a cliff as if to kill herself: "Then some ten feet from the edge ... she gave a sudden shriek and flung herself sideways—plunged from her horse and, rolling over twice, landed in a pile of brush five feet from the edge" (221). By saving herself at the last minute, Eleanor acknowledges that her disaffection is at least part *affectation*; by extension, Amory must admit that just as he "had loved himself in Eleanor, so now what he hated was only a mirror. Their poses were strewn about the pale dawn like broken glass" (222). By depicting youth's anomic as a facade, a defensive reaction against its ill-defined social integration, such scenes reveal how the young are caught between caring and not wanting to care, how their poses are attempts to avoid the painful uncertainty of the future. In this sense, "Young Irony" is essential to *This Side of Paradise's* portrayal of the new conditions of youth, for it shows how spectacular or theatrical displays of shocking behavior are forms of both power and powerlessness that dramatize but do not provide and escape from the indeterminacy and liminality of being young.

As Stuart Hall and Tony Jefferson have argued, the strategies by which youths like Amory and Eleanor symbolically respond to their disenfranchisement are not necessarily rejections of "proper" adult behavior; rather, they exaggerate to the point of parody patterns of social behavior otherwise deemed normal. In particular, youth cultures articulate their sense of identity through flagrant pageants of conspicuous consumption that display affluence and prosperity while demonstrating their indifference to the value of frugality and thrift (57). What Acland calls "the spectacle of wasted youth" is in this sense part of a broader consumer attitude that Stewart Ewen describes as the "spectacle of waste," a "live-for-the-moment ideology that ... avoids the question of the future, except insofar as *future* is defined by *new, improved* items" and experiences promising novel pleasures (245). In a culture that celebrates wastage as a privilege of abundance, the old adage about youth's being wasted on the young takes on a slightly different meaning: while the culture defines it as a quality that is conserved and sheltered, youth is precious to the young not for its fleetingness but for the very ease with which it can be lost. While elders covet the flame of adolescence, the young treat youth as a commodity to be exhausted. Wasting one's youth becomes a quintessential form of youth-culture display, for by utilizing the one quality that is uniquely their own, the young appropriate the central reward of the "promise"—the pleasure of consumption—from which they are otherwise alienated. Intriguingly, Zelda Fitzgerald alludes to this idea in her 1922 essay "Eulogy on the Flapper" when she dismisses the idea that disaffection and disillusion were detriments to her generation. By stripping youth of its innocence, she insists, they have taught young people to "capitalize their natural resources and get their money's worth." The lost generation is not really lost; is not "merely applying business methods to being young" (392–93).

The pleasure of wastage is a central motif in *This Side of Paradise*, for it represents the sensibility that Amory ultimately adopts when his Victorian ideals of adolescence fail him. As youth erodes into that "succession of quick, unrelated scenes," he struggles to acclimate himself to the lingering sense that maturation is a matter of loss rather than growth. At first Amory is demoralized, but gradually he assumes a pose of determined indifference toward the future. When Rosalind accuses him of being sentimental, he insists that he is a romantic, because "a sentimental, person thinks things will last ... [while] a romantic person hopes against hope that they won't" (166)— a line he later repeats to Eleanor (212). Of course, when Rosalind chooses to marry for security rather than passion, his wish comes true; the experience leaves him aware that "his youth seemed never so vanished as now" (226). The broken affair leaves him with "tireless passion, fierce jealousy, [and a] longing to possess and crush," which he feels are the only "payment for the loss of his youth—bitter calomel under the thin sugar of love's exaltation" (227). Likewise, he comes to understand that through his romance with Eleanor "he lost a further part of him that nothing could restore: and when he lost it he lost also the power of regretting it" (206). In effect, what Amory must learn here is that he will receive a fair return on his youth only if he transforms the loss ailing him into a proactive principle of self-depletion. No longer believing he possesses the "qualities that made him see clearer than the great crowd of people, that made him decide more firmly and able to influence and follow his own will" (88), Amory must accept that the definitive experience of youth is not moral growth or social achievement but the pleasure afforded by its consumption.

The realization comes to him on a rainy afternoon during which he aimlessly rides atop a bus rattling its way through Manhattan. Interrogating his motives and beliefs, he decides his cynicism is honest if not virtuous. The test of his corruption, he decides, would be "becoming really insincere" by "thinking I regretted my lost youth when I only envy the delights of losing it": "Youth is like having a big plate of candy. Sentimentalists think they want to be in the pure, simple state they were in before they are the candy. They don't. They just want the fun of eating it all over again.... I don't want to repeat my innocence. I want the pleasure of losing it again" (239). In many ways, the passage is even more central to Amory's education than the meditation that ends the novel, in which he declares that his generation has "grown up to find all Gods dead, all wars fought, all faiths in man shaken" (260). The bus-top monologue reveals that Amory has accepted the irrelevance of the bildungsroman in the modern world and that wastage is the lone compensation for one's inability to become "a certain type of artist.... a certain sort of man" (259). Youth, he realizes, is not a formative period of promise but a momentary pleasure whose entire raison d'être is defined by its own inevitable passing.

This Side of Paradise proved one of those rare novels that is ultimately remembered more as a part of a fad than as an artistic achievement. The book's initial printing of three thousand copies disappeared from bookstore shelves within a week, while total first-year sales neared fifty thousand, more than ten times the average amount for a debut novel in the 1920s. This unexpected success proved to publishers what other sectors of the commercial marketplace were at the same time discovering: that youth was a lucrative target audience as well as a topic of cultural concern. Savvy media manipulators realized that the prominence of the "rising generation" as a social problem offered unlimited potential for generating interest in their various products and ventures. Fitzgerald was among these skilled press agents. The popularity of *This Side of Paradise* allowed him to establish himself as a spokesman for modern youth. As he wrote his Scribner's editor Maxwell Perkins in May 1922. Amory Blaine's story created his "*own personal public*" composed of "countless flappers and college kids who think I am a sort of oracle" (Kuehl and Bryer 59).[8] And as he declared in interview after interview, he imagined it his duty to limn the attitudes and mores of his peers as accurately as possible. The three-paragraph aesthetic declaration entitled "The Author's Apology," composed in 1920 for the American Booksellers Association, offers Fitzgerald's most succinct statement of this intent: "An author ought to write for the youth of his own generation, the critics of the next, and the schoolmasters of ever after ward" (*F. Scott Fitzgerald on Authorship* 35).[9]

Yet almost immediately, the problem of following up the success of *This Side of Paradise* proved a formidable challenge. Fitzgerald wanted not only to retain his popular appeal but also to strengthen his standing among those literati who dismissed him as precious and pretentious—two seemingly conflicting goals that he intended to realize by reassessing his trademark theme of generational disaffection from the perspective of naturalistic writers whom he admired, including H.L. Mencken and Frank and Charles Norris. Even before *This Side of Paradise* was published, he spoke of at least four prospective projects that never materialized. Part of the reason that "The Demon Lover," "The Diary of a Literary Failure," "The Drunkard's Holiday," and "The Darling Heart" proved false starts may have been a growing need to move beyond the critique of the bildungsroman that had formed the plot of his first novel. "It seems to me that the overworked art-form at present in America is the 'history of the young man,'" Fitzgerald publicly declared in early 1921. "This writing ... consists chiefly in dumping all your youthful adventures into the readers' lap with a profound air of importance, keeping carefully within the formulas of Wells and James Joyce" (*E. Scott Fitzgerald on Authorship* 43). Fitzgerald was particularly irked by Floyd Dell's *Mooncalf*, which he repeatedly disparaged in 1920–21 for plagiarizing *Paradise* to cash in on its rightful popularity and praise (Bruccoli and Duggan 75). He also dismissed former influences: whereas *Stover at Yale* once served as a "textbook," Owen Johnson's *The Wasted Generation* (1921) struck him as "so obvious as to be painful," a pathetic attempt to palliate his generation's postwar disillusionment with an antiquated sentimentalism (*E. Scott Fitzgerald on Authorship* 50).

By August 1920, Fitzgerald had formulated a plot that freed him from the constraints of the "history of the young man": he would describe "the life of one Anthony Patch between his 25th and 33d years," showing how "he and his beautiful young wife are wrecked on the shoals of dissipation" (*Letters* 145). Ostensibly, in keeping with his ambition to produce naturalistic fiction, Fitzgerald planned to portray the Patches' wreckage as a symbolic testament to the amorality of the era's rampant consumerism. Yet wasted youth and its relationship to the dilemmas of maturation remained an insistent concern over the course of the composition process, albeit in a very different form than in *This Side of Paradise*. Fitzgerald's debut novel can be classified as a coming-of-age story in the sense that it attributes youth's problems to the uncertainty of the *paysage moralisé* into adulthood. But coming of age evokes something far more ominous in *The Beautiful and Damned*, as this second novel was eventually titled. If *This Side of Paradise* focuses on the difficulties of growing up. *The Beautiful and Damned* dramatizes the dread of growing old, for more than wealth or prodigality, it is the fear of aging that compels the wildly self-destructive behavior of the central characters. The result is a more complex and more compelling examination of the causes and consequences of wasted youth than the book's reception history would suggest.[10] In *This Side of Paradise*, displays of disaffection are compensation for Amory's inability to become "a certain type of artist" or "a certain sort of man." By contrast, *The Beautiful and Damned* projects a "use it or lose it" philosophy. Anthony and Gloria Patch so dread the chronological coming of senescence that they decide to squander their youth before its vibrant intensity naturally erodes. Measuring their self-wastage against clock and calendar, the couple ravage themselves prematurely because doing so is for them the only victory possible against the inevitable ravages of time. Their self-destruction is by no means as noble as Amory's; rather than rebel against the false promises of Victorian maturation, *The Beautiful and Damned* depicts wasted youth as a lifestyle adopted by dilettantes and bacchantes as well as romantic egotists. Nevertheless, the book elaborates upon Fitzgerald's belief that, given the temporal fixity of youth, its only practical value is the brief pleasure offered by its consumption.[11]

The novel builds toward a climactic revelation of this point by playing off connotations of youth as a standard of intensity, passion, and joie de vivre. Throughout the first third of the narrative, protagonists in their early twenties insist that they can retain their youthful energy and vigor as they exit their adolescence to assume adult responsibilities. Indeed, they initially believe that their enthusiasms will invigorate and transform stolid adult institutions, marriage in particular. Yet no sooner do Anthony and Gloria feel blessed with this power than an approaching birthday grips them with unrelenting age anxieties, and they are forced to acknowledge their imminent exile from the paradisiacal world of youth. Exploiting the desire to detach youth from time, Fitzgerald promptly insists it cannot be done. In the end, Anthony and Gloria succumb to a deterministic attitude toward age by dating their entry into senescence according to a specific chronological milestone—their thirtieth birthdays. Curiously, the Patches are not alone in dreading this approaching event. Fitzgerald's narrator frequently intrudes into the action with grandiloquent editorials that lament "the inevitable metamorphosis" that this milestone inaugurates. While one's twenties are "a play, most tragic and most divine," life after twenty-nine degenerates into "a succession of speeches, sweated over by the eternal plagiarist in the clammy hours and acted by men subject to cramps, cowardice, and manly sentiment" (170). By its final page, *The Beautiful and Damned* proves so insistent on this point that Fitzgerald might well have subtitled it "Life Ends at Thirty."

The yearning to believe that youth is an eternal quality that can transcend age is dramatized most vividly in the chapters detailing Anthony and Gloria's courtship. Fitzgerald introduces this desire in an atypical supernatural prelude that depicts youth as God's gift to humanity. In a dialogue with the spirit of beauty, the disembodied voice of the Lord announces his intention to reincarnate her as the "susciety gurl" Gloria Patch. "You will be known during your fifteen years as a ragtime kid, a flapper, a jazz-baby, and baby vamp," the deity declares. "You will dance new dances neither more nor less gracefully than you danced the old ones" (29). However inadvisable, this excursion into the fantastic offers Fitzgerald's most literal representation of juvenescence as a divine blessing. If beauty is youth and youth beauty, the scene implies, that is all we on earth need to know—except, as God assures Beauty, that being young is also a lot of fun. Originally, the novel was to conclude with Beauty's return to paradise, her spirit inexorably diminished by her tenure on earth. "How remote you are," God laments, "You seem to have no heart" (Bruccoli, *Some Sort of Epic Grandeur* 157). Fitzgerald cut this second scene shortly before publication, fearing that its lack of realism would diminish the tragedy of the Patches' dissolution. Had both dialogues remained, they would have served as narrative frames illustrating the point that youth is ephemeral, even in the afterlife. Without the concluding conversation, however, God and Beauty's first exchange serves an ironic function. While the early chapters suggest that youth's spirit is eternal, the rest of the story offers ample evidence of its fleetingness.

As Beauty's earthly incarnation, Gloria embodies the illusory allure of immortal youth in the novel's introductory episodes. On her first date with Anthony, when he tells her that, at twenty-two, she looks eighteen, she insists. "I'm going to start being that. I don't like being twenty-two" (64). She claims the power to reverse the clock; when Anthony asks, "It's your world, isn't it?" she replies, "As long as I'm—young" (66). Paradoxically, her unwillingness to act her age makes her seem wise beyond her years. Anthony is often surprised by how "she seemed to grow gradually older until at the end ruminations too deep for words would be wintering in her eyes" (113). Fitzgerald does not imply here that Gloria suddenly matures; rather, Anthony wants desperately to believe that her melodramatic immaturity embodies the age-old truth of the supremacy of youthful passions over adult contentment. A simple kiss from her convinces him that "he [is] young now," and that status makes him feel "more triumphant than death" (126).

Initially, Gloria resists Anthony's matrimonial advances, claiming incompetence in domestic matters. Once convinced that he shares her youthful fervor, she plots to rejuvenate marriage with juvenescent passion. A diary passage records her pledge not to succumb to "colorless" adult complacencies: "Marriage was created not to be a background but to need one. Mine is going to be outstanding. It can't, shan't be the setting—it's going to be the performance, the live, lovely, glamourous performance, and the world shall be the scenery." Nor will she relinquish her immature selfishness in the name of motherhood. Rather than "grow rotund and unseemly" and "lose [her] self-love" by "think[ing] in terms of milk, oatmeal, nurse, diapers," she will raise only "dream children ... dazzling little creatures who flutter ... on golden, golden wings" (147).

Yet this optimism erodes barely six months into the Patches' union when they realize that marriage is an "extortion of youth" (156). The revelation first comes during a honeymoon visit to the Virginia home of Robert E. Lee, where tourists flock to gape at the site's newly restored antebellum facade. To Gloria, the estate looks like "a blondined, rouged-up old woman of sixty" (167), an aged thing competing against its lost youth. The effort to reconstruct and preserve the past violates the natural tragedy of mutability: "Beautiful things grow to a certain height and then they fail and fade off, breathing out memories as they decay" (166), she declares. "I want this house to look back on its glamourous moment of youth.... [because] [t]here's no beauty without poignancy and there's no poignancy without the feeling that it's going, men, names, books, houses—bound for dust—mortal" (167). Fitzgerald offers little justification for why Gloria, the reincarnation of eternal beauty, should suddenly sing the praises of its mortality, yet the scene marks a turning point in the Patches' attitude toward youth. Oppressed by a sense of its ephemeralness, the couple begin "extracting poignancy from the memorable things of life and youth" (169) and pass their entire twenties measuring its slow disintegration. Certain to be soon dispossessed of it, Anthony and Gloria commence a countdown to thirty, the age at which they believe flaming youth gives way to the raked embers of middle age.

Intriguingly, the Patches' anxieties about aging are so strong that they date themselves not by their actual age but by the milestones looming on the horizon. As Fitzgerald implies, age phobias inspire the paradoxical tendency to soothe that fear by prematurely presuming oneself old. Anthony at twenty-six initiates this pattern when he bemoans his lack of accomplishment in life: "Here I am almost twenty-seven—" he declares in an argument with Gloria (211). At twenty-three, Gloria herself is "in an attractive but sincere panic" over turning twenty-four, because it means only "six years to thirty!" (192). At twenty-five, she fears turning twenty-six because she realizes that her adolescent narcissism has decayed into "something that she had hitherto never needed—the skeleton ... of her ancient abhorrence, a conscience" (278). And by her twenty-ninth birthday, she is reduced to wondering whether "she had not wasted her faintly tired beauty, whether there was such a thing as use for any quality bounded by a harsh and inevitable mortality" (391).[12] These frequent declarations not only insist that the butterfly of youth is broken on the wheel of time but that the most crushing blows come long before they are due.

Controversially, this attitude is reiterated by Fitzgerald's intrusive narrator, who often halts the advancing plot to offer his own ruminations on the significance of chronological milestones: "It is in the twenties that the actual momentum of life begins to slacken, and it is a simple soul indeed to whom as many things are significant and meaningful at thirty as at ten years before" (169). Pessimism about the middle years even leads to the occasional, bizarre reductio ad absurdum: "At thirty an organ-grinder is a more or less moth-eaten man who grinds an organ—and once he was an organ-grinder!" (169). Just when the organ-grinder's image seems to establish a new standard for idiosyncratic symbols, Fitzgerald conveys youth's dissipating energies by referencing another peculiar occupation: "After the sureties of youth there sets in a period of almost intense and intolerable complexity. With the soda–jerker this period is so short as to be almost negligible. Men higher in the scale hold out longer in the attempt to preserve the ultimate niceties of relationship, to retain 'impractical' ideas of integrity. But by the late twenties the business has grown too intricate, and what has hitherto been imminent and confusing has become gradually remote and dim" (283–84). Why an organ-grinder would suffer the loss of these sureties more than a soda jerk is an unresolved ambiguity; yet the interjections complement Anthony and Gloria's attitude by depicting aging as an unceasing erosion of youthful vivacity. Turning thirty, Fitzgerald concludes, marks the point at which "we value safety above romance, [and] we become, quite unconsciously, pragmatic" (284).

For most critics, this editorializing tendency reflects Fitzgerald's unfortunate training in the popular-fiction market of the 1920s, which encouraged authorial intrusions to minimize textual complexity and ensure recognition of a story's point. Matthew J. Bruccoli argues that the aforementioned asides diminish the novel's artistry and that Fitzgerald "would not become a complete novelist until he learned the techniques for controlling point of view and disciplining his habit of obtruding into the narrative" (*Some Sort of Epic Grandeur* 159), a prerogative he would not achieve until *The Great Gatsby* three years later. Yet, however aesthetically flawed, the running commentary on turning thirty in *The Beautiful and Damned* echoes a contemporaneous attitude toward aging popularly known as the "fixed period" theory. This view, disseminated throughout a range of scientific discourse and public policy, held that intellectual, moral, and economic potential decline with age. The early twentieth century witnessed a cottage industry in mathematical formulas and equations claiming to calculate the physiological and psychological effects of aging. Frequently advanced as "natural laws," these theories of senescence held that "a certain number of years mark the limit of human productivity, rationality, and efficiency," and they helped create the cultural presumption that "old age was irrelevant and burdensome" (Cole 169). Fitzgerald's interjections reflect a similar attitude. Not only is the enfeebling that age brings a biological inevitability, but that structure of decline is tied to a specific chronological sequence. Thirty may mark an earlier moment of erosion than most fixed-period advocates argued, but not by much—forty was the average age at which the irrevocable diminishment of capacities was said to begin. As the narrator of *The Beautiful and Damned* insists, age is a "force intangible as air" and "more definite than death" (414).

As if to compensate for their eroding youth, Anthony and Gloria begin to affect a "magnificent attitude of not giving a damn" and hurl themselves headlong into drinking and profligacy. They host endless fetes, wreck cars, and squander their finances, all in an effort "not to be sorry, not to loose one cry of regret, ... and to seek the moment's happiness as fervently and persistently as possible" (226). The Patches themselves are never quite able to articulate their motives for squandering what youth they still possess; Fitzgerald charges that duty to their close friend Maury Noble, who appears at select moments (much like the novel's narrator) to pontificate on the futility of ambition and effort in the adult world. In one long tirade against maturity, Maury recounts his initiation into the despair of senescence: "I grew up, and the beauty of succulent illusions fell away from me. The fibre of my mind coarsened me and my ears grew miserably keen. Life arose around my island like a sea, and presently I was swimming.... I reached maturity under the impression that I was gathering the experience to order my life for happiness. Indeed, I accomplished the not unusual feat of solving each question in my mind long before it presented itself to me in life—and of being beaten and bewildered just the same" (253–54). Growing up, the passage insists, offers little chance of triumphing over life's challenges. Instead, it ensures nothing but a sense of loss and defeat.

For their part, however, Anthony and Gloria fail to appreciate the significance of this dispiriting moral, and they continue their revelries with only slight awareness that both are "vaguely weaker in fibre" and that "things [have] been slipping" (278). But when Anthony's temperance-preaching grandfather happens upon one of their frequent debauches, they are disinherited and must cope suddenly with such adult inconveniences as paying their own bills. To meet expenses, Anthony embarks upon various careers but quits when he finds the work monotonous. Gloria also attempts to economize but grows bitter at her husband's laziness. By the final third of the novel, their marriage weathers adultery, alcoholism, and the humiliation of relocating to a working-class neighborhood. As refuge from this downward spiral, they act out increasingly empty gestures from their glamorous youth. Anthony resorts to drink to renew "those opalescent dreams of future [pleasure]—the mutual heritage of the happy and damned." But intoxication provides only a transitory escape from his fall: "As he grew drunker the dreams faded and he became a confused spectre, moving in odd crannies of his own mind ... harshly contemptuous at best and reaching sodden and dispiriting depths" (388). Gloria also reverts to her girlhood by dressing dolls and rereading the romantic novels which fuel "that illusion of young romantic love to which women look forever forward and forever back" (371). But whereas being young was once a matter of acting eighteen instead of twenty-two, Gloria can no longer maintain the fantasy. Her most debilitating moment of disillusion occurs when she discovers Anthony scrounging for loose change to buy his morning drink: "For a moment she received the impression that he was suddenly and definitely old" (424).

By their thirties, then, Anthony and Gloria waste their youth and beauty. But if their dissipation is a moral failure, the squandering also realizes perfectly the logic of planned obsolescence, for they consume and exhaust the precious commodity of their twenties and all that the age symbolizes before "harsh mortality" can. Not surprisingly, the toll taken by their wastage is not most visible in their marital discontent or economic misfortunes. The real tragedy of their ruin, Fitzgerald implies, is that they have made themselves old before their time. On her twenty-ninth birthday, Gloria is horrified to discover that she looks too old to star as a silent-film vamp, a part she once effortlessly played in high society. Told she is more suited for "*a small character part supposed to be a very haughty rich widow*" (403), she rushes to the mirror, where she is stunned by the wear and tear of her features. If her beauty once seemed the very essence of vitality, she recognizes now that her eyes are "tired": "Oh, my pretty face." she cries. "Oh, I don't want to live without my pretty face!" The episode concludes with Gloria prostrate on the floor, sobbing, "the first awkward movement she had ever made" {404}. As she later explains to Anthony, "I wasn't thirty; and I didn't think I—looked thirty" (428). Gloria's husband must likewise confront the withered youth in the mirror: "He faced his reflection ... contemplating dejectedly the wan, pasty face, the eyes with their crisscross of lines like shreds of dried blood, the stooped and flabby figure whose very sag was a document in lethargy." The vision leads to the book's strongest evidence of his decline: "He was thirty-three—[but] he looked forty" (444).

As with *This Side of Paradise*, Fitzgerald delivered his protagonists to a final recognition of their wasted youth only to confront his authorial uncertainty over the novel's ending. After discarding the episode in which Beauty, to God's dismay, returns dispirited to heaven, he crafted an orotund coda in which he praised the Patches' faith in the glory of youth. "In the search for happiness ... these two people were marked as guilty chiefly by the freshness and fullness of their desire. Their disillusion was always a comparative thing—they had sought glamor and color through their respective worlds with steadfast loyalty—sought it and it alone in kisses and in wine, sought it with the same ingenuousness in the wanton moonlight as under the cold sun of inviolate chastity. Their fault was not that they had doubted but that they had believed" (Bruccoli, *Some Sort of Epic Grandeur* 157–58). Praising Anthony and Gloria for their romantic idealism satisfied the sentimental dictates of *Metropolitan Magazine*, the high-paying periodical that serialized *The Beautiful and Damned* in the fall of 1921. Yet Fitzgerald eventually rejected this conclusion for violating the tragic tone he desired. Had it ended with this passage, the novel would have implied that the Patches' youth had been lost, not wasted.

At his wife's recommendation, Fitzgerald concluded the novel instead with the Patches sailing for Europe after winning an arduous court battle over his grandfather's thirty-million-dollar estate. Gloating over his replenished wealth and social status, Anthony congratulates himself for "show[ing] them.... It was a hard fight, but I didn't give up and I came through!" (448). All around him, passengers gossip about his poor health and the insanity said to accompany his courtroom travails. Their whispering confirms the long-term effects of the emotional breakdown that he suffers in the book's penultimate scene, just before their courtroom victory is announced. When a former mistress appears on his doorstep, Anthony suffers a violent blackout and reverts to his childhood. Gloria discovers him stretched out on his bedroom floor, poring over the stamp collection that he prized as a young boy. "Get out.... Or else I'll tell my grandfather," Anthony screams, his voice sounding "like a pert child" (447). Woefully unfit for adult responsibilities, he copes by escaping into a preadolescent world of simple, uncomplicated pleasures. The luxury of remaining childish is, of course, just what his newly refurnished wealth will allow. He can resume believing that youth is a lifestyle best enjoyed by the affluent. Yet the assumption is contradicted by his appearance, for he has been reduced to a "bundled figure seated in a wheel chair" (447). As Fitzgerald makes clear, Anthony and Gloria are neither young nor beautiful anymore, regardless of the fantasies that their fortune can now finance. Instead, they have been damned by the aging process.

The Beautiful and Damned hardly exhausted Fitzgerald's anxieties toward aging and lost youth. Rather, these issues remain a persistent—if unacknowledged—obsession throughout his major work as well as his more commercially minded short stories. In *The Great Gatsby*, Nick Carraway remembers in the midst of the climactic exchange between Gatsby, Daisy, and Tom that he has forgotten his thirtieth birthday: "Thirty—the promise of a decade of loneliness, a thinning list of single men to know, a thinning brief-case of enthusiasm, thinning hair" (106). And in a later story, "At Your Age" (1929), a fifty-year-old man hopes to revive the "warm sureties of his youth" by romancing a flapper young enough to be his daughter. The tale includes a line that could describe Fitzgerald's attitude toward the subject: "Youth! Youth! Youth!" Tom Squires tells himself. "I want it near me, all around me, just once more before I'm too old to care" (*The Short Stories* 482). Inevitably, however, such characters must admit that they have aged: "I'm thirty," Nick tells Jordan Baker when she accuses him of treating her inconsiderately. "I'm five years too old to lie to myself and call it honor" (*The Great Gatsby* 138). And as Tom Squires realizes that he has "lost the battle against youth and spring," he understands that the affair has stripped him of any illusions he had carried into middle age. "He could not have walked down wasted into the darkness without being used up a little; what he wanted, after all, was only to break his strong old heart" (*The Short Stories* 494). This age-consciousness even works its way into biographical legend. In 1950, Alice B. Toklas described Fitzgerald visiting Gertrude Stein on his thirtieth birthday complaining "that it was unbearable for him to have to face the fact that his youth was over" (I). While its accuracy is questionable—the Fitzgeralds were in Juan-les-Pins, not Paris, in September 1926—the story nevertheless furthers the myth of an artist who memorialized and moralized his generation's wasted youth. But rather than simply mourn the passing of youth, Fitzgerald was the first author to recognize the appeal of youth culture. Intrigued by and yet wary of the freedoms that new rites of passage allowed his peers, Fitzgerald poses in his early work a question that American writing would ask of its teens and twentysomethings for decades to come: Where are you going, and where have you been?

NOTES

1. Boyd's desire to rehabilitate Fitzgerald's "disillusioned youth" image may have been an effort to pay him back for recommending her manuscript *The Love Legend* to Scribner's in 1922. Fitzgerald also encouraged Maxwell Perkins to accept Boyd's husband Thomas's novel *Through the Wheat* (Bruccoli and Duggan 94).

2. The major exception is Berman's *"The Great Gatsby" and Modern Times*, which examines how Fitzgerald's most famous novel comments on various cultural phenomena of the 1920s, including the fascination with youth.

3. Held designed the book jackets for *Tales of the Jazz Age* (1922), Fitzgerald's second story collection, and *The Vegetable* (1923), his unsuccessful play. See Bruccoli, *Some Sort of Epic Grandeur* 171 and Le Vot 132.

4. It was long assumed that Fitzgerald's personal editor, Maxwell Perkins, wrote this letter (see Bruccoli and Duggan 32). Recently, however, West and others have suggested that William C. Brownell is the author (see *This Side of Paradise* xix).

5. His first reaction was hasty: before submitting the book again to Scribner's in late 1918, he "dispatched" Stephen Palms" to the war and callously slew him several thousand feet in the air, when he fell ... down **** down ****" (*This Side of Paradise* 394).

6. As West notes, this final dash turned into a period in the book's first edition. His introduction to the Cambridge edition of *Paradise* makes a convincing case for returning to the original punctuation (xxxi–xxx).

7. West's dissatisfaction arises largely from evidence that Fitzgerald spliced a portion of "The Romantic Egotist" into *This Side of Paradise* without revising minor inconsistencies like Stephen Palm's hair color (blond) to match Amory's (auburn) (*The Making of "This Side of Paradise"* 68–71).

8. For a brief but illuminating discussion of Fitzgerald's reputation as a generational spokesman, see Fass, who examines how the same periodical market that rewarded Fitzgerald handsomely for his Jazz Age short stories took up "the theme of youth ... like a literary leitmotif as it debated the effects of modernity on the emerging generation: "The central issue was always the failure of modern society; rarely were specific solutions for the youth problem more than an afterthought. The repetition of the catalogue of youth's faults was, in fact, not intended to describe or reform. It was, instead, a form of ritual incantation which, by bringing the problem forward again and again, created a painful consciousness that became a substitute for action, and indeed, even a way of coming to terms with the situation. "Like the countless articles sensationally entitled "The Revolt of Youth," "Has Youth Deteriorated?" or "These Wild Young People," both Fitzgerald's early novels and his short fiction employed the "technique of relief by exposure," for by "employing the symbols of his time to tease his readers' curiosity while he exploited their alarm," he "was able to best express the period's aching sense of frustration" (17).

9. Evidence suggests that Fitzgerald later regretted both this statement and his reputation as the voice of the "rising generation." In *The Beautiful and Damned* he attributes "The Author's Apology" to an unsympathetic character, the novelist Richard

Caramel, who complains about how his propensity for "strange pronouncements" pigeonholes him in the literary marketplace. "I believe a lot of it," Caramel admits. "It simply was a mistake to give it out" (189). Later, in what can only be regarded as a bizarre metafictional commentary on his public identity, Fitzgerald has Caramel complain that "Everywhere I go some silly girl asks me if I've read 'This Side of Paradise.' Are our girls really like that? If it's true to life, which I don't believe, the next generation is going to the dogs" (421).

10. With the exception of *The Vegetable*, *The Beautiful and Damned* has generated less critical interest than any other full-length work in its author's ocuvre. What commentary does exist treats the Patches' story as a critique of capitalist decadence. For a recent representative example of such criticism, see Craig Monk's "The Political F. Scott Fitzgerald."

11. Fitzgerald's age-consciousness surfaces in his stories as well. At times references may seem gratuitous, as in "The Ice Palace" when Sally Carrol Happer is described as "rest[ing] her nineteen-year-old chin on a fifty-two-year-old sill" (*Short Stories* 48). Elsewhere, the theme is more central to the plot. "The Curious Case of Benjamin Button" tells the story of a man born at seventy who grows younger throughout his life; the tale captures the era's belief that vitality and a healthy lifestyle could reverse the aging process. In "'O Russet Witch!'" a young man ages prematurely when he abandons his romantic illusions and settles for a dull but comfortable life whose equanimity is only occasionally interrupted by a woman who symbolizes for him the energy and power of youth. Only at sixty-five does he learn that this woman is not a supernatural being but a former dancer infamous for her role in a sensational divorce trial. The effect on Merlin is immediate. "He was an old man now indeed, so old that it was impossible for him to dream of ever having been young, so old that the glamour was gone out of the world.... He was too old now even for memories" (*Six Tales of the Jazz Age* 118–19).

12. In one of the novel's more glaring editorial oversights, Fitzgerald places Gloria's birthday in three different months (August, May, and February). When a reader, one George A. Kuyper, informed him of the inconsistency, Fitzgerald responded with exasperation: "My God! I can never straighten it out without rewriting the whole book. It is really a most embarrassing predicament. God! This bugbear of inconsistency!" (Bruccoli and Duggan 98).

R Y U I C H I   Y A M A G U C H I

A Yoknapatawpha Pantheon:
Light in August

Some six months after the publication of *Sanctuary*, Faulkner began a new novel that no one could call cheap: *Light in August*. This much longer and denser work still has much in common with its predecessor: shocking violence, a criminal hero, and attacks on puritanism, small-town gossip, and mob rule. In place of the twinned plots of Horace and Temple in *Sanctuary*, *Light in August* features the contrasted plots of Lena Grove and Joe Christmas, a formal experiment in counterpoint that Faulkner would extend in *The Wild Palms*. Like *Flags in the Dust*, *Light in August* depicts Yoknapatawpha as a world teeming with both people and stories. And with its multitude of narrators and points of view, *Light in August* evokes the rich polyphony that distinguishes *The Sound and the Fury* and *As I Lay Dying*. In all of these ways, *Light in August* is vintage Faulkner: Faulkner at his most luxuriant and, arguably at his most characteristic.[1]

For a Faulknerian masterwork, *Light in August* is relatively approachable. The stories of Lena Grove and Joe Christmas, mediated by Gail Hightower and Byron Bunch, are told mainly by means of dialogue and omniscient third-person narration. The reasons for this choice of presentation are both technical and thematic. In the first place, there is simply too much material to be presented by stream-of-consciousness narration, or by any one first-person narrator. No one character in the novel possesses the complete story. In the second place, *Light in August* probes

From *Fualkner's Artistic Vision: the Bizarre and the Terrible* by Ryuichi Yamaguchi. © 2004 by Rosemont Publishing & Printing Corp.

several religious questions, each one of which has a multitude of possible answers. Each of the major characters, and many of the minor ones, embody responses to these questions. And no one character's responses are definitive or complete. Thus, while *Light in August* may seem less boldly experimental in form than some of the earlier novels, its enterprise is no less demanding.[2]

This enterprise is above all a religious one, as all other concerns—race, sexuality, identity, even community—are saturated with religious significance for the characters. It is not simply a matter of providing what Alfred Kazin calls "a study in religious pathology" or an affirmation of the power of faith; in fact, *Light in August* does both, and more besides.[3] Essentially, this novel explores three related religious questions. First, did God create humankind in his image, or vice versa? Second, where does the human mind end and the mind of God begin? In other words, where is the boundary between the human and the divine consciousness? Finally, what is God the god of: of providence, of love, of wrathful hosts?

In its themes, its action, its characterization, and its discourse, *Light in August* is so thoroughly permeated with divinity that, as Virginia Hlavsa and K.J. Phillips have shown, it at least invites a mythic reading. It examines its religious concerns by beginning from the opposite premise to that which operates in *As I Lay Dying*. In the earlier novel, no one is God, and no one, including Darl, knows everything. In *Light in August*, however, nearly everyone partakes of the divine, and at some point, nearly everyone is omniscient or infallible. The characters read each other's minds; they pursue each other with superhuman accuracy; they see visions of eternity: they glow and glitter with divine light: they preach their respective truths on race, sexuality, justice, and the nature of God. They initiate and celebrate their own mythic ritual holiday, a Jefferson Saturnalia, announced by the column of smoke from Joanna Burden's burning house, and culminating in the castration and murder of Joe Christmas. In all of these activities, the characters present their individual responses—whether sublime, ridiculous, or horrific—to the essential questions posed by the novel.[4]

These are portentous matters and activities indeed; yet they are also the stuff of jokes. The gods of *Light in August* can be both awesome and ludicrous, sometimes simultaneously. Their visions are as often comical as profound. Their pronouncements range from the sardonic to the psychotic. And their carnival, their "Roman holiday," is indisputably a feast of misrule, from the arrival of the useless fire engine to the heroic bicycle ride of Percy Grimm.[5] As they converge on Jefferson, the "numberless avatars" (226) of *Light in August* suggest that if God is the highest aspiration of the human mind, he may also be the most dangerous. Their divinity gives them powers both bizarre and terrible, and their use of those powers propels both the violence and the benevolence of *Light in August*.[6]

"A Roman Holiday"

The "yellow pillar of smoke" (53) rising from Joanna's house on the Saturday morning after her death summons the people of Jefferson to a festival of sacrifice. This deadly holiday begins with the spectacle of the fire, moves immediately to a search for "someone to crucify" (289), and proceeds erratically to the inevitable castration and murder of Joe Christmas, Joanna's supposedly mulatto lover and murderer. Like the original Saturnalia, Jefferson's Roman holiday features a world turned upside down. Joanna Burden, the detested Yankee "Nigger lover" (292), is transformed by her death to a martyred southern woman, the innocent white victim of a black brute. Byron Bunch and Gail Hightower find their quiet personal lives turned upside down both by the murder and by the arrival in Jefferson of the pregnant and unwed Lena Grove. Jefferson's Saturnalia also includes a feast of misrule: the authorities are helpless, even with the best of equipment, to put out the fire or to find Joe before he is ready to be caught. Their efforts at crowd control are useless; in the prevailing atmosphere of festive excitement, the crowds act for their own unfathomable reasons. Finally, the Saturnalia ends, as traditionally it must, in the ritual killing (castration discretionary) of the king of the festivities—customarily, a convict or a slave.[7]

The murder of a scapegoat is not funny. But in *Light in August*, the local authorities—the police and the firefighters—are. First, while Joanna's old wooden house burns to the ground, the town's elaborate fire engine arrives with a noisy flourish. But its state-of-the-art ladders and hoses are useless at this fire. The upper story of the house has already gone up in smoke; worse yet, the Burden place is unequipped with a fire hydrant. All the shiny new fire engine can do is to stand idle while the volunteer firemen stare dumbly at the blaze and finger their pistols, wishing they could find the culprit. The feast of misrule has begun.[8]

The manhunt with the borrowed bloodhounds is a more sustained joke on the failure of law and order during this chaotic period. The dogs themselves are unimpressive, regarding "with sad abjectness" (296) the eager posse that meets them at the railroad station. Their performance is even worse than their appearance. They can find old garbage pits; they can find Joanna's ancient pistol; they can even follow the tracks of Joe's shoes, as long as he keeps wearing the same shoes. When they catch a scent, they bay hysterically—at deserted cabins or bewildered children. But they ignore visual clues, cannot hear the posse's shouts above their own woebegone howls, and, being dogs, are sadly lacking in the divine gift for unerring pursuit that belongs to the human characters. Eventually the sheriff decides that they are not even worth kicking. As for the fugitive himself, he speculates in amazement that there must be some "rule" (337) of the chase that forbids any solution so simple as accepting his surrender. Indeed, Joe is not caught until he goes into Mottstown, gets a shave and a haircut and new clothes, and admits to a local man that he is the fugitive.[9]

The signals that end Jefferson's Saturnalia are similar to those with which it began. To the accompaniment of the town fire alarm, a column or pillar—the "black blast," "like the rush of sparks from a rising rocket" (465) of Joe's blood as he dies—appears to the holiday celebrants. Like Joanna's column of smoke, Joe's rocket-rush of blood becomes a kind of monument, fixed permanently in the community's memory.[10]

Like the fire, too, the spurt of blood indicates a failure of established authority. Joe's escape from the sheriff's deputy gives Percy Grimm his chance to act as angelic vigilante. Percy has already usurped the authority of the state and even the federal government. He wants to wear his National Guard captain's uniform to show that "Uncle Sam is present in more than spirit" (453), in the lone but all-sufficient person of Percy Grimm. By the day of Joe's indictment, Percy's air of authority has convinced the milling crowds on the square that "He's the head of the whole thing" (458). Thus Percy shares with Joe the role of lord of misrule. And it is Percy who, by his savage extralegal act of mutilation and murder, brings forth the black blast that signals both the end of the Saturnalia and Joe's apotheosis.[11]

The holiday atmosphere of Jefferson's Saturnalia combines festivity and horror. Indeed, the festivity celebrates the horror. As they watch the smoke from the Burden house, the workers at the planing mill joke about "how fifty years ago folks said it ought to be burned, and with a little human fat meat to start it good" (49). The countryman who tells Byron of Joe's murder complains of having to miss the accompanying "excitement" (442): "Durn the luck. Just when I had to get started for home" (442) Jefferson's Roman holiday, even when solemnized in church, demands and celebrates "death as though death were the boon" (367). The sacrifice of Joanna Burden and Joe Christmas is the sacred and joyous task of the Saturnalia, and it requires the failures of the fire engine, the bloodhounds, and Sheriff Kennedy's authority for its completion.[12]

At the same time, however, there is a quiet celebration of new life in Jefferson. Apart from the outsiders—Lena, Byron, Hightower, Mrs. Hines—this celebration involves only Byron's landlady, the sheriff and his deputy, and a local doctor. But Lena's arrival in Jefferson, which coincides with the fire, involves Byron in love and life as he tries to help her, while Hightower, who delivers Lena's baby, feels a surge of triumphant vitality at his success. Joe's grandmother, Mrs. Hines, seizes a chance to start over, holding and protecting Lena's baby as she had wanted to protect her own grandson. And in calling the baby Joey; Mrs. Hines promises a new life to her condemned grandson: this time; Joey will be loved, happy, and at home. Thus Lena turns the world upside down. A birth, and four resurrections (Byron, Hightower, Mrs. Hines, Joe): these are the "luck and life" (406) that Lena brings to Jefferson.[13]

The Roman holiday offers Jefferson a chance to celebrate either life or death. Though a few, such as Mrs. Beard, choose the former, and one or two, including Sheriff Kennedy and Deputy Buford, take part in both, most of the community ratifies the young priest Percy's celebration of the sacrifice.[14]

GALLERY OF THE GODS

The word "avatars"—incarnations or manifestations of a god—occurs frequently in *Light in August*. It is associated explicitly with Lena, Joe, and Joanna, but so many characters in the novel exhibit symptoms of divinity that it might apply to almost anyone. The novel's one professional divine, the Reverend Dr. Gail Hightower, sits in the "attitude ... of an eastern idol" (90). The anonymous African American woman whom Lucas meets in the woods just before he jumps the train "contemplate[s] him with a detachment almost godlike but not at all benign" (434). Even Alice, the little girl at the orphanage who tries to mother Joe, undergoes an apotheosis when she is adopted," fading without diminution of size into something nameless and splendid, like a sunset (137). All of them are divine beings, propelling and illuminating the novel.

The gods of *Light in August* may reveal themselves in any number of ways. One of the most basic, as Virginia Hlavsa notes, is to identify themselves by name, especially by the formula "I Am," which the Old Testament God called himself when speaking to Moses (Exod. 3:14). The "I-Am" is a divine act of self-definition; its content is an assertion of transcendent existence. It is most likely to be a partial selective, of deliberately ambiguous revelation. The various "I-Ams" of *Light in August* follow this rule, as they usually respond to some specific occasion. Perhaps the most memorable example is five-year-old Joe's remark as he vomits the dietitian's toothpaste: "Well, here I am" (122). As Michel Gresset suggests, Joe proves the proposition *"vomito ergo sum."* The boy's revelation—his birth as the dietitian's enemy, and his subsequent definition as black—need not have occurred had he not vomited. Yet this revelation is the episode that determines the entire future course of Joe's life, including, eventually, his fate as a dying god.[15]

A subtler act of naming consists of a joke twice told, once on Lena and again, in converse form, on Joanna. Lena, heavily pregnant, climbing out her window to begin her journey, calmly reflects, "If it had been this hard to [climb out] before, I reckon I would not be doing it now" (6) As for Joanna, her joke is reported by Byron as he tells Hightower about the countryman who rescued Joanna's corpse from her burning house. Seeing her body facing one way and her severed head facing exactly the opposite direction, the countryman "said how if she could just have done that when she was alive, she might not have been doing it now" (92).

In both instances, this is a form of the "before and after" joke, which, in Arthur Asa Berger's taxonomy, is a type of identity joke. The remarks on Lena's and Joanna's past and present abilities serve two important functions. In the first place, they help to characterize the two contrasted goddesses. Lena's joke is calm and sunny, even in the dead of night, but the joke on Joanna is stated with sickened pity, and casts a pall of horror over her even under the midday sun. In the second place, the naming of both Lena and Joanna with essentially the same joke is a means of linking the two. They become the avatars of two deities with the same name: Diana.[16]

The gods of *Light in August*, even the least of them, also see visions of eternity. The farm boys at the schoolhouse dance with Joe and Bobbie carry their humble vision in the expression of their eyes "a heritage of patient brooding upon endless furrows and the slow buttocks of mules" (206). This vision is as far removed as possible from the dreams of sudden apocalyptic violence that seize the imaginations of the novel's puritan deities. The farm boys will plow their way imperceptibly into eternity through long, monotonous, and peaceful lives. What their vision lacks in divine melodrama, it makes up in godlike steadfastness. And if it heightens the aesthetic temptations of violence, it also inspires a certain awe of any god who can face those mules' buttocks through an entire lifetime.

Five-year-old Joe has a nightmare vision of eternity on the third day after his nauseous epiphany. When the dietitian unexpectedly offers him a bribe to keep her secret—a dollar with which to buy enough toothpaste to last him a week—an outraged Joe envisions "ranked tubes of toothpaste like corded wood, endless and terrifying" (125). The promise of an eternity of toothpaste to vomit: to little Joe, it is a vision of pure hell, infinitely worse than the beating he had expected. From this day on, he will always prefer inevitable beatings from predictable men to unexpected bribes from unpredictable women.[17]

The most portentous visions, however, belong to Joanna and Hightower. Joanna has her formative vision at the age of four. Like Joe, she suffers a terrifying vision of hell, but hers is a vision of eternal crucifixion and suffocation by the entire race of Africans and their descendants. The rest of Joanna's life is devoted to her struggle to escape that terrible black shadow, or at least to raise it, as her father commands. She joins in the project of "uplift" that had been begun by African American leaders in the late nineteenth century. But when she offers to educate Joe so that he can learn to embezzle, if only he will claim his uncertain African ancestry publicly, Joanna unwittingly echoes the dietitian's offer of a bribe. Here, Joanna's childhood vision of torment collides head-on with Joe's, and the results are fatal to both. Joanna makes her last prophecy in a scene strikingly similar to that which prompts the countryman's sick joke: Lying on her side, with her head turned and her mouth bleeding, she tells Joe, "Maybe it would be better if we both were dead" (278). Joanna is right: only death brings them peace, and a release from their respective visions of eternal torment.[18]

Hightower, like Joe and Joanna, experiences his vision in his early childhood. His, however, is a vision of heroism: the vision of his grandfather's gloriously fatal chicken-house raid. The pursuit of this vision has determined the course of Hightower's life since he was four years old: his insistence on being called to the Presbyterian church in Jefferson; his use of his wife's connections and strategy to obtain that call; and his subsequent abandonment of both his wife and his church in order, not to live, but to die in Jefferson. Once his wife has died and he has resigned his pulpit, Hightower can devote his remaining years solely to the contemplation of his vision, that aesthetically perfect but theologically suspect blend of heavenly hosts, horses, and his grandfather's death that has held him spellbound since childhood. To Hightower, the "shape of eternal youth and virginal desire which makes heroes" (483) is the death of an elderly soldier "in somebody else's henhouse wid a han'full of feathers" (485). This is the vision to which Hightower sacrifices everything: his vocation, his congregation, his dignity, his wife's mental health, and finally her life. As for his own, he had considered it lost already, "shot from the saddle of a galloping horse.... one night twenty years before it was ever born" (478).[19]

Hightower's final vision of the wheel of faces acts as a corrective to the complacent solipsism of his vision of his grandfather's death. At last he discovers his own responsibility for his actions and his choices, and the shock is so great that Hightower believes he is dying. In fact, this last vision is the first Hightower has ever bad of his own life, made possible by his willy-nilly involvement in both the birth of Lena's baby and the death of Joe Christmas. Finally, it is no longer as if his "life had already ceased before it began" (478). Hightower has come to understand that, possessed or not, his life is and always has been his own.

Not only are they visionaries; the characters of *Light in August* also have powers of divination. That is, they can be clairvoyant or telepathic. Their divination can have either comic or tragic results. For example, Lena knows from the first which road will lead her to Lucas. She follows him to northern Mississippi, not detouring toward Florida or Texas, without his having sent word to her. Byron knows in exactly which room he will find the sleeping Hightower when it is time to summon him to Lena's childbed. Joe's clairvoyance, by contrast, seals his doom: knows in advance that he will find some candylike treat in the dietitian's room. The dietitian's divination in turn not only identifies Hines as the person who had brought baby Joe to the orphanage; it leads to Joe's emergency placement with the McEacherns. Hines's divination in pursuit of his daughter and her lover results in murder, while Mrs. Hines's telepathic understanding of her husband enables her to thwart his effort to kill Joe. Finally, Percy's unerring anticipation of Joe's every move in his last flight enables him to shoot Joe, "almost before he could have seen" (464) him crouched behind Hightower's kitchen table. Like their visions of eternity, these Olympians' powers of divination are apt to bring them into conflict. And since these godlike powers are combined with equally crucial failures of knowledge, and are most often used to murderous ends, that conflict is likely to be fatal.[20]

Finally, each of the characters of *Light in August* has the attributes of some specific divine being, phenomenon, or function. Gods, angels, and apostles, often in caricature, populate the world of this novel. Lucas Burch, for one simple example, is manifest as both the Word that begets the virgin's son, and the mercenary tattletale "disciple" (45) who, like Judas, betrays his master for money. As Byron tells Lena about the new mill hand, Lucas alias Joe Brown, he comments especially on Lucas's incessant talk. Out of all that chatter, Lucas's one well-calculated word is the one that inspires the manhunt for Joe after Joanna's murder: "nigger" (97). This word is sufficient to establish Luca's innocence of the murder in the collective white mind of Yoknapatawpha. It is the one word from Lucas that even Byron will believe. And once having dropped it, Lucas is convinced, against all reason, that this magic word alone is worth the thousand-dollar reward for the capture of Joanna's murderer. He still believes the reward belongs to him even as be waits beside the railroad tracks to make his final escape from Lena.[21]

Lucas's apotheosis, ironically, consists of a wordless action. Byron, its sole witness, sees Lucas "materialise apparently out of air" (440), hopping the northbound freight train with consummate skill, to disappear between the cars. Lost in wonder and praise, Byron can say only, "Great God in the mountain....; he sho knows how to jump a train" (441). Even the unlikely Lucas thus displays superhuman power and inspires a momentary reverence. His apotheosis is also his one act of (unintentional) sacrificial generosity: he has left Lena to Byron, who loves her, and whom Lena herself now seems to prefer.[22]

At the opposite end of the pantheon from Lucas stands Simon McEachern, Joe's foster father. McEachern is a ruthless God the Father, who shapes Joe in his own image, with a new name and "a very kinship of stubbornness" (148) in the all-but-genetic similarity of Joe's stiff-backed walk. As the incarnation of "the Shalt Not" (207), McEachern dispenses the law, and judges and punishes Joe's every action with absolute consistency: a beating, no matter for what.

Like other retributive deities in *Light in August*, McEachern has powers of divination. Having once seen that Joe's new suit has been worn, "within about thirty minutes of intensive thinking he knew almost as much of Joe's doings as Joe himself could have told him" (201–2). He hunts down Joe and Bobbie with supernatural efficiency and accuracy. Possessed by his powers, McEachern is transformed into "the actual representative of the wrathful and retributive Throne" (204). He is still thinking and acting in this capacity when he achieves his apotheosis, meeting the blow of Joe's chair and being rapt into "nothingness" (205). McEachern loses the mental boundary between himself and God. No one, least of all McEachern himself, knows whether he serves the divine will or employs divine powers in the service of his own will. This question, inevitably left unanswered for all the divinities in the novel, is the source of the psychotic spookiness of *Light in August*.[23]

Doc Hines is a more extreme god than McEachern, for Hines is a god of wrath undisguised as justice. His wrath is directed at "Bitchery and abomination!" (370)—that is, at feminine sexuality and the existence of dark-skinned people. But the wrath does not belong to Hines; it belongs to God. It is "God's abomination of womanflesh!" (373), and "the black curse of God Almighty" (374). It is God, not Hines, who pronounces Joe Christmas "a pollution and a abomination on My earth" (386). Hines himself is merely God's confidant and instrument.

As God's confidant and instrument, however, Hines is given godlike powers and privileges. He has an infallible instinct for the detection of sex and blackness. Never having seen Joe's father by daylight, Hines still knows the man's racial background immediately. (In practice, it scarcely matters whether his intuition is correct.) Hines knows that Milly is pregnant before she herself can possibly know it. Hines knows all about the dietitian's clandestine sex life, of which the orphanage matron knows nothing. Hines is also granted the earthly privilege of judging and punishing abomination and bitchery: murdering Joe's father, cursing the African American congregations on whose charity he depends, allowing his daughter to die, kidnapping Joe in order to prevent his being sent to the Jim Crow orphanage. Hines's judgment and his actions in these cases are clearly privileged; he is never punished, even for the murder.[24]

Hines is one of Faulkner's most frightening villains, but even this self-appointed god of vengeance has his ludicrous features. Hines's Mottstown acquaintances sense something amiss about his vague intimations of past glory. When they joke (always behind his back) about Uncle Doc's career as a Memphis railroad and newspaper magnate, the Mottstown wits only echo Hines's own style. Who else would describe janitorial work in an orphanage as monitoring "the devil's walking seed" (383) from the sacred threshold of "God's own boiler room" (383)? Who else treats God as fairly as His intimate Doc Hines does: "God give old Doc Hines his chance and so old Doc Hines give God His chance too" (371). While white people snicker behind Hines's back, the black people of Mottstown recognize Hines as crazy and idle, and tolerate him as they tolerate God, "since God to them was a white man too and His doings also a little inexplicable" (344). If Hines does not inspire their reverence, at least he is a familiar type of divine presence in their lives.

Finally, Hines, the scourge of "Womanfilth" (132), is "incredibly dirty" (382), living in "filthy poverty" (340). The man who has set himself the task of ridding the world of pollution can see no need to cleanse his own body. (His filthiness, by the way, connects him with ancient and medieval Christian ascetics who also chose to mortify their flesh with its own odor and grime.) Hines is filthy alike in mind and body, irresistibly attracted to the pollution and abomination he pursues so zealously. "Devil or no devil" (373), he mutters, as he sets off in quest of more bitchery. And, as Mrs. Hines realizes, here alone has he named his true master.[25]

Like McEachern and Hines, Percy Grimm represents a combative god. Percy is a captain in the wrathful host, his god "the uniform of the United States" (453). That uniform magically confers on its wearer the full authority "To show these people right off just where the government of the country stands" (452). Better still, the man in uniform can dictate just where the federal government stands. But even without his khaki, Percy assumes divine authority, his face shining with the "serene, unearthly luminousness of angels in church windows" (462) as he joyfully fulfills his mission.

Percy too has superhuman powers. He needs neither food nor sleep, and has a holy contempt for anyone who does need them. He has an "irresistible and prophetlike" (453) charisma that enables him to win converts, and he can keep them from straying with the merest cold glance. By Sunday night, Percy has attracted not only a platoon of the heavenly host but also a devout congregation of the faithful: the good people of Jefferson. The next day, when Joe escapes from Deputy Buford on the square, Percy justifies the townspeople's faith. As he leaps into action, his every move swift and precise, Percy epitomizes the spirit of festive horror that has been growing in the town since the discovery of the fire. Astride his gallant two-wheeled steed, emanating his angelic radiance, unmoved alike by stones, potholes, and offers of a lift, Percy blends the burlesque, the horrific, and the divine.[26]

Percy is at his most horrifically divine when he and his three lesser angels burst into Hightower's house, exuding haloes of sunlight. Martial, he displays his marksmanship by filling Joe's chest with lead. Seraphic and priestly, he celebrates a sacrificial rite, castrating Joe and thereby exorcising the twin demons of miscegenation and black blood from Jefferson.[27]

Having fulfilled his divine purpose, Percy disappears, not in his own apotheosis but in Joe's. He even has to share his place in Hightower's vision of the halo of faces with Joe. The fact is that Percy's divinity depends on Joe. Without someone to hunt down, castrate, and kill, Percy could be neither lord of misrule nor martial seraph nor priest. And once the sound of the siren dies down and the excitement is over, Percy's moment is over as well. No longer a lone angelic priest, he becomes just one of the witnesses to Joe's apotheosis, all of whom will be haunted by the vision of his dying face for the rest of their long, uneventful lives.[28]

Hightower doubles both Percy and Hines: the former as a priestly celebrant of sacrifice with visions of martial glory; the latter as an unwashed heretic preacher living in idleness and poverty. Unlike the others, however, Hightower is contemplative rather than active. Hightower is an aesthetic apostle of the civil religion of the Lost Cause. But his patron saint is irreligious and meets his martyrdom in an act of theft against a friendly civilian. "Any soldier can be killed by the enemy in the heat of battle" (485), Hightower remarks to his wife. "But not with a shotgun, a fowling piece, in a henhouse" (486). By virtue of the sublime stupidity of his death, the elder

Gail Hightower becomes the apotheosis of supreme daring and southern Cavalier sportsmanship. But he has only one worshiper: his grandson. He can be a god—even an object of more than momentary interest—to no one else. And Hightower treats him just as the puritan fanatics treat their Jehovah: as a bloodthirsty demon god who demands human sacrifice and who offers nothing in return but an apocalyptic vision of death. Like his violent colleagues, too, Hightower loses the boundary between himself as apostle and the god he proclaims, calling himself the "instrument of someone outside myself" (491), namely his dying grandfather. In short, Hightower expects his congregation to worship Gail Hightower. The minister of this gospel of the chicken-house can only be a caricature: "a figure antic as a showman, a little wild" (488). Combining the manic, otherworldly incoherence of a sincere fanatic with the self-serving shrewdness of a patent medicine salesman, the youthful Hightower becomes the worst sort of twentieth-century American religious charlatan.[29]

Nonetheless, in his later life, Hightower can and does act as confessor, advisor, and even midwife. He tries to give Joe an alibi, although Percy spurns it. He also becomes one of the sanest religious thinkers in the novel, recognizing that the church's worst enemy is its own preference for "adjuration, threat, and doom" (487). After the birth of Lena's baby, Hightower begins to see the religious value of life as, walking home through the woods, newly aware of the natural world, he wonders whether "this itself be not the same as prayer" (406). Although he still awaits the ghostly cavalry charge every evening, Hightower is finally capable of immersing himself in life as well.[30]

Hightower's one lifeline since his retirement has been his friendship with the prosaic Byron Bunch. Byron's divine role is that of Joseph to Lena's Mary: a devout and just man with a job at the planing mill, he undertakes the care of the virgin mother and child. In doing so, like Joseph, he follows his dream rather than the harsh voice of clerical common sense (Hightower) that would urge him to set Lena aside. Byron has also been seen as an ironic Adonis figure: ironic indeed, in view of Byron's nondescript appearance. But Hightower envisions Byron as fertile—the father of Lena's future children—and Lena, the goddess of love and fertility, mourns her new Adonis when she believes she has lost him.[31]

In the pantheon of holy crackpots that populate *Light in August*, Byron is outstanding in his benign normality. His apocalyptic vision of falling off the edge of the earth and burning through space like a meteor is tempered with sanity: he knows that beyond this timbered hill he will find another. He never confuses himself with God; even as he moves unerringly to

Hightower's room, he knows that Hightower and Lena "would both have a different name for" (393) the spirit that guided him. As he gallops off on his trusty mule to fight Lucas, Byron has no delusions of possession or omnipotence. He knows Lucas can and probably will beat him, but he is willing to risk the beating for Lena's sake.

Byron's good common sense is the source of both his humor and his heroism. He can be beaten by Lucas and fought off by Lena, but this prosy little mill-hand drags Hightower back into life, reunites not only Lena and Lucas but Joe and his grandmother, and protects Lena from prying eyes and wagging tongues. Byron's heroism is comic rather than tragic because it fosters peace and life rather than violence and death. In the world of *Light in August*, this is a most inglorious sort of heroism. It leads to no apotheosis; instead, it elicits Hightower's vision of Byron, Lena, and their children: a vision not of eternity but of the future.[32]

Lena's role too is to foster life and peace. The gift of life that she carries, along with her "inwardlighted" (18) radiance and her divine serenity—"the untroubled unhaste of a change of season" (52)—marks her as a fertility goddess, like the Ephesian Diana, to whom she has often been compared. In her blue dress and sunbonnet, she calls to mind the Virgin Mary. Even her name has mythic connotations. Lena means lambency or radiance, as does the root of the name Diana, while Grove suggests the site of the Roman festival of Diana, which was celebrated in August.[33]

Lena's divinity is more than a matter of allusions, however. She has an innocence unlike any other in Faulkner's work: a generous innocence that believes the best even while knowing the worst. Seeing through Lucas's final lie, she lets him go. Even her pregnancy seems innocent; she calmly accepts it as "just my luck" (6). To Lena, pregnancy is neither a matter of bitchery and abomination nor a dirty little secret; it is a self-evident fact of life. The wholesome purity of her attitude toward her pregnancy also allies her with fertility goddesses and with the Virgin Mary. Lena is no nymphomaniac; she is just a young mother-to-be with the innocence of a virgin.[34]

Lena's comedy has several elements. First, and most conventionally, there is the purpose of her journey: she comes to marry Lucas, not to slay him, and she intends to reunite a family. Second, there is her innocent pleasure in life. Lena lives in a continuous state of happy wonder at how "A body does get around" (30). The serenity that accompanies Lena's innocence is another source of her comedy. She neither struggles nor surrenders when Byron attempts to rape her, but simply puts him outside, chiding him. "You might have woke the baby" (503). In all of these features, Lena offers a neat comic contrast to Joe, who cannot agree to marry Joanna but feels compelled to kill her, whose experience in every place is unvarying ennui followed by disaster, and who suffers physical assault without resistance and even with relief.[35]

Finally, Lena's unshakable faith in the success of what Cleanth Brooks calls her "obviously ridiculous quest" contrasts comically with the determinism of her colleagues in divinity. In her benign inexorability, Lena is as terrifying to Lucas as Hines in his mania is to Joe. Yet Lena is as infallible as Hines, and this point is crucial. She carries the promise that opposes the lethal determinism of Hines and Percy. For while Hines and Percy ensure that there will always be more violent deaths, Lena guarantees that life will go on nonetheless. She does so, fittingly, without coercing anyone. And in the end, Lena's sweet invincibility outlasts the puritans' spooky infallibility.[36]

The "night sister" (262) of this radiant earth mother is Joanna Burden, the inviolably virgin goddess of the chase, of the moon, and of death and the underworld. Joanna's Diana of Nemi, with her "physical purity which had been preserved too long now even to be lost" (261), forces Joe to hunt for her about the house and the oak grove. As moon goddess, she is infinitely mutable, "pass[ing] through every avatar of a woman in love" (259), measuring her life in phases and tides, and lying awake at night to pray in the moonlight. As goddess of death and the underworld, she proposes a suicide pact, loads both chambers of her ancient pistol, and, without a trace of personal malice, she offers Joe a choice between life with salvation and death with eternal damnation. And when she is killed, her festival, her Roman holiday, requires a human sacrifice in her name.[37]

Joanna's own destruction is a matter of being turn in two. Even before Joe dramatizes her plight by severing her head from her body, Joanna's puritan upbringing both magnifies and recoils from the power of her long-repressed femininity. The god of Joanna's head, the Burdens' wrathful Jehovah, has damned the urges of her body so thoroughly that she is simply incapable of accepting sex as an ordinary element of life. To Joanna, sex is inherently, inescapably depraved, and the more depraved it is, the sexier it is. It is precisely the puritan in Joanna that, in the second phase of her affair with Joe, insists on "living not alone in sin but in filth" (258). And it is the puritan that drives Joanna mad when middle age overtakes her, leaving her barren of both children and desire. In Joanna's third phase, the puritan Jehovah destroys the moon goddess, reclaims the virgin and the death goddess, and finally employs the exhausted phantom Joanna as yet another of his inexorable psychotic instruments.[38]

As with the other dark deities, Joanna's funny feature is also her most frightening. That one funny feature is the terrible purity, the reverse of Lena's, that makes her so fascinating to Joe. "She's trying to be a woman and she dont know how" (240). Joe muses on the day she comes to the cabin to talk to him. And her behavior during the wild second phase of their affair proves him right. She does what her masculine puritan education has taught her that a woman in love must do. Joanna throws fits of jealous rage, apparently just "for the purpose of playing it out like a play" (259). She hides notes for Joe, and lurks in wait for him in the house or even in the bushes. She strikes stereotyped and decadent poses as if for ancient erotic pagan art. Everything Joanna does in the second phase is utterly artificial, theatrical, or literary; she does nothing spontaneous or unrehearsed. Joanna's behavior is laughably bizarre because it is incorrigibly naive. Not only sex, but womanhood itself, is monstrous to her because she knows it only in puritan theory. The mysterious source of her corruption is precisely her invincibly virgin purity: a purity she shares with the typical Faulknerian male innocent.[39]

Joanna's apotheosis in the mind of the community is a cruel irony. She departs from the novel ignominiously as a mutilated corpse in a nightgown, and is granted life after death by her neighbors for the sake of excitement and the reward money offered by her nephew. Those neighbors worship her as a demon goddess of death and the underworld, but in doing so, they subordinate her to their own death-dealing Jehovah. It is the narrator who sends Joanna off with a benediction to "an attained bourne beyond the hurt and harm of man" (289). Joanna has earned her rest, and she has earned it on terms of which her neighbors know nothing. For a Faulknerian femme fatale, she is unusual in that she never whines, never cringes, and cannot be called a hypocrite (for she is honestly divided). She is far more generous and understanding to the townspeople than they are to her, and not because they are inherently more deserving of understanding. Finally, a vestige of the "untearful and unselfpitying" (234) Roman survives in Joanna, in that she is as prepared to kill herself as she is to kill Joe. Joanna holds no double standard. She feels as keenly as Joe does the necessity of her death. The tragedy of that necessity is made explicit in the narrator's blistering satire of the town's refusal to allow her to rest even in death.[40]

The longest and hardest battle between the self as god and an external god is fought between Joe Christmas and that same puritan Jehovah that propels the other gods of death. Joe as a god is prepared to defend his sovereignty against all comers. He can be neither bought nor broken. He spurns all offerings and is indifferent to beatings, because to be moved by either is to admit another god's jurisdiction in his life. It is in defense of his sovereignty that Joe refuses to surrender to either McEachern's or Joanna's Jehovah. He will have no other god before himself; he will be no other god than the irreducibly ambiguous Joe Christmas.[41]

Just as Joe the man is both dark and light, Joe the god has affinities with both Dionysus (a god of night and of wine) and Christ, "the light of men," according to John 1:4. Joe is a bootlegger and a furious reveler by night, and is associated with snakes, sacred to Dionysus and employed by the devil. Since the white puritan mind of *Light in August* recognizes no distinction between the Dionysian and the diabolical, and paints both black. Joe's affinities with the night god mark him as an Antichrist figure. As for Christ, the analogies are both more frequently observed and more controversial. Whatever objections the devout may raise against the portrayal of a violent criminal as a Christ figure, it cannot be disputed that Joe is betrayed by his "disciple" (45) for money, and that he suffers a scapegoat's painful and ignominious death. As an avatar of both Christ and Dionysus, Joe has no choice but to insist on his duality. And that duality can be healed only by his death, which includes features of both Christ's and Dionysus's deaths.[42]

Both of the crucial issues of Joe's divinity—his sovereignty and his ambiguity—are at stake in his relationship with Joanna. Diana to his Dionysus and, oddly, Jehovah to his reluctant Jesus, Joanna is at once a formidable adversary and a perfect nightmare match to Joe. Both deities are divided; both are ambivalent puritans, simultaneously obsessed with purity and fascinated with corruption; both struggle valiantly to maintain a sovereignty they cannot define. Each feeds the other's deepest needs and greatest fears. Joe brings the shadow of the black cross directly into Joanna's house, embodying both her damnation and her hope of redemption. General Joanna makes war on Joe's ambiguity by demanding that he identify himself unequivocally as African American, and on his sovereignty by insisting that he surrender it to the god of her fathers. And Joe can neither yield to Joanna nor flee her. The only way to preserve his divinity is to accept Joanna's alternative proposal, that both of them die.[43]

Joe's insistence on maintaining a sovereign ambiguity, "never act[ing] like either a nigger or a white man" (350), does more than anything else to brand him as Antichrist. The puritan urge to demonize difference makes race (as well as gender) a theological issue in *Light in August*, and Joe appears different—and differently demonic—to white and black observers. Among whites, the maybe-mulatto Joe is Antichrist; among African Americans, the apparently white Joe is "the devil! It's Satan himself!" (322). In either case, he is an anomalous presence of terrifying theological significance: the diabolical shape-changer, the Other as uncanny counterfeit Us.[44]

Joe's scapegoating and murder—his most Christlike features—are in fact the direct results of his being cast as Antichrist. Hightower makes the connection, as he bears in the Jefferson churchgoer's hymns the consecration of their already fixed intention to crucify Joe Christmas in God's name. As is the case with Jesus, Joe's acceptance of his scapegoating and murder affirms his divine sovereignty at last. By refusing to defend himself against Hines's blows or to shoot at Percy, Joe turns the tables on them. He finds his own peace on his own terms, while Hines is dismissed as crazy and Percy's men recoil, nauseated, from their seraphic leader's action. The divine lightning from Joe's hands and from his gun shows that Joe has the power to shoot and escape again if he chooses. Instead, he chooses the peace of accepting death, and, like his incarnate divine models, he achieves immortality in that choice.[45]

Where can the humor be in so tormented a figure? As with Joanna, it lies in the very source of his torment. Joe is so charged with demonic significance by nearly everyone he meets, white or black, that a normal human life in either of his two putative races is unavailable to him. Joe himself can see the joke, dimly, while he is on the run: "Any of them could have captured me, if that's what they want.... But they all run first" (337). Hungry, exhausted, and disoriented, Joe feels anything but superhuman; yet he is still universally regarded as a demonic menace. His last flight epitomizes his entire life since his conception: whatever his intentions, he invariably arouses hysteria. Joe's bizarre and terrible predicament is that he is the one terrifying and incomprehensible enemy against whom all others in his life define themselves. When he makes this discovery, Joe understands that the sovereignty on which he has insisted so stubbornly all his life is nothing more than the freedom to mind his own peaceful business among neighbors who mind theirs. He does not want to be a demon god; he wants to be human.[46]

The gathering of this Yoknapatawpha pantheon is bound to be violent, yet each of the deities depends on the others for recognition, definition, and purpose. Byron needs Lena; Percy needs Joe; Hightower needs all four of them. Without bitchery and abomination, both incarnate in Joe, to fight, Hines is drained of life. Joe and Joanna objectify, demonize, and yet cling compulsively to each other. Even their deaths can only make sense together. Lena and Joe, too, depend on each other for definition. The sunlit Olympian height of Lena's blessedness can be measured fully only from the bottomless black morass of Joe's torment. The clashing of opposites, real and imagined, propels *Light in August* and its divinities. As with Jefferson's Saturnalia, so with the gods themselves: they may celebrate either life or death, and most of them choose the latter. But the novel ends with the flight of the holy family, Byron, Lena, and Child, from the scene of death to a new life in Tennessee.

THE ORACLES OF YOKNAPATAWPHA

The gods and the worshipers of *Light in August* act on belief: beliefs about themselves, their neighbors, and the puritan Jehovah who dominates the religious life of Jefferson. They meditate, they pray, they preach, and they instruct their children. Their beliefs cover the whole range of potentially religious concern, and may be expressed by any believer, child or servant, woman, or patriarch. Most of the characters aspire to what the narrator calls "nice believing" (289): that which serves the believer's own needs for excitement, divine vindication, or a feeling of power or superiority.[47]

Whether they like it or not, all of the characters live and think in reference to the Jehovah they either serve, neglect, or defy. Nearly everyone, therefore, expresses some view of the nature and capacities of that God. The puritans emphasize God's power and his righteous aloofness from the filthy carnal world. But in this puritan-dominated novel, there is also a southern Cavalier view of God, the view expressed by Hightower's revered grandfather and his slave Cinthy. The Cavalier God has limits. He is continually confounded by human barbarity, perversity, and stupidity. This God serves as a hyperbolic court of final appeal for the vindication of one's own tastes and opinions. Thus the elder Gail Hightower declares that "even the good Lord Himself couldn't squeeze ... any music" (471) into a Presbyterian hymnal, while the bereaved and unemployed Cinthy claims that emancipation "made a bigger fool outen Pawmp [her husband] den even de Lawd Hisself could do" (477). The Cavalier God is restrained by gentlemanly good taste and simple kindness from even comprehending, let alone duplicating, the excesses of his more outlandish creatures.[48]

As for doctrine, by far the most popular belief in *Light in August* is that Joe Christmas really does have some African ancestry. This assumption has to be taken on faith, because neither Joe nor even Hines has conclusive proof. But Joe bases his life on that belief, as he confides sardonically to Joanna: "I don't know it ... If I'm not [of mixed race], damned if I haven't wasted a lot of time" (254). Joe finds a host of enthusiastic coreligionists, most of whom, like Lucas, claim in retrospect to have detected Joe's racial background immediately. Joanna too believes, embracing Joe ecstatically as "Negro! Negro! Negro!" (260).[49]

Among the believers in Joe's blackness, Gavin Stevens is notable for his erudition, which he employs in expounding his blood theory of Joe's behavior to his learned friend. Stevens facilely attributes Joe's violence to his "black blood" (449) and his restraint to his "white blood" (449). During the course of Stevens's Harvard education, he probably was exposed to some of the vast literature of "scientific racism" that was current at the time. Furthermore, he makes a modest contribution to the tragic-mulatto genre of American fiction with his version of Joe's inner conflict. The only thing Stevens's explanation of Joe lacks is an anchor in reality. It is based on an uncritical acceptance of prevailing pseudoscientific theory in preference to concrete reality: in a word, scholasticism. This bookish faith attributes Joe's attack on Hightower to his unproven black blood, and his failure to shoot anyone to his white blood, even though Stevens knows full well that Joe's white grandfather is a homicidal maniac. Stevens's nice believing has the full weight of contemporary scientific, theological, and artistic authority behind it. His black-blood/white-blood theory employs civilization, faith, and culture in the service of official barbarism.[50]

All faith requires some nurture, and the puritan fathers of *Light in August* assume this task with great vigor though with mixed success. Calvin Burden's method involves loud drunken lectures to his son late on Saturday nights, adjuring him to hate "two things" (243), namely "bell and slaveholders" (243). Nathaniel's response is strictly earthly: "Get on to bed and let me sleep" (243). Simon McEachern, the other puritan father with a "son" to instruct, announces to Joe on the day of his adoption that "the two abominations are sloth and idle thinking, the two virtues are work and the fear of God" (144): Joe, famously, has no concept yet of the fear of God, who is known to him only as music on Sundays.[51]

In both of these instances of religious instruction, the humor of innocence shows that puritans are made, not born. As children, Nathaniel and Joe recognize their own needs and limitations before all else, and the adults' gibberish enters their ears but not their minds. To the boys, God is still an unknown being; he will become a wrathful intimate only after Nathaniel and Joe lose their childish innocence.

Prayer too is an essential element of religious life. In *Light in August*, most people speak to their own belief when they pray: not to the God who made them, but to a god they have made. McEachern's prayer is a clear example, as he sets himself up as a model for God, "requesting that Almighty be as magnanimous as himself" (152) in forgiving Joe for refusing to learn his catechism. Doc Hines's prayers are even weirder, as they are two-way communications. Not only does he ask God's instructions; he receives them.

Worse, God's replies to Hines's prayers do not always suit Hines. When the holy janitor complains that the children's verbal cruelty to Joe is insufficient, God replies impatiently, "You wait and you watch" (371). Thus the answers to Hines's prayers actually do seem to come from some external source beyond his control. Furthermore, God entrusts the sacred task of Joe's murder to Percy rather than to Hines, who has always believed that he was the divinely ordained instrument of Joe's death. Hines too is praying to a God he has fashioned in his own image, but this God has taken on a frightening life of his own.

The element of humor in the prayers of *Light in August* is parody. Conventionally, Christian prayer should be fully conscious of the petitioner's own propensity for sin and need for mercy. Most importantly, it acknowledges the precedence of God's will over that of the speaker. But the prayerful deities of *Light in August* pray with absolute confidence in their own righteousness, and the only answer they expect is swift and perfect compliance with their demands. Their prayers are not conscious parodies involving irreverence or flippancy, but the result is an unconscious subversion of the conventions of prayer. Instead of an act of devotion, their prayer becomes a contest of will between two divine beings.[52]

Sermons—the divinely inspired preaching of the Word—have their place in *Light in August* as well. The preachers within the novel are oracular: they are controlled by, rather than in control of, their messages. At the same time, however, these oracular utterances are convincing and relevant only to the preachers themselves. The oracular pronouncement is an honored feature of both religious tradition, pagan and Judeo-Christian, that appear in *Light in August*. The sermons of the seminary-educated Hightower, "with his wild hands and his wild rapt eager voice" (65), fit into it no less neatly than do those of Hines, who is subject to fits and trances and who has the oracular Dixie frontier preacher's aptitude for "twofisted evangelism" (343). Calvin Burden who preaches when moved by spirits, is likewise a two-fisted frontier evangelist. Joe, as he seizes the pulpit of the rural African-American church and curses both God and the congregation in unconscious emulation of his grandfather, seems to the observers to be propelled by supernatural forces. Even Lucas delivers his sermon with the nearly hysterical emotionalism of a convert at a camp meeting, between laughter and tears.[53]

As for the content of these oracles, it is as cryptic as any Delphic utterance. Hightower's chaotic sermons leave his congregation "puzzled and outraged" (66). When Hines preaches white superiority, incarnate in himself, in black churches, his audience "probably did not listen to, could not understand much of, what he said" (344). As Joe delivers his inexplicable anathema, the congregation actually—prudently—flees. Lucas is moved nearly to tears by the eloquence of his own jeremiad—"I be dog if it aint enough to make a man turn downright bowlsheyvick" (438)—but his congregation, Byron and the Opponent remain unconverted. Ultimately, the oracles of *Light in August* end up talking to themselves. Their nice believing impresses their audience only as blasphemy, insanity, or mere stupidity. Thus the oracles as well as the prayers of *Light in August* are unintentionally parodic: in their helpless solipsism, they become sacrilegious.

In all of their devotional activities, the divinities of *Light in August* only obscure the essential religious questions of the novel. God's nature his ontological status in relation to his creatures, and the boundaries of identity between believer and God, all become confused when the characters try to worship. Apart from the mob and the church members, no two gods or believers can quite comprehend each other, let alone agree. They are bound to conflict, whether in the benign terms of Lena Grove and Martha Armstid about God's providence, or in the poisonous mutual obsessions of Joe and Joanna. And this conflict only reinforces each believer in his or her nice belief, for in *Light in August* the martyr's "*How Long, O Lord*" (490) is not so much a complaint as an exaltation of the cost of discipleship. The world's hostility, ideally culminating in martyrdom, provides infallible proof of the believer's own righteousness. In this way, nice believing in *Light in August* does indeed impel the believers "*to crucifixion of themselves and one another*" (368).

Yet nice believing can also express an orientation toward life. The holy manias of the puritans are countered by the holy folly of the virgin mother Lena, a folly whose holiness others acknowledge with offerings even as they ridicule Lena's faith. The elder Gail Hightower's facetious dread of being "corrupt[ed] ... into heaven" (472) reflects his joy in the pleasures of life on God's earth—which adds another twist of irony to his grandson's celebration of his death. Lucas may be converted to a kind of puritanism by his failure to collect the reward money; his Opponent is as omnipotent, inscrutable, and cruel as anybody's Jehovah. But still, Lucas is above all a survivor. Not every god in *Light in August* seeks a crucifixion; not all nice believing demands one.

In the light of August—Lena's warm inward light, Joanna's pouring moonlight, Percy's savage summer sunlight, Joe's lightning—a pantheon of divine beings gathers in Jefferson to celebrate a Roman holiday. In effect, there are two holidays, occurring side by side, with generally separate sets of celebrants. The more popular is the holiday of death, initiated by the dying gods Joe and Joanna, and observed by Hines, Percy, the churches, and the mob at the fire. The alternative is the holiday of new life, observed by Lena, Byron, and Lucas. Hightower, the living dead, has his share in both. Each holiday has its own proper rites in honor of its own nice believing. And each is celebrated with its own proper humor, whether of burning flesh or of a circus parade of telephone poles.

Each holiday also makes its demand on the individual celebrant. For each confronts the individual believer with the task of defining his or her own humanity and divinity. Each of these imperfect deities embodies one personal approach to the essential questions of humanity and divinity: who am I, and who is God to me? And within the novel, those who think they have found any more than a personal answer prove to be demon gods.

Yet although *Light in August* despairs of universal answers, it will not let the questions rest. Byron, who can accept an uncertain future provided it includes love and Lena; Hightower, whose meditations (with timely jolts from Byron, Lena, Percy, and Joe) finally bring him a moment of truth; Joe, who never rests in any imposed symbolic identity, but chooses his own at the moment of his death—all suggest the importance of the questioning itself. The questioning process may be painful and frightening, sad and funny, even all at once. But it must be approached somehow, and as they struggle to engage it, the human gods of *Light in August* appear at their most heroic, their most sinister, and their most divinely comic.[54]

NOTES

1. For the purpose of discussing Protestant religious fanaticism in *Light in August*, I have chosen the word "puritanism." The terms "Calvinism" and "fundamentalism," which are popular choices in *"Light in August* criticism, are too specific to serve. For descriptions and definitions of all anti- or otherworldly -isms in *Light in August*, see Berland, *Black and White*, 33–34; Bleikasten, *Ink of Melancholy*, 323–25 ("Puritanism"); Kazin, "Stillness," 158; King, "World-Rejection," 71–72; Mortimer, *Rhetoric of Loss*, 22, 25; Taylor, *Search*, 52–57; Vickery, *Novels*, 75; and Wilson, "Religious Culture," 22–25. For *Light in August* as characteristically Faulknerian, see Brooks, *Yoknapatawpha Country*, 47–49, and Millgate, introduction to *New Essays*, 12, 14. Millgate, 4–5, also discusses similarities between *Light in August* and *Sanctuary*, while Brylowski, *Olympian Laugh*, 91–117, discusses the two novels in the same-chapter. For the formal similarities between *Light in August* and *The Wild Palms*, see Millgate, "Not an Anecdote," 50; for a comparison with *Flags in the Dust*, 33–34. Wittenberg, *Transfiguration*, 117, calls *Light in August* "a 'companion work' to *As I Lay Dying*."

2. For the relative conventionality of the narrative technique of *Light in August*, see Millgate, introduction to *New Essays*, 5; Millgate, *Achievement*, 124; and Vickery, *Novels*, 66. Reed, *"Light in August*, 70–71, discusses technical reasons for the use of omniscient third-person narration in *Light in August*. Howe, *Faulkner*, 203, and Davis, *Faulkner's "Negro,"* 129, comment on Hightower's function in relation to Lena and Joe. Powers,

Yoknapatawpha Comedy, 89, discusses Byron's and Hightower's mediation between Lena's and Joe's stories.

3. For the former view, and the quoted phrase, see Kazin, "Faulkner and Religion," 5; Wilson, "Religious Culture," 35, and Berland, *Black and White*, share Kazin's view. For *Light in August* as a celebration of the power of faith, see Fowler, *Vision*, 37, 39.

4. Mythic readings of *Light in August* include Hlavsa, *Thoroughly Modern Novel*, and Phillips, *Dying Gods*, 83–93.

5. William Faulkner, *Light in August The Corrected Text* (New York: Vintage, 1990), 289. Hereafter cited with page numbers in parentheses immediately following quotes. All italics in all quotes are in original.

6. For Olympians and other gods in *Light in August* see Hlavsa, *Thoroughly Modern Novel*, 26, for a cast of characters with both pagan and biblical archetypes; Bleikasten, "In Praise of Helen," 128–43: Millgate, *Achievement*, 133–34; and Phillips, *Dying Gods*, 83–93. On humor in *Light in August*, see Brooks, *Yoknapatawpha country*, 71–74; Hlavsa, "Levity," 47–56; and Timms, "Carnival Yoknapatawpha," 134–35. Bleikasten, "In Praise of Helen," 132, notes that "nearly all gods and goddesses, especially when they involve themselves in human affairs, turn out to be ambiguous and contradictory figures."

7. For the Saturnalian features of the events from the discovery of the fire to Joe's death, see Hlavsa, *Thoroughly Modern Novel*, 146; Phillips, *Dying Gods*, 88; and Timms, "Carnival Yoknapatawpha," 144. Castration was not customary at Saturnalia, but it was a common feature of other ancient festivals of similar character. Phillips, *Dying Gods*, 83, and Hlavsa, *Thoroughly Modern Novel*, 187, 190–91, point out the parallels between Jefferson's Roman holiday and the ancient Phrygian festival of Attis and Cybele, as described in *The Golden Bough*. On the significance of the column of smoke, see Reed, *Light in August*," 68.

8. Berland, *Black and White*, 95, Hlavsa, *Thoroughly Modern Novel*, 137–38; and Ruppersburg, *Reading Faulkner*, 172, comment on the fire engine. Welsh, "Prevailing and Enduring," 134, observes that "The community comes alive ... when there is a fire to watch and a murderer to be hunted down."

9. On the bloodhounds, see Berland, *Black and White*, 94, and Ruppersburg, *Reading Faulkner*, 177–78.

10. On Joe's death as a monument, see Wadlington, *Reading Faulknerian Tragedy*, 162.

11. On Percy's usurpation as an indication of "the absence or suspension of rule," see Hlavsa, *Thoroughly Modern Novel*, 187–88, and Ruppersburg, *Reading Faulkner*, 258–59. Fowler, *Vision*, 36, notes the magical power of Percy's conviction. On the extralegal and sacrificial aspects of the castration and murder, see Sundquist, *House Divided*, 93–94, and Vickery, *Novels*, 74. Howe, *Faulkner*, 207, comments on the inevitability of Joe's death.

12. On the "sacrifice" of both Joanna and Joe, see Bleikasten, *Ink of Melancholy*, 303, 320; and, on Jefferson's worship of death, 325; Fowler, "Womanshenegro," 159; Porter, "Reified Reader" 61, and Wadlington, *Reading Faulknerian Tragedy*, 135–36.

13. On Lena, life, and resurrection, see Bleikasten, *Ink of Melancholy*, 298, 348; Brylowski, *Olympian Laugh*,, 111–12; Hlavsa, *Thoroughly Modern Novel*, 168, 174; Kartiganer, *Fragile Thread*, 52; Kazin, "Stillness," 150; Kazin, "Faulkner and Religion," 4; and Powers, *Yoknapatawpha Comedy*, 99.

14. On the castration and murder of Joe Christmas, see Bleikasten, *Ink of Melancholy*, 315; and Sundquist, *House Divided*, 93–94; cf. Brooks, *Yoknapatawpha Country*, 51–52, 61.

15. For the ontological implications of the toothpaste episode, see Hlavsa, *Thoroughly Modern Novel*, 94–96; and, for "*vomito ergo sum*," Gresset, *Fascination*, 231.

16. For the "before and after" joke, and its place in the taxonomy, see Berger, *Anatomy of Humor*, 18, 23–24. For Lena as the Ephesian Diana (a fertility goddess), and Joanna as Diana of Nemi (the virgin huntress and moon goddess), see Millgate, *Achievement*, 134. Bleikasten, "In Praise of Helen," 132, also draws the analogy between Lena and Diana, and, 134, refers to Joanna as Lena's "negative double." Hlavsa, *Thoroughly Modern Novel*, 126, and Phillips, *Dying Gods*, 86, 87, 93, discuss parallels between Joanna and Diana of Nemi. For descriptions of the two Dianas, see Jobes, *Dictionary*, 1:441–42. On Lena's joke, see Timms, "Carnival Yoknapatawpha," 135. On Joanna's, see Timms, "Carnival Yoknapatawpha," 135, and Brooks, *Yoknapatawpha Country*, 72.

17. On this episode, see Hlavsa, *Thoroughly Modern Novel*, 96.

18. On Joanna's activities, see Parker, *Novelistic Imagination*, 109; on her need to raise Joe, see Taylor, *Search*, 77–78, and Vickery, *Novels*, 76. Phillips, *Dying Gods*, 86 comments on Joanna as "a wise woman." On the commandments of the father in *Light in August*, see Bleikasten, *Ink of Melancholy*, 332–34, and Tully, "Dead Folks," 360–63.

19. On Hightower's sacrifices to his vision, see Vickery, *Novels*, 77–78; on his final vision, see Fowler, *Return*, 64–74.

20. See Berland, *Black and White*, 59–62; Bleikasten, *Ink of Melancholy*, 340; and Fowler, *Vision*, 36, on the infallible pursuit motif.

21. On Lucas, see Hlavsa, *Thoroughly Modern Novel*, 26, 62, 67, 70, 72. On his use of the magic word, see Davis, *Faulkner's "Negro,"* 65, and Dondlinger, "Getting Around," 102.

22. On Lucas's leaving the "holy family" of Byron as Joseph, Lena as Mary, and the baby as a new Christ figure to their travels, see Kerr, *Gothic Domain*, 134, and Hlavsa, *Thoroughly Modern Novel*, 62. On "Great God in the mountain," see Hlavsa, *Thoroughly Modern Novel*, 179, and Ruppersburg, *Reading Faulkner*, 250. For Lena's preference for Byron, see Hlavsa, *Thoroughly Modern Novel*, 168. The discussions of chapter 21 in Chappell, *Detective Dupin*, 330–36, and LaLonde, "Trap," tend to confirm Hlavsa.

23. For the godlike attributes of the (white) father, see Bleikasten, "Fathers in Faulkner", 133; Bleikasten, *Ink of Melancholy*, 332–33; and Taylor, *Search*, 57. Bleikasten, *Ink of Melancholy*, 332, comments on the monstrosity of Hines and McEachern as "the docile servants of God's will."

24. On society's approval of Hines's judgments and actions, see Bleikasten, *Ink of Melancholy*, 321; Brooks, *Yoknapatawpha Country*, 63; Dondlinger, "Getting Around," 100–101; and Wilson, "Religious Culture," 28–29.

25. On the violence inherent in puritanism in *Light in August*, set Bleikasten, "Fathers in Faulkner," 133; Bleikasten, *Ink of Melancholy*, 302, 308, 321–23; Hirshleifer, "Whirlwinds," 248; King, "World-Rejection," 65–66, 72, 82; Phillips, *Dying Gods*, 86; and Wilson, "Religious Culture," 31–32. On the puritan fascination with evil, see Taylor, *Search*, 54; and for Hines's lecherous dirtiness, see Bleikasten, *Ink of Melancholy*, 333.

26. On the "burlesque horror" of the bicycle chase, see Sundquist, *House Divided*, 87; see also Bleikasten, *Ink of Metancholy*, 313, for Percy as a caricatured knight.

27. On Joe's "black blood" and sex, see Berland, *Black and White*, 40–41; on southern hysteria about miscegenation in relation to Joe, see Sundquist, *House Divided*, 68, 70, 93.

28. On Percy's divinity and the ironies of his triumph, see Hlavsa, *Thoroughly Modern Novel*, 187–91. Watson, "Writing Blood," 89, notes the limits of Percy's priestly authority. See Bleikasten, "Fathers in Faulkner," 132, and Phillips, *Dying Gods*, 90, on the interdependence of Percy and Joe. On the castration and murder as a ritual sacrifice, and

on the self-perpetuating tendency of violent sacrifice, see Bleikasten, *Ink of Melancholy*, 328–29, 334, and Sundquist, *House Divided*, 92–94.

29. Bleikasten, *Ink of Melancholy*, 313, draws the parallels between Percy and Hightower. On the quoted remarks, see Ruppersburg, *Reading Faulkner*, 284–85. For Hightower and the southern civil religion, see Wilson, "Religious Culture," 33–35; for fuller discussions of southern filiopietisin, see Wilson, *Baptized in Blood*, and Foster, *Ghosts*. Bleikasten, *Ink of Melancholy*, 305, remarks that "Hightower stands at exactly the intersection of Faulkner's two youthful temptations, the heroic and the aesthetic." On the two Gail Hightowers, see also Wadlington, *Reading Faulknerian Tragedy*, 152–53. On southern religious charlatans, see Wilson, "Religious Culture," 21. Morcy, *Religion and Sexuality*, 172–73, comments on Hightower's immaturity and his "circusy" (173) antics.

30. Again, on Hightower, see Fowler, *Return*, 64–74.

31. On Joseph and his dream versus society, see Matthew 1:18–21; on Byron and Lena versus Hightower, see Duvall, *Marginal Couple*, 33–35. For Byron as Adonis, see Hlavsa, *Thoroughly Modern Novel*, 202–5; for the original Adonis, see Jobes, *Dictionary*, 1:34–35.

32. On Byron as a gently caricatured knight-errant, see Kerr, *Gothic Domain*, 128, and Wadlington, *Reading Faulknerian Tragedy*, 137. On Byron and Lena as "a rebuke and a check to the heroic," see Welsh, "Prevailing and Enduring," 135–37 (quote from 137).

33. On Lena as an avatar of the Ephesian Diana, see Millgate, *Achievement*, 134; Kerr, *Gothic Domain*, 115; and Bleikasten, "In Praise of Helen," 131–33. For Lena as the Virgin Mary, see Hlavsa, *Thoroughly Modern Novel*, 62–63. For the etymology of the name Diana, see Jobes, *Dictionary*, 1:442.

34. On the quality of Lena's innocence, see Kerr, *Gothic Domain*, 120; and see Bleikasten, *Ink of Melancholy*, 253, which observes that in Faulkner's fiction, innocence typically "appears as evil's most fertile ground." On Lena's attitude toward her pregnancy, see Wadlington, *Reading Faulknerian Tragedy*, 136–37; cf. Dondlinger, "Getting Around," 120.

35. On the family–as a conspicuous absence–in *Light in August*, see Berland, *Black and White*, 49: Bleikasten, *Ink of Melancholy*, 315; and Hirshleifer, "Whirlwinds," 247–48. On the conventionally comic alliance between family and community in *Light in August*, see Books, *Yoknapatawpha Country*, 72, and Kreiswirth, "Plots and Counterplots," 61. On Lena's delight in her travels, see Dondlinger, "Getting Around," 118, 122–23, and Wadlington, *Reading Faulknerian Tragedy*, 143–44. Faulkner later expressed admiration for Lena's calm in repelling Byron's rape attempt; see Faulkner, *Lion in the Garden*, 253–54.

36. For the similarity-in-contrast between Lena and Hines, see Kartiganer, *Fragile Thread*, 59. For a contrast with Percy, see Phillips, *Dying Gods*, 84. The phrase "obviously ridiculous quest" is quoted from Brooks, *Yoknapatawpha Country*, 55. Bleikasten, "In Praise of Helen," 131–32, discusses Lena as "a new avatar ... of the primal mother" (quote from 131).

37. On the impersonality of Joanna's offer to Joe, see Brooks, *Yoknapatawpha Country*, 58. For Joanna's persistent purity, see Bleikasten, *Ink of Melancholy*, 309; for her renewable virginity, see Phillips, *Dying Gods*, 86–87; for her lunar associations, see Bleikasten, *Ink of Melancholy*, 289. On the complementary relation between Lena and Joanna see Millgate, *Achievement*, 134; Bleikasten, *Ink of Melancholy*, 298; and for a view that is kinder to Joanna, Phillips, *Dying Gods*, 86–87. On the presentation of Joanna's debauchery, Bleikasten, *Ink of Melancholy*, 310, notes that the "angel plays, in the end, the beast, but it is a beast only *in the eye* of the beholding angel. And we all know this angel's gender" (emphasis

Bleikasten's). For human sacrifice in the festival of Diana, see Jobes, *Dictionary*, 1:442.

38. For the persistence of Joanna's puritanism even in the second phase of the affair, and for her final reversion to her fathers' god, see Bleikasten, *Ink of Melancholy*, 309–10 and Bleikasten, "Fathers in Faulkner," 133; for the conflict within Joanna between her sexuality and her moral training, see Bleikasten, *Ink of Melancholy*, 322; Brooks; *Yoknapatawpha Country*, 58 and Parker, *Novelistic Imagination*, 102–2. For the importance of the romance of taboo and transgression in Joe's and Joanna's affair, see Bleikasten, *Ink of Melancholy*, 310, and King, "World-Rejection," 78. For the contrast between Joanna's sexuality and Lena's, see Morey, *Religion and Sexuality*, 183–84. For Joanna's irreconcilable duality, see Fowler, *Return*, 83–85; Mortimer, *Rhetoric of Loss*, 31–33; and Vickery, *Novels*, 75–76. Wittenberg, "Women," 118, discusses the significance of the Janus-like position of Joanna's corpse.

39. On Joanna's play-acting as a symptom of her practical ignorance of womanhood, see Tully, "Dead Folks," 368–69. On her gender stereotyping, see Parker, *Novelistic Imagination*, 106. Bleikasten, *Ink of Melancholy*, 287, 301, compares Joe to Horace Benbow and Quentin Compson. Brooks, *Yoknapatawpha Country*, 68, identifies "callow idealism" as a common feature of Faulkner's male characters. For Joanna's invincible naiveté, see Bleikasten, *Ink of Melancholy*, 308. On Joe's fascination with Joanna's "script," see Wadlington, *Reading Faulknerian Tragedy*, 158–59.

40. On Joanna's posthumous transformation, see Davis, *Faulkner's "Negro,"* 148–49. The most vigorous argument for viewing Joanna as a figure of "grandeur" is Phillips *Dying Gods*, 88–91 (quote from 89). Bleikasten, *Ink of Melancholy*, 298, identifies Joanna as a femme fatale; more charitably, he also regards her as a victim of her fathers and of Joe's misogyny. Berland, *Black and White*, 49, and Reed, *"Light in August,"* 84, comment on the discrepancy between the reader's and the townspeople's knowledge of Joanna. Brooks, *Yoknapatawpha Country*, 57, 70, remarks Joanna's tragic dignity, but see Bleikasten, "Fathers in Faulkner, 129–30, on the outsiders in *Light in August*.

41. For Joe as an irreducible and menacing ambiguity, see Bleikasten, "Fathers in Faulkner," 130; Bleikasten, *Ink of Melancholy*, 316–17, 327; Brylowski, *Olympian Laugh*, 104; Dondlinger, "Getting Around," 111–12; Fowler, *Return*, 88; Kartiganer, *Fragile Thread*, 37–38, 41–42, 47–48; Rio-Jelliffe, *Obscurity's Myriad Components*, 59–73; Snead, *Figures of Division*, 88; and dazzlingly, Watson, "Writing Blood," 78–94. On Joe and sovereignty, see Fowler, "Womanshenegro," 148; Gresset, *Fascination*, 206; and Kazin, "Stillness," 158.

42. For the parallels between *Light in August* and John's gospel, see Hlavsa, *Thoroughly Modern Novel*. For Joe as an avatar of Dionysus, see Hlavsa, *Thoroughly Modern Novel*, 16, 27, 70, and 115. Bleikasten, "In Praise of Helen," 137, notes the importance of the Dionysian element in *Light in August* as a counterpoint to Lena. For Dionysus, see Jobes, *Dictionary*, 1:447–49. On Joe and the threat of chaos, see Bleikasten, *Ink of Melancholy*, 320, and Fowler, "Womanshenegro," 158. On Joe as a Christ figure, see Bleikasten, "Fathers in Faulkner," 131; Bleikasten, *Ink of Melancholy*, 330; Hirshleifer, "Whirlwinds," 247; Hlavsa, *Thoroughly Modern Novel*, 182; Kartiganer, *Fragile Thread*, 48; Kazin, "Stillness," 159; and Ruppersburg, *Reading Faulkner*, 265–66.

43. On the doubling of Joe and Joanna see Bleikasten, *Ink of Melancholy*, 318–20; Davis, *Faulkner's "Negro,"* 146; Fowler, *Return*, 83–85; Kazin, "Stillness," 155; Kinney, *Poetics*, 114; Reed, *"Light in August,"* 79–80; Sundquist, *House Divided*, 80–81; and Vickery, *Novels*, 71–72. For Joe's fascination with Joanna, see Mortimer, *Rhetoric of Loss*, 32; Powers.

Yoknapatawpha Comedy, 94–95; Reed, "*Light in August*," 70, and Wadlington, *Reading Faulknerian Tragedy*, 158–59. I assume that it was indeed Joe who killed Joanna, on the grounds of the logic of their characterization (as well as Lucas's) and the trajectory of their relationship. Cf. Meats, "Who Killed Joanna Burden?"

44. For the significance in *Light in August* of dividing the world into dichotomous sets of phenomena—white/black, male/female, good/evil—see Berland, *Black and White*, 40–41; Bleikasten, *Ink of Melancholy*, 326–27; Kartiganer, *Fragile Thread*, 38–39; Porter, "Reified Reader," 61–62: Snead, "Rhetorics," 152–56; Taylor, *Search*, 54–57; and Vickery, *Novels*, 67–69. For the terror of confusion between self and other, see Fowler, "Womanshenegro," 153–56; Mortimer, *Rhetoric of Loss*, 12–40; and Sundquist, *House Divided*, 71. For Joe as a supernatural shape-changer, see Hlavsa, *Thoroughly Modern Novel*, 121; for Joe as a earthly shape-changer, see Watson, "Writing Blood," 78–94.

45. On Joe's apotheosis, see Bleikasten, *Ink of Melancholy*, 329–30; Dondlinger, "Getting Around," 112, Fowler, *Return*, 87–88; Gresset, *Fascination*, 210; Phillips, *Dying Gods*, 90–91; Taylor, *Search*, 83; and Watson, "Writing Blood." 87–88.

46. On Joe's resistance to symbolic signification, see Dondlinger, "Getting Around," 108–12; Fowler, *Return*, 74–88 (here, resistance to the symbolic); Kazin, "Stillness," 151–52; Parker, *Novelistic Imagination*, 97–98; Rio-Jelliffe, *Obscurity's Myriad Components*, 70–72; Snead, *Figures of Division*, 88–89; Sundquist, *House Divided*, 75, 88; Vickery, *Novels*. 73–74; and Wadlington. *Reading Faulknerian Tragedy*, 155–60.

47. On the pervasiveness and power of faith in *Light in August*, see Fowler, *Vision*, 33–39.

48. On the Cavalier presence in *Light in August*, see Taylor, *Search*, 61.

49. On the "wasted time" joke, see Davis, *Faulkner's "Negro*," 133; and Sundquist, *House Divided*, 70.

50. On Gavin Steven's blood theory, see Davis, *Faulkner's "Negro*," 167–70; Lutz, "Parable," 464–65; Taylor, *Search*, 81–82; and Watson, "Writing Blood," 84–86. For an introduction to scientific racism in nineteenth- and early twentieth-century America, see Coben, *Rebellion*, 33–34, 38–40. On tragic-mulatto fiction, see Karcher, "Rape, Murder, and Revenge," 58–72, and Sundquist, "Forms of American Fiction," 5–13.

51. On Calvin and Nathaniel, see Ruppersburg, *Reading Faulkner*, 145 (with the comparison to McEachern and Joe), and Tully, "Dead Folks," 358–60.

52. On parody in *Light in August*, see Parker, *Novelistic Imagination*, 108.

53. On the oracle of Delphi and its priestess, see "Delphi," in Jobes, *Dictionary*, 1:428, and "Pythia," 2:1308. On the oracular tradition of preaching in the South and the Old Southwest, see Bruce, "Revivalism," in Wilson and Ferris, eds., *Encyclopedia of Southern Culture*, 1306–7; Bailey, "Frontier Religion," in *Encyclopedia of Southern Culture*, 1287–88 (including two-fisted evangelists); Peacock, "Folk Religion," in *Encyclopedia of Southern Culture*, 1285–86; and Dick, *Dixie Frontier*, 190–92. For the emotional and physical afflictions of camp-meeting converts, see Dick, *Dixie Frontier*, 196–98; and Ahlstrom, *Religious History*, 434–35. For Doc Hines as a sacred mad seer, see Hlavsa, *Thoroughly Modern Novel*, 96. Wilson, "Religious Culture," 35, compares Hightower and Hines as oracular preachers.

54. For various views on the importance of the search for the self and God in *Light in August*, see Hlavsa, *Thoroughly Modern Novel*, 38: Howe, *Faulkner*, 205: Kazin, "Stillness," 155; and Mortimer, *Rhetoric of Loss*, 12. On the continuance of questioning in *Light in August*, see Bleikasten, *Ink of Melancholy*, 347. Berland, *Black and White*, 68, and Fowler, *Vision*, 33, 38–39, discuss the place of *Light in August* in Faulkner's own search.

Chronology

1862	Edith Wharton is born on January 24 in New York, New York.
1871	Herman Theodore Dreiser is born on August 27 in Terre Haute, Indiana.
1873	Birth of Willa Cather on December 7 in Winchester, Virginia
1874	Gertrude Stein is born on February 3 in Allegheny, Pennsylvania, to Daniel Stein and Amelia ("Milly") Keyser.
1876	Jack London is born on January 12 in San Francisco, California. Sherwood Anderson is born in Camden, Ohio on September 13.
1885	Birth of Harry Sinclair Lewis on February 7 in Sauk Center, Minnesota. Birth of Ezra Weston Loomis Pound on October 30 in Hailey, Idaho.
1893	Stein registers at Harvard Annex, the college for women that in 1894 will become Radcliffe College.
1894	Stein studies philosophy and psychology with William James, the brother of Henry James, and works with the German professor, Hugh Münsterberg, at Harvard Psychological Laboratory.
1896	Francis Scott Key Fitzgerald is born on September 24, the first surviving child (two others having died) of Edward

	Fitzgerald and Mollie McQuillan, at 481 Laurel Avenue, St. Paul, Minnesota.
1897	William Cuthbert Falkner is born on September 25 in New Albany, Mississippi to Murry Falkner and Maud Butler Falkner. (The family name will be spelled "Falkner" until 1919 when William adds a "u.")
1899	Ernest Miller Hemingway is born in Oak Park, Illinois to Dr. Clarence Edmonds Hemingway and Grace Hall Hemingway.
1900	The Hemingway family goes to Windemere, their summer house in northern Michigan. It is here that Ernest will learn to fish and hunt from his father, a devoted outdoorsman. L. Frank Baum publishes *The Wonderful Wizard of Oz*.
1902	John Ernst Steinbeck is born on February 27. The Falkner family moves to Oxford, Mississippi. Stein and her brother Leo settle at Bloomsbury Square in London.
1903	Stein begins a first version of *The Making of Americans*. In the fall, Stein joins brother Leo in Paris, at 27, rue de Fleurus, the artists' quarter of Montparnasse.
1905	Ernest Hemingway begins the first grade. Stein begins *Three Lives*, the Saturday night salon at 27, rue de Fleurus begins.
1906	Stein sits for Picasso's portrait of her. In February, she finishes *Three Lives*. She continues working on her first novel, *The Making of Americans*.
1907	Picasso's African period piques with *Les Demoiselles d'Avignon*, the first announcement of abstract painting. In September, Alice B. Toklas arrives in Paris.
1908	Stein and Toklas secretly marry. Stein writes her first "Cubist" word portraits. One of these texts, "Ada," is a portrait of Toklas.
1909	Fitzgerald's first story, "The Mystery of the Raymond Mortgage," is published in the St. Paul Academy's *Now and Then*. Stein's *Three Lives* is published at her own expense by Grafton Press in New York.
1910	The Mann Act is adopted by Congress. The Mexican revolution against Porfirio Diaz begins. The Boy Scouts are established in the U.S. and Halley's Comet makes an

appearance. Falkner accepts a mentor relationship with Phil Stone, reading widely in the classics and contemporary literature. Stone will help Falkner get his early works published. Mark Twain dies.

1911   On March 25, fire breaks out at the Triangle Shirtwaist Factory in New York City. Arizona is admitted as a state. Frederick Taylor publishes *The Principles of Scientific Management*. Stein finishes *The Making of Americans*. She and Toklas visit the American patroness, Mabel Dodge, at her Medici place near Florence. Stein writes her "Portrait of Mabel Dodge at the Villa Curonia." Wharton publishes *Ethan Fromme*; Dreiser publishes *Jennie Gerhardt*.

1911–13   Fitzgerald enrolls in the Newman School in Hackensack, New Jersey. During this time, he writes and produces four plays and publishes three stories in the *Newman School News* before graduating in 1913.

1912   On April 15, the *Titanic* sinks. Woodrow Wilson is elected in a landslide by 435 electoral votes. Stein's 1909 portraits of "Picasso" and "Matisse" are published by Alfred Stieglitz in *Camera Work*, the first English texts on these painters. Wharton publishes *The Reef*; Dreiser publishes *The Financier*; Zane Grey publishes *Riders of the Purple Sage*; James Weldon Johnson publishes *The Autobiography of an Ex-Colored Man*; *Poetry* magazine is founded.

1913   The Sixteenth Amendment is ratified, providing for a graduated national income tax. The Seventeenth Amendment, which provides for the popular election rather than the appointment of senators, is passed. Henry Ford adopts the conveyor-belt technology developed by the meat-packers. The Armory Show in New York City introduces modern European art to the United States.

Fitzgerald enters Princeton University as a member of the Class of 1917. Here he meets Edmund Wilson and John Peal Bishop and begins to participate in literary and dramatic activities. Fitzgerald writes the book and lyrics for a Triangle Club Show and contributes the lyrics for two others. His stories, plays, and poems are published in the *Nassau Literary Magazine* and *Princeton Tiger* between 1914 and 1918. Hemingway attends Oak Park and River Forest high school, where he distinguishes himself as an aspiring journalist/writer. Wharton publishes *The Custom of the Country*; Cather publishes *O Pioneers!*; London publishes *The Valley of the Moon*; and James publishes *A Small Boy and Others*

1914   American Society of Composers, Authors, and Publishers (ASCAP) is formed in New York City. On April 20, the Ludlow Massacre gives rise to demonstrations across the country. Archduke Francis Ferdinand is assassinated. In August, Germany declares war on Russia and France, and Great Britain declares war on Germany as German troops invade Belgium. Japan also declares war on Germany. The Panama Canal opens for shipping. On September 5, the Allies are victorious at the Battle of the Marne. Charlie Chaplin makes his first appearance as the Little Tramp.

Stein's *Tender Buttons* is published in London. Dreiser's *The Titan*; James's *Notes of a Son and Brother*; Carl Sandburg's *Chicago*; Frank Norris's *Vandover and the Brute*; and Sinclair Lewis's *Our Mr. Wrenn* are published.

1915   On May 7, the Lusitania is sunk without warning by a German U-Boat, losing 1,198 out of 1,924 passengers. On August 17, Leo Frank is lynched in Marietta, Georgia by the Knights of Mary Phagan, which becomes a revived Ku Klux Klan. The Iron and Steelworkers strike for the 8-hour day. D.W. Griffith's *The Birth of a Nation* is released.

Fitzgerald leaves Princeton. In an effort to flee from the zeppelin raids on Paris, Stein and Toklas travel to Barcelona and Mallorca. Stein develops her specific language mixture of inner monologues and dialogues, her poetic "plays," and her eroticism. Cather publishes *the Song of the Lark*; Dreiser publishes *The "Genius"*; T.S. Eliot publishes "The Love Song of J. Alfred Prufrock"; and Edgar Lee Masters publishes *Spoon River Anthology*.

1916   In Mexico, Pancho Villa kills eighteen Americans and later raids towns in New Mexico. General John Pershing pursues Villa across the border. Wilson wins re-election. The Workman's Compensation act is enacted by Congress. Jeannette Rankin of Montana is the first woman elected to the House of Representatives. Mexican President Carranza orders U.S. Troops out of Mexico. Fitzgerald returns to Princeton, planning to graduate in 1918. Stein and Toklas return to Paris.

1916–17   Faulkner begins to write verse and to submit graphic and literary work for the University of Mississippi yearbook. Hemingway graduates high school in June. In October, he takes as job as a cub reporter for the *Kansas City Star*.

1917   On February 5, the Immigration Act is passed. On April 2, stating "the world must be made safe for democracy," Wilson asks Congress to declare war on Germany. On May 18, the Selective Service Act is passed. The first American troops arrive in France in October.

            In October, Fitzgerald joins the army as a second lieutenant, reporting for training to Fort Leavenworth, Kansas in November. Fitzgerald begins a novel he calls "The Romantic Egotist." Hemingway sails for Italy on May 23rd to assume his duties as a Red Cross ambulance driver. On July 8 he is badly wounded in Fossalta while distributing chocolate to the troops. While recuperating in Milan, he meets and falls in love with a nurse, Agnes von Kurowsky. Lewis publishes *The Job*; Eliot publishes *Prufrock and Other Observations*; Wharton publishes *Summer*; the Pulitzer Prizes are established.

1918   Wilson proposes "Fourteen Points" for peace in the world. On July 17, the Second Battle of the Marne takes place. On September 26, 896,000 American troops join 135,000 French soldiers in an attack at Argonne Forest. In the fall of 1918, a deadly influenza epidemic strikes, before it ends in 1919, the influenza epidemic will kill an estimated twenty to forty million people worldwide. On November 11, Germany signs the armistice treaty.

            Faulkner attempts to enlist in the U.S. Air Corps to fight in World War I—he is rejected due to insufficient height. Faulkner enlists in the Royal Air Force training program. He returns to Oxford after the war, feigning wounds and military experience when, in fact, his training ends in December, a month after the armistice. In February, Fitzgerald completes a first draft of "The Romantic Egotist" and sends it to Charles Scribner's Sons for publication. In July, Fitzgerald meets Zelda Sayre. Scribner's rejects his novel in August. Cather publishes *My Ántonia*; Wharton publishes *The Marne*; Henry Adams publishes *The Education of Henry Adams*; Booth Tarkington publishes *The Magnificent Ambersons*; the O. Henry Award is established.

1919   The Prohibition Act becomes law. On June 26, the Versailles Treaty is signed, which the Senate later refuses to ratify. On September 25, President Wilson suffers a stroke and never fully recovers.

After a brief stint in an advertising agency in New York City, Fitzgerald resigns and leaves for St. Paul, where he will live with his parents while rewriting his novel, now called *This Side of Paradise*. In September, Scribners accepts *This Side of Paradise* as well as magazine stories that were previously rejected. Hemingway returns to the United States. Stein and Toklas return to Paris. Sherwood Anderson publishes *Winesburg, Ohio*.

1919   On January 1, Jerome David Salinger is born in New York City to Sol and Miriam Salinger. Faulkner enrolls as a special student at the University of Mississippi. He studies French and writes a play entitled Marionettes. He also completes his first volume of verse, *The Marble Faun*. Lyman Frank Baum dies on May 6.

1919-24   Steinbeck graduates from Salinas High School and attends Stanford University sporadically, publishing "Fingers of Cloud" and "Adventures in Arcademy" in *The Stanford Spectator*.

1920   On January 16, the eighteenth Amendment (Prohibition Amendment) goes into effect at midnight. The 19th Amendment (voting rights for women) goes into effect. On May 5, Sacco and Vanzetti are arrested, and Warren G. Harding wins the presidential election by a wide margin. Ray Douglas Bradbury is born August 22 in Waukeagan, Illinois to Leonard Spaulding Bradbury and Esther Marie Moberg Bradbury.

Fitzgerald and Zelda are married and move to New York City in October. Stein becomes the first America subscriber to the circulating library connected to Sylvia Beach's Latin

Quarter bookstore, *Shakespeare and Company*. Following the war and Appollinaire's death (1918), the group of cubists at Stein's salon disperse and are replaced by young American's. Eliot publishes *Poems*, Wharton publishes *The Age of Innocence*, Lewis publishes *Main Street*, Fitzgerald publishes *This Side of Paradise* along with a short story collection *Flappers and Philosophers*.

1921   On April 2, Albert Einstein lectures in New York about his theory of relativity. The Emergency Quota Act restricts immigration by setting limits based on the number of foreign-born people already in the country in 1910. Immigration must not exceed three percent of each nationality already in the United States in that year. In July-September, wage cuts and massive unemployment cause unrest and an increase in violence. The newly formed Hoover Commission suggests price cuts and shorter hours rather than an increase in wages; the average working day is 12–14 hours.

In May, the Fitzgeralds travel to England, France and Italy. In September, they return to St. Paul, where in October their daughter, Frances Scott (Scottie) is born. Hemingway marries Hadley Richardson on September 3rd. Provided with letters by Sherwood Anderson, they leave for Paris after Thanksgiving. While in Paris, Hemingway will write dispatches for the *Toronto Star* and develop a unique American prose style. Sylvia Beach introduces Stein to Sherwood Anderson. Gertrude secretly undergoes surgery to remove a lump from her breast. Cather publishes *Alexander's Bridge*.

1921–23   Faulkner works in a New York bookstore managed by Elizabeth Prall, Sherwood Anderson's future wife. He returns to Oxford to serve as university postmaster, a job at which he notoriously fails and which ends in 1923 with his being fired.

1922   The World War Foreign Debt commission tries to sort out the issue of war debts owed to the United States, which insists on full payment and thereby causes ill will among European nations. The Supreme Court declares the nineteenth Amendment (votes for women) to be constitutional. The John Newbery Medal is awarded for the first time.

Fitzgerald's second novel, *The Beautiful and Damned*, is published in March, and his second collection of short stories, *Tales of the Jazz Age*, appears in September. In October, the Fitzgeralds move to a rented house in the wealthy community of Great Neck, Long Island, about 25 miles from New York City. Hemingway meets other expatriates in Paris—Ezra Pound and Gertrude Stein. Stein reads a fragment of his novel-in-progress, advising him to concentrate and begin anew. In December, Hadley takes a train to Lausanne where Hemingway is on assignment during which trip she loses some manuscript pages of his unpublished fiction. Stein meets Man Ray, which leads to the first of many photo sessions at his Montparnasse studio. Stein becomes temporarily estranged from Sylvia Beach when Beach publishes James Joyce's *Ulysses*. At her own expense, Stein publishes *Geography and Plays*, a collection of poems and prose from the prewar and war years, with a foreword by Sherwood Anderson. Kurt Vonnegut Jr. is born on November 22.

1923   On August 2, President Harding dies of an embolism after suffering ptomaine poisoning followed by pneumonia. Coolidge is sworn in on August 3. The FBI begins investigating an unusually high rate of murders and mysterious deaths among the Osage Indians in what Oklahoma newspapers call the "Osage Reign of Terror." U.S. Steel implements the 8-hour day, a victory for labor.

In April, Fitzgerald's play, *The Vegetable*, is published, but in November it fails in a trial production in Atlantic City, New Jersey. Cather publishes *A Lost Lady*. Hemingway goes to Spain for the bullfights at Pamplona, returning briefly to Toronto for the birth of his first son, John Hadley ("Bumby") in October. He publishes *Three Stories and Ten Poems*. Stein and Toklas become godmothers of John Hadley. Stein meets and becomes friends with Jane Heap and Margaret Anderson, publishers of *Little Review*, who regularly publish her texts. The Hotel Pernollet in Belley becomes the summer meeting place for the circle of friends.

1924   Congress passes a new and more restrictive immigration law; quotas are now set at two percent of existing nationalities in the U.S. in 1920, and Japanese immigration is suspended. Calvin Coolidge is elected by a large margin over the Democratic candidate, John W. Davis, and the Progressive candidate, Robert La Follette. Nellie Ross of Wyoming and Miriam Ferguson of Texas are elected governors of their states.

In April, the Fitzgeralds leave for France where they reside in St. Raphael on the French Riviera. That summer, Zelda and Edouard Jozan, a French aviator, become romantically attached. In late October, the family travels to Italy where Fitzgerald revises his new novel. Hemingway helps Ford Madox Ford in editing the *transatlantic review* which publishes "Indian Camp" and other stories. He brings out a small volume, *In Our Time*. Gertrude Stein writes *A Birthday Book* for Picasso's son, Paolo. Stein meets and becomes friends with the British writer, Edith Sitwell. Hemingway arranges for the serialized publication of a part of *The Making of Americans* in Ford Madox Ford's *Transatlantic Review* from April to December. Faulkner publishes *The Marble Faun* in December. Mark Twain publishes *The Autobiography of Mark Twain*. Wharton publishes *The Old Maid*.

1925   In July, Clarence Darrow defends John T. Scopes of Tennessee for his teaching Darwin's theory of evolution; William Jennings Bryan heads the prosecution, and in an unusual move, Bryan takes the witness stand to defend his strict interpretation of the Bible. Scopes loses the trial and is fined $100, but the trial publicity gives the debate over evolution national attention.

Faulkner travels to New Orleans where he is introduced (through Elizabeth Prall) to Sherwood Anderson and his literary circle, a group associated with the avant-garde literary magazine, *The Double Dealer*. He will spend six months with this group, developing an interest in writing fiction, and completing his first novel, *Soldiers' Pay*, a "lost generation" story. Anderson's publisher, Horace Liveright, accepts the manuscript for publication. Faulkner spends the second half of the year traveling to Europe, living in Paris, reading contemporary literature and writing reviews, until he returns to Oxford at Christmas. On March 5, Mary Flannery O'Connor is born to Edward F. O'Connor and Regina L. (Cline) O'Connor, in Savannah, Georgia. April 10, Fitzgerald publishes *The Great Gatsby*. A few weeks later, the Fitzgeralds rent a Paris apartment. In May, Fitzgerald meets Ernest Hemingway at the Dingo Bar in Montparnasse. In July, Fitzgerald meets Edith Wharton at her home outside Paris. Hemingway's *In Our Time* appears. It contains several stories set in Michigan, the subject of which is the maturation of Nick Adams, and concludes with "Big Two-Hearted River." Gertrude Stein's *The Making of Americans* is published in Robert McAlmon's *Contact Editions*, in Paris. Through Hemingway, Stein befriends F. Scott and Zelda Fitzgerald.

1925–26   Steinbeck leaves Stanford without a degree, moves to New York and works for the *American*; writes short stories but finds no publisher; returns to California where he continues to write and has several jobs, among them a caretaker of a lodge at Lake Tahoe.

1926   The Army Air Corps is established. A land boom in Florida comes to a halt as a massive tornado causes enormous damage. Richard Byrd makes the first flight over the North Pole. U.S. Marines land in Nicaragua to suppress a revolt and will stay until 1933. Gertrude Ederle swims the English Channel in 14 hours, 31 minutes.

In February, Faulkner's *Soldier's Pay* is published. In February, Fitzgerald's third collection of short stores, *All the Sad Young Men*, is published. The Fitzgeralds return to the Riviera where they reside until they return to America in December. Hemingway begins long-standing relationship with Scribner's and their editor, Maxwell Perkins, beginning with *Torrents of Spring*, a satire on Anderson, and *The Sun Also Rises*, his novel about expatriate life in Paris and Pamplona. Gertrude Stein's first estrangement from Hemingway. Her work, *A Book Concluding With As a Wife Has a Cow as Love Story* is published by the art dealer Daniel-Henry Kahnweiler and illustrated with lithographs by Juan Gris. Edith Sitwell tries, but fails, to get Leonard and Virginia Woolf to publish *The Making of Americans*.

However, Sitwell arranges invitations for Gertrude at the Oxford and Cambridge literary societies. Stein gives a lecture, "Composition as Explanation," which is published by the Woolf's Hogarth Press.

1927   On May 20–21, Charles Lindbergh flies *The Spirit of St. Louis* from New York to Paris, traveling 3,600 miles in 33 and a half hours. Refusing a nomination for re-election in what will become a famous statement, Calvin Coolidge says, "I do not choose to run." On August 23, while still protesting their innocence, Sacco and Vanzetti are executed after judicial appeals are exhausted. In October, *The Jazz Singer*, starring Broadway star Al Jolson, debuts as the "first" talking picture show, and its success spells the beginning of the end for silent movies.

The Fitzgeralds travel to Hollywood, where F. Scott has been hired to write a screenplay for a flapper film entitled, *Lipstick*. Faulkner's second novel, *Mosquitoes*, is published in April by Liveright. Hemingway publishes *Men without Women*, a story collection which includes "Hills like White Elephants" and "The Killers." Divorced by Hadley, he marries Pauline Pfeiffer. Following the death of Juan Gris, Gertrude Stein publishes "The Life and Death of Juan Gris" in *transition*. Gertrude is now interested in young painters such as the Russian exile Pavel Tcheltichev and the English aristocrat, Francis Rose. Random House Publishers is founded in New York City by Bennett Cerf and Donald Klopfer. Steinbeck publishes *Cup of Gold*. Cather publishes *Death Comes for the Archbishop*.

1928   In the presidential election, Republican Herbert Hoover, whose party's slogan is "A chicken in every pot, a car in every garage," beats Democratic candidate Al Smith. Democrat Franklin D. Roosevelt is elected governor of New York. The Kellogg-Briand Pact proposes to substitute diplomacy for warfare as a means of settling international disputes—sixty-two nations ultimately sign the pact, which the U.S. Senate approves in 1929.

Faulkner's third novel, *Flags in the Dust*, is rejected by Liveright. This novel marks the beginning of Faulkner's fictional history of his own region. It is eventually accepted for publication by Harcourt, Brace, with the stipulation that it be shortened. Faulkner begins writing *The Sound and the Fury* in the spring and finishes it by early fall. In April, the Fitzgeralds return to Paris and then return to Ellerslie in September. Hemingway leaves Paris and moves to Key West. His son, Patrick, is born and his father, Dr. Hemingway, commits suicide. Stein publishes, on her own, a second collection of short texts, *Useful Knowledge*. She writes *How to Write*, reflections on language, grammar, sentences and paragraphs. Kahnweiler publishes Stein's *A Village Are you Ready Not Yet*.

1929   On February 14, the "St. Valentine's Day Massacre," takes place in which six gangsters from the "Bugs" Moran mob and another man are gunned down in a Chicago garage. On February 17 Herman Harold Potok (Chaim) is born to Benjamin Max and Mollie (Friedman) Potok in the Bronx, New York. On July 1, enforcement of the Immigration Act of 1924 begins. On October 24, a date which will be known as "Black Thursday," thirteen million shares are sold on the New York Stock Exchange. Despite efforts to shore up prices by J.P. Morgan and John D. Rockefeller, prices fall again on October 29, "Black Tuesday," as sixteen million shares are sold. By November 13, $30 billion have been lost in devalued stocks; the stock market crash marks the beginning of the Great Depression. The Academy of Motions Picture Arts and Sciences gives out its first awards, although they will not be called "Oscars" until 1931.

Faulkner publishes *Sartoris*, a shorter and renamed version of *Flags in the Dust* in January. He beings working on *Sanctuary*. However, his first masterpiece, *The Sound and the Fury*, is rejected by Harcourt, Brace, but is accepted by Cape and Smith. In June, Faulkner marries Estelle Oldham Franklin following her divorce in April. *The Sound and the Fury* is published in October. In the fall, Faulkner works nights at a power plant, while completing a first draft of *As I Lay Dying* in less than seven weeks. In March, the Fitzgeralds return to Europe, traveling to Italy and the Riviera before renting an apartment in Paris in October. In September, Hemingway publishes *A Farewell to Arms*, a novel of love and war in Italy during World War I. Despite censorship in Boston of a serialized version in *Scribner's* magazine, both sales and reviews are good. Excerpts from Stein's *The Making of Americans* appear in French, translated by Georges Hugnet in his Editions de la Montagne. Stein writes stanzas, ballads, and her first French text, a film script: "*Film deuz soeurs qui ne sont pas soeurs.*"

1930   President Hoover says the worst effects of the Depression will be over within 90 days, stating that "Prosperity is just around the corner." The New York Police Commissioner gives employers a black list of Communists. Al Capone is released from jail. On February 13, Greta Garbo's first talkie (Anna Christie) opens. On March 16, WEAF in New York City carries the first opera broadcast directly from a stage in Europe. In July, Washington head dedicated at Mt. Rushmore by Gutzon Borglum. At $80,000 a year, Babe Ruth is making more than President Hoover. On September 14, the Nazis become the second-largest party in Germany over the communists as Hitler claims he would scrap Versailles treaty if in charge. CBS begins live Sunday radio broadcasts of the New York Philharmonic with Toscanini as conductor. *All Quiet on the Western Front* wins the Academy Award for Outstanding Motion Picture.

On December 10, Sinclair Lewis wins Nobel Prize for Literature for *Babbitt*, becoming the first American to do so. Faulkner publishes *As I Lay Dying* in October, giving a fictional county its name of Yoknapatawpha. Faulkner buys Rowan Oak, an elegant Oxford estate. In need of funds, he embarks on a mission to market his short stories along with his novels, the former offering better pay. The Fitzgeralds travel to North Africa in February, returning to Paris in March. Fitzgerald tries to focus on his new novel, and writes several short stories that defray their expenses. In late April, Zelda suffers her first nervous breakdown and is admitted to the Malmaison Clinic outside Paris. Steinbeck marries Carol Henning. Stein has her first and only meeting with James Joyce, arranged by Sylvia Beach. Stein promises George Hugnet the English translation of his

long poem "Enfances," but reneges, writing her own
"mirror" version of the text. This precipitates a breach in
their friendship, which breach causes her to entitle her
version "Before the Flowers of Friendship Faded
Friendship Faded." Stein sells Picasso's *Woman with a Fan*
in order to finance her publishing company, Plain Edition;
Toklas is the director. They publish their first volume, *Lucy
Church Amiably*, in an edition of one thousand copies.

1931   President Hoover proposes a one-year moratorium on all
international war debts and reparations. In May, the
Empire State Building, the world's tallest structure, is
dedicated in New York City. Great Britain goes off gold
standard, provoking fear amongst Americans that the
United States will do the same. 827 banks close over the
next two months as fear inspires widespread withdrawals. Al
Capone is found guilty of tax evasion in Federal Court in
Chicago and is sentenced to eleven years in prison and fined
$50,000. Hundreds of "hunger marchers" are turned away
from the White House after trying to petition for
employment at a minimum wage. Hoover seeks the
creation of an emergency reconstruction finance
corporation to lend money to lending institutions to bolster
industry and provide jobs.

February 18, Chloe Anthony Wofford (Toni Morrison)
is born to George and Ramah Willis Wofford in Lorain,
Ohio. Also in February, Fitzgerald returns to the United
States for his father's funeral. He will visit Montgomery to
inform Zelda's family of her condition. In the fall,
Fitzgerald accepts an offer from MGM's and returns to
Hollywood to work on a screenplay for Jean Harlow.
Faulkner does extensive revisions on *Sanctuary* before its
publication in February. The sexual violence of *Sanctuary*
captures Hollywood's attention and Faulkner begins his
twenty-year history as a scriptwriter for MGM and Warner
Bros. In September, *These Thirteen*, a collection of his short
stories, is published. Hemingway's son, Gregory Hancock,
is born. Stein and Toklas's publishing company, Plain
Edition, publishes "Before the Flowers of Friendship Faded
Friendship Faded". The critic Edmund Wilson (in *Axel's*

Castle) places Stein at the same level with Joyce, Proust, Yeats, and T.S. Eliot. Pearl S. Buck publishes *The Good Earth*

1932   The Reconstruction Finance Corporation is established by the Hoover administration as an attempt to restart the economy. In Albany, Franklin D. Roosevelt enters presidential race. His campaign Song is "Happy Days Are Here Again." Four protesters are killed during a riot at the Ford plant in Dearborn, Michigan. The Twentieth Amendment, which will move the presidential inauguration to January 20, is sent to the states for ratification. Amelia Earhart becomes the first woman to make a solo flight across the Atlantic. *Buck Rogers* airs on CBS radio. Radio City Music Hall opens. Academy Awards are given to *Grand Hotel* (best picture), Fredric March for *Dr. Jekyll and Mr. Hyde* (best actor), Helen Hayes for *The Sin of Madelon Claudet* (best actress), and Walt Disney, for inventing the character Mickey Mouse.

In February, *Light in August*, Faulkner's first major treatment of racial turmoil, is published by Smith and Haas. Zelda Fitzgerald is admitted to Phipps Clinic at Johns Hopkins University Hospital in Baltimore. Fitzgerald returns to his daughter in Montgomery and, in May, rents La Paix, a house near Baltimore. Zelda joins them in June after her release from Phipps. Zelda's novel, *Save Me the Waltz*, completed while at Phipps, is published. Steinbeck moves to Los Angeles and publishes the *Pastures of Heaven*. Hemingway publishes *Death in the Afternoon*, his book on bullfighting. In Paris, Stein's *The Making of Americans* appears in a complete translation by Bernard Fay. Plain Edition publishes *Operas and Plays*. During a stay at her summer residence in Bilignin, Stein writes *The Autobiography of Alice B. Toklas* in six weeks. At the same time, in *Stanzas in Meditation and Other Poems*, she reflects on having written her first accessible book, "a real achievement of the commonplace."

1933   Adolph Hitler becomes chancellor of Germany and reports come in regarding Nazi mistreatment of Jews, including dismissals from government and business positions, shop boycotts, raiding of homes, and physical violence. Fay Wray co-stars with a giant mechanical ape in *King Kong*. Wiley Post completes solo flight around the world in 7 days, 18 hours, 49 minutes with the aid of such technology as automatic pilot. A fleet of Italian seaplanes touches down on Lake Michigan as part of the Chicago Exposition. Marconi announces discovery of micro-waves. In December, Manhattan Federal Judge John M. Woolsey rules in favor of author James Joyce in *The U.S. v. One Book Entitled Ulysses*, a decisive victory for freedom of publishing that narrows the definition of pornography. The United States and the U.S.S.R. establish diplomatic relations for the first time.

Faulkner's second volume of poems, *A Green Bough*, is published in April. Jill Faulkner is born in June. A film version of *Sanctuary*, entitled *The Story of Temple Drake*, is released. Steinbeck returns to Pacific Grove and publishes *To a God Unknown* and parts one and two of *The Red Pony*. Hemingway publishes a collection of stories, *Winner Take Nothing*, which includes "A Clean, Well-Lighted Place" and goes on a safari which provides the setting for his two long stories, "The Snows of Kilimanjaro" and "The Short Happy Life of Francis Macomber," both of which will be published in 1936. Stein's *The Autobiography of Alice B. Toklas* becomes a bestseller. Stein is temporarily estranged from Picasso because Olga Picasso dislikes the book, and her friendship with Hemingway ends. Plain Edition publishes *Matisse*, *Picasso* and *Gertrude Stein with Two Shorter Stories*. In New York, *Three Lives* goes into its second edition.

1933–34   In December, upon completing *Tender is the Night*, Fitzgerald moves from La Paix to a townhouse in Baltimore; Zelda has another breakdown in January of 1934. *Tender is the Night* is published in April.

1934   In January, Congress passes Gold Reserve Act, empowering the president to regulate the value of the U.S. dollar. In February, Congress passes Civil Works Emergency Relief Act. In March, Henry Ford restores $5.00 per day minimum wage. Thousands battle the police in New York protesting the Scottsboro Trial which involved the alleged gang rape of two white girls, Victoria Price and Ruby Bates, by nine black boys. Shirley Temple appears in her first movie *Bright Eyes* and sings "On the Good Ship Lollipop." In June, Roosevelt establishes the Securities and Exchange Commission; its first chairman is Joseph Kennedy. June 30 becomes known as the "Night of Long Knives" when Hitler eliminates embarrassing friends and foes alike. President Paul von Hindenburg of Germany dies and is succeeded by Adolf Hitler as Reichsfuhrer. In July, the first general strike in U.S. history takes place in San Francisco in support of 12,000 striking members of International Longshoreman's Association. The comic strip, "Li'l Abner," created by Al Capp, makes its debut. In November, the Nobel Prize in Chemistry is awarded to Harold Clayton Urey for his discovery of deuterium, or heavy hydrogen, a major advance in atomic physics.

Steinbeck's "The Murder" is chosen for the O. Henry Prize Story. His mother, Olive Hamilton Steinbeck, dies. Stein writes her first and only detective novel, *Blood on the Dining-Room Floor*. On February 8, John Houseman directs the world premiere of *Four Saints in Three Acts* in Hartford, Connecticut. Stein appears for a lecture tour in the United States, published as *Lectures in America*. Her collection of hermetic texts *Portraits and Prayers* appears in New York. Stein meets and befriends Thornton Wilder; at Christmas she visits Zelda and Scott Fitzgerald in Baltimore. On December 30, Stein attends a reception at the White House, given by Eleanor Roosevelt.

1934–35	In April, Faulkner publishes a collection of detective stories, entitled *Martino and Other Stories*. Faulkner works on *Absalom, Absalom!*, an ambitious novel of the South, both in Hollywood and Oxford. He interrupts his work on *Absalom* for a few months in order to complete *Pylon*, a brief novel about stunt pilots. He will resume working on *Absalom* following the death of his youngest brother, Dean, in an air crash. *Pylon* is published in March 1935.
1935	U.S. Senate refuses to participate in the World Court by a vote of 52–36. Amelia Earhart becomes the first person to

fly solo across the Pacific Ocean. Robert E. Sherwood's play, *The Petrified Forest*, starring Humphrey Bogart and Leslie Howard, opens at the Broadhurst Theatre in New York City. The first round-the-world telephone conversation is routed from New York to San Francisco, Indonesia, Holland, England, and back to New York. "Flash Gordon," a science fiction radio program starring Gale Gordon, debuts. The League of Nations censures Germany's rearmament policy. Babe Ruth retires from professional baseball. Heinrich Himmler begins the Society for Research into the Spiritual Roots of Germany's Ancestral Heritage in Berlin. The Social Security Act establishes old-age retirement insurance and a federal payroll tax to finance federal-state unemployment insurance. Religious leaders discourage Americans from participating in Berlin Olympics. Nazi government revokes German citizenship of Jews. The United States makes the Philippines a commonwealth. In December, Congress passes the United States Neutrality Act.

Fitzgerald, now ill, stays at a hotel in Tryon and then in Asheville, North Carolina. His fourth collection of short stores, *Taps at Reveille*, is published in March. In September, he moves to an apartment in downtown Baltimore, and then moves to Hendersonville, North Carolina, for the winter, where he starts writing the *Crack-Up* essays. Steinbeck publishers *Tortilla Flat* and is awarded the Commonwealth Club of California Gold Medal. Steinbeck's father dies. Hemingway publishes *Green Hills of Africa*, an account of his safari experiences. Stein delivers a special lecture, "How Writing Is Written," at Choate School in Wallingford, later published as *How Writing is Written*. In Los Angeles, Stein meets Upton Sinclair and at a lecture in Pasadena she meets William Saroyan. At a party in Beverly Hills, arranged by Carl Van Vechten, Stein meets Dashiell Hammett, Lillian Hellman, Charlie Chaplin, Paulette Goddard, and Anita Loos. She also declines a movie offer by Warner Brothers. Following a few final days in New York, on May 4 she and Toklas return to Paris on May 12. Stein writes *The Geographical History of America or*

The Relation of Human Nature to the Human Mind (published in 1936) and *What Are Masterpieces* (published in 1940). Both books are introduced by Thornton Wilder, who will visit her many times in Paris and Bilignin. Stein refuses to believe first indications of war; Toklas decides to ship copies of Stein's work to America for safekeeping.

1936   Adolph Hitler is infuriated when African-American athlete Jesse Owens wins four gold medals at the Olympic Games in Munich; Hitler had intended to use the games as proof of his theory of "Aryan supremacy." Franklin D. Roosevelt is re-elected by a landslide to the presidency. Playwright Eugene O'Neill is awarded the Nobel Prize for literature. Ty Cobb becomes the first player elected to the National Baseball Hall of Fame.

Faulkner's *Absalom, Absalom!* is published in October by Random House, his permanent publisher from this time forward. In April, Zelda Fitzgerald is hospitalized in Asheville and, in July, Fitzgerald returns to the Grove Park Inn in Asheville where he has previously stayed. Fitzgerald's mother dies in September. Steinbeck publishes *In Dubious Battle* and "The Harvest Gypsies," as well as articles on migrants for the *San Francisco News*. Stein lectures again at Oxford and Cambridge. She meets and befriends the photographer Cecil Beaton who takes a series of photographs of her and Toklas. In March, Stein begins writing her second autobiographical account, *Everybody's Autobiography*.

1937   William H. Hastie becomes the first African-American jurist to be appointed to the federal bench.

Fitzgerald moves to the Oak Park Inn in Tryon for six months. In need of money, he enters into a six-month contract with MGM. In July, he meets gossip columnist Sheilah Graham, and they begin a relationship that lasts until his death. In the summer, he starts the script for *Three Comrades* (the only screen credit he will receive). In December, MGM renews his contract for another year. Steinbeck publishes *Of Mice and Men*, which will become a bestseller and a Book-of-the-Month Club selection. The play production *Of Mice and Men* wins the Drama Critics

Circle Award. Hemingway serves as a war correspondent during the Spanish civil war and works on *The Spanish Earth*, a propaganda film. *To Have and Have Not*, his most overtly political novel. Zora Neale Hurston publishes *Their Eyes Were Watching God*. August 11, Edith Wharton dies. The lease at 27, rue de Fleurus runs out. In December, *Everybody's Autobiography* is published in New York.

1938   Germany invades Poland; Britain and France declare war on Germany. The conflict escalates into a world war; the U.S. remains neutral. Walt Disney releases *Snow White and the Seven Dwarfs*, the first full-length animated film. American novelist Pearl S. Buck wins the Nobel Prize for Literature. The film *Gone With the Wind* is released. Terminally ill Lou Gehrig retires from baseball after playing 2,130 consecutive league games.

In February, Faulkner publishes *The Unvanquished*, a collection of Civil War stories. He writes *The Wild Palms*, a novel comprised of two intertwined stories and purchases a farm outside of Oxford. Fitzgerald moves several times in California, from the Garden of Allah Hotel, to Malibu, to Encino, where he lives in a cottage on the estate of actor Edward Everett Horton. However, his MGM contract is not renewed in December. Steinbeck publishes *The Long Valley* and *Their Blood Is Strong* (a reprint of the migrant articles with a postscript). Hemingway publishes *The Fifth Column and the First Forty-nine Stories*, which includes a play about the war in Spain. Stein moves to 5, rue Christine, in the *quartier* St. Germain. She writes *Picasso*, the play *Doctor Faustus Lights the Lights*, and a children's book, *The World Is Round*.

1939   After being refused the use of Constitution Hall by the Daughters of the American Revolution, the opera singer Marian Anderson overcomes racial discrimination to be known as one of the finest singers of all time. With the intervention of First Lady Eleanor Roosevelt, a replacement concert is arranged to take place on the steps of the Lincoln Memorial. The concert is attended by seventy-five thousand people.

In January, Faulkner publishes *The Wild Palms*. He is

elected to the National Institute of Arts and Letters. Nevertheless, despite reviews from French critics such as Malraux and Sartre, Faulkner only begins to receive serious commentary from American critics. In February, producer Walter Wanger hires Fitzgerald to work with writer Budd Schulberg on a script for a new film, *Winter Carnival*. The two go to Dartmouth College where Wanger fires Fitzgerald for drinking. Fitzgerald recovers in a New York City hospital, returns to California, and works as a freelance scriptwriter. In October, Fitzgerald begins work on a new novel about Hollywood. Steinbeck publishes *The Grapes of Wrath*, which becomes a number one national bestseller, and is elected to the National Institute of Arts and Letters. Hemingway separates from Pauline and moves to Finca Vigia, a house near Havana Cuba. Stein is warned by the American consulate to leave France, but she and Toklas remain. She writes her homage to Paris, *Paris France*. After France declares war, Stein and Toklas close the apartment in Paris and spend the winter in the country.

1940   Roosevelt is the first president elected to a third term. Physicist Albert Einstein, who fled his native Germany after Hitler came to power, becomes a U.S. citizen. Benjamin O. Davis, Sr. becomes the first black general in the U.S. armed forces.

In April, Faulkner publishes *The Hamlet*, the first novel of the Snopes trilogy. Also in April, Zelda Fitzgerald is released from Highland Hospital in North Carolina and returns to her mother's home in Montgomery. On December 21, F. Scott Fitzgerald dies of a heart attack, at Sheilah Graham's apartment in Hollywood. He is buried in Rockville Union Cemetery, Maryland, on December 27. Steinbeck receives the Pulitzer Prize for *The Grapes of Wrath*, and writes *The Forgotten Village*, a film script. Hemingway marries Martha Gellhorn and publishes *For Whom the Bell Tolls*, a novel about a band of guerillas during the war in Spain. On June 14, Paris is occupied. Stein and Toklas decide to wait out the war in Bilignin. *Paris France* is published in London. Stein writes the novels *Ida* and *Mrs. Reynolds*, as well as *The Winner Loses: A Picture of Occupied France*.

1941   Asa Philip Randolph threatens to march on Washington,
                D.C., with one hundred thousand blacks to protest
                segregation in the defense industry and the military.
                President Roosevelt issues Executive Order 8802, which
                bans segregation in military industries and in training
                programs. Despite opposition from isolationists, Congress
                authorizes the Lend-Lease Act, which allows for the
                shipment of war materials to Britain and the Soviet Union.
                Joe DiMaggio, the "Yankee Clipper," sets a baseball record
                for hitting safely in fifty-six consecutive games. On Sunday,
                December 7, at dawn, the Japanese attack the U.S. naval
                base at Pearl Harbor. The next day, President Roosevelt
                asks Congress to declare war on Japan; Congress grants
                Roosevelt's request nearly unanimously. The lone voice of
                opposition came from Representative Jeannette Rankin, a
                pacifist and feminist who had been elected to Congress in
                1916 as the first woman ever to attain that office. Italy and
                Germany declare war on the U.S., and the U.S. issues a
                declaration of war on Nazi Germany and Italy.

                Steinbeck publishes *Sea of Cortez*, with Edward F.
                Ricketts.

1941–42   Concerned about France, Stein sympathizes with Marshal
                Pétain's politics of the armistice. During the occupation,
                Stein and Toklas's friend, Bernard Fay, intervenes with the
                Vichy régime in order to secure their protection. Stein and
                Toklas manage to survive these years of deprivation with
                their vegetable garden, fishing with the help of an umbrella,
                Toklas's cooking skills, and Stein's black-market deals.

1942   General Douglas MacArthur is named commander of the
                armed forces in the southwest Pacific. Despite resistance by
                Filipino and American forces, the Philippines fall to Japan.
                U.S. naval forces halt the Japanese in the Battle of Midway,
                and U.S. troops land on Guadalcanal in the Solomon
                Islands. J. Robert Oppenheimer leads research on atomic
                weapons at Los Alamos, New Mexico. More than 110,000
                Japanese Americans are incarcerated by the U.S.
                government. Actor Humphrey Bogart stars in *Casablanca*.

                In May, Faulkner's *Go Down, Moses and Other Stories*, his
                most penetrating scrutiny of black–white relations, is

published. Steinbeck publishes *The Moon is Down* (also a play) and *Bombs Away*. He divorces Carol Henning. Hemingway outfits his boat, the *Pilar*, to hunt down German submarines in the Caribbean. However, no German submarines are found.

1943   After six months of combat, the U.S. Marines secure Guadalcanal Island; the U.S. Navy and Marines employ an "island hopping" strategy to gain control of the Pacific. U.S. troops invade North Africa led by Dwight D. Eisenhower and George S. Patton. The Allies land in Sicily; Italy surrenders. Leonard Bernstein conducts the New York Philharmonic Orchestra for the first time. Paul Robeson plays the title role in a record-breaking run of Shakespeare's *Othello* on Broadway.

Steinbeck marries Gwendolyn Conger and moves to New York, where he serves as a war correspondent for New York *Herald Tribune*. Stein and Toklas lose their lease on Bilignin. They also ignore another warning to leave France and move to a house near the town of Culoz. During the summer, a German office and his subordinates are billeted in their house, followed by Italian troops. Ayn Rand publishes *The Fountainhead*.

1944   The D-Day invasion of Europe begins. On June 6, Allies penetrate the Normandy coastline of German-occupied France. U.S. forces begin to retake the Philippines from Japan. President Roosevelt is reelected for a fourth term over Republican challenger Thomas Dewey. Congress authorizes the Missouri River Basin Project—the building of dams and reservoirs becomes an important issue between Indian reservations and the government. Along with saxophonist Charlie Parker and others, trumpeter Dizzy Gillespie launches the bebop movement in jazz. Evangelist Billy Graham holds the first of his massive revivals.

Steinbeck writes an unpublished film story for *Lifeboat*, and his first son, Thom, is born. While working as a correspondent, Hemingway observes D-Day and attaches himself to the 22nd Regiment, 4th Infantry Division, for operations leading to the liberation of Paris and the battle of Hürtgenwald. He begins a relationship with Mary

Welsh, a newswoman. At the end of August, the first American soldiers land in Culoz. The American press reports Stein's "liberation." Stein writes a theater play about life in an occupied country, *In Savoy: A Play of the Resistance in France*. In mid-December, Stein and Toklas return to Paris. With Picasso, they examine the unharmed paintings at rue Christine. There is a brief reconciliatory meeting with Hemingway, who is now on assignment in Paris as a war correspondent.

1945   The Allies liberate Paris. Roosevelt meets with Soviet leader Joseph Stalin and British Prime Minister Winston Churchill at the Yalta Conference. The U.S. Marines occupy Iwo Jima and Okinawa. Ernie Pyle, the best-known war correspondent of World War II, is killed in action. The city of Dresden is firebombed. President Roosevelt dies and Vice President Harry S. Truman succeeds him. Berlin falls and Germany surrenders. The Potsdam Conference begins—Truman, Stalin, and British prime minister Clement Attlee attend. The U.S., Great Britain, and the Soviet Union demand the unconditional surrender of Japan, but Japan refuses. The U.S. drops atomic bombs on Hiroshima and Nagasaki. Japan surrenders, ending World War II. The United Nations is created and Eleanor Roosevelt is named U.S. delegate to the U.N. and becomes chairperson of the Committee on Human Rights.

Steinbeck publishes *Cannery Row*, "The Red Pony" (with a fourth part included), "The Pearl of the World" (The Pearl), and a film story, *A Medal for Benny*. In December, Martha Gellhorn divorces Hemingway. In the spring, Stein's *Wars I Have Seen* appears and becomes one of her most successful books. Stein writes *Brewsie and Willie*, a critical portrait of GIs in Europe and starts a second opera libretto for Virgil Thomson, *The Mother of Us All*, about the suffragette Susan B. Anthony. In November, while lecturing to GIs in Brussels, Stein suffers a severe attack of intestinal problems, but does not take it seriously.

1946   President Harry S. Truman issues Executive Order 9808, which creates the President's Committee on Civil Rights. Congress creates the Indian Claims Commission to settle old disputes. John H. Johnson begins publishing *Ebony* magazine. One of the magazine's early features was an article by Eleanor Roosevelt entitled, "If I Were a Negro." Bernard Baruch represents the U.S. on the United Nations Atomic Energy Commission, which issues a joint declaration on the control of atomic energy. Eudora Welty publishes *Delta Wedding*, her first full-length novel.

In May, Malcolm Cowley's edition of *The Portable Faulkner* is published by the Viking Press. With the benefit of Cowley's introduction, this volume makes Faulkner's work inexpensive and available to a large reading audience. Steinbeck is awarded King Haakon Liberty Cross in Norway for *The Moon is Down*, and his second son, John IV, is born. Hemingway marries Mary Welsh. They live in Cuba and in Ketchum, Idaho. Robert Penn Warren publishes *All the King's Men*. Stein finishes her opera *The Mother of Us All*. *Yes Is for a Very Young Man* premieres in Pasadena. On July 27, Stein is diagnosed with colon cancer. She dies that afternoon while under anesthesia. Stein is buried in the Paris cemetery of Père Lachaise.

1947	Secretary of State George Marshall proposes his Marshall Plan, a massive program of aid for the devastated nations of Europe, both allies and enemies. Announced by Secretary of State George Marshall, the program was successful in preventing Communism from infiltrating the region. Republican senator Robert Taft sponsors the Taft-Hartley Act, which restricts the power of organized labor and enlarges the role of the National Labor Relations Board in labor-management disputes. Jackie Robinson joins the Brooklyn Dodgers and becomes the first black baseball player in the major leagues. Edwin Land invents the one-step instant camera. Tennessee Williams's play, *A Streetcar Named Desire*, is produced.

Steinbeck publishes *The Pearl* and *The Wayward Bus* and visits Russia with photographer Robert Capa. Ralph Ellison publishes *The Invisible Man*. On April 24 Willa Cather dies in New York. On July 29, Leon Stein dies in Florence.

1947–48	In November, Zelda Fitzgerald is readmitted to Highland Hospital. She will die in a fire there on March 10, 1948.

1948   The U.S. begins the Berlin Airlift to circumvent the Soviet
              Union's blockade of Berlin. President Truman issues
              Executive Order 9981 and segregation in the Armed Forces
              ends. Truman also issues an order making the U.S.
              government an equal opportunity employer. The Supreme
              Court voids a California statute that prohibits interracial
              marriages. Former diplomat Alger Hiss is accused of
              passing government documents to the Soviet Union; two
              years later he is convicted of perjury. Norman Mailer
              publishes his first novel, *The Naked and the Dead*. Andrew
              Wyeth paints *Christina's World*. *Cantos* by Ezra Pound wins
              the Bollingen Prize for poetry. Pound had been deported to
              the United States and tried for treason because of his
              broadcasts of Italian Fascist propaganda. He is confined to
              a mental hospital for twelve years after he is ruled unfit to
              stand trial. William Shockley invents the transistor, which
              leads to the miniaturization of many electronic devices and
              appliances.

                  In September, Faulkner publishes *Intruder in the Dust*, a
              sequel to the Lucas Beauchamp materials of *Go Down,
              Moses*. With its open treatment of Southern racial tensions,
              sales are large and Faulkner is encouraged to speak out on
              social issues. Faulkner is elected to the American Academy
              of Arts and Letters. November 4, T.S. Eliot is awarded the
              Nobel Prize in Literature. With Robert Capa, Steinbeck
              publishes *A Russian Journal* and is elected to the American
              Academy of Arts and Letters. Steinbeck is divorced from
              Gwendolyn Conger.

1949   NATO, the North Atlantic Treaty Organization, is formed
              under the guidance of Secretary of State Dean Acheson.
              Arthur Miller writes a Pulitzer Prize–winning play, *Death of
              a Salesman*. *Male and Female*, an anthropological study by
              Margaret Mead, examines gender roles in different
              societies.

                  In November, Faulkner publishes *Knight's Gambit*, a
              collection of detective stories.

1950   The United States becomes involved in the Korean War. A
              senate committee led by Joseph McCarthy accuses many
              Americans of being Communists or having ties to

Communist organizations. Many careers are ruined before McCarthy is discredited. Gwendolyn Brooks wins the Pulitzer Prize in poetry for her collection *Annie Allen*—she is the first African American to receive a Pulitzer.

In August, Faulkner publishes *Collected Stories*. Faulkner is awarded the Nobel Prize for Literature, travels with his daughter Jill to Stockholm, and delivers his famous Nobel Prize acceptance speech. Steinbeck publishes *Burning Bright*, writes *Viva Zapata!* for film, and marries Elaine Scott. Hemingway publishes *Across the River and into the Trees*, a novel about a December-May romance which receives very unfavorable reviews.

1951   Faulkner's *Collected Stories* is awarded the National Book Award. In September, *Requiem for a Nun*, a reprise of the Temple Drake materials in *Sanctuary*, written in both novelistic and theatrical form, is published. France awards Faulkner the Legion of Honor. From this point forward, Faulkner achieves serious and "canonical" attention, an acclaim that brings him financial security. He continues to write and speak out on political and racial issues, a position that costs him support from many of his fellow Southerners because of his attack on racism, and creates disappointment in liberals because of his advocacy of a gradual approach to desegregation. Steinbeck publishes *The Log from the Sea of Cortez*, including a tribute to Ricketts. J.D. Salinger publishes *The Catcher in the Rye*. February 7 Sinclair Lewis dies.

1952   Steinbeck publishes *East of Eden*. Hemingway publishes *The Old Man and the Sea*, a short book about the trials of the Cuban fisherman Santiago, which is printed in *Life* magazine. E.B. White publishes *Charlotte's Web*.

1953   January 22 *The Crucible* by Arthur Miller opens on Broadway. Hemingway and Mary go on a safari in Africa. James Baldwin publishes *Go Tell it on the Mountain*. Ray Bradbury publishes *Fahrenheit 451*.

1954   In August, Faulkner publishes *A Fable*, a story of World War I in terms of the Christ fable. It wins the Pulitzer prize. Steinbeck publishes *Sweet Thursday*. In January, Hemingway is severely injured by two successive plane

	crashes in Africa. He is awarded the Nobel Prize for literature.
1955	The first issue of the *Guinness Book of World Records* is published. Faulkner publishes *Big Woods*, a collection of stories. Steinbeck publishes *Pipe Dream*, a musical comedy based on *Sweet Thursday*, which is produced by Rodgers and Hammerstein. Flannery O'Connor publishes *A Good Man is Hard to Find*. Vladimir Nabokov publishes *Lolita*.
1956	Steinbeck publishes *The Short Reign of Pippin IV*; Allen Ginsberg publishes *Howl*.
1957	Jack Kerouc publishes *On the Road*. Ayn Rand publishes *Atlas Shrugged*. Dr. Seuss (Theodor Seuss Geisel) publishes *The Cat in the Hat*. February 10 Laura Ingalls Wilder dies.
1958	Steinbeck publishes *Once There Was a War*.
1959	Hemingway is in declining health and spends his sixtieth birthday in Spain.
1960	January 28, Zora Neale Hurston dies.
1961	Steinbeck publishes *The Winter of Our Discontent*. Hemingway undergoes shock treatment for depression. On July 2, he shoots himself and is buried in Sun Valley, Idaho. Joseph Heller publishes *Catch-22*.
1962	In June, Faulkner publishes *The Reivers*, his last and deliberately lighthearted novel. One month late, on July 6, Faulkner dies unexpectedly in a clinic in Byhalia, Mississippi, where he had been recurrently hospitalized for alcoholism and horseback-riding accidents. Faulkner is buried in Oxford on July 7. Steinbeck publishes *Travels with Charley in Search of America* and is awarded the Nobel Prize for Literature.
1963	Faulkner's *The Reivers* wins the Pulitzer prize. Sylvia Plath publishes *The Bell Jar* and on February 11 Plath dies.
1964	Steinbeck receives the Presidential Medal of Freedom. Hemingway's *A Moveable Feast* is published. August 3 Flannery O'Connor dies.
1965	January 4, T.S. Eliot dies.
1967	On March 7, Toklas dies. She is buried next to Stein in Père Lachaise Chaim Potok publishes *The Chosen*.

1968	Steinbeck dies December 20.
1969	October 29 Jack Kerouc dies. Kurt Vonnegut publishes *Slaughterhouse Five*.
1970	Hemingway's semi-autobiographical novel, *Islands in the Stream*, about the painter Thomas Hudson, is published.
1972	Hemingway's *The Nick Adams Stories* are gathered together in a single volume.
1973	Pearl S. Buck dies March 6.
1975	F. Scott Fitzgerald and his wife, Zelda, are reburied in the cemetery of St. Mary's Church, Rockville, Maryland. In 1986, their daughter Scottie was buried with her parents.

Contributors

HAROLD BLOOM is Sterling Professor of the Humanities at Yale University. He is the author of over 20 books, including *Shelley's Mythmaking* (1959), *The Visionary Company* (1961), *Blake's Apocalypse* (1963), *Yeats* (1970), *A Map of Misreading* (1975), *Kabbalah and Criticism* (1975), *Agon: Toward a Theory of Revisionism* (1982), *The American Religion* (1992), *The Western Canon* (1994), and *Omens of Millennium: The Gnosis of Angels, Dreams, and Resurrection* (1996). *The Anxiety of Influence* (1973) sets forth Professor Bloom's provocative theory of the literary relationships between the great writers and their predecessors. His most recent books include *Shakespeare: The Invention of the Human* (1998), a 1998 National Book Award finalist, *How to Read and Why* (2000), *Genius: A Mosaic of One Hundred Exemplary Creative Minds* (2002), *Hamlet: Poem Unlimited* (2003), and *Where Shall Wisdom be Found* (2004). In 1999, Professor Bloom received the prestigious American Academy of Arts and Letters Gold Medal for Criticism, and in 2002 he received the Catalonia International Prize.

SERGIO PEROSA has been a distinguished Professor of American Literature at the University of Venice. He is the author of *From Islands to Portraits: Four Literary Variations* (2000) and *Henry James and the Experimental Novel* (1978).

BENJAMIN T. SPENCER taught for almost 40 years at Ohio Wesleyan University. Among his works are *Patterns of Nationality: Twentieth Century*

Literary Visions of America (1981), and *The Quest for Nationality: An American Literary Campaign* (1957)

JAMES LEA is the author of *Katzanzakis: The Politics of Salvation.*

HOWARD LEVANT is the author of "John Steinbeck's *The Red Pony*: A Study in Narrative Technique" (1971), as well as *The Novels of John Steinbeck* (1974).

CHARLES MARZ has written on Dos Passos for *Studies in the Novel.*

PHYLLIS ROSE has taught English at Wesleyan University. Her publications include *Women of Letters: A Life of Virginia Woolf* and articles on Huxley and Woolf in *Victorian Newsletter* and *Women's Studies.*

BARBARA JOHNSON has taught at Harvard University, and her publications include a translation of Derrida's *Dissemination*, and an edition of *The Pedagogical Imperitive: Teaching as a Literary Genre.*

MAX PUTZEL (1910–2003) was a Professor of English and American literature and held the position of associate dean of the graduate school at the University of Connecticut at Storrs. He is the author of *The Man in the Mirror: William Marion Reedy and his Magazine* (1998).

TOM QUIRK has been Professor of English at the University of Missouri-Columbia. He is the author of *Nothing Abstract: Investigations in the American Literary Imagination* (2001); *Mark Twain: A Study of the Short Fiction* (1997); and *Coming to Grips with Huckleberry Finn: Essays on a Book, a Boy, and a Man* (1993).

RANDA DUBNICK has been a Professor and Vice President of Student Services at Montserrat College of Art, Beverly, Masssachusetts. She is the author of *Women and Literature: Four Studies* (1976).

ROBERT A. MARTIN is Emeritus Professor of English and American Literature at Michigan State University. He is a contributing editor of *The Theater Essays of Arthur Miller* (1996); *The Writer's Craft: Hopwood Lectures, 1965–81* (1982); and *Arthur Miller: New Perspectives* (1982).

D.G. KEHL has been a Professor of English at Arizona State University. He is the author of *Poetry and the Visual Arts* and has presented papers entitled "'Illegal Chuckles' for 'Humorless Times': Steinbeck's *Grapes of Wrath*" (2002) and "From Gestural Tableau to Idea: Fitzgerald's 'Unbroken Series of Successful Gestures'" (2002).

LISA KERR has taught at the University of South Carolina, Columbia. She won the 2002 Thomas Wolfe Student Essay Prize, which was adapted from a portion of her dissertation, "Climbing Parnassus: Thomas Wolfe's *O Lost* as Kunstlerroman."

RONALD BERMAN is professor of English Literature at Yale University. His published works include *Fitzgerald's Intellectual Context*, *Fitzgerald-Wilson-Hemingway*, and *Public Policy and the Aesthetic Interest*.

KIRK CURNUTT has been an Associate Professor of English at Troy State University in Montgomery, Alabama. He is the author of *Wise Economies: Brevity and Storytelling in American Short Stories* (1997) and *The Critical Response to Gertrude Stein* (2000).

RYUICHI YAMAGUCHI has been a Professor of English and American Literature at Aichi University, Toyohashi, Japan. In 1975, he was awarded a British Council Fellowship to participate in the International Shakespeare Seminar at the Shakespeare Centre in Stratford-upon-Avon. He has published extensively in Japanese on Donne, Shakespeare, and Faulkner.

Bibliography

Allen, Joan M. *Candles and Carnival Lights: The Catholic Sensibility of F. Scott Fitzgerald*. New York: New York University Press, 1978.

Astro, Richard. *John Steinbeck and Edward F. Ricketts: The Shaping of a Novelist*. Minneapolis: University of Minnesota Press, 1973.

Baker, Carlos. *Ernest Hemingwa: A Life Story*. New York, Scribner, 1969.

———. *Ernest Hemingway: Critiques of Four Major Novels*. New York, Scribner, 1962.

Baughman, Judith S., ed. *American Decades: 1920–1929*. Detroit: Manly/Gale Research, 1995.

Baughman, Judith S. and Matthew J. Bruccoli. *Literary Masters: F. Scott Fitzgerald*. Detroit: Manly/Gale Group, 2000.

Berman, Ronald. *The Great Gatsby and Modern Times*. Urbana: University of Illinois Press, 1994.

———. *Fitzgerald-Wilson-Hemingway: Language and Experience*. Tuscaloosa: University of Alabama Press, 2003.

———. *The Great Gatsby and Fitzgerald's World of Ideas*. Tuscaloosa: University of Alabama Press, 1997.

Bondi, Victor, ed. *American Decades: 1930–1939*. Detroit: Manly/Gale Research, 1995.

Bruccoli, Matthew J. *Classes on F. Scott Fitzgerald*. Columbia: Thomas Cooper Library, University of South Carolina, 2001.

————. *The Composition of Tender Is the Night.* Pittsburgh, Pa.: University of Pittsburgh Press, 1963.

————. *The Last of the Novelists: F. Scott Fitzgerald and "The Last Tycoon."* Carbondale and Edwardsville: Southern Illinois University Press, 1977.

Bruccoli, with Judith S. Baughman. *Reader's Companion to F. Scott Fitzgerald's Tender Is the Night.* Columbia: University of South Carolina Press, 1996.

Benson, Jackson J., ed. *The Short Novels Of John Steinbeck: Critical Essays with a Checklist to Steinbeck Criticism.* Durham: Duke University Press, 1990.

————. "Background of *The Grapes of Wrath.*" *Journal of Modern Literature* 5 (April, 1976): 194–216.

Bleikasten, André. *The Ink of Melancholy: Faulkner's Novels from* The Sound and the Fury *to* Light in August. Bloomgington: Indiana University Press, 1990.

Bloom, Harold, ed. *Modern Critical Views: William Faulkner.* Modern Critical Views Series. New York: Chelsea House, 1986.

————, ed. *Modern Critical Views: Ernest Hemingway.* Modern Critical Views Series. New York: Chelsea House, 1985.

————, ed. *Ernest Hemingway's the Sun Also Rises.* Bloom's Modern Critical Interpretations.

————. *F. Scott Fitzgerald.* New York: Chelsea House, 1985.

————. *F. Scott Fitzgerald's "The Great Gatsby."* New York: Chelsea House, 1986.

————, ed. *Gatsby.* New York: Chelsea House, 1991.

Bockting, Ineke. *Character and Personality in the Novels of William Faulkner: A Study in Psychostylistics.* Lanham, Md.: University Press of America, 1995.

Brooks, Cleanth. *William Faulkner: First Encounters.* New Haven: Yale University Press, 1983.

———— *William Faulkner: Toward Yoknapatawpha and Beyond.* Baton Rouge: Louisiana State University Press, 1978.

————. *William Faulkner: The Yoknapatawpha Country.* Baton Rouge: Louisiana State University Press, 1963.

Blotner, Joseph. *Faulkner: A Biography.* 2 vols. New York: Random House, 1974. Rev. ed. New York: Random House, 1984.

Bowers, Jane Palatini. *Gertrude Stein.* New York: St. Martin's Press, 1993.

Brodsky, Louis Daniel. *William Faulkner: Life Glimpses*. Austin: University of Texas Press, 1990.

Bruccoli, Matthew J. *Classes on Ernest Hemingway*. Columbia, S.C.: Thomas Cooper Library, University of South Carolina, 2002.

———. *Fitzgerald and Hemingway: A Dangerous Friendship*. New York: Carroll & Graf, 1994.

———, ed. *New Essays on "The Great Gatsby."* Cambridge: Cambridge University Press, 1985.

———. *Profile of F. Scott Fitzgerald*. Columbus, Ohio: Merrill, 1971.

Bryer, Jackson R., ed. *F. Scott Fitzgerald: The Critical Reception*. New York: Burt Franklin, 1978.

Carey, Glenn O., ed. *Faulkner, the Unappeased Imagination: A Collection of Critical Essays*. Troy, N.Y.: Whitston, 1980.

Chabrier, Gwendolyn. *Faulkner's Families: A Southern Saga*. New York: Gordian, 1993.

Chambers, John B. *The Novels of F. Scott Fitzgerald*. London: Macmillan; New York: St. Martin's Press, 1989.

Claridge, Henry, ed. *F. Scott Fitzgerald: Critical Assessments*, 4 vols. Near Robertsbridge, East Sussex, U.K.: Helm Information, 1991.

Clarke, Deborah. *Robbing the Mother: Women in Faulkner*. Jackson: University Press of Missisippi, 1994.

Coers, Donald V. *John Steinbeck as Propagandist: "The Moon is Down" Goes to War*. Tuscaloosa: University of Alabama Press, 1991.

Coffee, James M. *Faulkner's Un-Christlike Christians: Biblical Allusions in the Novels*. Ann Arbor: UMI Research Press, 1983.

Cowley, Malcolm. *Exile's Return: A Literary Odyssey of the 1920s*. New York: Norton, 1934. Rev. ed., New York: Viking, 1951.

Cross, K.G.W. *Scott Fitzgerald*. New York: Grove, 1964.

Davis, Robert M. *Steinbeck: A Collection of Critical Essays*. Englewood Cliffs, New Jersey: Prentice-Hall, 1972.

Davis, Thadious M. *Faulkner's "Negro": Art and the Southern Context*. Baton Rouge: Louisiana State University Press, 1983.

Dillon-Malone, Aubrey. *Hemingway: The Grace and The Pressure*. London: Robson, 1999.

Ditsky, John. *John Steinbeck and the Critics*. Rochester, N.Y.: Camden House, 2000.

———, ed. *Critical Essays on Steinbeck's The Grapes of Wrath*. Boston: Hall, 1989.

———. *John Steinbeck: Life, Work and Criticism*. Fredericton, N.B., Canada: York Press, 1985.

Crosland, Andrew T. *A Concordance to F. Scott Fitzgerald's* The Great Gatsby. Detroit, Mich.: Bruccoli Clark/Gale Research, 1975.

Dowling, David. *William Faulkner*. New York: St. Martin's, 1989.

Eble, Kenneth, ed. *F. Scott Fitzgerald: A Collection of Criticism*. New York: McGraw-Hill, 1973.

———. *F. Scott Fitzgerald*. New York: Twayne, 1963. Revised edition, 1977.

Edel, Leon, ed. *The Twenties*. New York: Farrar, Straus and Giroux, 1975.

Fahey, William A. *F. Scott Fitzgerald and the American Dream*. New York, Crowell, 1973.

Fayen, Tanya T. *In Search of the Latin American Faulkner*. Lanham, MD.: University Press of America, 1995.

Ford, Dan, ed. *Heir and Prototype: Original and Derived Characterizations in Faulkner*. Conway: University of Central Arkansas Press, 1988.

Ford, Sara J. *Gertrude Stein and Wallace Stevens: The Performance of Modern Consciousness*. New York: Routledge, 2002.

Fowler, Doreen. *Faulkner's Changing Vision: From Outrage to Affirmation*. Ann Arbor: UMI Research Press, 1983.

Fowler, Doreen, and Ann J. Abadie, eds. *Faulkner and Race: Faulkner and Yoknapatawpha 1986*. Jackson: University Press of Mississippi, 1987.

———. *Faulkner and Religion: Faulkner and Yoknapatawpha 1989*. Jackson: University Press of Mississippi, 1991.

———. *Faulkner and the Craft of Fiction: Faulkner and Yoknapatawpha 1987*. Jackson: University Press of Mississippi, 1989.

———. *Faulkner and Humor: Faulkner and Yoknapatawpha 1984*. Jackson: University Press of Mississippi, 1986.

———. *Faulkner and the Southern Renaissance: Faulkner and Yoknapatawpha 1981*. Jackson: University Press of Mississippi, 1982.

French, Warren, ed. *A Companion to* The Grapes of Wrath. New York: Penguin, 1989

———. *John Steinbeck*. Boston, Twayne, 1975.

———. *John Steinbeck's Fiction Revisited*. New York: Twayne Publishers, 1994.

Friedman, Alan Warren. *William Faulkner*. New York: Ungar, 1984.

George, Stephen K. *John Steinbeck: A Centennial Tribute*. Westport, Connecticut: Praeger, 2002.

Gray, Richard J. *The Life of William Faulkner: A Critical Biography*. Oxford and Cambridge, Mass.: Blackwell Publishers, 1994.

Griffin, Robert J. and William E. Freeman. "Machines and Animals: Pervasive Motifs *in The Grapes of Wrath.*" *Journal of English and Germanic Philology* 62 (April, 1963): 569–80.

Grimwood, Michael. *Heart in Conflict: Faulkner's Struggles with Vocation.* Athens: University of Georgia Press, 1987.

Gurko, Leo. *Ernest Hemingway and the Pursuit of Heroism.* New York, Crowell, 1968.

Hansen, Arlen J. *Expatriate Paris: A Cultural and Literary Guide to Paris in the 1920s.* New York: Arcade, 1990.

Hayashi, Tetsumaro, ed. *John Steinbeck: The Years of Greatness, 1936-1939.* Tuscaloosa: University of Alabama Press, 1993.

Harrington, Evans and Ann J. Abadie, eds. *The Maker and the Myth: Faulkner and Yoknapatawpha 1977.* Jackson: University Press of Mississippi, 1978.

———. *The South and Faulkner's Yoknapatawpha: TheActual and the Apocryphal: Faulkner and Yoknapatawpha 1976.* Jackson: University Press of Mississippi, 1977.

Higgins, John A. *F. Scott Fitzgerald: A Study of the Stories.* New York: St. John's University Press, 1971.

Hook, Andrew. *F. Scott Fitzgerald: A Literary Life.* Houndmills, Basingstoke, Hampshire; New York: Palgrave Macmillan, 2002.

Hines, Thomas S. *William Faulkner and the Tangible Past: The Architecture of Yoknapatawpha.* Berkeley: University of California Press, 1996.

Hlavsa, Virginia V. James. *Faulkner and the Thoroughly Modern Novel.* Charlottesville: University Press of Virginia, 1991.

Hoffman, Frederick J. *William Faulkner.* 2nd ed. New York: Twayne, 1966.

———. *The Twenties: American Writing in the Postwar Decade.* Rev. ed., New York: Collier, 1962.

Hoffman, Michael J. *Gertrude Stein.* Boston: Twayne Publishers, 1976.

Honnighausen, Lothar, ed. *Faulkner's Discourse: An International Symposium.* Tübingen: Max Niemeyer Verlag, 1989.

Hughes, R.S. *John Steinbeck: A Study of the Short Fiction.* R.S. Hughes. Boston: Twayne, 1989.

Hunter, Edwin R. *William Faulkner: Narrative Practice and Prose Style.* Washington, D.C.: Windhover, 1973.

Inge, M. Thomas. *William Faulkner: The Contemporary Reviews.* Cambridge: Cambridge University Press, 1995.

Irwin, John T. *Doubling and Incest/Repetition and Revenge: A Speculative Reading of Faulkner.* 1975. Expanded ed. Baltimore: Johns Hopkins University Press, 1996.

Karl, Frederick Robert. *William Faulkner, American Writer: A Biography.* New York: Weidenfeld & Nicolson, 1989.

Kartiganer, Donald M. *The Fragile Thread: The Meaning of Form in Faulkner's Novels.* Amherst: University of Massachusetts Press, 1979.

Kartiganer, Donald M., and Ann J. Abadie, ed. *Faulkner and Gender.* (Faulkner and Yoknapatawpha Conference, 1994.) Jackson: University Press of Mississippi, 1996.

———, ed. *Faulkner and Ideology.* Jackson: University Press of Mississippi, 1995.

———, ed. *Faukner and Psychology.* Jackson: University Press of Mississippi, 1994.

———, ed. *Faulkner and the Artist.* Jackson: University Press of Mississippi, 1996.

Kazin, Alfred, ed. *F. Scott Fitzgerald: The Man and His Work.* Cleveland: World, 1951.

Kennedy, J. Gerald and Jackson R. Bryer, eds. *French Connections: Hemingway and Fitzgerald Abroad.* New York: St. Martin's Press, 1998.

Kerr, Elizabeth M. *William Faulkner's Yoknapatawpha: "A Kind of Keystone in the Universe."* New York: Fordham University Press, 1983.

Kerr, Elizabeth M. *Yoknapatawpha: Faulkner's "Little Postage Stamp of Native Soil."* Rev. ed. New York: Fordham University Press, 1976.

Kinney, Arthur F., ed. *Critical Essays on William Faulkner: The Compson Family.* Boston: Hall, 1982.

Knapp, Bettina L. *Gertrude Stein.* New York: Continuum, 1990.

Kreiswirth, Martin. *William Faulkner: The Making of a Novelist.* Athens: University of Georgia Press, 1983.

Kuehl, John. "Scott Fitzgerald's Reading." *The Princeton University Library Chronicle,* 22 (Winter 1961): 58–89.

LaLonde, Christopher A. *William Faulkner and the Rites of Passage.* Macon, Georgia: Mercer University Press, 1995.

Lathbury, Roger. *Literary Masterpieces:* The Great Gatsby. Detroit: Manly/Gale Group, 2000.

Lee, Robert, ed. *William Faulkner: The Yoknapatawpha Fiction.* New York: St. Martin's, 1990.

———, ed. *Scott Fitzgerald: The Promises of Life*. London: Vision; New York: St. Martin's Press, 1989.

Levant, Howard. *The Novels of John Steinbeck: A Critical Study*. Columbia: University of Missouri Press, 1974.

Leff, Leonard J. *Hemingway and His Conspirators: Hollywood, Scribners, and the Making of American Celebrity Culture*. Lanham, Md.: Rowman & Littlefield, 1997.

LeVot, André. "Fitzgerald in Paris." *Fitzgerald/Hemingway Annual* (1973): 49–68.

Lewis, Robert W., ed. *Hemingway in Italy and Other Essays*. New York: Praeger, 1990.

———. *Hemingway on Love*. Austin: University of Texas Press, 1965.

Lisca, Peter. *John Steinbeck, Nature and Myth*. New York: Crowell, 1978.

Lehan, Richard D. *F. Scott Fitzgerald and the Craft of Fiction*. Carbondale: Southern Illinois University Press, 1966.

———. *"The Great Gatsby": The Limits of Wonder*. Boston: Twayne, 1990.

———. *F. Scott Fitzgerald and the Craft of Fiction*. Carbondale: Southern Illinois University Press, 1966.

Lockridge, Ernest, ed. *Twentieth Century Interpretations of "The Great Gatsby."* Englewood Cliffs, N.J.: Prentice-Hall, 1968.

Long, Robert Emmet. *The Achieving of "The Great Gatsby."* Lewisburg, Pa.: Bucknell University Press, 1979.

Lynn, Kenneth Schuyler. *Hemingway*. New York: Simon and Schuster, 1987.

Malin, Irving. *William Faulkner: An Interpretation*. Stanford, California: Stanford University Press, 1957.

Margolies, Alan. "Fitzgerald's Work in the Film Studios." *The Princeton University Library Chronicle* 32 (Winter 1971): 81–110.

McElrath, Joseph R., Jr., Jesse S. Crisler and Susan Shillinglaw. *John Steinbeck: The Contemporary Reviews*. Cambridge and New York: Cambridge University Press, 1996.

Mellow, James R. *Hemingway: A Life Without Consequences*. Boston: Houghton Mifflin, 1992.

Messent, Peter. *Ernest Hemingway*. New York: St. Martin's Press, 1992.

Meyers, Jeffrey. *Hemingway: Life into Art*. New York: Cooper Square Press; Lanham, Md.: Distributed by National Book Network, 2000.

Millgate, Michael. *The Achievement of William Faulkner*. Lincoln: University of Nebraska Press, 1978.

Minter, David L. *A Cultural History of the American Novel: Henry James to William Faulkner*. Cambridge: Cambridge University Press, 1994.

Minter, David. *William Faulkner: His Life and Work*. Baltimore, Maryland: Johns Hopkins University Press, 1980.

Mizener, Arthur, ed. *F. Scott Fitzgerald: A Collection of Critical Essays*. Englewood Cliffs, N.J.: Prentice-Hall, 1963.

Moreland, Richard C. *Faulkner and Modernism: Rereading and Rewriting*. Madison: University of Wisconsin Press, 1990.

Mortimer, Gail L. *Faulkner's Rhetoric of Loss: A Study in Perception and Meaning*. Austin: University of Texas Press, 1983.

Nagel, James, ed. *Ernest Hemingway, The Writer in Context*. Madison, Wisconsin: University of Wisconsin Press, 1984.

Neuman, Shirley C. *Gertrude Stein: Autobiography and the Problem of Narration*. Victoria, B.C.: English Literary Studies, University of Victoria, 1979.

Neuman, Shirley and Ira B. Nadel, eds. *Gertrude Stein and the Making of Literature*. Boston, Mass.: Northeastern University Press, 1988.

Noble, Donald R., ed. *The Steinbeck Question: New Essays in Criticism*. Troy, N.Y.: Whitson Publishing, 1993.

———, ed. *Hemingway: A Revaluation*. Troy, New York: Whitston, 1983.

Oates, Stephen B. *William Faulkner: The Man and the Artist*. New York: Harper & Row, 1987.

Oliver, Charles M. *Ernest Hemingway A to Z: The Essential Reference to the Life and Work*. New York: Facts on File, 1999.

Owens, Louis & Hector Torres. "Dialogic Structure and Levels of Discourse in Steinbeck's *The Grapes of Wrath*." *Arizona Quarterly* 45, no. 4 (1989): 75–94.

Owens, Louis. *John Steinbeck's Re-vision of America*. Athens: University of Georgia Press, 1985.

Parini, Jay. *John Steinbeck: A Biography*. New York: H. Holt, 1995.

Parker, Robert Dale. *Faulkner and the Novelistic Imagination*. Urbana: University of Illinois Press, 1985.

Parkinson, Kathleen. *F. Scott Fitzgerald: "Tender Is the Night."* Harmondsworth, U.K.: Penguin, 1986.

———. *F. Scott Fitzgerald: "The Great Gatsby."* Harmondsworth, U.K.: Penguin, 1987.

Pendleton, Thomas A. *I'm Sorry about the Clock: Chronology, Composition, and*

Narrative Technique in "The Great Gatsby." Selinsgrove, Pa.: Susquehanna University Press, 1993.

Perosa, Sergio. *The Art of F. Scott Fitzgerald*. Ann Arbor, Mich.: University of Michigan Press, 1965.

Piper, Henry Dan. *F. Scott Fitzgerald: A Critical Portrait*. New York: Holt, Rinehart & Winston, 1965.

———, ed. *Fitzgerald's "The Great Gatsby": The Novel, The Critics, The Background*. New York: Scribners, 1970.

Pivano, Fernanda. *Hemingway*. Milano: Rusconi, 1985.

Polk, Noel. *Children of the Dark House: Text and Context in Faulkner*. Jackson: University Press of Mississippi, 1996.

Parker, Robert Dale. *Faulkner and the Novelistic Imagination*. Urbana: University of Illinois Press, 1985.

Polk, Noel. *Children of the Dark House: Text and Context in Faulkner*. Jackson: University Press of Mississippi, 1996.

Prigozy, Ruth. *F. Scott Fitzgerald*. Woodstock, NY: Overlook Press, 2002.

Rao, E. Nageswara. *Ernest Hemingway: A Study of His Rhetoric*. Atlantic Highlands, New Jersey: Humanities Press, 1983.

Reynolds, Michael S. *Hemingway: An Annotated Chronology: An Outline of the Author's Life and Career Detailing Significant Events, Friendships, Travels, and Achievements*. Detroit, Michigan: Omnigraphics, Inc., 1991.

———. *Hemingway: The 1930s*. New York: W.W. Norton, 1997.

———. *Hemingway: The American Homecoming*. Cambridge, Mass.: Blackwell, 1992.

———. *Hemingway: The Paris Years*. Oxford, UK; Cambridge, Mass.: Blackwell, 1989.

———. *Hemingway: The Final Years*. New York: W.W. Norton & Co., 1999.

Roberts, Diane. *Faulkner and Southern Womenhood*. Athens: University of Georgia Press, 1994.

Rombold, Tamara. "Biblical Inversion in *The Grapes of Wrath*." *College Literature* 14, no. 2 (1987): 146–66.

Rovit, Earl and Gerry Brenner. *Ernest Hemingway*. Rev. ed. Boston, Mass.: Twayne Publishers, 1986.

Ruppersburg, Hugh M. *Voice and Eye in Faulkner's Fiction*. Athens: University of Georgia Press, 1983.

Scafella, Frank. *Hemingway: Essays of Reassessment*. New York: Oxford University Press, 1991.

Seiters, Dan. *Image Patterns in the Novels of F. Scott Fitzgerald*. Ann Arbor, Mich.: UMI, 1986.

Shain, Charles E. *F. Scott Fitzgerald*. Minneapolis: University of Minnesota Press, 1961.

Simon, Linda, ed. *Gertrude Stein: A Composite Portrait*. New York: Avon, 1974.

Simmonds, Roy S. *John Steinbeck: The War Years, 1939–1945*. Lewisburg: Bucknell University Press; London; Cranbury, New Jersey: Associated University Presses, 1996.

Singer, Kurt D. *Ernest Hemingway, Man of Courage*. Minneapolis, Minn.: T. S. Denison, 1963.

Sklar, Robert. *F. Scott Fitzgerald: The Last Laocoön*. New York: University Press, 1967.

Stavola, Thomas J. *Scott Fitzgerald: Crisis in an American Identity*. New York: Barnes & Noble, 1979.

Stern, Milton R. *The Golden Moment: The Novels of F. Scott Fitzgerald*. Urbana: University of Illinois Press, 1970.

———. *"Tender Is the Night": The Broken Universe*. New York: Twayne, 1994.

Sojka, Gregory S. *Ernest Hemingway: The Angler as Artist*. New York: Peter Lang, 1985.

St. Pierre, Brian. *John Steinbeck, the California Years*. San Francisco: Chronicle Books, 1983.

Stanton, Edward Feagler. *Hemingway and Spain: A Pursuit*. Seattle: University of Washington Press, 1989.

Stern, Milton R., ed. *Critical Essays on F. Scott Fitzgerald's "Tender Is the Night."* Boston: Hall, 1986.

Stewart, Allegra. *Gertrude Stein and The Present*. Cambridge: Harvard University Press, 1967.

Sundquist, Eric J. *Faulkner: The House Divided*. Baltimore, Md.: Johns Hopkins University Press, 1983.

Sutherland, Donald. *Gertrude Stein: A Biography of Her Work*. New Haven, Yale University Press, 1951.

Svoboda, Frederic Joseph. Hemingway & The Sun Also Rises: The Crafting of a Style. Lawrence, KS: University Press of Kansas, 1983.

Tate, Mary Jo. *F. Scott Fitzgerald A to Z: The Essential Reference to his Life and Work*. New York: Facts on File, 1998.

Taylor, Walter. *Faulkner's Search for a South*. Urbana: University of Illinois Press, 1983.

Timmerman, John H. *John Steinbeck's Fiction: The Aesthetics of the Road Taken.* Norman: University of Oklahoma Press, 1986.

———. "The Squatter's Circle in *The Grapes of Wrath.*" *Studies in American Fiction* 17 no. 2 (1989): 203–11.

Trilling, Lionel. "F. Scott Fitzgerald." From *The Liberal Imagination.* New York: Viking, (1950): 243–54.

Valjean, Nelson. *John Steinbeck, The Errant Knight: An Intimate Biography of His California Years.* San Francisco: Chronicle Books, 1975.

Vickery, Olga W. *The Novels of William Faulkner: A Critical Interpretation.* Rev. ed. Baton Rouge: Louisiana State University Press, 1964.

Visser, Irene. *Compassion in Faulkner's Fiction.* Lewiston, N.Y.: Edwin Mellen, 1996.

Wadlington, Warwick. *Reading Faulknerian Tragedy.* Ithaca: Cornell University Press, 1987.

Wagner-Martin, Linda, ed. *Ernest Hemingway: Seven Decades of Criticism.* East Lansing: Michigan State University Press, 1998.

———, ed. Ernest Hemingway's A Farewell to Arms: A Reference Guide. Westport, Conn.: Greenwood Press, 2003.

———, ed. Ernest Hemingway's The Sun Also Rises: A Casebook. Oxford, England; New York: Oxford University Press, 2002.

———. *Hemingway and Faulkner: Inventors/Masters.* Metuchen, N.J.: Scarecrow Press, 1975.

———. *"Favored Strangers": Gertrude Stein and Her Family.* Mew Brunswick, N.J.: Rutgers University Press, 1995.

Way, Brian. *F. Scott Fitzgerald and the Art of Social Fiction.* London: Arnold, 1980; New York: St. Martin's Press, 1980.

Weinstein, Norman. *Gertrude Stein and the Literature of the Modern Consciousness.* New York: Ungar, 1970.

Weinstein, Philip M., ed. *The Cambridge Companion to William Faulkner.* Cambridge: Cambridge University Press, 1995.

Weiss, M. Lynn. *Gertrude Stein and Richard Wright: The Poetics and Politics of Modernism.* Jackson: University Press of Mississippi, 1998.

Whitley, John S. *F. Scott Fitzgerald: "The Great Gatsby."* London: Arnold, 1976.

Williams, David. *Faulkner's Women: The Myth and the Muse.* Montreal: McGill-Queen's University Press, 1977.

Williamson, Joel. *William Faulkner and Southern History.* New York: Oxford University Press, 1993.

Wilson, Edmund. *Letters on Literature and Politics 1912–1972.* New York: Farrar, Straus and Giroux, 1977.

———. *The Thirties: From Notebooks and Diaries of the Period.* New York: Farrar, Straus and Giroux, 1980.

Wittenberg, Judith Bryant. *Faulkner: The Transfiguration of Biography.* Lincoln: University of Nebraska Press, 1979.

Young, Philip. *Ernest Hemingway.* New York: Rinehard, 1952.

———. *Ernest Hemingway: A Reconsideration.* University Park, PA: Pennsylvania State University Press, 1966.

Zender, Karl F. *The Crossing of the Ways: William Faulkner, the South, and the Modern World.* New Brunswick, N.J.: Rutgers University Press, 1989.

Acknowledgments

The "Tragic Pastoral" by Sergio Perosa. From *The Art of F. Scott Fitzgerald*, translated by Charles Matz and the author. © 1965 by the University of Michigan. Pp. 52–82, 203–208.

"Sherwood Anderson: American Mythopoeist" by Benjamin T. Spencer. From *American Fiction 1914 to 1945*, Harold Bloom, ed. Originally published in *American Literature* 41, no. 1 (March 1969). © 1969 by Duke University Press. Pp. 101–113.

"Sinclair Lewis and the Implied America" by James Lea. From *American Fiction 1914 to 1945*, Harold Bloom, ed. Originally published in *Clio* 3, no. 1 (October 1973). © 1973 by Robert H. Canary and Henry Kozicki. Pp. 115–125. Reprinted by permission of Cilo.

"The Fully Matured Art: The Grapes of Wrath" by Howard Levant. From *John Steinbeck*, Harold Bloom, ed. Originally published in *The Novels of John Steinbeck: A Critical Study*. © 1974 by The Curators of the University of Missouri. Pp. 93–129.

"Dos Passos's U.S.A.: Chronicle and Performance" by Charles Marz. From *American Fiction 1914 to 1945*, Harold Bloom, ed. Originally published under the title "U.S.A.: Chronicle and Performance," in *Modern Fiction Studies* 26, no. 3 (1980). © 1980 by the Purdue Research Foundation. Pp. 179–193. Reprinted with permission of The Johns Hopkins University Press.

"Modernism: The Case of Willa Cather" by Phyllis Rose. From *American Fiction 1914 to 1945*, Harold Bloom, ed. Originally published in *Modernism Reconsidered*. © 1983 by the President and Fellows of Harvard College. Pp. 61–76.

"Metaphor, Metonymy and Voice in Zora Neale Hurston's Their Eyes Were Watching God" by Barbara Johnson. From *American Fiction 1914 to 1945*, Harold Bloom, ed. Originally published under the title "Metaphor, Metonymy and Voice in *Their Eyes Were Watching God*" in *Black Literature and Literary Theory.* © 1984 by Methuen, Inc. Pp. 361–374.

"De Profundis: The Sound and the Fury I" by Max Putzel. From *Genius of Place: William Faulkner's Triumphant Beginnings.* © 1985 by Louisiana State University Press. Reprinted by permission of Louisiana State University Press.

"Fitzgerald and Cather: The Great Gatsby" by Tom Quirk. From *American Literature* 54, no. 4 (December 1982). © 1982 by Duke University Press. Pp. 576–591.

"Clarity Returns: Ida and The Geographical History of America" by Randa Dubnick. From *The Structure of Obscurity: Gertrude Stein, Language, and Cubism.* © 1984 by the Board of Trustees of the University of Illinois. Pp. 65–85, 140–143. Reprinted by permission of the author.

"The Expatriate Predicament in The Sun Also Rises" by Robert A. Martin. From *French Connections: Hemingway and Fitzgerald Abroad*, J. Gerald Kennedy and Jackson R. Bryer, ed. © 1998 J. Gerald Kennedy and Jackson R. Bryer. Pp. 61–73. Reprinted with permission of Palgrave Macmillan.

"Writing the Long Desire: The Function of Sehnsucht in The Great Gatsby and Look Homeward, Angel" by D.G. Kehl. From *Journal of Modern Literature* 24, no. 2 (Winter 2000/2001). © 2001 by Indiana University Press. Pp. 309–319.

"Order and Will in A Farewell to Arms" by Ronald Berman. From *Fitzgerald, Hemingway, and the Twenties.* © 2001 The University of Alabama Press. Pp. 99–115, 160–163.

"Lost Gods: Pan, Milton, and the Pastoral Tradition in Thomas Wolfe's O Lost" by Lisa Kerr. From *The Thomas Wolfe Review* 26, nos. 1 & 2 (2002). © 2002 by the Thomas Wolfe Society. Pp. 77–89.

"Youth Culture and the Spectacle of Waste: *This Side of Paradise* and *The Beautiful and Damned*" by Kirk Curnutt. From *F. Scott Fitzgerald in the Twenty-first Century*, Jackson R. Bryer, Ruth Progozy, and Milton R. Stern, ed. © 2003 The University of Alabama Press. Pp. 79–103.

"A Yoknapatawpha Pantheon: Light in August" by Ryuichi Yamaguchi. From *Faulkner's Artisitic Vision: The Bizarre and the Terrible.* © 2004 by Rosemont Publishing & Printing Corp. Pp. 166–188, 272–278.

Index